AFTERMATHS

AFTERMATHS

COLONIALISM, VIOLENCE AND MEMORY IN AUSTRALIA, NEW ZEALAND AND THE PACIFIC

Edited by Angela Wanhalla, Lyndall Ryan and Camille Nurka

OTAGO UNIVERSITY PRESS
Te Whare Tā o Te Wānanga o Ōtākou

Published by Otago University Press
Te Whare Tā o Te Wānanga o Ōtākou
533 Castle Street, Dunedin, New Zealand
university.press@otago.ac.nz
www.otago.ac.nz/press

First published 2023
Copyright © Individual authors as listed in the contents list
The moral rights of the authors have been asserted.

ISBN 978-1-99-004844-9

A catalogue record for this book is available from the National Library of New Zealand. This book is copyright. Except for the purpose of fair review, no part may be stored or transmitted in any form or by any means, electronic or mechanical, including recording or storage in any information retrieval system, without permission in writing from the publishers. No reproduction may be made, whether by photocopying or by any other means, unless a licence has been obtained from the publisher.

Published with the assistance of Creative New Zealand

Editor: Imogen Coxhead
Index: Lee Slater

Cover illustration: John Pule, Untitled, 2001, oil on unstretched canvas, 2110 x 1810mm.
Photo courtesy of Gow Langsford Gallery and the artist.

Printed in Hong Kong through Asia Pacific Offset

CONTENTS

LIST OF CONTRIBUTORS 9
ACKNOWLEDGEMENTS 15
A NOTE ON THE TEXT 17

INTRODUCTION

    COLONIALISM, VIOLENCE AND MEMORY   19
    ANGELA WANHALLA AND LYNDALL RYAN

PART I: CONFRONTING HISTORICAL SILENCES

01   **WAR STORIES OUR TEACHERS NEVER TOLD US:**   29
    Documenting New Zealand Wars: Narratives and silences
    JOANNA KIDMAN AND VINCENT O'MALLEY

02   **REGIONAL MEMORIALS AND FRONTIER VIOLENCE:**   39
    Reconciling with the Australian frontier
    AMANDA NETTELBECK

03   **THE BONES IN THE CLOSET:**   49
    Colonial violence in Pākehā family histories
    KERI MILLS

04   **WĒTERE TE RERENGA AND THE MURDER OF**   59
    REV. JOHN WHITELEY
    ANARU EKETONE

PART II: WOMEN AND COLONIAL VIOLENCE

05   **THE GRANDMOTHER DRESS:**   71
    Violence and world renewal in Northern California
    VICTORIA HASKINS

06 **MR AND MRS FLOWERS:** War, marriage and mobility 79
ANGELA WANHALLA

07 **VIOLENCE OF THE LAW:** 87
Prosecuting gendered violence in colonial Fiji
KATE STEVENS

08 **THE CODE OF SILENCE ON THE MACINTYRE** 97
RIVER FRONTIER:
Margaret Young's attempt to achieve justice for the murder
of her Aboriginal servant, Maimie, in 1848
LYNDALL RYAN

PART III: INTIMATE VIOLENCE

09 **'WOLVES ABOUT THEIR PREY':** 107
Intimacy and violence in Eyre's expeditions
SHINO KONISHI

10 **A HIDDEN VIOLENCE:** The sexual abuse of the Stolen Generations 117
STEPHANIE GILBERT

11 **FIJI'S COLONIAL ORPHANAGES** 127
ERICA NEWMAN

12 **WEBS OF SEX, COLONIES AND MYTH:** 139
A Pacific and Hollywood tale
PATRICIA O'BRIEN

PART IV: CRITIQUING COLONIALISM

13 **'CONFUSION TO ALL SNEAKS':** 149
Protection and punishment on the 1880s Western Australian frontier
JANE LYDON

14 **RACE AND REVOLUTION:** Haiti and the Kīngitanga, 1863 157
LACHY PATERSON

15 **'A MISFORTUNE IN THE DISTANCE'**: 167
Violence against the bush in the writings of Louisa Atkinson
GRACE MOORE

16 **'THE PIRATES OF PARIHAKA'**: Parody as a response to violence 179
KIRSTINE MOFFAT

PART V: CREATIVE RESISTANCE

17 **GOORDBELAYIN**: 193
The Bedford Downs massacre paintings of Rover Thomas
RACHEL BURGESS

18 **MAPPING MASSACRES**: 207
Art, history and artefacts in Judy Watson's *the names of places*
ANNA JOHNSTON

19 **ART, MEMORY AND THE AFTERMATHS OF** 217
IMPERIAL VIOLENCE: The life and death of Te Maro
TONY BALLANTYNE

20 **TREATY-MAKER ON TRIAL:** Contesting the Batman monuments 227
PENELOPE EDMONDS

21 ***REWI'S LAST STAND* AND DECOLONISING WAR HISTORY** 235
CAITLIN LYNCH AND SIAN SMITH

CONCLUSION 245
LYNDALL RYAN AND CAMILLE NURKA

NOTES 249
BIBLIOGRAPHY 283
INDEX 302

LIST OF CONTRIBUTORS

Tony Ballantyne is a professor of history and deputy vice-chancellor external engagement at the University of Otago, where he was the co-director of the Centre for Research on Colonial Culture. He has published widely on the cultural history of the British Empire, and his most recent sole-authored book is the award-winning *Entanglements of Empire: Missionaries, Māori, and the question of the body* (Duke University Press, 2014).

Rachel Burgess is a conjoint fellow in Australian history with the Centre for the Study of Violence, School of Humanities and Social Science, College of Human and Social Futures at the University of Newcastle. Rachel descends from the Wonnarua people of the Hunter Valley region of New South Wales. She holds a doctorate in fine art from the Australian National University. Her work is held in significant national and international collections including the Art Gallery of New South Wales and National Gallery of Australia. Rachel lives in the remote Kimberley region of Western Australia and works extensively with Aboriginal artists and custodians on books, exhibitions, community development and research projects.

Penelope Edmonds is Matthew Flinders professor and dean (research) in the College of Humanities, Arts and Social Sciences, Flinders University. Her recent publications include *Settler Colonialism and (Re)Conciliation: Frontier violence, affective performances, and imaginative refoundings* (Palgrave UK, 2016), which examines the performative life of reconciliation and its discontents in settler societies, and *Intimacies of Violence in the Settler Colony* (co-edited with Amanda Nettelbeck, Palgrave Macmillan, 2018).

Anaru Eketone (Ngāti Maniapoto, Waikato) is an associate professor in social work at the University of Otago. While his research interests are in Māori economic and social development, he also has an interest in the impact of religious movements in his tribal area.

Stephanie Gilbert is an associate professor in Indigenous studies at the University of Queensland. Her publications include the edited collection *Our Voices: Aboriginal and Torres Strait Islander social work* (co-edited with Bindi Bennett, Sue Green and Dawn Bessarab, Palgrave Macmillan, 2013) and book chapters on the historical experiences of Indigenous women and the Stolen Generations in New South Wales and Queensland.

Victoria Haskins is a professor of history and co-director of the Purai Global Indigenous History Centre at the University of Newcastle. She works on histories of gender, labour and colonialism, with a focus on cross-cultural relationships in domestic service. Her publications include *Colonialism and Male Domestic Service Across the Asia Pacific* (with Julia Martinez, Claire Lowrie and Frances Steel, Bloomsbury, 2018); *Living with the Locals* (with John Maynard, National Library of Australia, 2017); *Colonization and Domestic Service* (with Claire Lowrie, Routledge, 2014); and *Matrons and Maids: Regulating Indian domestic service in Tucson 1914–1934* (Arizona University Press, 2012).

Anna Johnston is an associate professor in English literature in the School of Communication and Arts at the University of Queensland, and former Australian Research Council Future Fellow and deputy director at the Institute for Advanced Studies in the Humanities. She has published widely on missionary writing and empire, colonial knowledge production, and the aftermath of colonialism in literary and cultural history.

Joanna Kidman (Ngāti Maniapoto, Ngāti Raukawa, Ngāti Toa Rangatira) is a professor of Māori education working in the field of Indigenous sociology at Te Herenga Waka Victoria University of Wellington. Her research focuses on the politics of Indigeneity, Māori youth and settler-colonial nationhood. She has worked extensively in Māori communities across Aotearoa and with Indigenous communities in central Taiwan.

Shino Konishi is a historian at the University of Western Australia and the Australian Catholic University, and the recipient of an Australian Research Council Discovery Indigenous Fellowship, funded by the Australian government. Her books include *The Aboriginal Male in the Enlightenment World* (Pickering and Chatto, 2012) and *Indigenous Intermediaries: New perspectives on exploration archives* (co-edited with Maria Nugent and Tiffany Shellam, ANU Press, 2015). Shino is Aboriginal and identifies with the Yawuru people of Broome, Western Australia.

Jane Lydon holds the Wesfarmers Chair of Australian History at the University of Western Australia. Her book, *Imperial Emotions: The politics of empathy across the British Empire* (Cambridge University Press, 2019), examines the way that emotional narratives created relationships across the British Empire throughout the nineteenth century and into the present. Her latest project, a study of the relationship between the abolition of British slavery and Australian colonisation, was published as *Anti-Slavery and Australia: No slavery in a free land?* (Routledge, 2021).

Caitlin Lynch has an MA in film studies and a BA in history from Te Herenga Waka Victoria University of Wellington. Her master's thesis, 'Revenge Remix: TERROR NULLIUS and the politics of sample filmmaking' (2020), investigates reworking historic cinema and archival footage to critique ongoing colonial culture. Caitlin currently works as a Poutaki Taonga/Collections Manager at Ngā Taonga Sound & Vision, Aotearoa New Zealand's television, film and sound archive.

Keri Mills is a senior lecturer at the Auckland University of Technology and a research fellow at the James Henare Māori Research Centre, University of Auckland. She has a background in academia and the public service. Her research interests are in Indigenous–settler relationships and environmental history.

Kirstine Moffat is an associate professor in the English programme at the University of Waikato. She has published widely on nineteenth-century New Zealand literature, music and culture and is the author of *Piano Forte: Stories and soundscapes from colonial New Zealand* (Otago University Press, 2011).

Grace Moore is an associate professor of English at the University of Otago. Her books include *Dickens and Empire* (Ashgate, 2004), *The Victorian Novel in Context* (Continuum, 2012) and *Victorian Environments* (co-edited with Michelle J. Smith, Palgrave Macmillan, 2018). She is completing a book on settlers and bushfires, *Arcady in Flames*, and another on Trollope and ecology.

Amanda Nettelbeck is a professor in the Institute for Humanities and Social Sciences at the Australian Catholic University and professor of history at the University of Adelaide. Her recent publications include *Indigenous Rights and Colonial Subjecthood* (Cambridge University Press, 2019), *Intimacies of Violence in the Settler Colony* (co-edited with Penelope Edmonds, Palgrave Macmillan, 2018) and *Violence, Colonialism and Empire in the Modern World* (co-edited with Philip Dwyer, Palgrave Macmillan, 2017).

Erica Newman (Ngāti Hine, Ngāpuhi) is a lecturer at Te Tumu: School of Māori, Pacific and Indigenous Studies, University of Otago. Her research is in the area of adoption, Indigenous methods of child circulation, cross-cultural adoption and kinship structures. She is currently leading a Marsden-funded project on the generational legacies of transracial adoption in Aotearoa.

Camille Nurka is a gender studies scholar and professional copyeditor for academics in the humanities, specialising in history. She is the author of *Female Genital Cosmetic Surgery: Deviance, desire and the pursuit of perfection* (Palgrave Macmillan, 2019).

Patricia O'Brien is an associate professor and the author of *Tautai: Sāmoa, world history and the life of Ta`isi O.F. Nelson* (University of Hawai`i Press, 2017) and *The Pacific Muse: Exotic femininity and the colonial Pacific* (University of Washington Press, 2006). She is co-editor, with Joy Damousi, of *League of Nations: Histories, legacies and impact* (Melbourne University Press, 2018) and numerous other Pacific-focused works. She was the resident Australian and Pacific historian at

Georgetown University from 2000 to 2013, the Jay I. Kislak Fellow in American Studies at the John W. Kluge Center at the Library of Congress, Washington DC, in 2011, and J.D. Stout Fellow in New Zealand Studies at Te Herenga Waka Victoria University of Wellington in 2012. From 2014 to 2019 Patricia was an Australian Research Council Future Fellow in the School of History, Australian National University, where she remains a visiting fellow. In 2020 she returned to Georgetown University to teach on Pacific pasts and presents in the Asian Studies programme.

Vincent O'Malley is a professional historian and founding partner of the Wellington research consultancy HistoryWorks. He has published widely on New Zealand history, including *The Great War for New Zealand: Waikato 1800–2000* (Bridget Williams Books, 2016), *Voices from the New Zealand Wars/He Reo nō ngā Pakanga o Aotearoa* (Bridget Williams Books, 2021), and (with Joanna Kidman and other members of their Marsden Fund project team on remembering and forgetting difficult histories) *Fragments from a Contested Past: Remembrance, denial and New Zealand history* (Bridget Williams Books, 2022).

Lachy Paterson is a professor at Te Tumu: School of Māori, Pacific and Indigenous Studies at the University of Otago. He has published widely in the area of Māori history, in particular on Māori-language newspapers, literacy and the use of texts in the nineteenth century. His books include *Colonial Discourses: Niupepa Māori 1855–1863* (Otago University Press, 2006), *He Reo Wāhine: Māori women's voices from the nineteenth century* (with Angela Wanhalla, Auckland University Press, 2017), and the edited collection *Indigenous Textual Cultures: Reading and writing in the age of global empire* (co-edited with Tony Ballantyne and Angela Wanhalla, Duke University Press, 2020). He currently co-leads, with Angela Wanhalla, a Marsden-funded research project exploring the impact of World War II at home on Māori families and communities, and on Māori society more broadly.

Lyndall Ryan is an emeritus professor of history at the University of Newcastle. She has published widely on frontier violence in colonial Australia and is best known for *Tasmanian Aborigines: A history since 1803* (Allen & Unwin, 2012). In 2022 she led the research team that released stage four of the award-winning online map of frontier massacres across Australia: https://c21ch.newcastle.edu.au/colonialmassacres

Sian Smith (Kāi Tahu, Kāti Māmoe) grew up in Aotearoa, Fiji and Singapore and studied history at Te Herenga Waka Victoria University of Wellington. Sian is interested in the works of wāhine Māori filmmakers, kaupapa Māori filmmaking, and issues of voice and authorship in history. Since graduating with a master of arts in 2020, Sian has worked as a research assistant and historian at Te Arawhiti Office for Māori Crown Relations. In her current position as Poutaki Taonga Māori Collections Manager at Ngā Taonga Sound and Vision, Sian is committed to kaipupuritanga for audiovisual taonga Māori. Sian lives in Te Whanganui-a-Tara/Wellington with her tāne and her son.

Kate Stevens (Pākehā/settler) is a senior lecturer at the University of Waikato. Her research focuses on cultural, legal and environmental histories of the colonial and postcolonial Pacific. She has published on interracial whaling communities in Aotearoa New Zealand, sexual violence and colonial criminal justice, and coconut commodities across the Pacific. She completed her PhD at the University of Cambridge in 2015 and was subsequently a postdoctoral fellow at the University of Otago and a research assessor at the Royal Society Te Apārangi.

Angela Wanhalla (Ngāi Te Ruahikihiki, Ngāi Tahu, Pākehā) is a professor in the history programme at the University of Otago. She is a historian of race, gender, intimacy and colonialism and has published on the history of cross-cultural families and interracial marriage in Aotearoa New Zealand. Her book *Matters of the Heart: A history of interracial marriage in New Zealand* (Auckland University Press, 2013) was awarded the Ernest Scott Prize in 2014. Angela also has an interest in colonial visual cultures, particularly the history of photography.

ACKNOWLEDGEMENTS

This book first took shape at the 'Afterlives: Intimacy, Violence and Colonialism' symposium, held at the Museum of New Zealand Te Papa Tongarewa in November 2019. Lyndall and Angela especially acknowledge all who supported the event by presenting papers and attending. This volume has benefited enormously from the opportunity to share ideas in a collegial environment, and we thank Te Papa for hosting our event and providing an inspiring space for conversation. We are also particularly grateful to Camille Nurka for bringing her editorial expertise, intellectual generosity, management skills and collaborative spirit to the project. Camille has been critical to transforming the book from an idea into a reality. She thanks the authors of *Aftermaths* for their hard work, grace and patience over multiple edits to ensure precision, consistency and clarity of meaning.

Special mention must be made of the financial support for the symposium and this volume. Both are outcomes from a collaborative Australian Research Council Discovery Project Grant 'Intimacy and violence in settler societies on the Anglophone Pacific rim 1830–1930'(DP150100914), led by Lyndall at the University of Newcastle, which sought to explore the connections between the broad-scale dynamics of colonial rule and the violent and intimate domains of its implementation on the ground. We also had assistance from the Centre for the 21st Century Humanities, University of Newcastle, the Royal Society Te Apārangi's Rutherford Discovery Fellowship programme and the University of Otago's Centre for Research on Colonial Culture.

Many of the photographs and artworks featured in *Aftermaths* come from libraries, archives, museums and other institutions in New Zealand, Australia, Fiji and the United States. We would like to acknowledge them and particularly thank those people who have contributed images from private collections.

We consider ourselves fortunate to have worked with Imogen Coxhead, Allan Kynaston, who produced the wonderful maps, and the whole Otago University Press team, to bring this book to completion.

A NOTE ON THE TEXT

Readers are advised that due to the sensitive nature of its subject matter – the experiences of colonialism by colonised peoples – this book contains accounts of physical and sexual violence that may be traumatising to some readers. The book also includes representations of deceased persons in New Zealand, Australia and the United States who have living descendants. We would like to take the opportunity to acknowledge the different protocols and interests of the many distinct cultural and linguistic groups whose stories appear in this volume, and we wish to pay tribute to the strength and resilience of Indigenous peoples around the world, who have kept their culture, traditions and identity alive in the aftermaths of colonialism.

Introduction

COLONIALISM, VIOLENCE AND MEMORY

Angela Wanhalla and Lyndall Ryan

> What we choose to remember and what we choose to forget about the violent past tell us something about the society we live in now. But whether we like it or not, we're part of each other's story. So how do we talk about the past?
>
> —Joanna Kidman and Vincent O'Malley

Aftermaths is concerned with the ongoing consequences of settler colonialism in Australia, New Zealand and the Pacific, including the Western United States. Originally an agricultural term, aftermath referred to the effects of crop harvesting and gathering, and the possibilities of renewal these enabled.[1] With its deep ties to land, agriculture and settlement, aftermath seems an apt metaphor for settler colonialism and the aspirations of the men and women who colonised what they perceived to be 'new' lands. As settlers, however, they were usurping locations already occupied by Indigenous peoples and sought to obtain ownership of land and resources through a variety of means, including armed conflict.

We prefer the modern interpretation of 'aftermath', which is concerned with the consequences of a traumatic event. Our aim is to unravel the historical roots of colonial violence in settler societies and address, in the words of Māori lawyer and scholar Moana Jackson, settler colonialism's 'ongoing presence'. Jackson reminds us that 'colonisation is a *process* of dispossession and control rather than a historical artefact', and that it is often 'written [about] in a stubborn past tense' when it is very much a part of the present.[2] Likewise, the editors of *Violence and Indigenous Communities: Confronting the past and engaging the present* argue that violence is 'one of the most important and challenging issues in Native American and Indigenous Studies', a contemporary reality and not something that can be relegated to the past.[3] Australian Indigenous scholar Chelsea Watego also draws attention to the daily violence of settler colonialism on Indigenous communities across Australia. As she explains, this is 'not just of the physical kind, but the emotional, spiritual, economic, intellectual and cultural kind'.[4]

One of the aftermaths of colonialism is the power to define how the past is interpreted. As Moana Jackson has written, 'Although in the simplest sense colonisation is the violent denial of the right of Indigenous peoples to continue governing themselves in their own lands, the colonisers have told stories that redefine its causes and costs.'[5] Other Indigenous writers, scholars and activists have identified similar patterns in Australia and the United States because, for them, colonialism is not an abstract concept but a lived experience. As Yawuru historian Shino Konishi points out, 'for us, these histories of colonisation by settlers feel more recent, more tangible, and are usually more emotionally affecting and less abstracted by theory'. This immediacy of feeling and lived experience means that Indigenous scholars 'are keenly aware of the impact of the colonial past on the present, so their work actively engages with the political ramifications of historical perspectives'.[6]

Settler colonialism is often written about as a process, and usually about the political decision-makers. As Keri Mills argues in her chapter in this volume, academic colonial history is often abstracted from the personal spheres of family, ancestry and inheritance that are enmeshed in the 'ongoing narratives' of colonisation. Because stories about ordinary civilian life seem divorced from the larger story of imperial exploration, war and settlement, 'it isn't hard', Mills suggests, 'for us to disassociate, to think of it as a story that has little to do with us today'. This volume, comprising contributions from Indigenous and settler scholars, seeks to reconnect the colonial past to our lives in the present by offering personal and collective experiences of the settler colonial process and its contradictions, and building upon the work of Indigenous thinkers and scholars who have long argued that colonialism is lived, embodied and felt. Many of our contributors honour this approach by sharing their personal experiences, family stories and collaborative research.

Aftermaths illustrates the many ways colonial violence was carried out in settler societies in Australia, New Zealand and the Pacific, and how that violence has been remembered, silenced and contested in the development of new settler states that emerged in the aftermath of colonial wars.[7] Typically, settler colonies are locations where English-speaking colonists quickly gained demographic and political dominance over Indigenous peoples and put in place destructive policies of assimilation. Assimilation refers to the disappearance of Indigenous communities through deliberate policies that targeted the eradication of language and culture. Settler colonies such as Australia, New Zealand and the United States also developed economic and military interests in the South Pacific from the second half of the nineteenth century. Settler colonies, though, are not homogenous: they do not all look the same. In the South Pacific, for instance, Papua and Fiji were not numerically dominated by British, Australian or New Zealand settlers, but they were nonetheless subjected to European cultural norms, customs, beliefs and laws, as Erica Newman, Kate Stevens and Patricia O'Brien reveal in this volume. Even within settler states, colonialism was carried out in many ways, including the use of unfree labour. In parts of Australia, for instance, colonial economies relied on indentured labourers from the Pacific; in Fiji, most labourers were imported from India.

Colonial violence is not a new area of research, but in recent years Indigenous and non-Indigenous scholars from the United States, Australia and New Zealand have challenged the dominant focus on conflict and war.[8] Historical and popular understandings have predominantly focused on massacre and warfare against Indigenous peoples as enacted only between strangers. In focusing on the specifics of colonial violence and its ongoing presence, our volume contests this standard interpretation and demonstrates that the development of modern settler states like Australia and New Zealand was not only grounded in violent dispossession and subjugation of Indigenous landowners but also shaped by complex relationships between displaced Indigenous peoples and the settler colonists. As several contributors to this volume highlight, violence was all too often enacted between those known to each other.[9] Neighbours, employers or caregivers deployed violence against Indigenous peoples, including children and people of colour in Australia, New Zealand, California, Fiji and Papua New Guinea.

Colonial violence inhabits our present in multiple ways. It is part of our landscape, referenced in street and place names, but also in family memory. *Aftermaths* is concerned with historical memory and the many ways in which colonial history is encountered, discussed, depicted, contested and misremembered within families and at the local level.[10] Contributions to this volume examine the expression of these histories in oral, literary, visual and material cultures, through commemoration and re-enactment, and in contemporary artworks.[11] They incorporate traditional scholarly essays and more personal accounts of historical memory – both approaches are equally powerful in their impact. Contributors show how historical silence continues to affect victims and perpetrators, and how the development of a settler 'code of silence' has lent credibility to perpetrator narratives and invalidated those of the peoples who have been, and still are, harmed by colonialism.

Aftermaths opens with a series of chapters on strategies of colonial mythmaking and historical forgetting in family accounts, popular memory and regional monuments. Joanna Kidman, Vincent O'Malley, Amanda Nettelbeck, Anaru Eketone and Keri Mills detail how new historical interpretations of colonial violence have influenced how we think about private memory and informed a growing, if uneven, public consciousness about the colonial past. The opening chapters demonstrate how the silences about the frontier wars in Australia (1820–1930) and the New Zealand Wars (1860–72) have proved difficult to shift in popular discourse in the twenty-first century. Joanna Kidman and Vincent O'Malley detail the collective amnesia associated with the New Zealand Wars and how memory and silence about this difficult past permeate people's lives in the present. In Australia, some local communities have established their own memorials to critical moments in the frontier wars. Nettelbeck explores two regional memorials as models of reconciliation that recognise colonial violence as present and ongoing, rather than belonging to a history now past.

Anaru Eketone and Keri Mills return to the New Zealand Wars and share personal accounts of how histories of violence are transmitted, or not, across generations. Colonial history is contested in family memory. Eketone details the competing narratives surrounding a missionary's death at the hands of Māori in 1869 during the New Zealand Wars and compares it to his own family narrative. Mills turns to settler memory of the New Zealand Wars, arguing that it is time non-Māori recognised their family stories in the ongoing narratives of colonisation.[12] In recent years, memoirs have appeared recounting the horror and shame of familial connections to colonial violence and the benefits of settler colonialism, in the form of land. Helpfully, these detail the complicated entwined histories of familial success and Indigenous dispossession, and recount processes of historical amnesia and mythmaking in the settler colonies.

The chapters that follow are case studies of individuals or groups and particular localities, which look to expand our understanding of colonialism and violence, including sexual violence, the power of colonial justice systems and massacre. Kate Stevens, Victoria Haskins, Angela Wanhalla and Lyndall Ryan address the impacts of colonial violence on Indigenous women and women of colour as told through court records, a memoir, a studio photograph and the return of a sacred dress.

The next set of chapters, by Shino Konishi, Stephanie Gilbert, Erica Newman and Patricia O'Brien, explore adult physical, sexual and cultural violence against children in intimate and exploitative master–servant relationships, in mobile and indentured labour settings, 'training' homes, orphanages and private family homes. As Konishi's chapter argues, young Indigenous men occupied a dangerously ambiguous place in the psychic space of settler colonialism, where they were invited into unequal yet companionate relationships with white male employers. Underpinning this unstable confluence of servant, employee and family member was the white fear that young Aboriginal 'companions' might resent and resist their servitude.

Gilbert and Newman look at the intersection between family and labour in institutions for children, who were the main targets of assimilation in the aftermath of colonisation. Our volume shows that, far from being a benign attempt to integrate Indigenous peoples into a new social and cultural regime, assimilation policies committed further violence against Indigenous peoples. Fiji's colonial orphanages, for instance, sought to assimilate the children of Indian indentured labourers into a new colonial regime that dismantled their existing kinship relations and cultural connections. In Australia, the assimilation era is synonymous with the Stolen Generation, where children were removed from their families and placed in institutions. Other settler societies practised child removal – and still do. Colonial views that assimilation was a 'benevolent' policy have encouraged public amnesia about its violent past and its ongoing presence in policy and practice today, as Gilbert demonstrates in her powerful contribution about institutionalised sexual abuse.

Sexual abuse is one part of a pattern of colonising violence, and its repercussions for those who live with its consequences daily are immense. Sexual violence took place during colonial warfare in Australia and New Zealand but historians rarely speak of its existence, thus rendering mute the experiences of Indigenous women and children. In recent years, accounts given to New Zealand's Waitangi Tribunal have broken that silence to speak of how descendants and communities have lived with the consequences of rape and sexual abuse on the cross-cultural frontier. Characterisations of the New Zealand Wars as 'chivalrous', for instance, which were left unchallenged until the late twentieth century, linked colonial violence with celebrations of white colonial masculinity that, in turn, helped to hide a terrible truth. Patricia O'Brien exposes the consequences of such celebratory narratives through a confronting account of sexual violence involving the Australian film actor Errol Flynn. She exposes the rampant racism of many Australians of the period and the assumption of white superiority and entitlement of sexual access to Indigenous women that come with it.

Settler violence on the colonial frontier was critiqued at the time and afterwards, and Jane Lydon, Lachy Paterson, Kirstine Moffat and Grace Moore shed light on the critics and their writing. Jane Lydon considers official investigations into abusive labour practices and instruments of punishment in Western Australia that looked akin to slavery. Critiques of slavery and colonialism were also informed by earlier struggles, as Lachy Paterson shows in his chapter on the connections between the revolutionary ideas of Haiti (1791–1804) and the Kīngitanga, a pan-tribal Māori movement, in 1863. That year the movement's newspaper, *Te Hokioi e Rere Atu na*, imagined a Māori future and employed the Haitian state as an example of a non-white society successfully displacing their colonial masters.

Grace Moore confronts the environmental violence wrought by settlers on the Australian landscape through the writings of Louisa Atkinson, for whom destruction of the environment represented one of the excesses of colonisation – one we are still dealing with today. Kirstine Moffat offers a scintillating account of the parody composed in reaction to the invasion of the pacifist Māori community of Parihaka on 5 November 1881, at a time when settler voices of dissent were rare. As she notes, the use of parody raises important questions about both the potential of satire to expose injustice and hypocrisy and the appropriateness of humour as a response to violence.

Aftermaths closes with a series of chapters on how contemporary Indigenous artists and activists in Australia and New Zealand have creatively reflected on the violence of the colonial past and how it determines the present. Rachel Burgess explores the Aboriginal artist Rover Thomas, whose paintings of the 1924 Bedford Downs massacre in the East Kimberley of northwestern Australia are now considered not only important and accurate records of the massacre but also accounts that demonstrate the impact on the survivors. Anna Johnston offers an account of the personal, powerful and deeply moving artwork *the names of places* by Waanyi artist Judy Watson, who deploys the strategy of palimpsest to show how mapping place names can hide as well as reveal sites of massacre of Aboriginal people across Australia. Through the artistic representations of Te Maro, one of the men killed by James Cook's crew in October 1769, Tony Ballantyne shows how artists Nick Tūpara and Michel Tuffery refuse to define Te Maro's life in relation to his death, and instead place him at the centre of public memory. Penny Edmonds reviews the ongoing debate about John Batman, the 'founder' of Melbourne, and his allegedly deceitful role in signing a treaty with the Kulin leaders to purchase several hundred thousand acres of their land in 1835. In particular, she focuses on the public trial of Batman in 1991 by Aboriginal activists who sought to make him accountable to history and to Aboriginal peoples.

Our volume closes by returning to the New Zealand Wars through the reappraisal of a well-known New Zealand film and the question of whether it should still be used for educational purposes. Caitlin Lynch and Sian Smith consider *Rewi's Last Stand*, first made as a silent movie by Rudall Hayward in 1925 and later remade in 1940 as a 'talkie' version with a new cast but the same director. Although the 1940 film has been heavily critiqued for its assimilationist message and romanticisation of war, the authors draw attention to its use in educational settings as a text that enables contemporary audiences to appreciate the active participation of Indigenous peoples in historical storytelling. In doing so, we come face-to-face with our ancestors and our collective past.

PART I
CONFRONTING HISTORICAL SILENCES

Chapter 1

WAR STORIES OUR TEACHERS NEVER TOLD US

DOCUMENTING NEW ZEALAND WARS NARRATIVES AND SILENCES

Joanna Kidman and Vincent O'Malley

It is quiet at the frontier, the only sounds the scrape of shovels as saps are dug and muffled voices down the trail beyond the orchard, where peach trees still bear fruit at the end of a long warm season.[1] But the crescent moon, passing behind clouds as the evening star Meremere-tū-ahiahi rises high and bright in the darkening sky in the days before the fighting begins, is a portent and a warning.[2] This will not end well.

The battle at Ōrākau pā has left a powerful legacy for generations of Māori. For many who have come later, this centres on the solidarity the defenders forged inside the pā (fort) during the siege when the people they loved lay dying around them and they were given the choice to surrender or die. But none of them could imagine a life without land and kin, so they chose to die together rather than live alone. That is a great and terrible intimacy, and for many Māori, that is the story of Ōrākau.

The invasion of the Waikato by British and colonial troops, which began in the winter of 1863 and ended with the fall of Ōrākau pā in April 1864, has been described elsewhere.[3] It is enough to say here that, for nearly nine months, Māori communities in the region had been subjected to a state of almost constant siege. By the autumn of 1864, the war was drawing to a close and as the death toll mounted, Waikato Māori were increasingly isolated and vulnerable. The battle at Ōrākau was the final armed conflict in the area, in a war fought by two unevenly matched forces: a massive, highly weaponised invading army and small groups of Māori, many of whom were members of the same families.

Most war stories speak to battles lost and won, of heroes and villains or the deeds of clever military strategists and generals. Years after the assault on Ōrākau, Pākehā commentators couched it as a conquest of Māori 'rebels' who had fought nobly and with great honour against a larger army. But for many Māori, who live in the aftermath of those events, the siege is remembered as a story about the tūpuna (ancestors) who lived and died there and the choices they made at gunpoint. It is a story about those ancestors. Importantly, it is a story about violence and love.

KA WHAWHAI TONU MĀTOU: THE BATTLE OF ŌRĀKAU

During the late summer of 1864, in the final weeks of the Waikato War, British and colonial troops occupied the small settlement of Kihikihi on the southern border of the Waikato. By the time they arrived there the kāinga (village) had been abandoned, as Māori had earlier fled the area to the relative safety of the lands beyond the Puniu River. In their haste, they left behind storage pits filled with fruit and vegetables from the summer harvest, sufficient to feed the entire army through the coming winter.[4] There the occupying forces made preparations for the final assault, which took place a short distance away in the orchard gardens of a place called Ōrākau.

A fighting pā was hurriedly built but the site was not ideal for armed conflict: the area could be easily surrounded, there was no clear escape route and the water supply was vulnerable. Each of these factors played a part in what was to come. The defenders of the pā were joined by iwi (tribe) allies from outside the Waikato. Around 100 women and children were also present. The battle at Ōrākau lasted three days and ended in acts of extraordinary violence. More than half the 300 Māori who defended the pā were killed. Most died not during the siege but on the third and final day when food, water and ammunition were nearly exhausted and the people of the pā made a desperate bid to break through British lines and run to safety.

At around noon on that day, it was clear that the pā would fall. With a British victory seemingly assured and the pā surrounded, Lieutenant-General Duncan Cameron, the commanding officer of British forces in New Zealand, declared a ceasefire through his translator William Mair and urged the defenders to surrender in order to save their lives. He was refused, with words of courage and defiance that have since passed into Māori history: 'E hoa, ka whawhai tonu mātou. Āke! Āke! Āke!' (Friend, we will fight on forever and ever and ever).

Cameron then called on the women and children to leave before the final assault. Again, the people refused. Ngāti Raukawa woman Ahumai Te Paerata stepped forward and replied, 'Ki te mate ngā tāne, me mate anō ngā wāhine me ngā tamariki!' (If the men die, then the women and children must also die). Ahumai's words delivered a clear message to the waiting army that those inside the pā, knowing that defeat was certain, chose to die together as free men and women, forever united. It was an act of defiance and desperation. It was also an act of solidarity and love.

And so, the onslaught began.

In the late afternoon those inside the pā prepared to leave. They gathered in tight formation with women, children, the wounded, and surviving rangatira (leaders) at the centre to protect them as much as possible. As they ran towards open ground, the troops opened fire and a number of defenders were killed. The group scattered as people fled for their lives. Hitiri Te Paerata, son of Ngāti Raukawa rangatira Te Paerata and brother of Ahumai, was shot four times but survived. He later described the chaotic scenes that ensued:

> As we fled before them they tried, by outmarching on our flanks, to cut off our retreat, and poured a storm of bullets which seemed to encircle us like hail. It became as a forlorn hope with us; none expected to escape, nor did we desire to; were we not all the children of one parent? [T]herefore we all wished to die together.[5]

Under heavy gunfire, some ran towards the nearby mānuka swamp. There were scenes of extraordinary brutality as the invading forces pursued those fleeing for their lives. Snipers on the ridge opened fire, and members of the cavalry rode the people down and bayoneted them where they fell. Others were killed or injured as they ran toward the soldiers in a desperate bid to breach the line. One contemporary newspaper reported:

> *Women – many women –* slaughtered, and many children slain, are amongst the trophies of Orakau, and 'civilization' in pursuit, or as it returned from the chase, *amused itself by shooting the wounded 'barbarians'* as they lay upon the ground where they had fallen [emphasis in original].[6]

AFTERMATHS

This is how the assault ended in terror and bloodshed, and the violence of these events echoes over time. British and colonial troops complained for weeks afterwards about the smell of decomposing corpses in the nearby swamps, where many of the more than 150 Māori killed had fallen. Later, a road would be built through the middle of the pā, obliterating the physical remnants and reminders of this terrible history as if it had never happened, and in time, new myths around the chivalrous and noble conflict fought at Ōrākau would be created.

The siege and its bloody conclusion also gave rise to new stories that are handed down in many Māori communities. These stories, about the collective stance taken in the pā, are seen as a legacy and gift. Today the words 'Ka whawhai tonu mātou' have become a catch cry for Māori resistance and are regularly chanted when Māori protest against Crown injustices. Each time they are uttered, the defenders of Ōrākau are summoned into being.

The contrast with how Pākehā have (mis)remembered and forgotten these events is jarring.

REMEMBERING AND FORGETTING ŌRĀKAU

On 1 April 1914, as war clouds loomed over Europe, some 5000 people gathered at Ōrākau, a few kilometres up the road from Kihikihi, to mark the fiftieth anniversary of the most famous battle of the New Zealand Wars. Cabinet ministers, MPs, the head of the armed forces, numerous dignitaries and a smattering of elderly Māori and Pākehā veterans were present at the unveiling of a memorial on the site where Ōrākau pā once stood.[7] An early-morning train from Auckland to Te Awamutu had been organised for the big day, and veterans had received free rail passes to allow them to attend. The Auckland Education Board granted a special holiday to all children attending schools in the Waikato and Waipā counties. Those schools unable to take part in the ceremony were instructed to assemble their pupils, hoist the national flag and give a lesson on 'the difficulties of early settlement in New Zealand'.[8]

Newspapers throughout the dominion reported at length on the Ōrākau 'celebrations'. And for

OPPOSITE: *Ngāti Raukawa wahine toa Ahumai Te Paerata became renowned for her defiant response to the British invitation for women and children to surrender during the Ōrākau siege. But her own subsequent fate – shot four times while attempting to flee – highlighted a much darker side to the battle than many Pākehā preferred to remember.*

Portrait by Irene Hill, 1913. A-472-040. Cowan Family: Collection. Courtesy of Alexander Turnbull Library, Wellington

War stories our teachers never told us

Pākehā New Zealand, it was precisely that. As the *New Zealand Herald* explained, the Ōrākau battle marked 'the final acceptance of the British mana by a heroic and warlike native people' that had been met by 'a just and generous reciprocity which is everywhere regarded as an example to the civilised world'.[9] Something of that view was reflected in the jubilee souvenir programme, which described the anniversary as a 'commemoration of 50 years of peace'.[10] But as the *Herald* editorial suggested, this was no ordinary peace. Ōrākau gave birth to the myth of New Zealand as a country with the greatest race relations in the world. And for a land that many Pākehā felt was lacking in suitable legends, what better tales to immortalise than those that emanated from Ōrākau? In this way, a highly sentimentalised version of Ōrākau was openly appropriated by Pākehā for their own nationalist and nation-building ends.

Just one thing was missing. The Ōrākau ceremony in 1914 had largely been a Pākehā affair. Waikato Māori had no interest in celebrating the brutal killing of as many as 150 of their ancestors, the sweeping confiscation of their lands and the destruction of their economy that condemned generations to lives of poverty. While Pākehā publicly celebrated Ōrākau, Waikato Māori privately grieved, recalling the history in waiata tangi (songs of lament) and sometimes even in the names they gave to their children: Muru (plunder), Mamae (pain) and even Raupatu (land confiscation) were not uncommon in some areas.

That Māori held a notably less sentimental view of the war than most Pākehā, even more than 50 years later, was evident in the exchanges around the provision of additional text for the memorial, on which the name 'Rewi Maniapoto' appeared without explanation or description.

In 1916 a member of the Te Heuheu family (possibly Tureiti Te Heuheu) supplied a draft inscription, which, when translated by the government, read:

> Rewi Maniapoto was one of the highest of the chiefs of Ngati-Maniapoto and Ngati-Raukawa. He was an upholder (or supporter) of the Kingdom (or Kingship) of Potatau te Wherowhero and Tawhiao, and at the time of the war waged by the Pakeha race against the Maori King he fought in the war on the side of the Maori King, with the result that he was defeated here at Orakau; his tribe subdued; and his lands taken by conquest.[11]

Edith Statham, the Inspector of Old Soldiers' Graves for the Department of Internal Affairs and a leading figure in the Victoria League, led the charge for a new monument and/or inscription at Ōrākau, but in response to the translation

Pākehā in their thousands flocked to the 1914 jubilee of the Battle of Ōrākau to celebrate what they imagined was a chivalrous and noble conflict that had given rise to 50 years of peace and unrivalled harmony. Meanwhile, many Waikato Māori privately grieved the loss of their tupuna, along with their lands and livelihood.

Commemoration of the Jubilee of the Battle of Orakau: The Celebrations on the Battlefield Near Te Awamutu, on April 1, Auckland Weekly News, 9 April 1914, p. 47. AWNS-19140409-47-1. Courtesy of Auckland Libraries Heritage Collections

---

of this text she wrote, 'I do not quite like it, as it does not set forth the main fact that I was anxious to give publicity to, viz., that Rewi was the Chief commanding the Maori troops and made such a gallant defence against our men.'[12] Te Heuheu had disrupted Pākehā myth-making around Ōrākau with awkward reminders of the Kīngitanga that Rewi Maniapoto had devoted much of his life to defending, to a war 'waged by the Pakeha race against the Maori King', and to the dreadful consequences of that conflict for the tribes involved. This was not what Pākehā wanted to hear. They preferred to frame Ōrākau in terms of a noble and heroic – if ultimately doomed – defence that had given rise to 50 years of unblemished and unrivalled peace and harmony between Māori and Pākehā. Their imagined

Ōrākau was conspicuous for chivalry, gallantry and mutual respect among contending fighters before final acceptance by Māori of their subservient position in relation to the government. A bland alternative inscription was solicited from Elsdon Best before the whole matter was quickly and quietly dropped.[13]

As the Great War drew to a close, there came renewed interest in New Zealand's own wars. Supporters lobbied the government to commission a history of these conflicts before the last survivors passed away. In 1918 the government finally agreed, and James Cowan, a bilingual journalist who grew up on a farm that included part of the Ōrākau site, was enlisted to write it. His two-volume work, published in 1922 and 1923, was invaluable for its extensive use of oral histories from Māori and Pākehā veterans of the wars and came to be seen as the definitive history for decades thereafter. Cowan's work was largely devoid of critical analysis and interpretation, and in this way did not constitute any kind of threat to the emergent myth of Ōrākau. If anything, the success of his book (with its emphasis on the 'mutual respect' of former adversaries forged through 'ordeal by battle') helped foster this development.[14]

Cowan's work inspired efforts to depict the wars through other mediums. Pākehā flocked in their thousands to Rudall Hayward's 1925 silent movie *Rewi's Last Stand*, later remade as a popular feature-length talkie.[15] The myths around Ōrākau that came to the fore around the time of the fiftieth anniversary became deeply embedded in Pākehā culture and endured for much of the twentieth century. At the 1964 centenary of the battle, guests were treated to a special screening of *Rewi's Last Stand*, a hāngī, kapa haka competitions and a concert featuring Kiri Te Kanawa.[16] Some Waikato elders wanted no part in proceedings, concerned that the whole affair had become something of a circus.[17] So long as Pākehā continued to use the war anniversaries as an excuse to pat themselves on the back for their supposedly superior race relations, that attitude was understandable. The Pākehā narrative of the Waikato War was out of sync with the still largely ignored Māori story of an unjustified invasion of their homeland followed by numerous and senseless killings, confiscations, exile and poverty.

Thanks to more forceful Māori voices, aided by a new generation of historians, the Pākehā version of the wars was becoming harder to sustain, and by the 1970s, it had been all but discredited. The problem was that no new narrative of the wars emerged, or at least none that was acceptable to the majority of Pākehā, and so we were left with a kind of uncomfortable silence. When that silence was challenged in ways that mainstream Pākehā opinion found difficult to ignore, significant

Poster for Rewi's Last Stand *(1940)*. Rudall Hayward's Ōrākau films were watched by many New Zealanders and helped to reinforce romanticised perceptions of the conflict as a gallant and respectful affair, a view at odds with the way many Māori remembered the conflict. *Illustration by Ramai Te Miha. P03845. Courtesy of Ngā Taonga Sound & Vision, Wellington*

controversy arose. *The Governor*, a highly ambitious six-part drama series that screened on TV One in 1977, presented the Waikato War as an unsavoury land grab while continuing to laud Māori bravery at Ōrākau. Prime Minister Robert Muldoon attacked the series, supposedly for its excessive expenditure – though his criticism probably reflected a deeper cultural unease at its troubling depiction of the colonial era.[18]

James Belich's *New Zealand Wars* documentary series, which screened just over 20 years later to critical acclaim, was also accompanied by a strong backlash from some sectors of the public.[19] 'How dare they say that stuff about our Pākehā ancestors?' seemed to be the attitude. For many Pākehā, it was just easier to forget the Waikato War had ever happened.

Arguably, only in the last few years has there been wider public acceptance of the need to engage with this history in an upfront and honest way. That change owes much to the students of Ōtorohanga College and their 2015 petition that called for New Zealand history to be taught in schools.[20]

What we choose to remember and what we choose to forget about the violent past tell us something about the society we live in now. Whether we like it or not, we're part of each other's story. So how do we talk about the past? And in particular, how do we talk about the past to children and young people at school?

The New Zealand school curriculum has not served us well in terms of understanding our own history. Generations of New Zealanders learned nothing of the bloody events at Ōrākau and elsewhere during the nineteenth-century New Zealand Wars. For the most part, these are war stories our teachers never told us. Those omissions and silences foreclosed the possibility of a more vibrant and informed national conversation about our difficult past. A recent government announcement that New Zealand history will be compulsorily taught in schools is heartening.

For this to work, iwi need to be central to the public drive to remember and tell the stories of the past; mana whenua should be empowered and resourced to tell these histories in their own way. This is important, because these stories have the potential to change our minds – and to change our lives and our future. They can bring us together in diverse ways as we forge new public intimacies around the difficult, violent, unresolved past. But if told carelessly, they will push us further apart. That is the power of stories and how they define us.

Chapter 2

REGIONAL MEMORIALS AND FRONTIER VIOLENCE

RECONCILING WITH THE AUSTRALIAN FRONTIER

Amanda Nettelbeck

The imperatives of truth-telling, articulated so powerfully in the 2017 Uluru Statement from the Heart, have become central to wider calls in contemporary Australia to reconcile with the nation's histories of colonial violence. Gabrielle Appleby and Megan Davis recently argued that the value of a truth-telling process lies not only in acknowledging injustice as a matter of historical record but also in reconstituting the contemporary relationship between Indigenous people and 'the rest of the nation'.[1] In this understanding of truth-telling as a politically generative process for the present rather than just a reckoning with the past, the focus is less on documenting a forensically exhaustive record of historical events than on the purposes and capacities of reconciliation. In October 2018, Reconciliation Australia and the Healing Foundation hosted a Truth-Telling Symposium that brought together Indigenous and non-Indigenous representatives from across multiple public sectors to discuss the forms that truth-telling might take.[2]

Australia now appears better prepared to invest in this process than it was two decades ago at the height of the history wars when public intellectuals, politicians and historians contested the degree to which settler state-building took place under conditions of violence.[3] Today, greater public recognition that violence underpinned the process of Indigenous dispossession is indicated by several recent initiatives that have carried nationwide impact. These include the 'Change the Date' campaign that seeks to unharness Australia Day from the anniversary of colonial arrivals; widespread attention to continental maps of Indigenous massacre sites; and a series of national press reports on the frontier wars by the *Guardian*.[4]

To the degree that there is now public appetite for greater knowledge about Australia's colonial frontier wars, it has a generational tilt towards younger Australians.[5] But more broadly, according to Reconciliation Australia's 2018 barometer of public opinion, 86 percent of the 'general' Australian community now agree that 'it is important for all Australians to learn more' about 'past issues of European settlement and government policies' affecting Indigenous people; and 81 percent agree on the importance of teaching Indigenous histories and cultures in Australian schools.[6] Notably, similar majorities of both 'general' and Indigenous community respondents expressed support for an Indigenous body within the Constitution, indicating public appreciation that reconciliation requires Indigenous political agency, as outlined in the Uluru Statement from the Heart.[7]

Yet despite these public trends, the foundational violence of Australia's frontiers remains a contested subject, especially at the national level, where the iconographies and commemorations of foundational moments are most laden with longstanding values and traditions.[8] As every Australia Day approaches, the Change the Date campaign is countered by a campaign to 'Save the Date'.[9] Likewise, annual calls to include a formal commemoration of colonial frontier wars at the Australian War Memorial continue to be deflected.[10]

National division about how to acknowledge foundational violence is also reflected in Reconciliation Australia's 2018 survey findings. Although a large majority of respondents support a truth-telling process in the service of reconciliation, many remain ambivalent about what historical truths might be told. Only 57 percent of respondents accept that 'frontier wars occurred across the Australian continent as a result of Indigenous people defending their traditional lands from European invasion', and another 35 percent remain unsure.[11] This numerical disjuncture between 86 percent support for a process of truth-telling and a combined 78 percent of continuing doubt about the frontier wars indicates a persistent pattern of 'unknowing' about the nature of national foundations. As scholars have argued, historical unknowing arises less from collective ignorance about the nature of the contested past than from a process of making the past intelligible in a way that reinforces a legitimising narrative of statehood.[12]

This national tension between support for historical truth-telling and reluctance to accept uncomfortable historical truths also suggests a deep-seated ambivalence about what and whom reconciliation is 'for'. Some critics of formal reconciliation agendas have pointed out that they seek to establish an account of shared national experience in a way that is more comforting for non-Indigenous Australians than empowering for Indigenous Australians.[13] Others note that any model of reconciliation that only 'remembers' the past to 'move on' from it can replicate historical amnesia. As Ravi de Costa observes, when interpreted principally as historical 'recognition', reconciliation does not necessarily transform relations in the present or challenge ongoing structural inequalities.[14] In this sense, reconciliation remains as contested a term in Australia as it does across the former settler colonial world.[15]

The degree to which the politics of reconciliation continue to be nationally contested was recently visible in relation to the federal government's plans to commemorate the 250th anniversary of Captain Cook's arrival on Australian shores. While the government interpreted heritage reinvestment in the Captain Cook anniversary as a reconciliation project to celebrate the meeting of European and Indigenous cultures, critics saw Cook as a divisive figure and a symbol of colonial conquest.[16] In a similar vein, the 2018 inauguration of Reconciliation Day as a public holiday in the nation's capital attracted argument about the inappropriateness of 'celebrations amid ongoing indigenous disadvantage'.[17]

Whereas the tension between a trend to remember and a desire to forget the histories and ongoing legacies of colonialism appears to be most entrenched at the national level, a community-led truth-telling process has arguably been more active at the regional level over a longer period. This is suggested by the growth of regional memorials and monuments to Australia's frontier wars, especially during the past two decades, alongside a growing tradition of public-space installations and exhibitions by Indigenous artists and curators.[18]

Many regional memorial projects began as community initiatives that developed from collaborations between local Indigenous and settler-descended groups and local heritage bodies or councils.[19] This trend towards remembering the conflicted frontier region by region reflects the fact that frontier violence was by definition a regional phenomenon, where hostilities and contestations over occupation of Country took place between settler and Indigenous groups who lived in close proximity and often knew one other, at least by reputation. As a result, accounts of frontier warfare and massacre have always had a stronger presence in local historical memory than in national historical narratives, carried forward intergenerationally by Indigenous and settler-descended communities whose historical experiences might have differed radically but whose roots remained mutually grounded in place.[20] In this sense, the 'great Australian silence' on Indigenous–settler relations in the colonial past was always fissured by a dense web of hairline fractures.[21]

This chapter addresses the uneven relationship between national and regional remembering of Australia's violent frontiers. It considers two regional memorials – established at opposite ends of Australia and more than two decades apart – to show how local communities have been reflecting upon Australia's histories of foundational violence in ways that are arguably more successful than has been true in the contested national space. As memorials that sit within an expanding field of regional engagement with the frontier wars, these two examples speak back to larger trends in the politics of memory that have been occurring in settler nations since the late twentieth century, and they highlight the power of regional projects to influence how national narratives of foundation can be revised.

The Explorers' Monument in Fremantle, Western Australia (first erected in 1913 and adapted as a counter-monument in 1994) is an example of a memorial project that offers a corrective to an older, orthodox account of pioneer foundation. The Reconciliation Cross in Toowoomba, Queensland (unveiled in 2016) is a newer memorial that commemorates Indigenous defence of Country as military action and highlights the moment of colonial foundation as a crossing of two sovereign cultures. Although these memorial projects were initiated decades apart on either side of the history wars debates, both commemorate the agency of Indigenous people in opposing colonial occupation of their Country and, in so doing, emphasise the ongoing significance of the past in the present. In this sense, they offer a model of reconciliation that does not attempt to resolve colonial dispossession and its related injustices as part of a history now gone; rather, they foreground contested Country as part of the permanent legacy of living within a settler nation.

REGIONAL MEMORIALS: RECONCILING WITH THE FRONTIER WARS

Since Federation in 1901, the Australian landscape has been dotted with monuments to the memory of individual settlers killed by Indigenous people. But until the end of the twentieth century, few memorials existed to prompt awareness of the 'other side of the frontier'.[22] The 1994 adaptation of Western Australia's 1913 Explorers' Monument is an early example of a regional memorial project designed to counteract this nationwide orthodoxy of wilful unknowing.

Explorers' Monument, with plaque depicting shackled Aboriginal prisoners.
Photograph by Graeme Saunders, 2014. Reproduced with kind permission of Graeme Saunders. Courtesy of Monument Australia, Creswick, Australia

The plaque adorning the original monument dedicates it to the memory of three white explorers fatally 'attacked at night by treacherous natives' near La Grange Bay in November 1864 and to the colonial magistrate and 'pioneer pastoralist' Maitland Brown who led the 'search and punitive party' after their deaths. According to local accounts from Karajarri people, the spearing of the explorers was provoked by earlier acts of abduction, murder and the violation of customary law by pastoral entrepreneurs and pearlers.[23] In retaliation, Brown's punitive party chased down and shot dead approximately 20 Karajarri people, a punishment he described in his journal in the elliptical terms of 'teach[ing] them a lesson'.[24] Erected some 50 years after these events, in a post-Federation climate when veneration of the colonial pioneer was at its peak, the Explorers' Monument applauded the punitive expedition as the assertion of order over Aboriginal 'treachery', rendered in an etching of shackled Aboriginal prisoners being brought to justice.

In 1988, the year of Australia's bicentenary, a collective of Indigenous community members and non-Indigenous historians formed a Public Action Project to turn the monument into a counter-monument that would prompt Australians to 'think more critically about their history, mindful that the way we see our past influences the way we act in the present'.[25] The counter-monument – a term made familiar by memory scholar James Young in relation to the renewed field of Holocaust memorialisation after the fall of the Soviet Bloc in the early 1990s – is designed not just to revise how the past can be remembered but also to encourage active dialogue on the nature of historical interpretation and to allow for the inclusion of different, potentially unreconciled points of view.[26] In this sense, counter-monuments differ fundamentally from anti-monument movements, such as the Rhodes Must Fall campaign, which seek to remove the statues of controversial foundational figures from public space.

Through the Public Action Project, researchers and Karajarri descendants of the La Grange Bay massacre worked together to determine the wording of a new plaque that was added to the original monument in 1994, one that tells 'the other side of the story'.[27] Australian historian and original Public Action Project member Bruce Scates describes this model of 'dialogical memorialisation' as a process that can bring orthodox (settler) and neglected (Indigenous) historical perspectives into conversation without necessarily reconciling them into a reassuring narrative of shared experience.[28]

Some scholars have expressed caution about the influence of counter-monuments. For instance, public policy scholar Elizabeth Strakosch suggests that while they have value in including previously neglected historical perspectives, they can also perpetuate a form of passive monumentalism that does little to challenge the state-building tendencies of monuments themselves.[29] Other commentators suggest that physical monuments can buttress a distinctly Western style of historical remembering; or, as a familiar part of public space, can serve as a kind of memory proxy that facilitates forgetting more than reflection.[30]

Aside from such debates about the value of counter-monuments, the Explorers' Monument demonstrates how local historical memory of the violent frontier can directly engage unsettled national debates (in this case emerging from Australia's bicentennial year) about uncomfortable historical truths.[31] This intent to mediate between regional history and national debate is reflected in the new plaque's script, which remembers the Karajarri people killed by Brown's party and 'all other Aboriginal people who died during the invasion of their country'.

Uncle Colin Isaacs (artist), Reconciliation Cross commemorating the Battle of One Tree Hill, 2016. Photograph by John Huth, 2017. Reproduced with kind permission of John Huth. Courtesy of Monument Australia, Creswick

Some two decades later, a similar symbiosis between a regional memorial project and current national debate informs the Reconciliation Cross, installed in 2016 in the Warriors Chapel of St Luke's Anglican Church, Toowoomba. While the Explorers' Monument revitalises a historically neglected history of a frontier massacre, the Reconciliation Cross commemorates a regionally well-known event: the 'Battle of One Tree Hill' near Table Top Mountain in southern Queensland. Through the early 1840s until his death in 1846 in a settler raid, the Jagera warrior Multuggerah led his people in an effective campaign against settler appropriation of Jagera Country, intimidating pastoralists, harassing stock and laying siege to local supply routes. In September 1843, Multuggerah initiated a successful ambush of an armed settler cavalcade on the overland supply route to the Darling Downs, forcing its retreat and leading the government to respond with a military counter-offensive.[32]

Unlike acts of settler violence, Indigenous campaigns of guerrilla warfare against settlers attracted intense public attention. Even in his own lifetime, Multuggerah's war on settlers was put to verse in the colonial press.[33] As a result, Indigenous resistance leaders like Multuggerah, Yagan and Jandamarra have maintained strong visibility in Australia's settler-descended histories of place, as well as in Indigenous community memory.[34] But while Indigenous military action traditionally tended to be read in terms of the outlaw or otherwise absorbed into European cultural traditions, a more exceptional depiction of the retributive violence that followed Multuggerah's campaign was recorded by the young colonial artist Thomas John Domville Taylor, who was resident in the Darling Downs in the early 1840s. In the pencil drawing opposite, inscribed with the words 'Blacks who robbed the drays … attacked by a party of Darling Downs squatters', Domville Taylor recorded in stark clarity the settler campaign of terror that followed Multuggerah's success at the 'Battle of One Tree Hill'. Echoing the kind of intimidatory violence that was widely deployed on Australia's frontiers, he depicts a camp of Aboriginal men, women and children fleeing before a moving line of squatters who shoot from their raised guns. Women run with small children on their backs and figures fall before the line of fire. National Library of Australia curator Marie-Louise Ayres suggests that the drawing could be a direct eyewitness account of this event in September 1843. Even if it were retrospectively imagined, it offers a rare contemporary record of the 'tragedy of dispossession' that unfolded here and everywhere around the continent.[35]

Emerging from a community initiative to commemorate this history, the Reconciliation Cross is a notable example of how European and Indigenous traditions can be brought together to acknowledge the frontier wars. Designed by Dharawal Elder and acclaimed artist Uncle Colin Isaacs, it was sponsored by a local descendant of an early settler family, Heather Johnston. Uncle Colin Isaacs's design draws together Indigenous and Christian spiritual systems in presenting two arms of the cross as the meeting point between two cultures and peoples. The warrior Multuggerah stands atop the vertical arm, representing 'all Aboriginal people of strength, wisdom and courage, who love their land and people and its Spirit'. The horizontal arm represents 'European settler culture, much less deep in Australia yet still real and vital'. Together the arms of the cross invite all

Thomas Domville Taylor, *Squatters Attack on an Aboriginal Camp, One Tree Hill, Queensland, 1843*. Courtesy of National Library of Australia, Canberra

Australians 'to honour those who have gone before us, to appreciate Aboriginal culture more deeply, and to work for justice and healing for all'. In placing the defence of Indigenous Country and continuity of Indigenous culture at the centre of the nation's foundational narrative, the Reconciliation Cross encourages reconciliation as a process that not only remembers the past but also prompts 'reflection and attention' in the present.[36]

CONCLUSION

These locally initiated memorial projects are just two examples from a growing number that emphasise an Indigenous experience of the frontier wars and of survival in the aftermath of colonial violence. Other memorials to the frontier wars draw upon the familiar lexicon of military memorials, reminding us that remembrance for those who fought and died for their country and culture applies as much to Aboriginal people killed on colonial frontiers as to soldiers lost in offshore battles.[37] Some memorial projects highlight the ways intimacy and violence were closely entangled on colonial frontiers, such as the 'Women in Pearling' monument, funded by the Broome Shire and Kimberley Development Commission and unveiled in 2010 on the Broome foreshore. The monument, which depicts an Aboriginal woman emerging from the sea, recalls the history of blackbirding, indenture and forced sexual servitude that marked Indigenous women's role in the pearling sector. It also celebrates their historical place as mothers and builders of the region's multiracial community.[38] All these projects capture the power of local memorials, as Stephen Gilchrist puts it, to inscribe the landscape with Indigenous as well as settler historical experiences and to assert their intergenerational significance.[39]

From place to place around the continent, regional memorial practices that prioritise an Indigenous experience of the frontier are helping to advance a broader national agenda of truth-telling about Australia's histories of colonial violence and their afterlives. In this sense, regional memorials to the frontier wars can serve as mnemonics that influence the national story. This is best demonstrated by the Myall Creek Memorial Site in Kamilaroi country (northeastern New South Wales), established in 2000 near the original location of the notorious Myall Creek massacre of June 1838. The plans for the memorial site emerged from a reconciliation conference initiated in 1998 by Aunty Sue Blacklock, Elder of the Kamilaroi nation. The project garnered wide community support and local reconciliation project funding, and the Myall Creek Memorial Site is now registered on the National Heritage List.[40] The commemoration that takes place there on the massacre's anniversary each June attracts participants from all over the country in ways that bridge regional and national levels of remembering.[41]

To the degree that the relationship between Australia's colonial history and its national self-image remains contested, a continuing tension persists between an imperative to remember and a drive to forget the truth that the nation's foundations were grounded in violence. But as Mark McKenna argues, although this truth has been 'a slow and traumatic realisation' for non-Indigenous Australians, it has also been unavoidable because Indigenous and settler histories have been entangled since the moment of first contact. In this sense, he notes, reconciliation with our colonial past is best approached 'from the ground up' or from a regional rather than national perspective because it is only through the 'telescopic eye' that we can 'see in fine detail' what is otherwise lost within the national frame.[42]

Chapter 3

THE BONES IN THE CLOSET

COLONIAL VIOLENCE IN PĀKEHĀ FAMILY HISTORIES

Keri Mills

Nō Kōterani tōku whaea
Nō Ingarani ngā tūpuna o tōku matua. I haere mai rātou ki Ngāmotu, ki
  Te Waipounamu hoki i te rautau tekau mā iwa. I whawhai tētahi o ōku
  tupuna i te pakanga i Taranaki, ā i riro i a ia ētahi whenua i raupatuhia ai
  i Urenui.
I tipu ake ahau i Te Whanganui a Tara, i te rohe o Taranaki Whānui ki te
  Upoko o te Ika, i raro i te maru o Tarikākā.
Ko Keri Mills tōku ingoa.
Nō reira, tēnā koutou, tēnā koutou, tēnā koutou katoa.

I am Pākehā. My mother is from Scotland and my father's ancestors came from England to Taranaki and Te Wai Pounamu in the nineteenth century. At least one of my ancestors fought in the New Zealand Wars and received stolen Māori land from the government in the wake of the fighting. This is something I have learned fairly recently and am still discovering more about. I grew up in Te Whanganui-a-Tara, around the base of Tarikākā, knowing only scraps of my family history. This chapter explores a common phenomenon among Pākehā New Zealanders – our lack of knowledge about our own families' complicity in the history of colonialism in this country – and tracks a nascent movement among Pākehā scholars and public figures to confront the violence in our family stories. It is primarily written for other Pākehā (Māori need no telling about this story, after all) and uses 'our' and 'we' throughout to refer to Pākehā. In te reo Māori there is a distinction between 'mātou' ('we' that excepts the listener) and 'tātou' ('we' that gathers the listener into the fold). If I were able to write an academic paper in te reo Māori, I would be using 'mātou', in the understanding that not everyone reading this will be Pākehā. All I have to choose from in English is the ambiguous 'we' or the distancing 'they', and I have been distanced from this story for too long.

*

Memory can be a heavy thing. As Te Herenga Waka academic Arini Loader reminds us forcefully in a 2018 briefing paper, Māori have been shouldering the memory burden of our two centuries of colonial history: telling, singing, walking and living these painful stories, keeping them warm.[1] Pākehā, on the other hand, tend to shrug off our history and deny a meaningful connection between ourselves today and the European arrivals of the nineteenth century, even if they were our own kin.

When Pākehā engage with our family histories it is often in a shallow way, absorbed with drawing family trees, documenting births, deaths and marriages, finding homelands back in Europe and discovering famous ancestors. Investigating how one's ancestors lived in Aotearoa, whose lands they lived on and how those lands were removed from their owners to arrive in Pākehā hands, is not a common focus of this genealogical research. Colonial history *is* a focus of academic history, but this is often about the bigger picture. It's not usually connected explicitly to Pākehā family stories and how these are part of the ongoing narratives of colonisation. As a result, for many, colonial history remains an abstract narrative. It isn't hard to disassociate, to think of it as a story that has little to do with life today.

This is in stark contrast to Māori historical traditions of connected kin-based histories, where whakapapa drives and informs research and provides a framework for organising not only histories but all forms of knowledge.[2] Takirirangi Smith has described whakapapa kōrero as 'discourses held by tangata whenua as … important narratives which define their identity. As taonga they also represent a knowledge base for the survival and welfare of the group.' He emphasises that they are neither genealogies nor myths and histories. Instead, whakapapa kōrero are the basis of Māori philosophy and identity.[3] To know your whakapapa is to know your world, your community and yourself. Joseph Te Rito describes learning his 400-year whakapapa as:

a highly exciting, extremely relevant and ... immensely empowering exercise ... it has helped [me] ground myself firmly in place and time. It connects me to my past and to my present. Such outcomes certainly confirm identity and a deep sense of 'being'.[4]

In a follow-up paper he catalogues his family's loss of land over generations through the alien institutions of Pākehā land and inheritance laws, and the damage this has done to whakapapa and identity.[5]

Stories like Te Rito's, of loss wrought by colonisation, are ones that Māori know intimately. The Waitangi Tribunal process has documented a thousand such narratives – of loss of land, resources, sustenance, burial grounds and other sacred places, of language and of identity itself. Many of these histories are in the easily accessible reports, but many, many more are filed away in the tribunal's archives in statements of claim and individual submissions to inquiries.[6] Often these submissions contain genealogical charts through which the writers connect themselves to their ancestors, to establish the ground from which they speak.

In her briefing paper, 'Te Pūtake o te Riri' (The cause of the wars/anger), Arini Loader expresses her anger and exhaustion with the fact that Pākehā do not bother to remember the atrocities of colonial history, such that sites of massacre become places that Pākehā treat as recreational grounds, even get married upon, in a literal dancing on graves. She writes:

> Māori have carried the weight of these 'awkward' episodes in our past on their own. Whānau tell and retell the narratives at tangi, at hura kōwhatu, at trust meetings, at committee meetings, on marae with tea and fried bread, in homes, in schools, in churches. Field trips built into language learning and other wānanga take in sites of significance to the people. History is both 'storied' and 'placed' ... The abusive relationship that the Māori partner is locked into will remain the status quo while their Tiriti partner continues to shirk their share of the labour, of the effort required to enjoy a meaningful, satisfying, respectful partnership.[7]

Historian Rachel Buchanan has written several books about Parihaka, the way it is remembered publicly and privately, and of her family's loss and resilience in the face of colonial onslaught. She makes a similar call for Pākehā to take up this memory work and specifies the importance of acknowledging where there are kinship connections to the colonial violence in our shared past. She notes the 'encouraging signs' that some Pākehā whose ancestors invaded Parihaka have since participated in reconciliation work. She describes the Parihaka reconciliation ceremony and Bill as an 'intimate, whānau-centred' model that all

New Zealanders might follow.⁸ One of the chapters in her book *Ko Taranaki Te Maunga* finishes with the question, 'Will people step up now and take the time to learn, know and feel the history of the places they call home?'⁹

Until recently, few Pākehā have stepped up to do this work, at least in the public eye, but in the last few years several scholars and public figures have published examinations of Pākehā roles in colonial violence and reflected on how it 'feels' to know these stories. Leah Bell, the ex-Otorohanga High School student who, with her classmate Waimarama Anderson, spearheaded the successful campaign to make New Zealand history a compulsory subject at secondary schools, is one of these. Bell delivered a conference paper in 2019 in which she spoke about discovering that two of her ancestors were imperial soldiers in the New Zealand Wars. Her essay is full of 'feeling'. She noted how, in the past, she had been present at commemorative events for atrocities that she later learned her ancestors had perpetrated. She reflects on the 'bitterly poignant demonstration of privilege' involved in being able to be there without knowing and her overpowering sense of guilt and shame, although she had previously disavowed those feelings as 'lifeless emotions to bring to history'.¹⁰

Another public figure looking into their problematic family past is Radio New Zealand podcast editor Tim Watkin. Watkin decided to delve into the story of one of his European ancestors, who arrived in Taranaki soon after the invasion of Parihaka. The result was a one-hour podcast about the wars in Taranaki and Watkin's attempts to find out how his ancestor had obtained land in the area (purchased from the Crown out of the huge tracts confiscated in the 1860s). The podcast culminates in Watkin meeting Anaru Marshall, a leader of Ngāti Maru. Together they visit the land, where he asks Marshall, 'How do you think your ancestors saw mine?'¹¹ Marshall answers generously, pointing out that Māori were initially welcoming of Pākehā settlers but noting that this welcome would have worn thin when 'it became apparent that you couldn't live the way you used to live, in your environment'. Nor could they live effectively in a Pākehā way, as all their resources were gone.

Environmental studies scholar Amanda Thomas writes about her ancestor Arthur Turnbull, who was a member of the armed forces that invaded Parihaka. She admits to feeling 'uncomfortable' about this history and notes that discomfort can be a productive emotion. The combination of guilt, shame and tension can drive action on 'how we might reciprocate the welcome extended by Māori and what it means to be held together within a Treaty relationship'. Thomas suggests one of the ways this might be done is by 'giving things up', considering redirecting inherited assets, and supporting Māori political struggles.[12]

In *This Pākehā Life* educational scholar Alison Jones details her complex (and occasionally imagined) interactions with Māori and reflects on the way these exchanges have shaped her own identity. Jones is the child of 1950s English immigrants but has discovered a genealogical link to colonial Aotearoa. Two of her relatives fought in the Taranaki and Waikato wars, and one attended the Treaty signing. She writes of this discovery: 'I had feelings that were very mixed but, strangely, largely positive. I felt that, somehow, if I had a claim to our past, I also had a claim to our future.'[13]

An increasing number of scholars are beginning to theorise more deeply in this area. Historian Miranda Johnson wrote a thoughtful piece on her ancestor Ormond Wilson, who, for many years, cared for the historic New Zealand Wars battle site of Te Pōrere in the central North Island, and on Wilson's grandfather J.D. Ormond, who was a government official in charge of operations in the area at the time of the battle. Rather than engaging directly with ideas of shame or discomfort, Johnson writes of the 'knotted' nature of histories and their entanglements in human relationships across time. She reflects on the way that Pākehā no longer 'live' their family histories and how the act of reviving these dormant familial connections from the past can remind us of the ongoing obligations to those in the present and future.[14]

An interesting example of a Pākehā scholar grappling with the complexities of family entanglements in the colonial past has come from sociologist Hugh Campbell. He devotes a chapter of his book to analysing the rise of the 'modern farm' in Aotearoa through a cluster of farms from around Aotearoa that feature in his own family's past. Campbell's chapter is lively with the 'possible futures' that existed in the early days of Pākehā farming, particularly his example of Heather's Homestead/Marotahei in the Waikato, where Campbell's Pākehā ancestor and his Māori wife lived in the area on Māori terms. Campbell documents a narrowing of these possible futures and the way the diverse farms of the nineteenth century all began to resemble each other in the extractive and environmentally damaging farm model that, in most places across Aotearoa, continues to the present. He argues that the Māori histories of these places have been 'made invisible' by Pākehā (though presumably not made invisible to Māori), thus enabling and justifying the Pākehā agricultural economy.[15]

Another growing cluster of Pākehā writers devoting deeper scholarly attention to their family's complicity in colonial violence have been influenced by the American educationalist Christine Sleeter. Sleeter identifies the issue of advocates for descendants of settlers to engage in 'critical family history' or family history that examines relationships of power in the past.[16] One of these scholars is sociologist Avril Bell. In a recent article Bell scrutinises the histories of her two 'middling' Pākehā family lines in Aotearoa to examine the ways they have benefited from the colonial regime. Bell focuses on her family's acquisition of land and the economic advantage that conveyed and juxtaposes this with the corresponding Māori loss of land and impoverishment. She uses Belinda Borell and colleagues' framework of five key elements of historical privilege to analyse the initial 'windfalls' of land and wealth received by her families in the past and to follow the trail of inheritance to her family in the present:

Five key elements of historical privilege
1. original windfall/s (benefits that are substantially delivered by forces outside the individuals' efforts)
2. ongoing acts of historical renewal (the social processes by which privilege is embedded over time)
3. experienced by groups
4. across generations
5. involving a combination of remembering and forgetting, especially forgetting.[17]

Bell then engages with Waitangi Tribunal reports relating to the Tāmaki and Taranaki rohe (regions), where the two lines of her family were based, and contrasts her family's establishment and maintenance of a 'modest' level of wealth with the forced landlessness of the iwi of those regions. In this article she doesn't dwell on how it 'feels' to know these histories, although she reflects on the evolution of her thought from unawareness to acknowledgement. She finishes by saying, 'It behooves us Pākehā to educate ourselves about our history ... and to support ongoing Māori struggles and initiatives, however our location and circumstances allow.'[18]

Another scholar in this group is political scientist Richard Shaw, whose book *The Forgotten Coast* follows three of his ancestors – one of whom, Andrew Gilhooly, was a member of the Armed Constabulary – at the time of the invasion of Parihaka. The confiscated lands Gilhooly received for his service created wealth for subsequent generations of his family, something Shaw reflects upon and attempts to trace in the same manner as Bell. Shaw was inspired to undertake this research after reading Rachel Buchanan's work.[19] Two other scholars, Rebecca Ream and Esther Fitzpatrick, also follow Sleeter's lead and reflect on their family entanglements in the colonial past. Ream and Fitzpatrick deal with the dual issues of difficult emotions and scant remaining historical evidence by delving into experimental methodologies of poetry and fictionalisation from a factual base.[20]

Young scholars appear to be picking up the wero (challenge) as well. PhD candidate Dani Pickering details a transformative experience that followed their discovery of the story of a Scottish Gaelic-speaking ancestor, Niall MacLeòid, who was a member of the Armed Constabulary in Taranaki during the years leading up to and possibly including the 1881 invasion of Parihaka. The research inspired Pickering to learn the Gaelic language and reflect deeply on the various complexities of a colonised person becoming a coloniser. Pickering's thesis is focused on how identity narratives might be used to inspire dominant settler groups to take action on decolonisation.[21]

These publications and research projects all appeared between 2017 and 2021, and though only the latter cluster of scholars are substantially in conversation with each other, all cover remarkably similar themes – the discovery of family entanglements in colonial violence, reflection on difficult-to-articulate feelings of guilt, shame, discomfort and complicity, and political resolution to commit to more honourable and supportive relationships with Māori in the present.

I was spurred into action to learn my own family's history by Arini Loader's call for Pākehā to stop 'shirking the labour' of remembering the New Zealand Wars. A few months before she published her briefing paper through the Policy Observatory (where I worked), I had discovered that my great-great-great-grandfather, Thomas Wills, had fought in the Taranaki wars of the 1860s. I chose to look into his life for a reo Māori assignment in a class I was taking at the time.[22] All I knew about Wills beforehand was a scrap of family memory that was passed down to me in the ordinary 'living' way: my great-grandmother remembered that Māori men came to her grandfather's house in Taranaki where he spoke with them in te reo. I began by typing his name into a search on the Puke Ariki website.

Immediately out of the ether leaped a photo of him sitting, white-bearded and resplendent, beside his wife Martha at their son's wedding. Under the photo was a caption saying that he had received the medal he wore on his chest as a result of participating in the Taranaki wars.[23] I was shocked – but not that he had fought

Wills family photo, with Martha and Thomas Wills seated at front. Private collection

in the wars. As a historian of Aotearoa New Zealand, this was not at all surprising to me when presented with the fact. What *was* shocking was the accessibility of this information – instant, on the internet – and the fact that I had not bothered to discover it until 2018, nearly 20 years after I began to study New Zealand history as a final-year subject in high school. I have since learned that he received confiscated land in Urenui as a government reward for his role in the fighting, though I'm yet to successfully trace how that 'windfall' percolated down through the generations of my family. I have not even begun to learn about the other wings of my Pākehā family, who mainly went to areas of Te Wai Pounamu (the South Island) also in the nineteenth century.

As Rachel Buchanan puts it, 'Forgetting is rarely innocent. People have to work hard not to know, recall, not to see, and to be truly ignorant.'[24] I was confronted by the fact that I had worked hard to avoid this information, partly stalled by the Pākehā academic historian's snobbery of family history but also, surely, by an unconscious, fear-driven looking-away. Sociologist Stanley Cohen has written about the many different forms denial takes, in individuals and particularly in communities, when faced with information that is 'disturbing, threatening or

Thomas and Martha Wills. Private collection

anomalous'.[25] He writes specifically about historical denial, saying it is usually not a planned campaign of forgetting but rather a 'gradual seepage of knowledge down some collective black hole', and emphasises the instrumental value, for 'perpetrator' societies, in leaving behind the memories of the violence they have wreaked on others. 'Historical skeletons are put in cupboards because of the political need to be innocent of a troubling recognition; they remain hidden because of the political absence of an inquiring mind.'[26] Over time, it seems, these skeletons can deteriorate, such that when dormant minds are jogged into inquiring, the only things that remain are small and disturbing bits of bone, hard to piece together.

Loader describes a 'bitter, confusing, traumatic legacy' of the New Zealand Wars. The fragments of history left lying in my family cupboard, and the further fragments I've managed to find in our national repositories, are nothing so coherent as a legacy. Where, for Māori, there is a living, collective memory from our colonial history, it seems that for Pākehā there is an unexamined and many-faceted *inheritance*. I am interested in the various meanings of the word 'inheritance'. First, there is the material inheritance of money, land, privilege, names, assets, heirlooms – the kind of inheritance Avril Bell traces in her work. There is also a genetic inheritance of the blood and body, a part of our ancestors literally alive in us today. Pākehā are not accustomed to thinking of genetics as significant for historical studies, though it speaks to a Māori understanding of the past. Last, there are inherited behaviours, what oral historian Maria Haenga-Collins calls the 'reproductions' of colonial practices.[27] This is the way Pākehā actions in the present mirror and continue those of the past, sometimes without our awareness.[28]

A world of inheritance and identity remains for Pākehā to explore, and it won't be entirely bound up in violence and shame. Poet Glenn Colquhoun captures some of the opportunity that is also a part of this re-enlivening of the past:

> As an immigrant culture it seems at times Pākehā are a book without a cover, one with the first chapter missing. For me, being Pākehā now is enormously exciting. It means we get a chance to write that chapter, or at least compile the stories that reveal it.[29]

What it is to be Pākehā is a question we need to keep returning to. Michael King's last word on the subject was offered a long while ago, and in a criticism of it Lydia Wevers suggested being Pākehā should be 'not an expression of fear and entitlement but an acceptance of a foundational relationship [with Māori] which describes why we choose to be here, the grounds on which we are here and what we should do about it'.[30] As to what to do about it: whaowhia te kete mātauranga. The first step is to learn.

Chapter 4

WĒTERE TE RERENGA AND THE MURDER OF REV. JOHN WHITELEY

Anaru Eketone

I remember, as a child, sitting in the kitchen talking to my mother about what, in those days, we called the Māori Wars. At that time, it was not uncommon to be teased by my Pākehā classmates, who claimed they were in charge because they had beaten us in the *Mowri* wars.

My mother is Pākehā and her grandparents had moved to New Zealand after the Highland clearances. My father is Māori from the Ngāti Maniapoto and Waikato iwi (tribes). I was probably worried about how unfair the wars were. I distinctly remember her mentioning that the 'Hauhaus' were 'terrible people', and I recall thinking, 'How does she know they were terrible?', 'How does she know about the Māori Wars?', and 'I can't believe we were in the wrong.'

I found out how she knew a few years later when she showed us an old school journal, where the story 'Children of the Forest', a memoir of the childhood of A.H. Messenger, had been serialised.[1] It told of Messenger's life as the son of an officer who was guarding a frontier post at Pukearuhe, north of New Plymouth, to stop Māori in the King Country from reaching through to Taranaki in the early 1880s. There was one particular description of a fearsome Māori leader, Te Wētere, who had led the attack at Pukearuhe that killed five men, a woman and three children in 1869. Messenger described how they had 'gazed fearfully at this tall sinister figure' and wrote, 'I remember that all that night in my dreams I was being chased by tattooed Maori warriors.'[2]

So this was where my mother had got her vision of the 'Hauhaus'. It had obviously made a lasting impression on her.

In the mid-1980s I was visiting home from Auckland and my mother pulled out a *Dunedin Weekender* article on the nineteenth-century photographers, the Burton Brothers.³ One photo stood out to her and she had saved it because the man in it looked exactly like my father in his mid-forties. The resemblance was so uncanny she had ordered extra copies of it. I looked at the caption and saw the name 'Wetere Te Rerenga Great Mokau chief'. It was the very same Te Wētere who had formed her image of the Hauhau some 30 years before. I looked at my mother and said, 'That is Dad's great-great-grandfather.' It was so ironic: the man she married was both the descendant and spitting image of the bogeyman that had such an impact on her as a child.

For over 150 years my great-great-great-grandfather Wētere Te Rerenga has been referred to as the murderer responsible for the death of the Methodist missionary Rev. John Whiteley, a claim that is disputed by the family to this day. Whiteley was among those killed in 1869 at Pukearuhe, a military redoubt at Parininihi, a natural boundary between Taranaki and the Tainui tribes of Ngāti Maniapoto and Waikato. The attack on Pukearuhe redoubt was a defining moment of the war against the Waikato–Tainui tribes because these were the last shots fired in anger in that conflict; the gunship rounds launched at Mōkau pā a few weeks later were the last shots of the Taranaki war.⁴

The first part of the attack on the redoubt is reasonably clear. Wētere Te Rerenga led a party of around 15 men to attack the Pukearuhe redoubt by deception. They pretended they had pigs to sell, and while the four soldiers stationed at the fort were separated from one another, the attackers killed them with tomahawks. They also killed the wife of one of the soldiers and her three children, aged five, three and three months. It was as grisly a scene as you can imagine.⁵ Even the dog was killed.⁶

The men gathered some of the bodies together and buried them in a shallow grave. They then searched for arms and ammunition and anything else of value that they could carry. But as the group prepared to leave, a lone rider was seen approaching. It was John Whiteley, on his regular visit to parishioners. Whiteley had previously been a missionary to the Ngāti Maniapoto and Waikato tribes for over 30 years.⁷ Now, while he still had Māori parishioners, he spent most of his time with the new settlers who had moved to Taranaki in search of land. Whiteley had become discouraged by the behaviour of Māori. In his view, God had

OPPOSITE: *Wētere Te Rerenga, Ngāti Maniapoto.*
Photograph by Burton Brothers, 1885. Box-096-022, Hocken Collections – Uare Taoka o Hākena. Courtesy of University of Otago, Dunedin

Reverend John Whiteley, Methodist missionary.

Unknown photographer, c. 1900. 'Rev. J. Whiteley, Killed White Cliffs Massacre Feb. 1869'. From William Francis Robert Gordon, Some 'Soldiers of the Queen' Who Served in the Maori Wars and Other Notable Persons Connected Herewith (photo album), p. 11. PHO2011-2458. Courtesy of Puke Ariki, New Plymouth

commanded mankind to go forth and replenish the earth, including turning wilderness into productive land. He believed that Māori were disobeying God by not selling land they weren't using to settlers who would fulfil God's commands.[8] So strongly did he feel about this that he had written to the *Times* in London, calling for resources to defeat Māori and put an end to their love of land, which he referred to as 'idolatry'.[9] His views were well publicised, and he was apparently also known for reporting to the government on the movement of rebel Māori forces.[10] Now, as he approached the redoubt, Whiteley's horse was shot from under him and he was hit by five bullets. The physician who later examined the body reported that each one would have been fatal.[11]

While these are the generally accepted facts, the minutes leading up to Whiteley's death are where accounts diverge. One source claimed that Wētere had said that whoever the rider was, they needed to die so they couldn't raise the alarm.[12] Other sources say that Wētere told Whiteley to go back, but he refused as he wanted to see what they had done.[13] Still others say Whiteley was hit by a volley of shots after someone said 'Dead cocks don't crow' and encouraged the men to shoot.[14] Another said Wētere himself fired two shots that hit Whiteley, then walked up to him with his pistol and shot him at close range as Whiteley knelt to pray.[15]

The attack on the military settlers was sudden, although there had apparently been warnings that were not heeded.[16] The murder of a woman and her three young children by axe was brutal. But the land wars had moved on from the so-called chivalrous engagements of the early Waikato War (1863–64). Colonial troops had killed Māori women and children at Rangiaowhia in February 1864; and nearby, at the other end of Ngāti Maniapoto country at the Battle of Ōrākau, captured women had been bayoneted.[17] However, the murder of John Whiteley seemed to cause the most consternation and have the longest-lasting effect. Here was the so-called 'friend of the Māori', supposedly murdered by the man he had baptised and given the new 'Christian' name Hone Wētere, John Wesley, the name of the founder of Methodism.[18] From that time until this, the Methodist Church has dominated the narrative. Whiteley wasn't just murdered, he was martyred: a true martyr killed because of his faith.[19] The Methodist version of this story is as self-serving as the family narrative I will discuss later.

The authorised version was written by William Morley, a young minister who had moved to Raglan to work originally with Waikato Māori and was to marry Hannah Buttle, the daughter of an early Methodist missionary to Ngāti Maniapoto.[20] Hannah would have known Whiteley well, as his old mission station in Kāwhia was also in Ngāti Maniapoto territory. Morley blames Wētere and repeats several times Whiteley's status as a martyr.[21] The need for a martyred John Whiteley, rather than a murdered one, was important. Tertullian, writing in the second century about how martyrdom makes Christianity strong, wrote, 'The blood of the martyrs is the seed of the church.'[22] Martyrdom is an important part of the history of the Christian church and is believed to lead to a purification of the church that will bring revival. Therefore, all the facts of Whiteley's death had to feed into this narrative: Whiteley's conversation with Wētere stressed his position as a shepherd looking after his flock; and he had died at the hands of his one-time acolyte who had turned from the faith, as he knelt in prayer beside his horse.

Yet there were other narratives as well. One of the stories that emerged was that a Pākehā member of the group had instigated the murder, had cried out 'Dead cocks don't crow' and fired first. This death at the hands of a Pākehā was reported early on by the *Daily Southern Cross* newspaper but dismissed as a lie. As one reporter said:

> There is a horrible report now current among the natives, and by them generally believed, which I trust, for the honour of our race, will prove utterly false. It is to the effect that the murderers at Pukearuhe, or White Cliffs, were accompanied by two white men, and that the Rev. Mr. Whiteley met his death at the hands of one of them … I give you this as I have heard it – a Māori report. I can hardly credit myself that any such bloodthirsty renegades, capable of such atrocities on their own countrymen, women, and children, can be in existence.[23]

In other words, it could not have been true as no white man would have done this sort of thing to another white man.

Wētere claimed David Cockburn killed Whiteley.[24] In this he was supported by Rewi Maniapoto, the most important chief at the other end of Maniapoto territory (although he was not at the scene at the time), who also claimed that Cockburn fired the first shot.[25] Benjamin Ashwell, an Anglican missionary in Waikato, reported to his superiors that two Pākehā had killed Whiteley; and Cort Schnackenberg, one of the missionaries who had served with Whiteley in Maniapoto territory, claimed from the outset that it was said a Pākehā was responsible for the death.[26]

The man in question was referred to as Wētere's white slave or 'taurekareka', though the more accurate term would be 'mōkai', which sometimes means slave but is closer in meaning to 'pet'.[27] Cockburn had deserted from the British army in 1865 from the very area that had been attacked.[28] He had gone to live with Ngāti Maniapoto, where he had five wives.[29] If Cockburn was indeed there, it makes sense that he would not have wanted any witnesses to his involvement. While many Māori would not have been afraid of British justice, as a soldier Cockburn would have had intimate knowledge of British military discipline and what he could expect if it became known that he had committed treason by taking up arms against his country. There would be little reason for the Māori involved to hide their identities. They would not have needed to worry about Whiteley warning other settlers, as the mere fact that they torched the buildings as they left would have drawn locals from far and wide. Also, Whiteley was killed by several bullets, the discharge of which could have raised the alarm. Upon their escape, they might have tied up Whiteley easily enough. It is more likely that the Pākehā man present, a deserter, was in most need of no witnesses.

In the eyes of Pākehā, the most damning account was by a 'half-caste', Henry Phillips, who signed a confession in September 1882 to a local shopkeeper and a farmer. Phillips claimed that he and some companions had come up from the south. Having been ferried across the Mimi River by Captain Messenger, they had met Wētere north of Pukearuhe, and Wētere had forced him to accompany his party as a translator. Phillips said he witnessed the killings but had not participated in them; Wētere, he claimed, had decided that whoever the rider was, he should be killed.[30]

It is doubtful that Wētere would have wanted a translator, as a number of contemporaries noted that he was fluent in both written and spoken English.[31] And there were other discrepancies in Phillips' story. Captain Messenger recalled talking to a man that day who had demanded to be ferried across the Mimi River with his friends. Messenger was concerned about the type of men they were and was suspicious of their motives.[32] Wētere also claimed that Phillips was one of the men who shot Whiteley.[33] In fact, Phillips is probably the person referred to as the second Pākehā, as it was not unusual for Māori to refer to 'half-castes' as Pākehā, just as Pākehā call 'half-castes' Māori.

The timing of Phillips' confession is interesting. A few weeks earlier, a telegram had fallen into the hands of the newspapers that claimed Wētere had made a full confession to the killing of Whiteley.[34] It was a fake produced by Whiteley's grandson, John Whiteley King.[35] King was angry that Wētere had been travelling freely to Wellington to meet with Cabinet minister John Bryce and had not been arrested by the government.[36] It may be that Phillips was rushing to get a competing story out. Within a week of Phillips' confession, Wētere, along with Te Kooti and others, had received a full pardon from the government for their wartime activities.[37] It would have been interesting to see Phillips' confession if he knew that he, too, was to be pardoned. As for Wētere, even though he now had a full pardon, he maintained until his death that he was not responsible for Whiteley's death.[38]

Wētere's pardon stunned the families of dead Pākehā, who were 'angry and disgusted' that the killers would benefit from the amnesty.[39] But the settler government was in a quandary: as one of the top three Ngāti Maniapoto chiefs, Wētere had the power to keep the King Country closed but instead had supported opening it up for the building of the main trunk railway.[40] Without an amnesty, this wouldn't have happened.

AFTERMATHS

THE FAMILY STORY

Wētere Te Rerenga led the attack but always maintained that he was not responsible for the death of John Whiteley.[41] However, family history is always contextual and can change in response to the dominant thinking of the time. One family narrative comes from Sister Heeni Wharemaru, one of Wētere's descendants, born in 1912.[42] Heeni wanted to do church work, but her parents were reluctant. However, after some discussion, they released her to the work of the Methodist Church. In an interview, Sister Heeni said, 'So without really understanding why at the time, I was given over to the Methodist Church partly as an offer to make reparations' for the death of Whiteley.[43] Sister Heeni became a well-known deaconess of the Methodist Church, where her service was seen as part of the family's response to Whiteley's death; while Sister Heeni knew of the association, she rarely mentioned it.[44]

I did not hear of it until 1983 at my grandmother's funeral. An uncle was teasing my grandmother's cousins about how our ancestor was a murderer and had killed a missionary. One of my relations snapped back that it was all wrong and Wētere was a great man. There was still some residual shame associated with this and the conversation stopped abruptly. I was interested to note the change in family demeanour at a family reunion in the late 1990s, where there was even some pride in the death of Whiteley. The revision of New Zealand history had taken place and the missionaries were no longer seen as the heroic workers of the past but often as land grabbers who used their influence to rob the natives. They were seen as the vanguard of the British colonising mission, sent by a greedy empire to prepare the way for a treaty to allow settlement to extend British power.[45] The death of a missionary who, at first glance, appeared to fit this profile was not only seen as justified, it had also become almost a badge of honour as an example of resistance to colonisation. As I was always interested in whakapapa (genealogy), I asked an uncle, Rongo Wetere, whether Wētere had indeed killed Whiteley. His reply was, 'Yeah, he did it.' I was dubious about this response, as it conflicted with other stories. Twenty years later, in 2018 I approached him again and questioned him about what he had said. He modified his explanation: although Wētere hadn't pulled the trigger, he was responsible because he was in charge. This less enthusiastic response maintained Wētere's innocence of the actual murder but retained a little of the reflected glory of someone who had been part of the resistance.

Wētere had not always been antagonistic towards Pākehā; both before and after the attack,

OPPOSITE: *Wētere Te Rerenga with one of his later wives and son.*
Photograph by Burton Brothers, 1885. C.010083. Courtesy of Museum of New Zealand Te Papa Tongarewa, Wellington

3621 WETERE TE RERENGA, WIFE, AND SON — BURTON BROS. DUNEDIN

he had proven protective of Europeans. He had protected the missionary Cort Schnackenberg in 1865 when tribal members wanted to harm him, as well as the military officer Charles Hutchinson, also in 1865.[46] The following year he had protected three white men who had entered the King Country from Taranaki, and had personally escorted one for three days to Te Awamutu to enable him to go to hospital.[47] He rescued a couple of surveyors from the followers of Te Kooti in 1883, and in 1886 he received a medal from the Royal Humane Society of Australasia for rescuing two surveyors whose boat had foundered on the Mōkau bar.[48] Wētere Te Rerenga was pardoned for his activities in the land wars in 1883 and worked to encourage settlement in his tribal area on his terms.[49] He ran unsuccessfully for Parliament in 1884, and when he died in 1889, he was receiving a £100 pension from the government, the same as that given to Whiteley's widow.[50]

John Whiteley was killed because he was in the wrong place at the wrong time: it didn't matter who he was. It was claimed he was killed so he would not raise the alarm, but he could have been tied up or locked in the blockhouse; the gunfire and smoke from the burning buildings would have been enough to alert people nearby. The idea that a white man had killed Whiteley was dismissed early on, as the reality was the church needed a martyr. The land wars had seen a great falling away from the church. The early missionary successes had been overtaken by ambivalence among many Māori, who had started turning their backs on the church. The land wars were seen by many in the church as a punishment from God for their turning away from Him.[51] The martyrdom of a longstanding significant missionary only served to prove the evil that lurked within the Māori race, and showed that the lack of success was due to Māori ourselves rather than any betrayal by the settlers.

The Europeans' rejection of the idea that a white person could do something as terrible as kill another white person was farcical. Methodist historian Rev. Morley wrote, 'Whiteley was told to go back, but an evil voice and surely not that of a Pākehā, cried out in the darkness "Kāhore e tangi ngā tikaokao mate", "Dead roosters do not crow".'[52]

This story was not something that was talked about in the family and was addressed only when I raised it. It had become almost obliterated from memory, a legacy of guilt. In the end, I don't think this silence was about the death of Whiteley, although his death was the last action of the Waikato wars. To my mind, it was about the death of a woman and three children, one of them a three-month-old baby. That doesn't rest easy with anyone.

PART II
WOMEN AND COLONIAL VIOLENCE

Chapter 5

THE GRANDMOTHER DRESS

VIOLENCE AND WORLD RENEWAL IN NORTHERN CALIFORNIA

Victoria Haskins

In 2014 a sacred deerskin dance skirt made a long journey across the United States, from the Smithsonian National Museum of the American Indian (NMAI) in Washington DC to the ancestral lands of the Wiyot Tribe on Indian Island in Humboldt Bay, California. The elaborately decorated skirt, which the Wiyot people today call the 'Grandmother Dress', was to be worn in a three-day 'World Renewal Ceremony', not performed by Wiyot people since 1860. It was escorted by NMAI conservator Susan Heald, who had determined that the fabric remained strong enough to be danced in. 'There's so much love put into making this dress,' Heald reflected. 'Plus, there's the sound it makes when worn by a dancer, shells moving together at the bottom of the dress and the larger shells at the hip level.' As tribal chair Cheryl A. Seidner recalled, 'It was mesmerizing seeing it come home to dance and sing.'[1]

The occasion was of tremendous significance to the Wiyot Tribe. The last World Renewal Ceremony had been terminated in the most brutal way imaginable. In the pre-dawn hours of 26 February 1860, as Wiyot women and children lay sleeping in their huts in the village of Tuluwat on the sacred island, unprotected by their men, they were set upon by a gang of settler vigilantes and hacked to death. That same night the marauders also laid waste to a village at the mouth of Eel River and attacked at least one other Wiyot community at South Spit. Over the coming days, in what was clearly a coordinated effort, parties of settlers carried out further deadly attacks on Indian villages along the Eel River. These atrocities against a Native tribe that was widely regarded as peaceful and even helpful to the settlers shattered whatever tentative possibilities there were for coexistence of the two cultures. In the wake of the killings, the handful of survivors and their grieving male relatives, and those Wiyots who remained in the Humboldt area, were rounded up and forcibly marched to reservations. Over the ensuing months, years and decades, the Wiyot people would be scattered and the island itself desecrated and poisoned.[2] The World Renewal Ceremony, performed since time immemorial, went into abeyance.

Many Wiyot ceremonial objects were lost or destroyed at the massacre site but the Grandmother Dress survived.[3] The return of the dress to its place of origin in 2014 was key to the transformative power of the revival of the World Renewal Ceremony. This was a way of restoring the true meaning of Indian Island, the centre of the Wiyot world; now, 'Indian Island is not just a place where a bloody massacre occurred; it is once again a place of world renewal.'[4] The revived ceremony is an important part of the Wiyot survivors' descendants' longstanding fight for redress and restoration. Throughout the twentieth century, keeping alive the memory of the infamous massacre on the island has been central to their efforts to secure restitution and reclaim their land. In 1992 Cheryl Seidner and her sister Leona Wilkinson, together with two local non-Native women, Peggy Betsels and Marylee Rohde, began holding annual vigils on neighbouring Woodley Island. By 2000 the tribe had raised enough money to buy the 1.5-acre (0.6ha) ceremony site at Tuluwat, where the massacre occurred. And in 2004 the City of Eureka (which had owned much of the island since about 1960) returned 60 acres (24ha) more to the Wiyot Tribe.[5] In that same year, remarkably, the Grandmother Dress was found languishing in the storage collection of the Smithsonian NMAI, which set in motion preparations for its return to Indian Island in 2014.

Speaking of the vigils to honour those killed in the massacre, Seidner said, 'It's a healing of two communities. It's not just us or them. We need to come together as a community of learning, to understand each other. That rip in our society needs to be mended.'[6] Her remark, with its allusion to the necessary repair of social fabric, evokes the history of invasion, destruction, dispossession, renewal and return that is woven into the story of the Grandmother Dress. As an item of material culture, the skirt can be understood as an agent shaping and mediating human relations through the powerful meanings that it carries – meanings that have only deepened over time. The object itself and its journeys have enabled people to make material and concrete sense of the most senseless of events and helped to restore order, harmony and balance. In a complex historical way, the skirt connected people of, in and with the past, and continues to do so.[7]

Wiyot Tribe women's decorated dance skirt – the Grandmother Dress.

Photograph by NMAI Photo Services. NMAI # 086522.000. Courtesy of National Museum of the American Indian (NMAI), Smithsonian Institution, Washington

---

'THEY COME HIGH'

The Wiyot skirt that was worn at the 2014 ceremony had been held in the NMAI since 1989, when it was legally transferred into the NMAI's possession, along with the major proportion of the NMAI's current collection, from millionaire George Heye's private museum in New York.[8] A small, neatly typed catalogue card record inherited from Heye's museum states that the skirt was 'Wishosk', an old term for Wiyot; that it came from the 'Mouth of Eel River' in Humboldt County; and that it had been collected by a Miss Grace Nicholson. Heye purchased the dress from Nicholson along with another dance skirt (from Trinity County) in 1918, commenting to Nicholson at the time on the quality of these 'specimens' and their expense – 'they come high but we must have them'.[9]

A major figure in the history of Native American collecting, Nicholson operated an Indian curio shop in Pasadena, California, and built a successful career collecting and selling Indian woven baskets to middle-class white women when the fashion for decorative exotic homeware was at its peak. She and her business partner, Carroll S. Hartman, supplied prestigious museums all around the country with thousands of artefacts from northwestern California, acquired in the course of annual collecting trips to the region. No record has been found of how Nicholson acquired the skirt. However, she would certainly have been aware of the story of the massacre on the island and the skirt's significance: her most well-known supplier was the famed basket-weaver Elizabeth Hickox, daughter of Wiyot survivor Polly Conrad Steve.[10]

Two more historical Wiyot dance skirts came to light after the Smithsonian skirt was found. A Wiyot skirt held in the Brooklyn Museum in New York was purchased from the son of a prominent businessman and early settler in Arcata, formerly Union Town on Humboldt Bay, in 1905; the other came into Harvard University's Peabody Museum in 1910, acquired by Nicholson and Hartman from another white man resident in Arcata.[11] It is possible that the Grandmother Dress, too, had been in the private hands of an Arcata resident. Arcata has a pitiful significance in the history of the massacre. The morning after the massacre, grieving Wiyot men rowed the mangled bodies of their wives and children across from the island to lay them out on the shore at Union before the horrified eyes of the townspeople. Some days later, those Wiyots who remained were ordered to leave the township at once and were given no time to gather their belongings.[12]

We can only wonder what meaning the Grandmother Dress and the two other skirts held for those settlers who first secured and then hoarded them. Yet the stories behind the skirts' survival and collection remain considerably less significant than their restoration to the Wiyot people.

'THAT SKIRT WAS READY TO BE FOUND'

In 2004 the Grandmother Dress was discovered in the storage collection of the NMAI by a group of Wiyot women who were there for the museum's official opening. Marnie Atkins, the Wiyot Tribe's then cultural director, had set up an appointment to go out to the NMAI's Cultural Resources Center in Suitland, Maryland:

I was told they had no Wiyot artifacts. But I thought I recognized some baskets. Sure enough, they were Wiyot! And I felt there was something Wiyot on a shelf up higher. So I looked. And there was a dance skirt! A very sacred item … Honestly, I didn't find it. It found me. I believe it came back into our lives because of the land. Because we can now return to Tuluwat. That skirt was ready to be found. To come home and dance again … From this, I knew things should go alright. Even if it takes us another 20 years.[13]

The Wiyot women recognised the skirt as an item of ceremonial regalia, traditionally kept by the aristocratic families of the Indian northwestern communities to be worn by young women in the World Renewal Ceremony. The rediscovered skirt became central to a project to revive the Wiyot women's coming-of-age ceremonies and served as the model for a ceremonial dress handmade by 14-year-old Michelle Hernandez, the daughter of tribal chair Ted Hernandez, to celebrate her passage to womanhood. On the Wiyots' Table Bluff rancheria, over the course of two years, guided by the older women and helped by her younger sister, Michelle made her own dress.

In 2006, for her three-day coming-of-age ceremony, Michelle fasted, bathed and danced in her new dress. Her 'Granddaughter Dress' has become a sacred and iconic object in its own right and was displayed with pride at the opening of the new Wiyot Heritage (now Cultural) Center in March 2007, where it remains today.[14] In reviving the ceremony, Michelle secured its meaningful place in Wiyot culture for future generations: 'I won't say we lost these ceremonies,' she said, 'but they were sleeping, and now they're awake again.'[15]

The Grandmother Dress remained at the NMAI until 2014, when it was loaned back to the Wiyots for the World Renewal Ceremony. As ethnographer Les W. Field explains, ceremonial garments such as the Grandmother Dress are meant to be danced in 'not only to fulfil their function, but also because of the sentient nature of these objects, their individual needs and destinies'.[16] The Grandmother Dress was invested with the energy and spirit, rituals and songs of those who made and sacralised it. In 2014, the energies that its return symbolised would inspire Eureka's then mayor, Frank Jager, to draft a letter of apology for the Indian Island massacre on behalf of the city. Hoping to 'heal old wounds', the apology backfired when the wording was watered down; but the ensuing controversy opened the door to justice. When incoming councillors Natalie Arroyo and Kim Bergel, concerned about the now inflamed state of Indian–white relations in the area, asked the Wiyot people what they wanted, the Wiyots answered simply:

Michelle Hernandez dresses for her coming-of-age ceremony.

Photographs Cheryl Seidner, 2006. Reproduced with kind permission of Michelle Hernandez

'Give us back the island.'[17]

The historic and long-awaited handover of Indian Island to the Wiyot was formalised in October 2019.[18] The Grandmother Dress's permanent return from the NMAI to the Wiyot Tribe was planned for March 2020.[19] This final journey home for the skirt was to occur in conjunction with the planned World Renewal ceremonies, to be held then to celebrate the Indian Island return. It is more than fitting that the Grandmother Dress should be repatriated to the Wiyot for that ceremony. And although a world pandemic intervened, the dress, and the Wiyots, have considerable patience.

The massacre that took place on that gloomy February night in 1860 was intended to destroy the Wiyot world. In targeting sleeping women and children resting at the very centre of their world, at the end of a week of major ceremonies for maintaining the balance of the world, the vigilantes unleashed a storm of horrific disorder. But the rediscovery of the Grandmother Dress by the Wiyot women and the reconnective ways in which it was used – first to revive the coming-of-age ceremonies and then to celebrate the revival of the World Renewal Ceremony – indicate the enduring power and strength not only of the dress itself but of the girls and women it embodies. The Grandmother Dress will remain the embodiment of the power of Native women's endurance and renewal. And as the Wiyots await the return of the Grandmother Dress to sing and dance their energies to life once more, we must all wait with them to see, once again, the world's renewal.

Chapter 6

MR AND MRS FLOWERS

WAR, MARRIAGE AND MOBILITY

Angela Wanhalla

On 8 February 1878, Nathaniel and Margaret Flowers visited the studio of William Harding in Whanganui, New Zealand, to have their photograph taken. Now held at the Alexander Turnbull Library, their image has been a source of fascination for me since I first encountered it in a 1976 book about Māori and photography.[1] As a historian interested in the connections between marriage, race and colonialism, I was intrigued by the photograph, the story behind its making and the lives of the couple themselves.

Harding's photograph is of a striking couple. Devoid of the props common to colonial portraiture, the plain composition and unfussy backdrop relies on the subjects, and their dog, for its appeal. No doubt the domestic charm of this interracial couple affirmed the photo's suitability for a volume about photographic history focused on Māori. Couples such as the Flowers appear rarely in New Zealand's public collections, and their presence in the book serves to confirm the assumption that most interracial couples in nineteenth-century New Zealand involved a white man and a Māori woman. Margaret was not Māori, though.[2] She was from St Helena, a small, isolated tropical volcanic island in the South Atlantic Ocean, and her life was intimately bound up with the history of slavery and colonial violence.

Margaret's husband, Nathaniel Flowers, was born in Coventry, England, where he enlisted in the British army on 29 December 1848 at the age of 17. Initially stationed on St Helena, by 1856 he had transferred to the 65th Regiment of Foot for service in New Zealand, and arrived

OPPOSITE: *Margaret and Nathaniel Flowers.*

Photograph by William Harding, 1878. 1/4-005003-G. Courtesy of Alexander Turnbull Library, Wellington at Wellington in January 1857 from Australia on the *Louis and Miriam*.[3] When he was discharged from service at the rank of private on 1 March 1860, Nathaniel became one of the thousands of men from the British imperial regiments who settled in New Zealand.[4] He and Margaret lived out their lives in Whanganui, a small colonial town that was garrisoned by imperial soldiers in the 1860s.

Nathaniel obtained permission to marry Margaret Ann March in April 1854.[5] Theirs was an interracial marriage enabled and shaped by the particularities of garrison life on St Helena. Its isolated location, combined with the stationing of a regiment at Jamestown, the capital and main settlement situated on a long, narrow strip of land set between steep cliffs, meant people could not escape the presence of military personnel and culture. Redcoats dominated life in the town. British soldiers dominated the marriage market too.

Nathaniel and Margaret's marriage and mobility form the focus of this chapter. It is possible to track soldiers like Nathaniel due to the detailed administrative records collated by the Victorian British army, notably the personnel file. As historians Charlotte Macdonald and Rebecca Lenihan argue, these records offer 'a means to explore the local, variable and connected nature of the British garrison world'.[6] Personnel files may help to trace the movement of an individual soldier but, as Macdonald and Lenihan point out, they offer little insight into marriage and domesticity within garrison life.

Marriage was an important component of British military strategy and because of this, it demands attention.[7] Soldiers had to obtain permission to marry from their commanding officer, but how marriage was regulated and who had access to it depended upon where one was stationed. For those based overseas, where long stints in one place were common, marriage – whether legal or according to the local custom, such as in British India – was not unusual. Until 1847, enlistment in the British army was for life or until granted a discharge on medical grounds. From that year, the term of enlistment changed to 21 years in the infantry, with the first term of service set at 10 years.[8] Given that for most of the second half of the nineteenth century over half the British army was stationed abroad in the colonies, military service needed to be made attractive in order to aid recruitment and sustain its numbers. Reducing the length of enlistment was one way to make a military career more appealing, but so was widening access to marriage to the rank and file.

In 1841, a regiment of infantry composed of two-thirds volunteers and one-third recruits was raised from Britain for service on St Helena. Those who volunteered were to be 'enlisted for General Service, and a proportion (not exceeding 8 per Company) after serving 5 years in the island, to be annually permitted to volunteer to other Regiments of Infantry at home and abroad. The men [were] to enjoy all the privileges of the Pension and Good Conduct Warrants, and to be entitled on discharge to free passages to England and the Cape of Good Hope.'[9] Rather than the standard 10 years for the first period of service, five were permitted, providing the man transferred to another regiment to complete the first term. At 1 December 1856, this applied to the 281 rank and file stationed on St Helena, one of whom was Nathaniel Flowers.[10]

It is not possible to detail marriage patterns for the mid-nineteenth-century British army 'as there are no figures available which take into account all the important considerations – rank, age, whether stationed at home or abroad, whether on or off the strength'.[11] Without this information, it is difficult to get a sense of the marriage patterns of soldiers who served overseas. Nonetheless, this was an era in which the married soldier was seen as an asset by the army, which provided facilities for wives and children as an incentive for married men to enlist (an alternative interpretation is that military service enabled the married man to avoid his responsibilities). Marriage was perceived as providing a steadying influence on garrison life. It helped to manage the spread of venereal disease and the presence of women expanded the pool of cheap labour available to the army.[12]

At St Helena, where a British regiment was stationed from 1842 to 1863, marriage was a regular feature of the garrison experience. This can be explained by its location and the role the regiment played there. In the popular imagination, the island is most associated with Napoleon, who was exiled there in 1815 and died on the island in 1821. For just over 200 years, St Helena was an East India Company (EIC) territory until control was transferred to the British Crown in 1834. Prior to this, the territory was protected by a garrison under the direction of the EIC, which had numerous economic interests on the island and deployed slave labour there.[13] One of the most significant New Zealand connections to the island is Thomas Gore Browne, who was governor of St Helena from July 1851 to December 1854, after which he was appointed to New Zealand in 1855, where he governed during the first phase of the war in Taranaki before being replaced by Sir George Grey. Browne would have been a familiar name or figure to Nathaniel.

The regiment was based at Jamestown and spent a great deal of time on guard duty, building defences, creating roads and doing other heavy labour. Jamestown was a busy port, as St Helena lay on key shipping routes that connected Asia,

Africa and South America. After British acquisition of Southern Africa in the late eighteenth century, St Helena took on extra significance for imperial defence. Due to its location near Southern Africa, and thus the Indian Ocean, Jamestown became a hub for the transfer of troops into India as Britain sought to shore up its military and economic predominance in the Indian and Atlantic Ocean worlds.[14] It was also a significant port for slavers. Its long history as a staging post on the route to India made it vital to the EIC, who used slave labour there long after Britain abolished the trade in 1807.

New arrivals encountered an island people whose lives were shaped by their location in the South Atlantic – an accident of geography that connected them to one of the most significant events in modern history. In 2008, archaeological work undertaken to prepare the way for the establishment of the island's first airport uncovered one of the largest mass graveyards of slaves in the world. It is estimated the graves contain the bodies of some 10,000 men, women and children who were forced into slavery and died in brutal conditions on board ships taking them to South America.[15] Due to monsoon winds and ocean currents, slavers had to pass by St Helena, where the Royal Navy had established a Liberation Depot that operated from 1840 to 1874.[16] The navy's role was to hunt the slavers in order to suppress the trade. A substantial scholarship on the history of slavery has addressed what is referred to as the West Africa, North America and Europe triangular model, but places like St Helena were on other significant slave-trade routes that connected West and East Africa with South America, notably Brazil.[17]

St Helena's location in the South Atlantic, then, was vital to the slave trade and also to bringing it to an end. In addition to the Liberation Depot, a Vice-Admiralty Court was set up on the island to place the slavers on trial. It 'condemned more slave ships and liberated more Africans than any other British possession, which in absolute terms amounts to 450 vessels and over 25,000 people'.[18] At depots, traders were arrested and the human cargo liberated, although analysis of the Vice Admiralty Court records has revealed that the pathways of these men, women and children rarely included going home. Instead, small numbers stayed on in the locations where they were liberated, and the majority were sent to South America or the British Caribbean, where their liberated status was constrained by the conditions of labour in which they found themselves. Of the around 75,000 who gained liberated status through British Vice-Admiralty Courts, including St Helena's, some entered conditions of work that looked and felt little different to slavery.[19]

Survivors of the slave ships who were liberated at St Helena were brought to Rupert's Valley, where a treatment and holding depot used by the navy's West Africa Squadron was located.[20] Many succumbed to disease. Those who survived were mostly shipped to Sierra Leone for further assessment and transferred to the Caribbean or South America; some stayed on the island, where they took up employment.[21] When slavery finally came to an end on the island in 1833, the 614 individuals who were part of the enslaved population were ethnically diverse, for during the EIC's control of the island 'three quarters of the island's slave population came from Madagascar, a number came from Madras', while 'St Helena also acted as a stopping point for ships carrying captives from West Africa to the slave plantations of Asia'.[22] Adding to the cosmopolitan demographic were Chinese indentured labourers who were brought to St Helena on contracts of three to five years' duration.[23]

Nathaniel joined the regiment on 5 January 1849.[24] When he arrived on the island from England on 28 July 1849, St Helena's population was made up of former slaves, Indian sailors and Chinese labourers, as well as British settlers.[25]

Local people are descendants of earlier residents brought to the island under a range of free and unfree conditions. We can only speculate on Margaret's origins as a woman of colour because those who were connected to slavery rarely left written records and are difficult to trace. Margaret has left a faint archival imprint in the form of her marriage record, her death record and the photograph taken at William Harding's Whanganui studio in 1878, which was most likely prompted by Nathaniel's impending departure for England the following month.[26]

As Margaret bore the surname of March, the name of an island family, it is reasonable to assume that she was a servant in their household. Perhaps it was under these conditions that Nathaniel encountered Margaret. According to the information on her death certificate, Margaret was born on St Helena in 1833, prior to the establishment of the Liberation Depot, meaning she was not among the thousands of Africans freed from the slavers. She was, however, born during a significant moment in the history of the British slave trade. That year the British government passed the Slavery Abolition Act, which abolished slavery in parts of the British Empire, including St Helena. Margaret was born free but into a world shaped by slavery and a culture of unfreedom based on race. Her parents are not recorded, but they were most likely born into slavery, or taken to the island by EIC traders, probably from India or Madagascar, and laboured under the conditions set by the company.

Margaret and Nathaniel's marriage appears as an anomaly in a class- and colour-conscious society such as St Helena. In a small society where the population rarely ever exceeded 5000, marital options were limited, so new arrivals were seized upon. Officers were regarded as excellent marriage material for the daughters of local white elites.[27] Many of these men took up land or roles within local government. Enlisted men, those in the rank and file, tended to marry servants employed by the elite families. Some of the servant class included liberated Africans. Despite the racial hierarchies inherent in a society forged out of slavery, interracial marriage was feasible. In Nathaniel and Margaret's case, it is possible they gained permission to marry because they had a son, William, who was born in 1850.

Upon serving five years with the regiment, an enlisted man was eligible for a free passage to England or the Cape of Good Hope. Marriage to a redcoat gave a woman the opportunity for mobility, which could also secure the future of any children, giving them access to opportunities not available on St Helena, whose economic, military and political importance would reduce dramatically from the 1870s with the opening of the Suez Canal and the introduction of steam shipping. Such technological and engineering innovations meant vessels increasingly bypassed the island's port.

Nathaniel's plan to return to England and transfer to another regiment probably also advanced their case to marry and thus ensured that Margaret and William would not be abandoned – a not uncommon practice in British military units stationed in the colonies. This is reinforced by the muster rolls, which show that after his marriage Nathaniel started to collect good-conduct pay regularly: marriage perhaps brought stability as well as discipline and a sense of responsibility.[28] By April 1855, after serving his five-year term overseas, Nathaniel was based at the St Helena Depot in the United Kingdom where he continued to receive good-conduct pay and was temporarily elevated to corporal. On 10 September 1856 he volunteered for and was transferred to the 65th Regiment of Foot, which was sent to New Zealand, via the Australian colonies, as a garrison force.

It is unclear if Nathaniel brought Margaret and William to England but they somehow made it to New Zealand, where they settled in Whanganui. Nathaniel did not divorce himself from military culture after being discharged in 1860; Whanganui was, after all, a garrison town. He joined the local volunteer force, but in 1868 he was shot in the knee during a private practice session and

Soldiers promenade along Castle Terrace, Jamestown, St Helena, 1815.
CO 1069-760-14. Courtesy of National Archives, Richmond (UK)

was incapacitated for four months.[29] Once recovered, he took up work as the signalman at the York Hill Station near the military stockade and supplemented his income by repairing umbrellas and china.[30] Margaret was a laundress, an area of employment generally dominated by women of colour in garrison towns across the colonial world.

Although the Flowers family left a light imprint on the public record, their lives and travels can be found in army records and newspapers, which also record their fate. Margaret died at home on 8 August 1887. At his death at the age of 80 in August 1906, Nathaniel Flowers was listed as a chimney sweep. Their son, William Robert Henry Flowers, worked as a labourer. He never married so there are no descendants to maintain their memory.

As a working-class interracial couple, Nathaniel and Margaret exist at the edges of written memory. As the record of their lives is scant, we have to rely on the administrative records of the British army to track their mobility. Even then,

Margaret is invisible because military records rarely remarked on family. However, marriage mattered to military command, as it could make troops more efficient and encourage discipline and stability in garrison towns where soldiers were often stationed for long periods of service.

Nathaniel may not have participated in war as part of a fighting force, but his trajectory from England to St Helena and thence to New Zealand was shaped by colonial violence. His stationing on St Helena demonstrates how the New Zealand Wars (1860–72) cannot be divorced from the wider imperial context, including the role of soldiers in expanding British interests overseas as an occupying force. While historical treatments of the New Zealand Wars are dominated by battles and military analysis, they also have a social history, which the lives of couples like Nathaniel and Margaret illustrate. Finally, and most significantly, Margaret's presence forces us to confront the invisibility of women – especially women of colour – in the story of military culture and colonial violence.[31] It is time their stories were told.

Chapter 7

VIOLENCE OF THE LAW

PROSECUTING GENDERED VIOLENCE IN COLONIAL FIJI

Kate Stevens

Trials of sexual violence cases in colonial Fiji demonstrate the gendered violence of both colonial society and the court system. Despite the rhetoric of legal equality for all, in practice the courtroom recentred male and European voices and reinforced policing of the behaviour and bodies of non-European women and children. The violence of assault was thus compounded by the violence of the colonial legal system. Given the challenges in accessing court archives and their intimate and violent content, these are stories that are not always exposed to public view. The issue of gendered violence and how it is addressed by the police and judicial system, however, remains a thorny problem into the present in Fiji, as in Australia and New Zealand.

RACE, SPACE AND LAW IN EARLY COLONIAL FIJI

Britain annexed Fiji in 1874. Disputes over land sales, conflict and political authority had increased to overcome British reluctance for formal intervention. Law was, therefore, a key justification of imperial rule, along with protectionist policies toward Indigenous Fijians that recognised 'traditional' chiefly authority, village culture and land tenure.[1] The colony nevertheless needed a cheap labour force on the sugar plantations, owned by Australian companies such as Colonial Sugar Refining Company, to be economically productive. Imported labour was initially sourced from neighbouring islands such as the Solomons and Vanuatu. But from 1879 to 1916, the government organised the migration of over 60,000 girmitiyas, or Indian indentured labourers, to work the sugar plantations on

Street Scene, Suva, 1900. Though colonial legislation sought to restrict Indigenous presence in the cities, the state's ability to constrain mobility was limited. Economic and social opportunities, as well as legal obligations, all brought iTaukei (Indigenous Fijians), Indian indentured labourers and others to Suva from its foundation.

From Richard John Seddon, compiler, and Frederick W. Sears, photographer, 'Premier's Trip to the Pacific Islands, May–June 1900' (photo album), p. 6. PH-ALB-249. Courtesy of Auckland War Memorial Museum

---

five-year contracts. Most remained in Fiji after the narak (hell) of indenture and set up communities on the outskirts of the plantations or migrated to towns and established agricultural and trading businesses.[2]

As the seat of colonial government from the 1880s, Fiji's capital Suva acted as a settler space in a non-settler colony. Legislation from both the colonial government and from the Bose Vakaturanga (Council of Chiefs) curtailed the mobility of non-white people in the town in attempts to designate urban space as white.[3] This helped to shape who was welcomed, valued and protected by colonial law, and the experience of going to court. However, the desired spatial separation was never achieved. Suva quickly became cosmopolitan in ways that were unexpected and problematic to officials, missionaries and chiefs.[4] By the 1911 census, for example, Suva's population of around 3500 was recorded as approximately 67 percent

Indian, 15 percent Fijian, 8 percent Polynesian and 7 percent European or 'part-European'.[5] Many others visited the town temporarily, including to attend trials.

The operation of the Supreme Court reflected British attempts to manage this diversity and mobility, and to assert its supremacy in the colony. Operating quarterly from Levuka and, after the capital shifted in 1882, from Suva too, the Supreme Court served as the heart of empire in the growing town. Officials believed that the law had the power to help 'civilise' the islands, despite the fact that the British were increasingly drawn into Fiji to control the unruly behaviour of their own subjects in the decades prior to annexation.[6] The court served as a symbolic and theatrical space, with architecture and courtroom rituals that reinforced the structures of colonialism.[7] However, like Suva itself, the court was also a place in which these hierarchies could be contested and challenged, as indicated by the presence in the court archives of the various men and women who possessed some ability to narrate their own story, even within the context of violence.

Government House, Suva, 1880s. The architecture of the colonial government reinforced the centrality of European laws. Though such spaces were also the sites of intimate and contested stories, few images capture the complex experience of those in the courtroom itself. Photograph by Burton Brothers. O.036857. Courtesy of Museum of New Zealand Te Papa Tongarewa, Wellington

In Fiji, criminal cases were divided along the boundaries of race as well as geography, frequently separating Indigenous and European subjects and Indian indentured labourers within the judicial system.[8] Lower-court sittings held in villages and on plantations were the primary means through which Fijians and Indian indentured labourers, respectively, interacted with the judicial system. Police courts, which operated in Suva and Levuka, dealt with crimes stemming from the problems of urban settlement (theft, drunkenness and offences to public order and morals) and operated like their equivalents in Britain or British settler colonies.

The Supreme Court adjudicated on all serious crime, including murder, assault, rape and sexual assault. Cases were forwarded from the lower courts to the criminal sittings held quarterly in Suva or Levuka. Trials were conducted by jury if all parties involved were European, or by 'assessors' who advised the Chief Justice but did not have a decisive vote in the outcome of the case.[9] The pattern of courts across the colony broadly reflected the attempted compartmentalisation of racial groups in different geographic and economic spaces.[10] Nevertheless, all serious criminal cases, such as murder, rape and sexual assault were heard in English before the Supreme Court in Suva.

INTIMATE VIOLENCE

Sexual and other serious violent crimes (such as murder and assault) were particularly significant because all individuals – regardless of race or social status – were, theoretically at least, brought before the same court and subject to the same law, procedure and punishment.[11] The adjudication of violent crimes revealed the intersections of gendered and racial hierarchies of the colonial era, despite the fact that colour-blind, legal equality was a cornerstone of narratives to justify imperial rule.[12]

Rape cases centred on questions of penetration and consent. Indecent assault (sexual assault short of penetrative rape) required proof of lack of consent, though the physical evidence required was less defined. Carnal knowledge, the charge for rape or indecent assault of (female) children, specified that if the victim was under 16 years or, more commonly, under 12 or 13 years, the question of consent was irrelevant.[13] Only physical proof of the assault was required, though this could be problematic to establish and was, therefore, the subject of speculation. Despite this, trials of sexual crime frequently involved both physical evidence and moral judgment, and gendered, racialised hierarchies of knowledge and reliability.

These cases provide a key source in which women's voices are heard directly in the colonial archive, though their stories are structured by the nature of the court process.[14] For example, both Indian and Fijian women stood up for their virtue when faced with insinuations or direct slurs against their morality. In a 1910 rape trial, an indentured labourer of the Vancouver Sugar Company testified, 'I am not a woman of loose character. I am not in the habit of alluring any men to have connection with them. I swear that with the exception of my man and the accused no one has had connection with me since my introduction to Fiji.'[15]

Occasionally, glimpses of the physical or emotional impact of the violence upon women are revealed. Many mentioned they felt afraid to report the crime, especially if the offender was a chief or an overseer. Others focused on the physicality of the attack. For example, one woman highlighted the violence of rape, describing how the accused 'lifted her bodily', 'fisted' her thighs and shoulders so she was 'rendered weak and he overcame me'.[16] Another emphasised her fear of her attacker, stating, 'When near I saw the expression of his eyes were not good. I was afraid and ran away.'[17] A female indentured labourer who was viciously assaulted and raped by a group of men on a plantation one night in 1907 described feeling she was 'silly' and lost her senses after the attack.[18]

Other cases drew attention to the feeling of shame caused by such assaults and to the emotional violence of the physical attack. After describing her physical wounds, one woman said simply, 'My mind also is in pain.'[19] In an 1881 rape case, a witness reported that a Solomon Islands labourer told her 'M has forced me and made a fool of me.'[20] A Tokelauan woman said, 'A Fijian has insulted me as if I were a pig.'[21] These accounts go beyond a description of the assault to hint at the devastating physical and psychological effects of sexual crime. Other accounts focus on the physical act alone, though it is unclear whether this reflected an inability or unwillingness to articulate emotional suffering in the public courtroom or that the process of translation and transcription of testimony obscured the victim's tone and emotion.

Trials, and the resulting archives, were in English, meaning the accounts we have were filtered through colonial clerks and translators. Victim testimony was often overshadowed by both colonial politics and the court's focus on the medical evidence, on the victim's body instead of the victim's words. And although the overwhelming majority of complainants in trials for sexual violence were non-European, official reports and newspapers reinforced narratives that centred on either the threats to white women by 'uncivilised' Indigenous men or the

So-called 'civilised' law provided an important justification for British colonisation. Photographs of orderly Fijian police circulated as an example of the progress towards order, again obscuring the judicial violence of the state.

'Soldiers of the King'. From J.W. Burton, The Fiji of Today *(London: Charles H. Kelly, 1910), facing p. 72. Courtesy of Internet Archive, San Francisco*

provocation and immorality of non-white women in Fiji as an explanation for violence.[22] Non-European accounts of violence were consistently overshadowed by colonial interpretations in the courtroom and beyond.

JUDICIAL VIOLENCE

The prioritisation of certain types of evidence in the Supreme Court – male, European and increasingly medicalised – parallels processes occurring across the British Empire in ways that continue to shape the perceptions of women's testimony and reliability in sexual violence trials today. Underpinning these factors, in the minds of European magistrates, was the pervasive afterlife of influential jurist Matthew Hale's 1778 warning that 'rape is … an accusation easily to be made and hard to prove, and harder to be defended by the party accused, tho never so innocent'.[23] Hale drew attention to his (unsubstantiated) fears of false and pernicious rape accusations, arguing the importance of a fresh complaint and corroborating evidence. As many contemporary commentators and historians on rape acknowledge, such implicit distrust of women's testimony disadvantaged female victims in courtrooms across the British Empire and frequently focused attention on the victim's actions, morality and credibility.[24] The female body had to be proved innocent in cases of sexual crime. More broadly, sexual cases involved complicated assessments of gender-appropriate behaviour and reputation.[25] Consequently, many women chose not to report sexual assaults, and even when they did, police and officials frequently dismissed or minimised their complaints.[26]

Overlaid on the mistrust of female testimony were racialised doubts regarding the validity of statements made by Fijians, Islanders and Indians in court. Non-European women were 'doubly suspect suspects'.[27] The 'native' witness was portrayed as either deceitful and untrustworthy, or naïve, confused and therefore unreliable. By contrast, judges, colonial officials and expert medical witnesses were considered part of the rational and objective court process. In general, non-European or Indigenous actors were perceived as unable to contribute to, and excluded from, the increasingly 'scientific' legal project on the basis of empire-wide concepts of racial difference. These perceived differences were themselves the products of an increasingly rigid and scientific discourse of race, further contributing to a damaging cycle that reinforced colonial hierarchies within the courts.[28] Both Indigenous Fijians and indentured Indians were subject to a discourse that equated whiteness with credibility and rationality, and non-whiteness with unreliability. This logic enabled colonial law to 'enunciate equality while fabricating a racial taxonomy through which to operate unequally'.[29] The questions of reliability contributed to the many sexual violence cases that never made it to the courtroom, especially at the level of the Supreme Court.[30]

European expert medical testimony was central in Supreme Court case *Rex v RB*.[31] The trial provides insight into the ways that ideas about race, age and gender were entwined in cases of sexual assault and the challenges experienced by non-Europeans appearing before the court. Around 6pm on Wednesday 3 August 1910, a local Fijian man indentured at Korovatu entered the empty labourers' house where a nine-year-old girl was playing with her two younger siblings. Her mother was cooking in the kitchen some 50 yards (45m) away. The girl, of Fiji-European descent, told the Labasa Police Court that although she tried to leave, the man carried her to the bed. Pulling her pinafore up, her sulu down and stuffing his own white sulu in her mouth to prevent her cries, he 'then had connection with me gently. He did not penetrate far and his semen was spent on my two thighs'.

The girl's mother arrived and, hearing her approaching, the man scrambled to cover himself. She confronted the man, who admitted the rape: 'Yes, it is true. I got on to her but I did not have connection: it is true I have committed an offence.' However, when questioned again, he asserted it 'was [the girl's] fault; she comes into our house and plays with [another labourer] and I indecently'. The man disappeared when the mother went to report the case to police. He was found and arrested the following day and brought before the Labasa Police Court on 10 August 1910.

The man was charged with carnal knowledge and Acting Chief Justice Ehrhardt heard the case in the Supreme Court on 21 September 1910. The depositions centred on the accounts of the victim and her mother, as well as the expert testimony provided by Labasa District Medical Officer (DMO), Gilbert Emerson Arnold. The accused's plea is missing from the Supreme Court file, but the perpetrator was found guilty and sentenced to 18 months hard labour and 20 lashes. The facts of the case were not in question. The man admitted what had occurred to the girl's mother, but he tried instead to place responsibility on the nine-year-old by insinuating she frequently sought to play 'indecently' with the Fijian labourers. The young victim denied this, stating, 'I am not in the habit of going in there every day and pulling down my sulu and lying on the bed and playing with you.' The case shows how sexual cases frequently centred on the victim's actions, comportment and character, even when they were of a very tender age.

Arnold's expert testimony is striking for his assessment of morality and sexual behaviour extrapolated from his physical examination of the little girl. Two days after the assault, Arnold first questioned her and, apparently with her permission, performed a physical genital examination in the presence of Constable Orisi. Presenting his findings, Arnold emphasised his belief that she demonstrated sexual knowledge and behaviour beyond her years. The DMO reported he was struck by her extreme precocity:

> She showed an intimate knowledge of all sexual matters about which she spoke in a matter-of-fact and deliberate way like a woman of the world; in a perfectly serious, and not ribald, way.

A perceived lack of reserve and her understanding in discussing sexual matters was problematic to the European DMO, who clearly felt that a child of nine could not and should not have such intimate knowledge except if gained through sexual experience. She contradicted gendered expectations about modesty and ignorance of sexual matters: the very act of speaking out against the perpetrator implicated her own character.

Arnold also reported on his physical examination of the girl's genitals. He noted that the hymen was intact and genitals too small for full penetration but found the vulva 'deep and dilated', a state consistent with molestation. Arnold further noted 'considerable redness and signs of irritation', yet these observations did not add weight to his view of the likelihood of assault. Instead, Arnold assumed that 'the child is sexually precocious and has probably been addicted to the habit of masturbation and possibly incomplete intercourse with boys and men'. Although this was an unfounded opinion, the physical examination was used to support the DMO's initial hypothesis of sexual precocity. Far from its purported objectivity, the medical evidence intersected with moral judgement.

Arnold concluded, 'I found her condition to be consistent with both their stories.' Yet the overwhelming tenor of his statement, and the frequent references to the girl's precocity, favoured the perpetrator's insinuation that the victim was a Lolita of sorts: sexually mature and encouraging of inappropriate intimacies with the older labourers. Ultimately, the perpetrator was found guilty because the girl's young age meant that the question of consent was not relevant to the case, despite the extensive and unnecessary interrogation of her words and body. However, the problematic narrative of sexual precocity likely contributed to the relatively short sentence. Arnold and the accused both focused the court's attention on the girl's sexual knowledge, suggesting her responsibility in participating or even encouraging sexual interaction.[32]

CONCLUSION

The experience of this nine-year-old in the colonial court system highlights the ongoing impact of Hale's warning and the violence of the judicial process, which examined female bodies in both violent and intimate ways. The retelling of her experience of intimate violence took place in the unfamiliar setting of courtrooms in Labasa and Suva and necessitated bodily examination by medical and police officials. While trials could provide a space for female and colonised voices in Fiji to speak out against the assaults they experienced, court cases also reinforced the colonial state's power and the violence of judicial process for those appearing before the court.

Beyond acknowledging the physical and emotional impact of violence and the strength to recount such experiences, sexual assault trials draw our attention to the troubling intersection of violence, consent and racialised gender expectations that permeated colonial society. Rape and sexual assault were frequently underreported and under-prosecuted because of these systemic prejudices as well as the shame associated with sexual violence, in Fiji and elsewhere. The accounts that made it to trial represent the tip of an iceberg and point toward the long aftermath of sexual violence, both for the individual recounting the violence in the courtroom and in the broader legacies of gendered and racialised legal biases in the British Empire.

Colonial law in Fiji limited physical and economic mobility for men and women, and paid particular attention to the private and intimate lives of women and Fijians, indentured Indian labourers and other non-European newcomers.[33] Law also created new hierarchies and interpretations of race, gender and age that played out in the courtrooms and continue to shape experiences of sexual violence and the criminal justice system into the present.

Chapter 8

THE CODE OF SILENCE ON THE MACINTYRE RIVER FRONTIER

MARGARET YOUNG'S ATTEMPT TO ACHIEVE JUSTICE FOR THE MURDER OF HER ABORIGINAL SERVANT, MAIMIE, IN 1848

Lyndall Ryan

Mr Marks and a team of men he gathered arrived at our house … shooting every native in sight, even our station [A]boriginals, even my house gins, one of which was my faithful Maimie, my loyal friend who had shared so many experiences with me, in the first hard years at Umbercollie. As these two gins were unarmed, and one was blind, they both had no chance to escape. Maimie dropped behind the house, and the other girl ran to the river and dived in, staying there all night, dying from cold as well as wounds. We were helpless to help, as the natives were now in a frenzy, as well as Marks' men shooting. After a while there was silence, and Marks' men had gone.[1]

On 11 June 1848, Margaret Young, then aged 34, and her husband Jonathan, aged 48, were living with their three daughters, aged one, four and six, in a bush hut at Umbercollie pastoral station on the northern side of the Macintyre River at present-day Goondiwindi in Queensland. The Youngs had leased the station three years before and, with the assistance of three white stockmen and the labour of Bigambul people living there, hoped to make their fortune raising sheep for wool export and grazing cattle for meat before retiring to Maitland, 500 kilometres to the south.[2] As the first settler woman on the Macintyre frontier, Margaret was reliant on a young Bigambul woman, Maimie, for friendship and support, and was totally unprepared for the brutal murder of her Aboriginal friend by white men and the code of silence that would prevent justice being served.

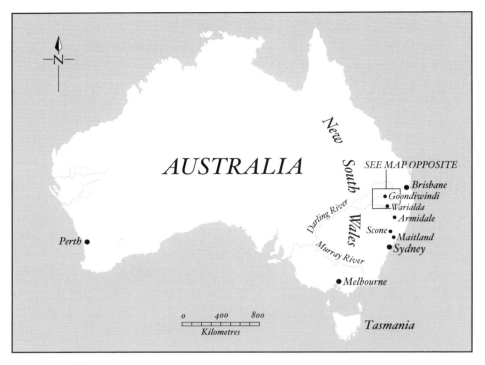

Location of the Macintyre River region. Map by Allan Kynaston

Margaret Young's memoir of her experiences on the Macintyre River frontier, 1841 to 1857, is a rare find for historians of the colonial frontier in Eastern Australia. In 1980 a descendant, Alice Edith Tonge, presented typed copies of the memoir to the Mitchell Library in Sydney and the John Oxley Library in Brisbane. I came across the memoir in the Mitchell Library as part of my research on the Macintyre River region for the digital map project of massacre sites on the Australian colonial frontier, 1788–1930. In the 1840s the region was the front line of a bloody war between the invading pastoral settlers and the Aboriginal owners, the Bigambul people, for possession of the land. The map documents 12 incidents of frontier massacre across the region between 1844 and 1849, with an estimated loss of more than 400 Bigambul and 10 settler lives.[3] As far as I am aware, Margaret Young was the first settler woman to witness such an attack.

At daylight, Margaret records, Jonathan 'went outside to get the two dead girls and bury them as already wild pigs were eating Maimie's body. This was a frightful

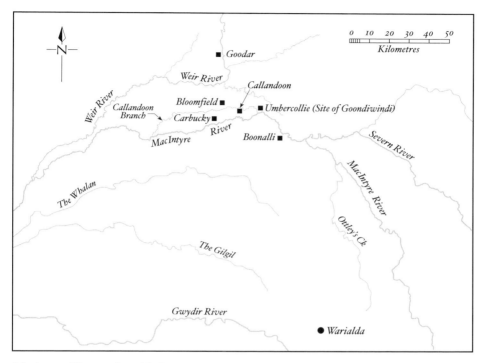

Macintyre River region, 1848. Map by Allan Kynaston

sight right beside our house. Jonathan had to dig their graves himself, close to our house, as it was not safe to venture far.'[4] In the aftermath, 'he wrote to police headquarters and later all these men were brought to trial, identified by Jonathan and the station natives'.[5] However, investigations of the official sources of the case carried out independently by historians Mark Copland and Heather Goodall reveal that, far from identifying the suspects, the Youngs avoided doing so. As a consequence, the ringleader, settler James Mark, escaped arrest; the five other suspects were arrested but escaped conviction.[6]

How, then, could Margaret Young consider that justice was exacted for Maimie's brutal murder? This chapter reviews the complexities of the case, in particular the power of the code of silence that prevented the men from being brought to justice, by combining Margaret Young's recollections of the aftermath with the investigations of Copland and Goodall and my own research on mapping the locations of frontier massacres.[7] Copland included the case as part of a wider study of the frontier war on the Macintyre River in 1837–50; Goodall cited the massacre as a case study of the failure of the rule of law on the Macintyre River frontier as experienced by the police magistrate, Richard Bligh; and the digital frontier massacre map provides important connections between the killings at Umbercollie and others in the region. In taking this approach, new insights emerge about the failure of Margaret Young's attempts to achieve justice for the murders of the Aboriginal people and, in particular, her friend Maimie.

The seeds of the massacre were sown on 10 September 1847, when Johnny, the seven-year-old son of settler James Mark from Goodar pastoral station on the Weir River, not far from Umbercollie, was brutally murdered by Bigambul warriors in reprisal for Mark's killing of a young Bigambul man who was conveying a message from one station to another some weeks earlier.[8] The murder was reported in the *Maitland Mercury* and on 2 October Richard Bligh, the newly appointed magistrate at the Warialda Police District, dispatched two constables to join Mark and a party of stockmen in 'apprehending' the murderer of his son. The operation appears to have finished at the end of October, and although it is known that several Bigambul were killed, the alleged murderer was not apprehended.[9]

Mark, however, was hell-bent on revenge. According to Margaret Young, 'Mr Mark was a hater of all [A]boriginals and would shoot any seen approaching his property.'[10] In early 1848, he 'travelled throughout the district recruiting white stockmen and landholders for a vigilante party' to track down the murderer and exact revenge.[11] Jonathan Young refused to join them on the grounds that Mark had brought the tragedy on himself.[12] Undaunted, Mark appears to have recruited at least seven stockmen from nearby stations, and they commenced 'a killing spree' that lasted several months.[13] According to the recollections of stockman William Telfer, they 'made their first attack at Boonall station', where 'they found about forty blacks encamped on the [Macintyre] River at night … they were shot down and burned on their camp fires being taken unawares.'[14] By early June, Mark was beginning to intimidate settlers who employed Bigambul people on their stations. On the night of 10 June he led an attack on some sleeping Bigambul women on Carbucky station, at least three of whom were killed.[15] The following night he led six stockmen onto Umbercollie station where the horrifying events recounted at the beginning of this chapter took place.

Following the killings, Jonathan Young sent a letter to magistrate Bligh at Warialda, reporting the dreadful events at Umbercollie and the murder of Maimie. Copland asserts that the letter never reached Bligh and suggests this 'was the first step taken to conceal the details of the attack and ultimately subvert the course of justice'.[16] Bligh did eventually investigate Maimie's death, and appears to have interviewed the Youngs at Umbercollie in early August; he collected more detailed information from the Bigambul workers, who provided a vivid description of the attack and the identity of the suspects. By law, however, Aboriginal people were not permitted to give evidence in court, so Bligh had to work with the limited information provided by the Youngs. Still, it was clear to him that they were intimidated by the code of silence imposed by the settlers and stockmen to protect James Mark from arrest.[17]

At the inquest at Warialda on 26 August, Jonathan stated that three of his Bigambul workers had identified five of the attackers as William Jones, Daniel Maclean, John Reardon, Stephen Holden and James Mark. He also stated that on the night of the attack, he heard at least 30 shots fired at the Bigambul people; the next day he found Maimie's body at the 'sliprail with her skull broken into six or seven pieces' along with the mutilated body of her favourite puppy.[18] Margaret stated that Ben, one of the Bigambul station workers, told her that during the attack Maclean called him by name, saying, 'Come here, Ben – Come here.'[19] Frustrated by the Youngs' refusal to identify the suspects directly, Bligh was forced to conclude in his coroner's report that Maimie had been 'murdered by persons unknown'.[20] Even so, he believed he had enough evidence to apprehend one of the suspects, Daniel Maclean.

News of Maclean's arrest spread across the region like wildfire. On 2 September, in an effort to intimidate other settlers and prevent them giving evidence, James Mark led six vigilantes in a night attack on Callandoon and Broomfield stations where they killed three Bigambul women and a boy. The following morning three of the vigilantes fired on a Bigambul camp at the station belonging to Margaret Young's stepbrother, Richard Chapman. The tactic worked. When Augustus Morris, the lessee of Callandoon station, wrote to the colonial secretary about the attacks, he refused to identify the killers.[21]

Bligh, however, refused to be intimidated. On 4 September he recorded a statement from Daniel Maclean, who named James Mark and the other five stockmen as the perpetrators of the premeditated attack at Umbercollie on 11 June.[22] Buoyed by the confession, Bligh lost no time in issuing warrants for the arrest of Mark and four of the five stockmen. The stockmen were quickly apprehended, but Mark evaded arrest and vanished from Goodar station on 15

September. Frustrated that the ringleader had slipped away, Bligh sent warrants for his arrest to magistrates at Armidale, Scone and Brisbane.[23]

When the four stockmen appeared before Bligh at Warialda Police Station on 16 September, they denied the evidence in Maclean's confession. Unconvinced by their story, Bligh remanded them in custody until Jonathan Young made another statement on 21 September. Once again, Jonathan failed to name the suspects directly and said his neighbours complained that he was providing too much assistance to the investigation.[24] With neither of the Youngs prepared to openly identify the killers, Bligh's case had reached a stalemate.

On 5 October Mark, now apparently in Brisbane, attempted to further undermine the case by persuading George Harris, a hutkeeper at the station from which the vigilantes had set off for their attack on Umbercollie, to appear before the bench of magistrates at Warialda and state that Maclean did not leave the station on the night in question.[25] Bligh doubted the veracity of the statement and wrote to the attorney general: 'You will observe that the man Harris … directly contradicts the evidence of the approver (Maclean). That Harris is perjuring himself I entertain not the slightest doubt and I am sorry to say that such perjury in a case of this sort will be deemed meritorious by his class.'[26]

Bligh charged the four stockmen with murder and committed them for trial at the district court in Maitland on 12 February 1849. In the interim, he held Maclean in protective custody at Warialda.[27] When he presented the papers for the prosecution to the attorney general in Sydney, however, he was warned that unless gentlemen settlers of the status of Morris and Young directly identified the killers, Harris's testimony would make a conviction unlikely.[28] By then Bligh had also become a target of intimidation: some of his horses were stolen and others were destroyed.[29] Further intimidation came from the now elusive James Mark. In December he complained to the governor, Sir Charles Fitzroy, that Bligh had unfairly accused him of murder and allowed the district to 'sink into chaos'.[30]

In early January 1849 Bligh defended his handling of the case to the Chief Commissioner of Crown Lands. He pointed out that had the Bigambul people been permitted to give evidence in court, 'the balance of injury and crime would be fearfully against the white population'.[31] He was shocked by both the systematic planning that had gone into the murders at Umbercollie and the power of the settlers' code of silence in protecting Mark from arrest. He considered the vigilante group of ex-convict stockmen the true ringleaders in Maimie's death by virtue of their uniting together 'by the bond of their common villainy [and] having an interest in exciting and maintaining the violence of the natives and exaggerating the dangers to which they were exposed' in order to demand excessive wages for themselves.³²

By then, Bligh understood the power of the code of silence on the Macintyre River frontier. It prevented Margaret and Jonathan Young from directly identifying Maimie's killers; it enabled Mark to evade arrest; and it secured freedom for the stockmen. In March 1849 the case at Maitland Court was dropped and the four stockmen were released on bail. Bligh and the Youngs did achieve one small victory, however. Three of the suspects – Holden, Cummins and Reardon – were prevented from returning to the Macintyre River district on the grounds that they could be runaway convicts.³³

Why, then, did Margaret Young record in her memoir that 'all the men were brought to trial, identified by Jonathan and the station natives'? She gives the impression that the men were convicted and punished, yet Jonathan never openly identified the killers. Perhaps Margaret believed she and Jonathan had presented as much evidence as they could without becoming targets themselves.

On the New South Wales frontier in the 1840s, the code of silence ensured that no settler of Mark's status was ever convicted of the murder of an Aboriginal person. As this case has demonstrated, this culture enabled Mark to prevent Jonathan from identifying him as the ringleader, even though there was sufficient evidence for a warrant to be issued for his arrest. Had Mark been arrested and the case proceeded to court, Jonathan would have been a key witness for the prosecution. It's likely that Margaret Young understood the power of the code of silence perfectly: the reaction of other settlers in the region would have placed Jonathan in an untenable position, and his life and that of his family would have been at risk.

Margaret Young may well have been satisfied that Richard Bligh had placed all the evidence of Maimie's death on the public record. The details certainly enabled historians like Copland and Goodall to access them more than 150 years later. Whatever her views about the evidence, however, her tribute to Maimie is testimony to her sorrow:

> Maimie was very intelligent, I treasured her friendship and happy nature, as it was many years before I saw another white woman or went away. Maimie would watch and quickly learn all the things I taught her. She loved the children, calling them her white piccaninnies, at every opportunity she played with them and taught them so much about the Australian bush, birds and animals; she would bring some of

the black children to play with them … I felt as though she belonged to our family. She was always so full of chatter and laughter and would talk of her own way of life and legends. I have always felt indeed lucky to have the companionship to help me in my first difficult years, as she was always beside me.[34]

Margaret Young's failure to secure justice for the brutal murder of Maimie reveals the limits of cross-cultural friendships among women on the Australian colonial frontier, where white settlers' allegiances favoured the reproduction of their own social dominance at the expense of the legal rights of Aboriginal people. Did Margaret imagine herself to be more powerless than she actually was? The friendship between the two women was always inherently unequal: the close bond Margaret formed with Maimie in forced circumstances was not what she would have *chosen* and suggests she was not prepared to pursue the preferred legal outcome. For Maimie, friendship with Margaret was fundamentally undermined by the brutal loss of her land and way of life to white settlers who were determined to preserve their fragile hold on their valuable acquisition, regardless of the cost to Aboriginal life.

PART III
INTIMATE VIOLENCE

Chapter 9

'WOLVES ABOUT THEIR PREY'

INTIMACY AND VIOLENCE IN EYRE'S EXPEDITIONS

Shino Konishi

> He loves the boys   especially Cootachah
> The youngest   now twelve
> who most often rides beside him
> as he checks the early routes
> —Miriel Lenore, 'Cootachah'[1]

> for safety Eyre plans to shoot Neramberein
> (never young Cootachah) but cannot
> —Miriel Lenore, 'the boys'[2]

On 28 June 1837, Edward Eyre 'reached the Goulburn river, about 51 miles [82km] from the Winding Swamp'. He was some three months into his first overlanding expedition, driving '78 head of cattle and 414 sheep' across a 600-kilometre stretch from Molonglo to Port Phillip. The river had 'considerable width' and a fast-moving current; crossing it was a daunting prospect. Camped on its bank was another party led by Mr Yalbone, who had already lost one horse and rider to its raging waters; a second man had barely survived the crossing. Among that group were Cootachah and Joshuing, 'two little black boys about eight years old' who were 'perfectly naked' and looked 'very hardy as well as full of life and spirits'. They had arrived earlier with another unnamed settler from the Murray, who promptly abandoned them when they refused to cross the flooded river. Finding that Yalbone 'did not know what to do' with the boys, Eyre eagerly 'attached them to [his] own party'.[3]

Eyre had been intrigued by Aboriginal people and culture since arriving in Australia four years earlier as a 17-year-old.[4] In the course of his overlanding journey he had benefited from the 'great use' of Aboriginal men's tracking skills, usually solicited in exchange for blankets, tobacco and 'other things'.[5] He had also learned that these savvy adults could easily give him 'the slip' once they had received their payment, which, in his eyes, proved them to be unreliable. Perhaps Eyre envisaged that the two vulnerable young boys, who had already seemingly attached themselves to Yalbone's party, could not slip away from him as easily as the men.[6]

Once they were in his service, Eyre found Cootachah and Joshuing some clothes and offered them 'a corner' of his tent to sleep in, but they preferred to sleep out by the fire. Eyre thought the boys soon seemed 'reconciled to their new master' and they proved 'very active and useful, especially in tracking lost animals'.[7] Eyre viewed the boys as more than just labourers or servants and treated them differently to the men he employed. When the overlanders were still 100 kilometres from their destination, Eyre left the teams with the livestock and took Joshuing and Cootachah, whom he called Yarry, with him onward to Port Phillip on horseback. After negotiating the sale of his sheep, they travelled together by boat from Port Phillip to Van Diemen's Land before sailing to Sydney. In Launceston the boys were treated as 'objects of great curiosity' because, as Eyre bluntly put it, Aboriginal people in Van Diemen's Land had 'been hunted down some years before when they were either destroyed or removed to a distant land'.[8] Despite referring to Cootachah and Joshuing only as the 'black boys', Eyre developed an affection for them during this trip. He often preferred for them to ride on horseback while he and his overseer, John Baxter, walked alongside, and treated them to theatre visits and an excursion to watch the troops parade during their time in Hobart.[9]

By December 1837 Eyre had organised an expedition overlanding cattle from New South Wales to Adelaide in the newly established colony of South Australia. His crew included Cootachah and Joshuing, a new Aboriginal guide from Gundaroo called Unmallie, and six white labourers prone to drink who quarrelled violently with one another.[10] Tensions within the expedition were exacerbated by the labourers' fear of encountering Aboriginal people on the journey and Eyre's refusal to give them 'guns and ammunition'.[11] After reuniting with Baxter on 15 January 1838, the overlanders approached the Murray River most likely somewhere in the lands of the Yorta Yorta and Bangerang Nations. Here they 'found a large tribe' that happened to include both Cootachah and Joshuing's parents, who were 'greatly delighted' to see the boys again. One father in particular showed 'a great deal of feeling and tenderness' towards his son. The Aboriginal group camped alongside the overlanders that night and again the next evening after following them throughout the day. Eyre 'did not quite like' this development as he was 'afraid of losing the two boys', whose company he had kept for six months. He set about convincing the parents to let him keep Cootachah and Joshuing by 'being very civil' and 'making them sundry little presents' until they eventually appeared to 'acquiesce in the children remaining' with him.[12]

A few days later Eyre took Cootachah to Port Phillip to obtain supplies. By the time he reunited with the teams on 8 February, five of his disgruntled crew had 'bolted, taking with them the black boy, Jos[h]uing'. Eyre did not seem all that dismayed by the loss, brightly adding, 'On the other hand, two other men had been added to our numbers.'[13] Despite the seemingly intimate attachment he had fostered with Joshuing over their seven months together, and knowing how prone to violence the absconders were, Eyre showed little concern for the whereabouts or welfare of the eight-year-old. On the frontier, Aboriginal boys were invaluable to colonists as servants and guides, yet ultimately considered disposable.[14]

The expedition arrived in South Australia in July, and Eyre achieved a significant profit from the sale of the livestock. In October he began organising his second overlanding expedition, which set off in early December. Three weeks into the journey, when he was in Wiradjuri Country near Gundagai on the Murrumbidgee River, he found another Aboriginal boy. Not much older than Cootachah, the boy was named Neramberein and often referred to as Joey. Having lost Joshuing some eleven months earlier, Eyre quickly attached Neramberein to his crew, taking him out on reconnoitring trips and then to Adelaide, in advance of the teams, to organise the livestock sale. Eyre evidently felt closest and most comfortable with the two Aboriginal boys: that Christmas he organised a feast of mutton, duck, fish, a rich plum pudding and 'a little grog … but not enough to make them tipsy' for all of his men, but chose to dine with the boys and an Aboriginal 'stranger' who had speared fish for them the day before.[15] This second overlanding endeavour also made a profit, which enabled Eyre to purchase land in Adelaide and build a weatherboard cottage for himself and the two boys.[16]

After undertaking two explorative expeditions in South Australia with Baxter and the boys, Cootachah and Neramberein, he set off on a third overlanding expedition in 1840, taking sheep from Albany to Perth. On his departure he met Wylie, a local Mineng youth, who helped drive the stock to Perth and accompanied Eyre back to Adelaide in April. Eyre spent much time with Cootachah, Neramberein and Wylie in Adelaide, and the four took most of their meals together.[17]

That winter Eyre embarked on an expedition into the South Australian interior to find an overland route to Western Australia. With financial contributions from the South Australian government and subscriptions, Eyre funded more than half of the expedition's costs and put together a small team: Baxter as overseer, Edward Bate Scott as his assistant and companion, Corporal John Coles, two drivers for the drays, and Neramberein and Cootachah. He had wanted Wylie to accompany them, but the young man was unwell at the time of their departure. The journey was difficult as the expedition had to keep circling great salt lakes, and water and food were hard to find. By late January 1841, after three attempts to get around the head of the Bight, Eyre realised he could only move forward with the horses; the drays would have to be left behind. The expedition went on to Fowler's Bay to meet their supply boat and Eyre soon discovered that Wylie, whom he had summoned from Port Lincoln, was aboard and delighted to join them.[18]

Here Eyre decided to abandon the officially sanctioned expedition and improvised a new route.[19] Along with writing his letter of termination, he had to decide whom to retain for the 'perilous attempt' to continue on to Western Australia. Admitting it was a 'painful' decision, he released Scott, for he 'had no right to lead a young enthusiastic friend into a peril from which escape seemed to be all but hopeless'. He explained to Baxter his plan to journey on through 'inhospitable' terrain and was relieved when the overseer decided to stay with him. The 'native boys', on the other hand, were given no choice; Eyre decided they would 'accompany' him on the journey because they 'would be better able to put up with the fatigues and privations we should have to go through, than Europeans', and 'their quickness of sight, habit of observation, and skill in tracking, might occasionally be of essential service' to him. He also expected that Wylie would 'be able to interpret to any tribes' they might encounter. Eyre briefly considered sending Cootachah back to Adelaide but felt that the youngest boy 'had been with me several years, and I did not like to send him away whilst he was willing to remain'. He also reasoned that since the boy 'was so young and so light in weight … his presence could cause but little extra difficulty'.[20]

Although Eyre believed that 'three natives' was more than he required, the boys were kept very busy performing a range of onerous tasks such as recovering

Wylie. Portrait by Robert Neill, 1845.

From Edward John Eyre, Journals of Expeditions of Discovery into Central Australia, and Overland from Adelaide to King George's Sound, in the years 1840–1 *(London: T. and W. Boone, 1845), opposite p. 295. Courtesy of State Library of South Australia, Adelaide* lost horses and livestock, hunting for game and digging wells for water to help provision the expedition. Such intensive labour, combined with the difficult conditions, quickly began to erode the expedition's morale. By April 1841 the situation was dire. They had little food and everyone felt miserable. Baxter was especially pessimistic about the expedition's future as they survived on 'sting-ray fish', which they had initially found palatable but which now made them feel 'ill and weak', and a paltry supply of flour.[21] Eyre feared that Wiley, Neramberein and Cootachah would hear the overseer's complaints and try to abscond. On 16 April Eyre ordered Baxter to slaughter one of their ailing horses so its meat could be salted to last them for a few days. Eyre could not bring himself to eat the 'horrible and revolting' horse flesh and persisted with the stingray even though it made him 'dreadfully sick'. Disgusted, he complained that the 'native boys gorged themselves to excess, remaining the whole afternoon by the carcass, where they made a fire, cutting off and roasting such portions as had been left'. To Eyre, they 'looked like ravenous wolves about their prey'.[22] He claimed to give the boys a larger share of the rations than he kept for himself, but perhaps their evident hunger was a sign of their greater exertions in performing their various duties. His description of them as wolf-like seemed to reflect his growing anxiety about their 'disaffection and discontent', which he considered a 'frightful' prospect.

This rationing sparked great tensions and the increasingly suspicious Eyre began weighing the horsemeat each night. Believing that any one of them could 'gratify his own appetite at the expense of the others', he maintained that it was 'necessary to enforce strict honesty towards each other'.[23] During his nightly weighing on 22 April, he decided that four pounds (1.8kg) were missing. Eyre blamed the boys and deducted the amount from their rations and proclaimed that whoever identified the thief would be spared this reduction.[24] Cootachah, who would only have been about 11 years of age, was adamant he was innocent, while the indignant Neramberein threatened that he and Wylie 'would leave [Eyre] and make their way themselves' if their rations were halved. Eyre tried to bluff the boys, 'pointing out to them the folly, in fact the impossibility almost, of their succeeding in any attempt of this kind' and 'advised them to remain where they were, and behave well for the future'.[25]

Despite his bravado, Eyre was increasingly anxious that the boys might leave, just as he had previously worried that Unmallie might leave him.[26] He was concerned that 'for some time past the two eldest of the boys, both of whom were now nearly grown up to manhood, have been far from obedient in their general conduct'. Resenting Eyre's attempt to discipline them, and despite his 'remonstrances and expostulations' for them to stay, Wylie and Neramberein prepared their spears and 'walked sulkily from the camp', planning to travel to King George's Sound by themselves. Cootachah tried to follow, but Eyre physically detained him, believing he 'was too young to know what he was doing'.[27] Three days later, however, the older boys returned. Wylie apologised for leaving and claimed that they 'could get nothing to eat for themselves', an unlikely excuse given that the boys had often hunted game for the expedition. Neramberein was more obstinate and sat 'silently and sullenly at the fire'.[28] Perhaps the boys returned because they felt guilty about leaving Cootachah behind with Eyre. After reprimanding Wylie and Neramberein, Eyre gave them some tea and bread. Over the next four days the expedition faced greater hardship as finding water became more challenging, and their only food was a wallaby shot by the boys.

On the night of 29 April, Eyre took the first watch over the horses while the others slept. At about 10.30pm he was 'startled by a sudden flash, followed by the report of a gun'. Upon his hasty return to the camp, he saw Wylie running towards him in a state of alarm and was 'horror-struck to find [his] poor overseer lying on the ground, weltering in his blood, and in the last agonies of death'.[29] Cootachah and Neramberein were missing and the camp's belongings were scattered. With Baxter gone, the 'frightful, the appalling truth now burst upon' Eyre: 'I was alone in the desert'.[30] Really, he meant he was now the only white man in the expedition, for Wylie remained by his side. However, Eyre felt he could not trust 'his fidelity' because he 'might be in league with the other two, who perhaps were even now, lurk[ed] about with the view of taking away my life'. Realising that they had taken his double-barrelled shot gun, Eyre 'ripped open the bag in which the pistols had been sewn up', only to discover that the boys had taken the ammunition as well as the bread, tea, sugar, tobacco, water and a second shotgun. Eyre was terrified that the boys would try to kill him next, so he and Wylie quickly set off away from the camp.[31] As Eyre had never witnessed Baxter ill-treating the boys, he guessed the overseer had interrupted the boys' plans to steal away in the night; when one of the younger boys killed him, Wylie decided to stay while Cootachah and Neramberein fled. Eyre spent the night keeping a look out for the boys, scared they might find and kill him: 'With an aching heart, and in most painful reflections, I passed this dreadful night.'[32]

The next day Eyre sneaked back to camp to gather the 'bare necessities' and mournfully 'enshroud' Baxter's body where it had fallen, since burial was impossible in the rocky ground. He and Wylie 'escape[d] from the melancholy scene' and 'travelled slowly and silently' west. The day after, as they packed up their makeshift camp, Wylie noticed 'the native boys', hidden behind their blankets, 'advancing towards' them, which 'alarmed' Eyre, who had assumed they would head back to Fowler's Bay where the expedition had previously buried provisions. Believing that 'as long as they followed like bloodhounds on our tracks our lives would be in their power at any moment that they chose to take them', Eyre felt he was 'sufficiently a match for them in an open country' with his rifle and pistols.[33] He soon made the extraordinary decision that the only way 'to save my own life … was to shoot the elder of the two. Painful as this would be.' Instructing Wylie to watch the horses, he advanced towards Neramberein and Cootachah, 'rifle in hand'. As he closed in, he saw they already had their guns trained on him. When he lowered his rifle, they advanced, calling out to Wylie 'incessantly'. Eyre tried to 'parley with them', but they quickly retorted, 'Oh massa, we don't want you, we want Wylie.' He now realised their 'only present object in following' was not to kill him but to get Wylie 'to join them'. A relieved Eyre returned to Wylie, who 'remained quietly' with the horses, and urged him to come away from the boys. Upon seeing Wylie leave, Cootachah and Neramberein 'set up a wild and plaintive cry' and followed at a distance, 'never ceasing in their importunities to Wylie'.[34] As the evening approached, Eyre and Wylie travelled through the undulating sands in the dark, covering 30 kilometres in an effort to outrun the boys. After holding that pace for the next five days, Eyre was finally confident that he had lost the boys: he believed Cootachah was not 'equal to so arduous a task'.[35] Assuming they had probably turned back, he grimly predicted that Cootachah and Neramberein would starve to death once they ran out of their plundered rations, still holding on to the belief that they lacked the bush skills necessary to survive in the desert.

Even though he had thought to kill Neramberein, Eyre 'could not help feeling for their sad condition', especially given 'the youngest of the two had been with me for four years, the elder for two years and a half, and both had accompanied me in all my travels'. Despite his sympathies, he nonetheless fantasised about 'the miseries and sufferings they would have to encounter and the probable fate that awaited them' – a 'dreadful and lingering death … aggravated in all its horrors by the consciousness they had brought it entirely upon themselves'.[36]

Eyre and Wylie continued their arduous journey and arrived in Albany more than two months later on 7 July 1841. Both were interviewed about Baxter's death by Justice of the Peace Peter Belches, and both testified that they never saw

Eyre's Journey to Albany. Engraving by Samuel Calvert, 1891.
IAN01/01/91/SUPP/12. Courtesy of State Library of Victoria, Melbourne

Cootachah or Neramberein again.[37] Eyre reportedly remained concerned about the boys, often enquiring if there was news of their whereabouts.[38] Aboriginal oral histories over time offer conflicting reports about what ultimately happened to Cootachah and Neramberein. In 1882 Aboriginal people brought Baxter's remains to William Graham, the station master at Eyre's Sandpatch, along with pieces of ironwork and saddle. They reported that 'the boys certainly reached Eucla on their way back' and were 'positive' that they had travelled to South Australia.[39] However, in 1912 when Daisy Bates was in Eucla, she was told by local Mirning that the 'moment they left' the 'protection of the whites' – Eyre and Baxter – the boys were 'descended upon and killed'.[40] In 1997, Ngadju-Mirning man Arthur Dimer similarly reported that the Mirning had speared the boys, but only after they had witnessed Eyre killing Baxter, from afar.[41]

Explorative expeditions were not only instrumental to the colonial enterprise; they also mirrored colonial power dynamics, in that they were spaces marked by racial boundaries, codes of discipline, social hierarchies and labour exploitation.

This tragic story palpably illustrates the claustrophobic microcosm of the expedition, whereby precariousness could quickly rupture its social dynamics and transform intimacies into violent antipathies at a moment's notice. With a single gunshot, Eyre's masquerade as a colonial master attempting to discipline his Aboriginal boys evaporated and he believed himself to be in a kill-or-be-killed situation against youths with whom he had lived and travelled for a number of years. Eyre narrated five desperate days in which he attempted to outrun Cootachah and Neramberein through the desert, hoping that they, guilt-ridden by their crimes, would starve to death before they had a chance to catch up with him.

Eyre's belief that he was their prey outweighed the intimacy he had forged with the boys over several years and, more importantly, the intimacy that they – as three Aboriginal youths removed from their family and Country – had forged with one another. Disregarding their plaintive cries to reunite with Wylie, Eyre drove Wylie onwards to outrun the seemingly predatory Cootachah and Neramberein to ensure that he would not be left truly alone in the desert.

The actual prey in this story was not Eyre as he imagined, but instead Cootachah, Neramberein and Wylie. They represent the hundreds, if not thousands, of Aboriginal children and youths unofficially taken from their families to reside with and work for settlers as domestics, servants, guides, labourers and companions on the Australian frontier.[42] Aboriginal children were favoured because they were seen as tractable; as Dane Kennedy explains, many were 'forced by circumstances of their estrangement to forge a new niche for themselves at the intersection of cultures'. Colonial violence resulted in untold numbers of Aboriginal orphans and other children cut off from their own communities who were 'easy prey for settlers'.[43] It can never be definitively known whether Cootachah and Neramberein made it back to their Country or met their demise in the desert. Either way, they were still victims of a colonial mentality that normalised the removal of Aboriginal children from their families. Their stories reveal how violence and intimacy were inextricably entangled on the colonial frontier.

Chapter 10

A Hidden Violence

The Sexual Abuse of the Stolen Generations

Stephanie Gilbert

Sexual violence is commonly reported in the testimonies of the Stolen Generations. These testimonies have been told, collected and recollected for inquiries and compensation claims as well as for entertainment. They have been collected by agencies such as Link-Up, which helps members of the Stolen Generations trace and reunite with their families, and used for analysis by industry professionals, including lawyers, psychologists, documentary filmmakers and storytellers. The telling and representation of these stories also sits across a multitude of ideological, legal and social frameworks.

The ways in which the stories of the Stolen Generations are constructed can appear almost formulaic at times. The central defining feature is the physical removal of children from their family of origin. However, other features occur frequently enough in the narratives to constitute core facets of the experience. These include physical and sexual abuse, emotional trauma, lack of self-worth and obstructed development of a core Aboriginal identity. This chapter focuses on how sexual abuse operated as a hidden and unaddressed violence, or silence. How it is spoken about, represented and visualised spatially, both in the past and in the present, is in part dependent upon the spaces and places where the abuse occurs. My aim here is to convey a sense of how important location is, while also giving voice to that violent silence.

I present the reader with the opportunity to be 'present' with the children who were abused in the Cootamundra Aboriginal Girls' Home. This Home – a site of former criminal activity and now a world heritage site – is an example of how spaces regulated girls' bodies, imposed upon their minds and circumscribed

AFTERMATHS

their movements. The repercussions of the sexual abuse that occurred there, and in other similar institutions throughout Australia, are immense. This discussion constructs these actions as crimes that operate as part of a foundation stone of colonising violence.

MAPPING THE SPACE: WHERE DID THESE CRIMES OCCUR?

Imagine, for a moment, that you are a child lying in bed in a dormitory at your children's home, fearing that you will be chosen that night to be led away by an adult who is meant to be caring for you. You know that a crime will be committed against a child in that room – against that child's body and mind – and yet, for self-preservation's sake, you hope it will not be you. At the same time, you are intimately aware of what will be suffered by the child who is chosen that night.

This was what it was like for the girls who were residents of the Cootamundra Aboriginal Girls' Training Home in the state of New South Wales (NSW) from 1911 to 1969. The Home was in an early federation-style building that had served, from its construction in 1887, as Cootamundra's first hospital.[1] The training home was established in 1911 and listed as a world heritage site in 2012.

George Edward Ardill, vice president of the Aborigines Protection Board, created the Cootamundra Aboriginal Girls' Home and instilled his own values into its processes. He was also the head of the Sydney Rescue Work Society and ran the Home of Hope for Friendless and Fallen Women. Ardill was raised a Baptist and committed to full-time charity work in his twenties. He joined the Aborigines Protection Board in 1897 and was instrumental in embedding into NSW legislation the idea that Aboriginal girls' futures lay in being taught domestic service. His beliefs guided the purpose of the Cootamundra Aboriginal Girls' Home, setting the course of, and presiding over, the lives of the girls in the Home, which would later be condemned for its 'slavery-like' conditions.[2]

The Home had two dormitories. The first had served as a hospital ward and the second was on the building's veranda. Both dormitories made use of the hospital's beds, which were lined up in neat rows.

As one woman testified to the National Inquiry into the Separation of Aboriginal and Torres Strait Islander Children from Their Families (hereafter the Inquiry), the dormitories were sites of sexual abuse. Abusive adults walked into these rooms and chose a child to accompany them.

A hidden violence

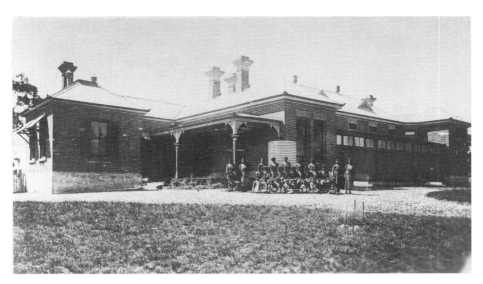

Cootamundra Aboriginal Girls' Home.

Government Architect, NRS 4346, Photographs of public buildings in New South Wales, 1880–1940. NRS-4346-1-[9/5879B]-1-13. Courtesy of NSW State Archives and Records, Kingswood

---

I didn't know what she was doing with me. I didn't know anything about sex or anything like that, we weren't told. I can remember a piece of wood shaped like a walking cane only on a smaller scale, like the candy-striped lollipops they make today approximately 30cms long. She was telling me all about the time she was with my mother when she died and how my mother had told her how much she loved me. She also had a large bag of puffed wheat near the bed, because she knew how much I loved it. All this time she was inserting this cane into my vagina. I guess I was about 9 or 10. I know she did this to me many times over the years until she left the Home when I was about 14 years old.

We were totally isolated in the Home. You never knew anything of the outside world. We didn't know if that was right or wrong. Every time I knew she was coming, when matron was going on holidays, I would beg to matron not to go, because I knew she'd be there. She was always there – in my life, in my life in the Home. Her bedroom used to open out onto the dormitory ... I'd hear my name being called ... It was always me ... One night I hid under the bed. I held onto the bed and she pulled me out and flogged me with the strap. She is my biggest memory of that home.

Confidential evidence 10, Queensland:
NSW woman removed to Cootamundra Girls' Home in the 1940s[3]

Doreen Webster describes the sexual abuse perpetrated by the staff of Cootamundra while she was there. 'It was inhumane, we were really abused horribly, we shouldn't never have been taken in the first place. We often talk about it, some of the girls still cry … It was too difficult, and it still is difficult, but we as Coota girls, we talk to each other about what happened', she says. 'I can't say much about the impacts of it, on me.'[4]

The Home also had a storeroom that doubled as a punishment room. Originally used as a morgue for the hospital, it has since been demolished, although the concrete foundation slab remains.[5] Webster spoke of a small external weatherboard building the size of a pantry and also known as 'the morgue', where girls were locked up overnight if they had run away or misbehaved.[6] The following testimony to the Inquiry describes the punitive use of this small space:

> They were very cruel to us, very cruel. I've done things in that home that I don't think prisoners in a jail would do today … I remember once, I must have been 8 or 9, and I was locked in the old morgue. The adults who worked there would tell us of the things that happened in there, so you can imagine what I went through. I screamed all night, but no one came to get me.
>
> *Confidential evidence 10, Queensland:*
> *NSW woman removed to Cootamundra Girls' Home in the 1940s*[7]

Girls described how others were put in the storeroom overnight and were never seen or heard of again.[8] Objecting to or resisting sexual abuse would likely incur physical and psychological punishment amounting to torture, which in some cases resulted in death.

Cootamundra Aboriginal Girls' Home was the site of sexual crimes against the girls who were placed there. Colonial subjection and its consequent horror created the opportunity for the Coota girls' lives to operate as a site of suffering – where they lay in their beds, physically vulnerable in what ought to have been a place of safety, knowing that the most heinous crimes may be about to be inflicted on them or one of their sisters.[9]

As girls left the Home to go into domestic service, the site of the crimes of sexual abuse shifted to the site of their domestic service: approximately 11 percent of girls in service became pregnant. Victoria Haskins argues that 'there is no doubt the board knew of the high rates of pregnancies to girls in service and was aware also of cases of alleged sexual abuse and rape'.[10] Some of these pregnant girls returned to Cootamundra, where they would lose their child to the same system they had been subjected to, and then be re-apprenticed. In some instances, they were returned to the placement where they had become pregnant.[11]

THE EFFECTS OF THIS WIDESPREAD SEXUAL ABUSE AND HOW IT HAS BEEN DEALT WITH

The Inquiry report states that its recommendations 'are directed to healing and reconciliation for the benefit of all Australians.'[12] At the time the report 'Bringing Them Home' was released, in 1997, it was possible to dream that the 51-odd recommendations would set a path for healing and reconciliation. Now, more than 20 years on, we know that neither healing nor reconciliation has occurred.

Why set a goal to want all Australians to heal from this past? Any process for healing surely starts with an acknowledgement of the crimes committed against Stolen Generations children. In the report, sexual assault sits alongside other 'effects' of child removal. Many commentators, including former Prime Minister Kevin Rudd in his apology speech in 2008, note that for healing to occur, the actions that created the situation would have to stop and 'the injustices of the past must never, never happen again'.[13] This goal has not been achieved, in part due to the continuation of the same philosophies in family and child services, which result in the crime of sexual abuse of children continuing with regularity in Australia today. These crimes were only minimally explored as a consequence of the Stolen Generations in the Inquiry's report, which showed that Aboriginal child removal is one of the pillars of colonising violence enacted over Aboriginal Australians. Very little thought has been given to the perpetrators of child removal and child sexual abuse. In this, it is perhaps timely to remind ourselves of former Prime Minister Paul Keating's words in his 1992 Redfern Park speech:

> We took the children from their mothers. We practised discrimination and exclusion. It was our ignorance and our prejudice, and our failure to imagine these things being done to us. With some noble exceptions, we failed to make the most basic human response and enter into their hearts and minds. We failed to ask, 'How would I feel if this were done to me?' As a consequence, we failed to see that what we were doing degraded all of us.[14]

CAN HEALING OCCUR IF THE PILLARS OF COLONISING VIOLENCE CONTINUE TO EXIST?

The importance of storytelling to the healing process has been debated extensively and yet remains ambiguous. It has, however, been the strategy that underpins many of the funding models for redress implemented by Australian governments. It could be argued that requiring the sharing of stories to be part of the redress processes embeds the ongoing violence against the child victim. If sharing your experience is a requirement for participation in processes like redress schemes, but there is no equal commitment to charging anyone with the crime you report, this is incredibly problematic and violent.

Table 1 outlines the state, territory and national redress schemes for reparations for Stolen Generations. The aims of this table are twofold. The first is to highlight how many times a Stolen Generations individual might be asked to engage in telling a version of their personal story as a removed child, including stories of their sexual abuse. The second is to highlight that each time a person is forced to recount a highly personal, and perhaps tragic, narrative, they then have it viewed through an analytical or testing framework. The professionals involved in witnessing and evaluating this narrative include lawyers, medical doctors, psychiatrists, psychologists and teachers who have no experience of hearing and understanding sexual abuse from within the gestalt of the experience.

Table 1 shows that each scheme for redress in the states and territories across Australia is different. In 2019–20 some national uniformity was brought to bear, but the rules strictly exclude many who have already been compensated at a state level. This is partly because the national redress scheme, of which all states and territories are part, is for all Australians who fit within its parameters, whereas the states have specific schemes for Stolen Generations peoples.

TABLE 1: STOLEN GENERATIONS REDRESS SCHEMES[15]

LOCATION	REQUIREMENTS	PAYMENT PER CLAIM	APPLICATION DATES	NOTES
Commonwealth National Redress	• you experienced sexual abuse when you were a child (under 18 years of age) • the abuse happened before 1 July 2018 • an institution was responsible for bringing you into contact with the person who abused you • you were born before 30 June 2010 • at the time you apply, you are an Australian citizen or a permanent resident	up to A$150,000 average payment is approx. A$76,000	30 June 2017	Created in response to the Royal Commission into Institutional Responses to Child Sexual Abuse This scheme has a number of disqualifiers, such as being in jail or having already accepted compensation.
Australian Capital Territory: Nil schemes				
New South Wales Stolen Generations Reparations Scheme and Funeral Assistance Fund	• you are on the Protection Board list • you were removed by, committed to, or otherwise came into the care of, the New South Wales Aborigines Protection or Welfare Boards under the Aborigines Protection Act 1909 up until the Act was repealed on 2 June 1969	A$75,000 Funeral Fund: A$7000	2 December 2016	
Northern Territory: Nil schemes				

TABLE 1 *continued*

LOCATION	REQUIREMENTS	PAYMENT PER CLAIM	APPLICATION DATES	NOTES
Queensland Redress Scheme	• you experienced abuse and neglect in a Queensland institution • your name is on the list of nominated institutions	Level 1: A$7000 Level 2: up to A$33,000	30 June 2008	
South Australia Stolen Generations Reparations Scheme		A$20,000 + A$10,000	2015	A$11 million package A$6 million paid to direct claims and the remainder to indirect reparations
Tasmania	• you are Aboriginal and were removed from your family between 1935 and 1975 for at least 12 months		2006	A$5 million package paid to 106 individuals or their children
Victoria Stolen Generations Redress Scheme			March 2022	March 2022 A$155 million package Includes redress payments, counselling support, and a funeral or memorial fund[16]
Western Australia Redress Scheme	• you experienced very severe abuse and/or neglect with ongoing symptoms and disability	Initially A$80,000, dropped to A$45,000 due to large number of claims	2007	

PROCESSES OF ONGOING VIOLENCE

In order to apply for the Queensland Redress Scheme, an individual had to visit a psychologist who would question them about their time in care, their psychological experience of that time and its ongoing impact, and then provide a document for the claims process. After that, the individual had to seek legal assistance to lodge a claim. The professionals themselves made claims from the scheme for their services. As Table 1 shows, an analytical process determined whether a claim was assessed as Level 1 alone or Levels 1 and 2: Level 2 assessments were for permanent injury and/or disablement. To qualify for this, an individual had to develop a legal document with evidence to show there had been abuse and permanent physical and/or psychological damage caused by the experience of being in care.

Creating each claim was traumatic. Each assessment was traumatic. Receiving the outcome was traumatic. Each time a person was asked to do this, they were forced to revisit their trauma. Would it have been possible to remember and recount these stories without being retraumatised? It seems it would not, as this is a history stored in each person's body. It also reinforced that person's Aboriginality as the very reason for their removal as a child. As a Stolen Generations child, the label identifies you as Aboriginal and indicates Aboriginality itself is the problem. Through bureaucratic, state-sponsored processes of assessment, analysis and decision-making, the now-adult is recolonised by the same violent colonising actions that created their removal. Once again, their body is a site of colonising violence. They are mapped as part of the colonial space and site.

A person cannot be anything but retraumatised if they are asked to revisit these stories repeatedly for the various institutional inquiries that are supposed to be 'healing' or compensating. In each state, as both a child and a Stolen Generations adult, you could be retraumatised, redefined and re-removed under different rules, new expectations and new or different Aboriginalities. I myself lived under 'child protection' in three states before leaving state care at the age of 18 and experienced the redress scheme as a new trauma experience confirming the older experiences. I have argued elsewhere that the Aboriginal child was removed as a body, as a site of intervention for the wishes and desires of non-Aboriginal Australians.[17] This chapter has mapped these stolen bodies into the colonising violence of sexual abuse and questioned why these crimes of sexual violence were not constructed as crimes.

Achille Mbembe writes that 'memory and remembrance put into play a structure of organs, a nervous system, an economy of emotions centred necessarily on the body and everything that exceeds it … All forms of memory therefore find consistent expression in the universe of the senses, imagination, and multiplicity.'[18] Mbembe suggests that memory is sensory and embodied and produced through multiple sites of experience. This chapter has explored what it continues to mean to be treated as an anonymised body available for removal – and a problematic identity – within the multiple spaces of colonial governance that serve as a site of persecution and then of traumatisation. Why have perpetrators not been charged if the children were victims of crime? If we accept Mbembe's proposition, we must understand that there will be a consistent expression of colonial trauma for these now-adults. For Mbembe, an 'event never simply takes place'; its repercussions are felt across time.[19] Perhaps he would agree that by witnessing the gestalt of these memories, readers will allow a possessing and repopulating of these abused bodies. Healing cannot occur without an end to the colonial violence explored here, or if it is not recognised as having occurred. Listening must happen 'at the intersection between an event, words, signs and images' to create remembering and understanding of these sexual assaults as they were experienced.[20]

In conclusion, while the repossession work of the Stolen Generations over their own bodies continues, colonising violence does as well. We must not let the crimes go unpunished, they must also be heard within a criminal framework. They must operate as more than narratives for a process of assessment for compensation where personal experience is independently weighed up. What use is testifying and witnessing time and again if it never leads to justice? This cannot be allowed to be about how much getting raped is worth in monetary compensation. The systematic removal of Aboriginal children continues in Australia today.

There are two things to consider, then. The first is that innocent child who lay in bed waiting for her rapist: she should not be forgotten and left behind, sacrificed for the rights of others. Second, understanding these removals as acts of colonising violence must create impetus for change in current policies and practices and an equal commitment to understanding the criminal nature of sexual violence against Aboriginal children.

Chapter 11

FIJI'S COLONIAL ORPHANAGES

Erica Newman

Orphanages, and ideas about guardianship of non-related children and adoption of children, were introduced to Indigenous societies with the arrival of Europeans. These were concepts that the Indigenous people did not require or understand. Fiji is no exception. The iTaukei, Indigenous Fijians, like all societies within the Pacific region, had a community kinship structure where child-raising was not the sole responsibility of the birth parents and all children were cared for.

When it comes to children's welfare and colonialism, many of us may immediately think of the Stolen Generations in Australia (discussed by Stephanie Gilbert in this volume), the impacts of residential schools and the Sixties Scoop in Canada, or the Royal Commission of Inquiry into Abuse in State Care in New Zealand. Orphanages in Fiji are different. Although they were a collaboration between churches and the state and were introduced colonial institutions implicated in cultural colonisation, that is where the comparison ends. In Fiji the establishment of orphanages, guardianship and adoption was a consequence of the Indian indentured labour scheme that was introduced in 1879 and ended in 1919. Orphanage care for Indian children during the colonial period was supported by the Wesleyan Methodist Church, the most influential religious body in Fiji during this period. Placement in an orphanage affected the cultural beliefs and practices of Indian children and altered the meaning of family for those raised within this institution.

AFTERMATHS

THE INTRODUCTION OF INDIAN INDENTURE LABOUR TO FIJI

Around the time Fiji became a British colony in 1874, European plantation owners were recruiting Polynesian labourers in indentured labour schemes, sometimes through dubious means of persuasion or kidnapping (blackbirding). Upon his arrival in Fiji in 1879, the new governor, Sir Arthur Gordon, introduced an Indian indentured labour scheme to meet the demands of the colonial plantation economy. Gordon already had experience of using Indians as indentured labour while he was governor in Trinidad and then in Mauritius and believed a system of supplying Indian workers would be of benefit to Fiji.

India had been a British colony since 1858, and the Indian population was familiar with Western ideals and institutions by the time Fiji's Indian indentured labour scheme began. The Indian population practised their own kinship and social structure within a strict caste system that defined social order.[1] Indian kinship and family clans were based on a joint family structure, common for both Hindus and Muslims. In this patrilineal structure, a family consisted of parents, their sons and their sons' wives and children. Aunts, uncles, cousins and other

An example of a 'Coolie' Line as Indian indentured labourers tried to establish themselves in their new home. From J.W. Burton, The Fiji of Today (London: Charles H. Kelly, 1910), opposite p. 257. Courtesy of Internet Archive, San Francisco

members of the extended family shared the responsibilities of caring for children. Families that did not have a son practised adoption by approaching the patrilineal line to adopt the son of the father's sister, or of the wife's sister. If a male child could not be adopted through these lines, the last option would be non-familial but from a sub-clan whose caste and religious affiliation were known.[2]

When indenture began, caste and religious structures were not taken into consideration during the long voyages or on the plantations. Labourers continued to practise their customs and traditions but altered them to accommodate their new environment.[3]

THE INTRODUCTION OF THE INDIAN ORPHANS ORDINANCE 1885

Following the introduction of the Indian indentured labour scheme, the occasional orphaned child needed guardianship. In these infrequent situations, the Colonial Office appointed a guardian. In 1884 nine orphaned Indian children arrived in Fiji with a shipment of indentured labourers. No guardians were available for these children. With no institutions or laws to cater for orphaned children in Fiji at this time, the colonial government introduced the Indian Orphans Ordinance, the first child guardianship and custody law of Fiji.[4]

The colonial secretary, who drafted the ordinance along with the attorney-general's office and the agent-general of immigration, believed it was the colony's responsibility to provide care arrangements for Indian orphans. Discussions focused on who would be the most appropriate guardians, and the need to establish a procedure to find guardians for orphaned Indian children. They felt orphans should ideally be cared for by Indian immigrants, but not exclusively so, and placement should be based on age: a child under the age of two would be placed with a married Indian couple of good repute (as supported by the manager of the plantation they were indentured to); a child who was over two but under 10 would be placed with a European couple; and those over the age of 10 would be indentured on a plantation in accordance with the 1878 Indian Immigration Ordinance.[5] These guardianships were temporary and limited initially to three years (this was later extended to five years or until the child reached the age of 15).

In 1885 the ordinance was approved and passed through legislation as the Ordinance to Provide for the Care and Maintenance of Orphan Indian Immigrants. It defined an orphan as:

any infant Indian immigrant under ten years of age whose parents or other lawful guardians have died during the voyage from India or after arrival in this Colony either before or after they were indentured or whose parents or lawful guardians have in the opinion of the Agent-General become incapable of taking care of such infant.[6]

Not only could a child be orphaned by the death of their parents, but the agent-general could also create 'orphans' if he believed the parents or guardians were unfit to care for a child. The offices of the agent-general and the colonial secretary vetted applications for guardianship. Applicants required a reference from their plantation manager, and if this did not support the couple, their application was denied. European couples were also vetted and were often supported by someone they knew within the colonial secretary's office. In the first few years of implementing this ordinance there was a high proportion of temporary European guardians compared with Indian, although this changed in later years.[7] The legislation provided procedures and processes for orphaned children of Indian indentured labourers, paid for by the Indian Immigration Fund and therefore only available for Indian children. No practice was formally established for any other indentured labourers within Fiji, such as orphans of Polynesian indentured labourers.

DILKUSHA AND THE OPERATIONS OF WESLEYAN METHODIST ORPHANAGES

The increasing numbers of orphaned Indian children arriving in Fiji or becoming orphaned on the plantation meant that sometimes there were not enough reputable people available to be guardians. In these instances, the agent-general of immigration would approach the church to become guardians. Although there were two primary Christian missions in Fiji at this time – Wesleyan Methodist and Roman Catholic – the colonial government of Fiji relied most on the Methodist Church. The church cared for orphaned children within unofficial orphanages attached to their mission stations.

Opened in 1905, Dilkusha was Fiji's first official orphanage; it is still in operation today as a children's home. John Burton was the first superintendent, and his wife and a missionary sister, Miss Austen, cared for the orphans.[8] During Burton's time as superintendent, from 1905 to 1910, the orphanage admitted 13 children. Of these, nine were actual orphans. Of the remaining four, one had been abandoned, and one was placed with a Christian Indian couple as legal guardians,

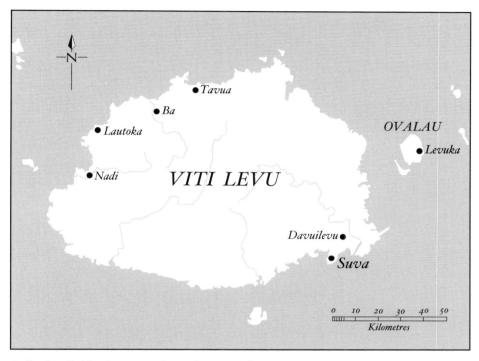

Dilkusha Children's Home is located at Davuilevu. Map by Allan Kynaston

with the agent-general's approval; there is no information regarding the other two.[9]

Dilkusha accepted the placement of children in its care either by private arrangement with the parents or relatives, or under negotiated terms with the agent-general of immigration following the procedures set by the Indian Orphans Ordinance. Initially, any private arrangements between the orphanage and the parents lasted until the parent completed their indenture period. Parents used the orphanage as a boarding school that provided their child with temporary accommodation, care and education, but had to agree to Christian teaching and have limited contact with their child until the end of their indenture, when they were able to collect them. This affected the religious beliefs, cultural practices and kinship structure of the Indian family.[10]

In 1911 Cyril Bavin became superintendent of Dilkusha and set about amending the placement procedures. He had two goals: the first was to ensure that all Indian orphans were placed at Dilkusha, or at least the orphanage should have first rights of guardianship with the government's support. The second was government implementation of legal sanctions to prevent parents from attempting to retrieve their children before the end of their indenture term. Bavin believed that 'after years of careful nursing and training, the parents came and claimed their child at the age when, in the opinions of the missionary, most care and protection was needed'.[11] The agent-general of immigration at the time, A.R. Coates, declined to recommend that the Methodist orphanage be offered guardianship of all orphans. Coates declared, 'On the whole children are better off and happier with their country-people who usually treat them very well, as Indians are fond of children'.[12] Coates surmised that Bavin was 'asking for measures to prevent parents gaining access to their own children while the latter were under mission control'.[13] Coates wanted parents to reclaim their children when they were able and to limit the Methodist mission's guardianship to cases where parents were destitute and absolutely unable to care for their child.

Although the government did not support or agree with Bavin's intended goals, the Methodist mission was open to trying his initiatives. They made parents sign a relinquishing agreement that transferred their parental rights to the orphanage. The format of the agreement is reproduced here:

10 September 1911
Agreed with [parent's name], ex [ship arrived on]
1. That the said [parent's name] of his own free will and accord shall hand over his infant child, about [age of child], to the care of the said Cyril Bavin.
2. That the said [parent's name] does here hereby constitute the said Cyril Bavin or whomever he shall appoint the guardian of his child, promising to relinquish all parental control of the child from the date hereof.
3. That the said [parent's name] promises that he will not henceforth claim his child, nor in any way interfere with or cause annoyance to the guardian of his child or in any way try to induce the child to return to him at any further date.[14]

This appears to be the permanent transfer of guardianship from the parent to the orphanage, and to state that a child would never be returned to their parent. How much of this a parent understood is not known; many signed these agreements with a symbol, not a name, an indication that they possibly were not able to read or write in English. Other parents entered private agreements with the orphanage for a period of no less than five years. Parents were able to visit once every three months.

Although parents may have signed the transfer of their parental rights to the orphanage, some changed their minds and wanted their child returned to them or wanted more access to their child. These parents had to go through the legal system to be heard, and because they had signed the transfer agreement, the courts did not always rule in their favour. Even though Coates had categorically stated that parents should be able to retrieve their child whenever they were able to without hindrance, Bavin's aggressive changes to the orphanage procedures seemed to have worked.[15]

Bavin continued his aggressive tactics, and in 1913 he approached the employers of Indian indentured labourers to promote the orphanage facilities. He advised of two separate processes that parents could follow in committing their child or children to the facilities:

> Either a child could be left by his parents for any amount of time at a cost of £5 per annum. Or an agreement, which must have the sanction of the Agent General of Immigration and the employer, could be drawn up to transfer the child to mission care free-of-charge and for a period of five years.[16]

This tactic also seemed to work, as there was an increase in children placed at the Methodist orphanages between 1913 and 1918. Of the total number of children in these orphanages, just under 45 percent were actual orphans; the remainder had been admitted by their parents through Bavin's process whereby the orphanage raised and educated the children at its own expense.[17]

In 1918 the Methodist mission decided it would only accept children if they were given over to its care until they reached 15 years of age. It was believed that children would only gain the benefits of being raised in the orphanage if they remained for this longer period of uninterrupted care and education. Parents agreed to these terms, particularly when they were unable to provide the support payments that would be required if their child were placed for a shorter time. The Methodist mission provided all financial support for a child when admitted to the orphanage in exchange for the parent signing a transfer of guardianship contract, such as this one dated 18 January 1919:

> I, [name of parent] (reg. no.____) ex [name of ship arrived on] now of [name of town residing in], do hereby agree to hand over my [daughter/son, child's name] aged [age of child] to the guardianship of Superintendent of the Methodist Mission, Dilkusha, Nausori, for education and maintenance until the said [daughter/son] shall have attained the age of fifteen years (15).

And I hereby agree that, should I in any way interfere with the aforesaid superintendent in the discharge of his guardianship I will refund to the said Superintendent at the rate of Eight (8) pounds per annum for each year or part of a year in which expense for said maintenance shall have been incurred.[18]

There is no way of knowing how much of this the parents understood, especially those who signed using a symbol. The agreements were witnessed by the Wesleyan Methodists who were affiliated with the orphanage at the time.[19]

A child could return to their family if they were to be raised within a Christian household. However, if the orphanage staff were not able to complete the reformation of a child within this time, and if they knew the child was not returning to a Christian family, they did everything they could to retain the child.[20] Superintendents of the orphanages 'had little faith in the ability of Indian parents to bring their children up adequately and unless a child was returning to a Christian environment opposition to a child's discharge intensified'.[21] In this instance, missionaries sought to persuade the child to tell their parents they did not want to leave and live in a non-Christian household. This provided the orphanage with a reason to fight for the child to remain in their care.[22] The superintendent created pre-prepared typed statements, with blank spaces to be completed, that expressed a child's desire not to return to their parents. The child and the superintendent signed the form, witnessed by staff or Wesleyan Methodist missionaries. When a parent arrived to collect their child, they would be presented with the following typed statement:

> I hereby state that I [child's name], having attained the age of fifteen years, and having been handed over at the age of [age when admitted] years in [year of admission] by [name of person admitting child] to the care of the Superintendent of the Methodist Mission Dilkusha until I shall have attained the age of fifteen years, –
>
> Of my own desire and choice wish to remain under the care of the said Superintendent and do not consent to any arrangement intended by my father for me which has not the full approval of the said Superintendent.
>
> Dated this [date statement made]
>
> Signed by [child's name]
>
> In the presence of [staff member].[23]

Miss Watson, who helped care for Indian orphans at Dilkusha.
From the 'Fiji Methodist Centenary Souvenir 1835–1935'. Courtesy of Fiji National Archives

Persuading a child would not have been a difficult task, especially if they had been admitted to the orphanage at a young age. Some children would have had little memory of their family and would have felt as though they were leaving with a stranger. Remaining in the orphanage, the only life the child knew, would almost always have been their preferred option.[24]

Through a well-structured education system, the missionaries in the orphanage prepared the boys for employment that would benefit the community. A number of boys went on to become teachers within the Methodist mission schools, catechists, government officers, medical practitioners, plumbers and carpenters.

The girls of Dilkusha were trained in the domestic duties of keeping a home; their objective was to marry a Christian Indian with a steady income. One of the missionaries' greatest fears was the arranged marriage of a young girl, since they knew she would be married to a Hindu or Muslim – a good Christian girl would be lost from their faith. The mission put in place regulations for Dilkusha girls regarding courtship and engagement. These stipulated that engagements were to be for at least six months and the intended groom had to be earning a salary of at least five pounds per month.²⁵ By this means, the mission hoped to establish the beginning of a family that would be self-sufficient and not succumb to destitution. These regulations were mostly successful, and in 1923, of the first 30 orphan girls who 'graduated' from Dilkusha, 19 were 'happily married to Christians'. There were three 'bad cases', however: two husbands had been involved with the police and a third girl had married a Hindu.²⁶

Reasons for committing children to an orphanage altered over time. In the early years, most of those committed had been orphaned when their indentured labourer parents died. Others were there because their parents viewed the orphanage as a safe haven for their children to board at while they either fulfilled their indenture contract obligations or until they could properly maintain their children.²⁷

But Fiji society was changing; at the end of indenture periods, many Indians decided to remain in Fiji as 'free Indians'. Indian merchants were also arriving who were not tied to the indenture scheme. Fiji's population was growing, especially within the urban centres. Children were still being placed in the orphanages, but the reasons for this were expanding to include, for example, children born to unmarried women who became pregnant due to an affair, incest or rape. If a wife left her husband, he might place all or at least some of his children into the orphanage. If the husband left a wife, she might place her children in the orphanage if she was unable to feed and care for them.

From its establishment in the colonial period right up until 1970, the orphanage took only Indian children. Raised as Christians, these young people had limited understanding of Indian kinship and social structure and followed a European way of life. iTaukei were not placed at the Methodist orphanages or indeed in any orphanage, and although there were talks of a possibility, the responsibility for these children remained within the village.²⁸ Indigenous peoples resisted the orphanage, but because indentured labourers could not call on familial and kinship support, they were vulnerable to the incursions of church aspirations for Christian reform.

The orphanage was a Western institution established and maintained in Fiji initially through religious affiliations. The purpose was to care for children who couldn't be cared for by their families. In reality, for the indentured Indians and free Indians, these were a means to an end during hardship where parents believed their children would be appropriately cared for until they could return to care for them themselves. Good intentions on both sides were not realised as the institutions followed Western ideals, morals and cultural and social practices, and imposed these on Indian children, who were raised as European Christians in order to best fit within a European colonial settlement. In effect, these institutions were removing, or at least altering, their Indian identity. The next step is for us to hear from those who experienced the orphanages themselves so that this aspect of colonial history is not forgotten in Fiji.

Chapter 12

WEBS OF SEX, COLONIES AND MYTH

A PACIFIC AND HOLLYWOOD TALE

Patricia O'Brien

Australian cinema icon Errol Flynn was a man with a storied past. This story emerges at the intersection between colonial myths about the Pacific and Flynn's own experiences there. His story fits into a larger one of pervasive colonial masculinity, premised on attitudes to sex and race, that shaped empire at this time.

Flynn was born in Battery Point, Hobart, in a hospital overlooking the Derwent River. His parents, Theodore Thompson Flynn and Marelle (née Young), had relocated from New South Wales to Tasmania just prior to his birth in June 1909, six months after the young couple's hasty wedding in Balmain on the shores of Sydney Harbour.[1] Twenty-six years later, Flynn found overnight Hollywood fame starring in the 1935 film *Captain Blood*, a tale of colonialism in the Caribbean, white slavery and imperial clashes between England and the Spanish Main. Flynn owed this transformative casting decision to his recent wedding to Lili Damita, a veteran actress who elevated his profile instantly and exponentially. The turbulent marriage killed Damita's career; Flynn's took flight.

Before he rocketed to the glamorous heights of celebrity in Hollywood's Golden Age, Flynn had starred in one slice of Australian cinematic history: Charles and Elsa Chauvel's *In the Wake of the Bounty*, which opened in 1933. This first cinematic attempt to capture the drama of the infamous 1789 mutiny on HMS *Bounty* in the Eastern Pacific cast the young Flynn as the story's chief protagonist and hero, Fletcher Christian. Through his maternal line, Flynn claimed a personal association with the mutiny as a descendant of one mutineer, Edward Young.[2] What Flynn (and his mother, who spurred the myth) neglected to contemplate was that if they were descendants of Edward Young, that also made them descendants of one of two Tahitian women – Maimiti and Toofaiti – with whom Young had seven children.

Edward Young was born on the West Indies island of St Kitts and was thought to have African as well as British parentage. Young's British bloodlines, some claim, included being nephew to Sir George Young of the British admiralty, who was one of the chief proponents of a British colony at Port Jackson (modern-day Sydney), a plan being executed at the very time the *Bounty* was in Tahiti in 1788.[3]

The purpose of the *Bounty* voyage was to transfer Tahitian breadfruit trees to the British slave colonies of the Caribbean, like the one Edward Young was born into, to provide cheap food for slaves. The ambitious plan went terribly awry in April 1789 when Christian launched a mutiny. Explanations for this piratical act varied, but the one that received the greatest popular traction was the fateful allure of the Tahitian women with whom the mutineers had formed intimate bonds. When the nine mutineers were in hiding on Pitcairn Island, they and the 11 Tahitian women, a little girl and six Tahitian men with them formed a tense colonial microcosm. Disparities of power, captivity, enforced work and seething resentments led to all the men being killed on the island except two mutineers, one of whom was Edward Young, who eventually died of natural causes. Three women also died during these killing years. Nine women were found living there when the community was discovered by the outside world in 1808.[4]

For Flynn, who would become a poster boy of eugenic white masculinity in the 1930s and 1940s, the possibility of a bloodline tie between himself and Edward Young would have been enticing. Yet it does not bear out. The four sons born to Young and Maimiti or Toofaiti are not Flynn's ancestors, as their names and birth years do not match those of Marelle Flynn's paternal line.

But Flynn nonetheless had strong familial connections to less celebrated episodes of colonial violence in the Pacific. His maternal grandfather and his great-uncle, Fredrick and Robert Young, were blackbirders at a particularly fraught time. They plied the Western Pacific 'capturing natives from the islands and selling them to work on the sugar plantations in Queensland', as Flynn's mother Marelle explained.[5] Her father's stint in this dangerous trade was short. Marelle's uncle Robert was caught up in a spate of 'outrages' in the Western Pacific in the late 1870s. Spurred by the cycle of violence between blackbirders and avenging islanders, the British Western Pacific High Commission (based in Suva) sent ships to unleash punitive action. Amid all this violence, in late 1878 Robert's ship called at Ambae Island in the New Hebrides (Vanuatu), which had endured seven years of recruiter attacks, kidnappings and islander attacks on subsequent crews.[6] On this occasion the islanders appeared 'friendly'; Robert dismissed warnings and landed on 3 November 1878 with 'the expressed purpose of having connection with a woman'. He was set upon and killed. Family lore maintained he was also cannibalised.[7]

Despite the violent death of Robert Young, future generations of Youngs also worked in Pacific colonial enterprises.[8] Fifty-five years after Robert's death, his great-nephew Errol was also on a Pacific labour recruiting expedition. In 1933, at the very time Flynn was appearing on Australian cinema screens as Fletcher Christian in *In the Wake of the Bounty*, he was living his own colonial adventure in New Guinea. Flynn was labour recruiting in the Finschhafen district, looking for men to work tobacco or copra plantations.[9] He was not only interested in men for labour, however: he was interested in local women too. We know this because he kept a diary. In it he detailed the plight of the German planter class following the expropriation of their assets as a settlement for Australia's war debt; he included a ledger of his labour recruits; and he also 'boasted of his sexual successes in New Guinea'.[10] But these critical pages were censored by Alice Allen Innes, the hotelier who found the diary in her New Guinea hotel with a number of Flynn's personal effects he had stored there. Innes explained that she destroyed part of the diary because it would have shown Flynn 'in very unfavourable light'.[11] By the time of Innes's censorious burning of incriminating pages in Flynn's 1933 diary – most likely in the 1950s – he was a man notorious for his promiscuous sexuality and his fetish for underage girls.[12] On the downward slide of his acting career, he did little to hide this aspect of his life from public view, further tarnishing his insouciant reputation that was fuelled by heavy alcohol and narcotic use. His excesses contributed to his sudden death in 1959 at age 50 in Vancouver. Flynn's disregard for social convention and, moreover, statutory rape laws (this had been tested by the state of California, as we shall see) made him both loathed and admired during his life and after his death, though he nevertheless attained a mythological status.

Flynn's posthumous myth was greatly enhanced by the publication of his memoir *My Wicked Wicked Ways*, which was rushed to press after his death and made waves for its unapologetic portrayal of his life and vicious score-settling. His first wife, Lili Damita, was a prominent recipient of his scorn. Given how unrepentant Flynn was about his life and how he had lived it – even before the appearance of his memoir – what could have been so shocking in his 1933 recruiting diary to warrant the destruction of certain 'purple passages'?[13] We can be fairly sure it concerned sex with New Guinean women or, most likely, with girls. In *My Wicked Wicked Ways*, Flynn had a lot to say about his New Guinea years where, he claimed, he became a 'man' in surviving headhunters, crocodiles and malaria, in partaking in colonial punitive expeditions, in his various quests to make money and, most tellingly, in having sex with 'little girls'. The terms 'women' and 'girls' in New Guinea are interchangeable, Flynn explained, 'as there is no such thing as age in New Guinea. A girl generally matures at about twelve.'[14] Flynn deployed romantic rhetoric to conjure up several relationships he claimed to have had. One relationship began after he found 'a pathetic creature, a girl … expecting to be killed' (by a rival tribe), hiding behind a bush on the copra plantation where he worked. She was 'absolutely exhausted, petrified, and as she looked up at me there was a sort of supplication in her eyes, as if she anticipated death instantly'. He claims he saved her, Maihiati, and permitted her to be trained in the cookhouse where 'this child became like a little puppy. She found my thatched house a haven, and I thought, Why not? Besides, she was so attractive.' But Flynn's attraction to 'this child' came with 'a horrible feeling of guilt', not due to her age but her race. Flynn's father, Theodore, had 'admonished' him in a recent letter: 'My boy, always remember a man who has anything to do with a native woman stinks in the nostrils of a decent white man.' Flynn conceded that 'shortly thereafter I wrote back, *Dad, I stink.*'[15] When Flynn's job ended, so did this relationship.

After this 'romance', Flynn returned to Sydney in 1929 to receive treatment for 'gonorrhea – or black pox, as they called it thereabouts'.[16] His infection with a venereal disease points to the realities of the sexual cultures in colonial New Guinea: sex was casual, transactional and replete with the endemic abuse of local women by colonial men. In order to further obscure these features of sex in the colonial worlds he inhabited, along with lavishly using romantic and chivalric self-representation, Flynn also promulgated oppositional, violent stereotypes of New Guinea men.[17] Flynn's last 'romance' occurred when he had settled in Papua as a tobacco planter, where the daughter of one of his workers caught his eye. From first seeing Tupersalai, Flynn wrote, 'I had to buy her … I had to have this downcast-eyed little woman or girl.' He bought her for two pigs, one fuse of English shillings and some seashell money. At first, she was 'sulky', Flynn would recall, as 'she had been sold into sexual slavery to me, for I knew that that was what it amounted to'. Flynn set about trying to change her opinion of him as a 'harsh owner' with a 'little kindness' and a 'little sweetness'. His gallantry charmed Tupersalai with the pair 'making love'; Flynn added, 'I can only say that I don't know whence again my heart pounded so.'[18] Though the attractions of Tupersalai were considerable, Flynn's last New Guinea romance ended when he left for Sydney in 1932 to make his acting debut as Fletcher Christian. Though he briefly returned to New Guinea in 1933 as a labour recruiter, Flynn did not elaborate in *My Wicked Wicked Ways* on the final colonial sexual escapades that were so damning as to have been censored from the diary he kept during his stay there.

Two years after Flynn left Papua and New Guinea, he arrived in the 'film colony' of Hollywood. Like Australia's tropical colonies in the Western Pacific, the burgeoning film colony in Los Angeles already displayed troubling sexual cultures. Though the film industry was still relatively young at the time Flynn arrived, sex scandals had featured in its short history since the three trials of actor Roscoe (Fatty) Arbuckle for the rape and manslaughter of Virginia Rappe in 1921 and 1922, for which he was eventually acquitted. After this formative episode, the Hollywood film industry was at great pains to project a wholesome image. Despite the extensive efforts of publicity teams at the big studios, however, glimpses of the systemic abuse of young women kept occurring.[19] Flynn entered this world in 1935, indulging in its existing sexual cultures and then taking them in new directions. Though married to Damita, Flynn's extramarital indulgences were common knowledge and launched what would become his epic reputation for promiscuity.

Flynn's Hollywood idyll of fame, fortune and uninhibited sexual privileges suffered a great test in September 1942 when authorities tracked down a 16-year-old Nebraska high school graduate who had run away to Los Angeles. She had quite a tale to tell, about how she, a casual worker in a drug store, was invited to a gentleman's party by a young Warner Brothers studio worker. She was promised film work (as in so many other girls' Hollywood abuse stories) if she 'played up' to Errol Flynn, who was a guest at the soirée. She did as instructed and then Flynn gave her a drink that made her ill. He took her upstairs, undressed her and had sex with her. After she reported this to the authorities, Flynn was arrested and appeared before a grand jury, which failed to indict him. The newly elected district attorney overruled and pressed forward with criminal proceedings for statutory rape. To bolster the case, a complaint made a year before against Flynn for twice raping a 15-year-old aboard his yacht while cruising in the Pacific around Catalina Island was revived. Flynn now faced three counts of statutory rape and was tried in the sensational court case, *The People of the State of California vs Errol Flynn*, which ran from late 1942 to February 1943.

Flynn's trial captivated global audiences with its salacious details, providing a welcome diversion from the gutting news from the European front and especially from across the Pacific as the Battle of Guadalcanal raged. The trial provided plenty to titillate, though many newspapers had to tone down evidence as the 'lurid' testimony was 'unprintable' in family newspapers.[20] In 1943, the *Los Angeles Times* published evidence by the complainant that had been deemed inadmissible by the judge (who clearly favoured the defendant). It was the graphic police testimony by the girl just after being attacked aboard Flynn's yacht in August 1941. She described Flynn coming to her room at 2am. 'I was very mad and scared and I fought him,' she said. 'I thought a prominent person like him would never think of attacking a person,' she continued. He 'got rougher' and as she 'hollered' she continued to fight him, 'but he was so savage … I was scared he would murder me.'[21] The court's erasure of this grotesque account likewise erased Flynn's sexual violence.

Flynn's defence team mounted a classic strategy of demolishing the stories and reputations of the young girls, who were cast as preying on an innocent man known to be wealthy and vulnerable to schemes designed to extract money. As a result, Flynn was acquitted of statutory rape. The excruciating spotlight of a rape trial, covered extensively by the media without concealing their names or appearances, wrecked these teenage girls' lives. Flynn's career soared after all the publicity, which only enhanced his box office appeal (why would a sex symbol resort to rape?), especially for women. In *My Wicked Wicked Ways*, Flynn would dub this chapter of his life 'Head Hunters of California', equating the state's government officials' vengeance towards him with the bloodthirsty act of war of New Guinea's Highlands. He also admitted that he indeed 'knew' the girl raped on his yacht 'very well, and I did not deny it' (he did, under oath). He also argued the sex was consensual and she could have passed for 'anywhere between twenty and twenty-five'. Besides, 'who had been hurt?' he would ask, nearly two decades after the trial at which his rape victim had testified that he was 'so savage' she was terrified he would kill her.[22]

Errol Flynn's backstory is one of sex and violence in numerous Pacific locales and temporal settings connecting Tahiti, Pitcairn Island, Hobart, Sydney, Vanuatu, New Guinea and Los Angeles. His lived experiences and self-mythologising weave disparate Pacific colonial pasts together – through his own family lore and his personal experiences of harsh colonial settings. These intertwined histories reveal deep, persistent and violent colonial ideas about sex, race and white masculinity.

Flynn brought these colonial cultures into Hollywood, where he became a global symbol of white manhood from the mid-1930s.

This chapter has pointed to vast and nefarious histories of sex and violence that lie beneath the surface of Flynn's image, life story and the worlds he inhabited. The sexual abuse of underage girls and sexual aggression are foremost among the troubling brand of masculinity Flynn embodied and helped to entrench in Hollywood.

PART IV
CRITIQUING COLONIALISM

Chapter 13

'CONFUSION TO ALL SNEAKS'

PROTECTION AND PUNISHMENT ON THE 1880s WESTERN AUSTRALIAN FRONTIER

Jane Lydon

Mr Brockman again charges me with deliberate misrepresentation with reference to the taking of native women from their natural protectors. I am not aware of any word in my report which would convey the idea that I meant taking or keeping them by force, but as Mr Brockman will ventilate this subject, I may very properly call upon him to explain the circumstances under which a young girl was tied up to a tree close to his house, and had her hair cropped short, only a few days before my visit. This perhaps looks something like keeping by force.

—Robert Fairbairn, *Government Gazette of Western Australia*, 1882[1]

Down with Gribble and all his supporters and confusion to all Sneaks.
—Placard posted around the town of Carnarvon, 1886[2]

In Western Australia in the late nineteenth century, Aboriginal labour was highly sought after in the northwestern pastoralist and pearling industries. To ensure a labour supply, the colonial government imposed a system of courts, police, prisons and punishment targeted at Aboriginal people. 'Humanitarians' like the Reverend John Brown Gribble raised concerns about the treatment of Aboriginal people, but coercive labour practices were ultimately condoned by authorities in the colony and in Britain. During the 1880s, the frontier regime of the Murchison–Gascoyne region entailed the forcible and perpetual 'assignment' of Aboriginal people to settlers, their arrest for 'absconding' or 'theft' of stock, their removal 'on the chain' to prison, and the appropriation of Aboriginal women by white settlers for sex. This looked very much like Caribbean slavery to some observers.

In 1881, for example, Governor Robinson wrote to the secretary of state that recent reports on the pearling industry had disclosed 'a state of things little short of slavery'.[3] Government Resident Robert Fairbairn was sent to investigate, and his 1882 report on the Murchison and Gascoyne districts identified violence perpetrated against Aboriginal people, particularly girls and women, as a source of racial conflict.[4] These claims were contested by prominent settlers like Charles Brockman, but public debate was minimal.

The official perspective, represented by Fairbairn's report, was that increased policing would curb the worst excesses of violence against Aboriginal workers yet ensure a docile labour force. But these aims stopped short of protecting Aboriginal women and children from abuse by white male employers. Together, Fairbairn and Gribble's reports of labour conditions in Western Australia's northwest revealed a culture of secrecy, or 'code of silence' (see Lyndall Ryan's chapter in this volume), that condoned coerced labour and especially the sexual exploitation of Aboriginal women and children. The legacies of this complicity are visible today in continuing sexual violence against Aboriginal women.

WESTERN AUSTRALIA'S NORTHERN FRONTIER

From the 1860s, as the pastoralist and pearling industries developed in tandem, Western Australian colonists moved steadily northwards, stimulating expansion into the region defined by the Murchison and Gascoyne Rivers and inevitably bringing settlers into conflict with Aboriginal people.[5] Under the Masters and Servants Act adopted after 1842 and amended in reference to Aborigines in 1868, 1882, 1886 and 1892, workers supposedly signed contracts as indentured servants. The reality, however, was that local Indigenous people were considered to belong to the lease, as a form of property, and those who did not comply with demands to work were termed 'absconders' and could be legally arrested and sentenced to imprisonment.[6]

As well as local Aboriginal labour, pearling quickly came to rely upon so-called Malays from the Indonesian archipelago in a harshly exploitative regime. This was how Robert Fairbairn (1841–1922) first came to the northwest in 1876, where he was to play a key role in consolidating colonial industry and law. Reports of abuse in the pearling industry at Shark Bay prompted the colonial Cabinet to send him to investigate. Fairbairn found that pearlers Charles E. Broadhurst and Captain Francis Cadell had ill-treated their workers and failed to

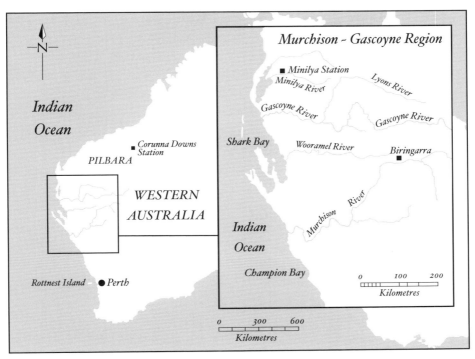

Location map showing the Murchison and Gascoyne rivers region. The Murchison and Gascoyne originated north and south of the Robinson Ranges and flowed west to the Indian Ocean around 500 kilometres away. Map by Allan Kynaston

pay them and that Indonesian workers were abandoned at the end of the pearling season.[7] Fairbairn's report led to reforms in pearling labour contracts to provide for healthier conditions, a better diet and yearly inspections by a magistrate.

In May 1882 Fairbairn was called upon again, this time to investigate 'from a disinterested side of the question, the true state of the relations that exist between the settlers and the [A]boriginals', in response to reports that 'the natives were committing serious depredations on the flocks, and even assaulting settlers' in the Murchison–Gascoyne region. He was instructed to visit the stations occupied by Frank Wittenoom, Archibald Campbell, Mr Aitken, Mr Birrell and Mr O'Grady and then to proceed to the Gascoyne. Well-supported by police constables and empowered to swear in settlers if needed, he was to punish all transgressions with 'severity, but yet with justice' by removing offenders to trial. By 12 July Fairbairn had sentenced 29 men to various terms at Rottnest Island for sheep stealing.[8]

He reported that complaints from the Murchison had been exaggerated; sheep had been lost to drought and wild dogs because female Aboriginal shepherds were left unsupervised over large areas. Violence from Aboriginal people was a threat only in unexpected encounters when both sides were taken by surprise. But some settlers disagreed: Fairbairn quoted 27-year-old Wittenoom, the owner of the largest flock on the Murchison, who believed that all police should be withdrawn and settlers should be enabled to take the law into their own hands to mete out their own punishments against 'the natives'. He argued that if 'half a dozen of the worst ringleaders were shot it would "soon put an end to the whole affair"'.[9] Likewise, Charles Gale and Robert Walcott both argued that if the government allowed settlers to shoot the 'ringleaders', the rest would submit. Walcott stated that 'in the early days of Champion Bay the natives were shot down right and left for sheep and cattle stealing'.[10]

Fairbairn also relayed stories of women being taken by settlers, quoting an Aboriginal man who complained that 'the young men could not get women now, because all the young women were living with the whites'.[11] At Irrida, an Aboriginal man came and complained that a settler travelling to the Gascoyne with sheep the previous summer had taken three girls from the Murchison, his woman being one of them, a story corroborated by settlers.[12] Finally, in August, Fairbairn wrote that he had uncovered 'the real cause of the numerous and very serious depredations committed by the natives'. Two white men had been murdered on the Lower Gascoyne, and the reason was found to be that shepherd Charles Brackle had kidnapped a woman named Kaluman, wife of the accused man Wangabiddie. Fairbairn noted that he had seen young Aboriginal women at every station but one, and at every sheep camp. He noted that Charles Brockman, Wittenoom's partner at Minilya Station on the Gascoyne, had said that 'his men keep women; he likes them to do so, as they warn them of danger, and the men themselves are more contented'.[13] Robinson agreed with Fairbairn, concluding that 'interference with native women on the part of the white shepherds is to a large extent at the bottom of the reprisals which have taken place. Their women are surely as valuable to them as our flocks and herds are to us.'[14]

Fairbairn's report prompted several significant outcomes. Perhaps most revealing was the response from prominent settlers, including George Brockman, Alexander Crawford, Richard Gale and Robert Walcott. These pastoralists wrote to the newspapers attacking Fairbairn and, in a letter to the *Herald*, Wittenoom asked that 'all police shall be withdrawn, and that settlers shall be allowed to deal with natives in their own way'.[15] Some questioned the veracity of Fairbairn's investigations, mounting a defence that unwittingly betrayed the prevailing sexual violence. In rejecting Brockman's allegation of 'deliberate misrepresentation with reference to the taking of native women', Fairbairn pointed out that he had not accused Brockman of kidnapping women, 'but as Mr Brockman will ventilate this subject, I may very properly call upon him to explain the circumstances under which a young girl was tied up to a tree close to his house, and had her hair cropped short, only a few days before my visit. This perhaps looks something like keeping by force.'[16]

In this, Fairbairn implied that where *he* had adhered to the gentleman's code of silence about frontier interracial sex, the settlers had broken it; he was therefore forced to 'ventilate the subject' of the kidnapping and rape of Aboriginal girls and young women. Fairbairn went on to note, 'As for taking and keeping native women, and often girls of very immature age, by sufficient inducements held out to them, from their natural protectors', he had heard considerable evidence and concluded that during his visit to the Murchison and Gascoyne, 'stories were told me of a most revolting nature, by some of the principal settlers, touching the treatment of girls of tender age by men on the stations'.[17]

Fairbairn recommended forming a new police station on the north side of the river near Biringarra, and Robinson approved the appointment of an itinerant stipendiary magistrate to the district. This was Charles Foss, a former pastoralist and sheep scab inspector, who became notorious for his ready sentencing: one newspaper suggested he would transport 'the whole of the native inhabitants to Rottnest'.[18] The application of sentencing laws in the region in 1884 led to a peak in the number of prisoners from these districts sent to Rottnest Island prison; this group accounted for more than 50 percent of the prisoners, most convicted for stock killing, reflecting the advance of the pastoral frontier.[19] One of Governor Broome's first actions after his arrival in mid-1883 was to introduce an Aboriginal Offenders Bill. The Aborigines Protection Act 1886 (WA) that followed introduced further regulations to Aboriginal employment and advanced the increasingly oppressive regime of regulatory oversight and control of Indigenous Western Australians.[20]

THE GRIBBLE AFFAIR

Fairbairn's report was overshadowed by the Reverend John Brown Gribble's sensational and disastrous 'affair' just a few years later. Gribble had established himself as a successful missionary in New South Wales and undertook a pilgrimage in 1884 to London's humanitarian centre, Exeter Hall, which immersed him in the antislavery tradition of missionary martyrdom. After returning to Australia in 1885, he was appointed by the Church of England to establish a new mission on the Gascoyne. Settlers who were already concerned that his presence might 'tamper … with their servants' were outraged by his outspoken denunciation of practices he termed slavery, and his 1886 booklet, *Dark Deeds in a Sunny Land*, prompted tremendous public scandal. In it, Gribble asked,

> If a native desires to go away when he has faithfully fulfilled the conditions of his engagement is he then discharged to enter the service of another, if he feels disposed? The truth is – No; he is not! The poor fellow is given to understand in a way he does not like, that once assigned he is for ever a slave in effect. Is it not a fact that some who have been for years in the same bond service run away repeatedly? And why do they run away? Simply because they know they cannot release themselves in any other way … I ask again, What does this go to prove? – verily that a species of slavery does exist in this part of the Queen's dominions!

Gribble also named the unnameable:

> I also found that women and girls were fully assigned to teamsters. It is quite a common thing to see them even in Carnarvon with such. Upon asking some of these men why they had girls and not boys attached to their teams, some said they 'preferred them'; others said they were 'better than boys', and that 'boys always run away'; but others frankly admitted that they had them for immoral purposes … Assignment of native females against their will for purposes of immorality is a sign of slavery.[21]

Gribble sued the pastoralist-owned *West Australian* newspaper for libel, for calling him a 'lying, canting humbug' and more. In doing so, he polarised colonial opinion and aligned liberals against conservative elite interests.[22] But Gribble lost his case and, for many observers, all credibility.

Fairbairn's adjudication of frontier relations was considered 'able and impartial' by the government; his report aimed to prevent homicide through greater oversight, but assaults on women and girls were harder to police. When Western Australia gained responsible government, section 70 of the 1889 Constitution established the Aborigines Protection Board under the direct control of the governor. However, this legislation, in implying that colonists could not be trusted to govern their Indigenous population, was considered a 'stain of dishonour', and in 1897 the Western Australian government repealed it.[23] Echoing Gribble, critics continued to point out the injustice of the brutal frontier punishment regime, its labour exploitation, and practices such as arrest, neck-chaining, imprisonment and exile by drawing on the powerful cultural repertoire of trans-Atlantic slavery. Over the years leading up to Federation in 1901, there was sporadic condemnation of the use of neck-chains for Aboriginal prisoners by witnesses horrified by what they saw.

In 1905 the findings of an inquiry into 'the condition of the natives', headed by Royal Commissioner Walter Roth, prompted public outcry in both Australia and Britain that was focused especially upon the shocking sight of gangs of neck-chained prisoners.[24] The pastoralist lobby argued that neck-chains were the most humane method of restraint, and Sir John Forrest, premier from 1890 to 1901 and then member of the new federal House of Representatives (a position he was to retain until 1918), questioned whether the neck-chain was as 'inconvenient to the [A]boriginal as the wrist-chain'. Forrest argued that the chains 'are not heavy and are protected by coverings so as to avoid that portion which presses close to the skin being unduly uncomfortable during the hot weather'.[25] Neck-chaining continued into the 1950s in parts of the north.[26]

CONCLUSION

In popular memory, the abolition of slavery across the British Empire in 1833 is a matter for celebration, but the history of Western Australia's northwestern frontier reveals significant continuities with slavery.[27] To meet the need for labour, white colonists used violent methods of domination such as massacre, flogging, chaining and sexual servitude, alongside seemingly more humane forms of punishment and constraint provided by the penal system.

Colonial law offered poor protection for Aboriginal women on the frontier; the kidnapping and sexual abuse of women and girls was normalised and condoned by a culture of secrecy that protected white settler men from prosecution and kept their abuses hidden. In a pattern common across colonial frontiers, violent conflict between Aboriginal and white men was entwined with the white settlers' sexual exploitation of black women. Pastoralist wealth shaped late nineteenth-century

Perth, and its legacies are still evident across the state's society and landscape. For example, Frank Wittenoom's 1890s Queen Anne-style mansion, The Terraces, still stands overlooking the Swan River at 63 Mount Street, West Perth, one of the city's most prestigious locations. Wittenoom retired here late in his career to enjoy Perth society. The violent and bloody conquest that fuelled such prosperity has been forgotten, omitted from heritage narratives.

As Indigenous women continue to point out, these legacies continue today: sexual violence in Australia is deeply grounded in the historical toleration of the systemic rape and sexual abuse of Indigenous women.[28] In her powerful memoir *My Place*, Sally Morgan reveals the continuing impact of pastoralist families' exploitation of Aboriginal women in the Pilbara through an account of her own journey of discovery of her Indigenous heritage. Her grandmother, Daisy Brockman/Corunna, had concealed her life story because she was ashamed of her abuse at the hands of Howden Drake-Brockman at Corunna Downs Station in the Pilbara. Daisy was taken from her mother in her early teens to work as a virtual domestic slave for her white natural father, Drake-Brockman and his family. In the same way, her own daughter, Gladys, also fathered by a Drake-Brockman (possibly Howden), was taken from her at the age of three and placed in a children's home. Fearing that Gladys's children would be taken away in turn, neither Gladys nor Daisy told them of their Aboriginal heritage. As Daisy told her granddaughter:

> Before I had Gladdie, I was carryin' another child, but I wasn't allowed to keep it. That was the way of it, then. They took our children one way or another. I never told anyone that I was carryin' Gladdie. Now how this all came about, that's my business. I'll only tell a little. Everyone knew who the father was, but they all pretended they didn't know. Aah, they knew, they knew. You didn't talk 'bout things then. You hid the truth.[29]

Chapter 14

RACE AND REVOLUTION

HAITI AND THE KĪNGITANGA, 1863

Lachy Paterson

In 1804, after a 13-year struggle, the ex-slaves of Saint-Domingue finally defeated their former colonial masters and established the independent state of Haiti. Their struggle reverberated at the time; Saint-Domingue's sugar plantations had made it one of the richest colonies of the Americas, and the disruption of war and the island's subsequent loss resulted in an economic blow to republican, then Napoleonic France. Moreover, the island remained surrounded by neighbouring states suspicious of, or antagonistic to, this new creation, whose very existence served as a rebuke to their own slave economies. Although the Haitian Revolution is often seen as of less historical importance than the American or French revolutions, or even 'suppressed in Western historiography', scholars have more recently endeavoured to draw attention to its significance within the Age of Revolution.[1]

According to Adom Getachew, the 'three sites of domination' facing Haiti in the late eighteenth century – 'the plantation, race and imperialism' – allowed its revolutionaries to visualise 'a previously unimaginable world order in which both slavery and colonial rule would finally be transcended'.[2] Whatever the revolution may have meant to its participants, its impacts have long been felt outside of Haiti itself as 'a source of both fear and inspiration to the world outside of its shores', spurring revolts or giving hope to slaves in the Caribbean and beyond, and providing justifications for the arguments of both abolitionists and their enemies.[3] Beyond the debates about and practices of slavery, the revolution also significantly influenced literary and intellection production, particularly pan-Africanist movements, into the twentieth century.[4] It is clear that most of the scholarly work on the immediate and subsequent effects of the Haitian Revolution has focused on the 'Atlantic world'.[5] This is hardly surprising, given that the Atlantic Ocean encompasses or borders the lands from where forced African labourers were sourced and to which they were transported, as well as the national economies that benefited from the slave trade. In addition, almost all the descendants of slaves continue to inhabit former slave-holding territories, or the metropoles of former colonial masters. Scholarly attention to the Haitian Revolution and its legacies is thus Atlantic-centric almost by default.

Yet could the Haitian example have resonated further afield, with non-Africans who sought to escape colonial chains? Colonialism is by its nature global, and ideas and knowledge flowed along with people and goods. For example, the notion that Māori were God's chosen people, the Jews, was pervasive through the nineteenth century and also adopted by other Indigenous peoples from reading the Old Testament.[6] The Kīngitanga, or the Māori King Movement, which emerged in the mid-1850s, was also derived from scripture, as well as from the increasing knowledge of Europe that Māori gained from their travels there.[7] This chapter looks at how the Haitian Revolution had relevance for the Kīngitanga in New Zealand as it sought to assert Māori autonomy against the new settler colony. It examines the movement's portrayal of the revolution through its newspaper, *Te Hokioi*, and the response in the government's own niupepa (Māori-language newspapers), as both sides anticipated war.

At first sight, Haiti appears an unlikely paradigm for New Zealand, as the latter has no history of chattel slavery or a plantation economy. Māori had traditionally enslaved captives from neighbouring tribes on a small scale; the practice peaked in the 1820s as muskets permeated Māori society, but by the late 1830s tribes had released most slaves, whether due to conversion to Christianity or more customary peace-making.[8] The formal inclusion of New Zealand within the British Empire, through the signing of the Treaty of Waitangi in 1840, post-dated the abolition of slavery and thus precluded the slavery experiences of earlier colonies. Besides, New Zealand was envisaged as a colony of independent British settlers, not one of plantations. Although the English and Māori texts contained significant discrepancies between how 'sovereignty' may have been defined (or not), the treaty, influenced by a cresting humanitarianism, extended to Māori 'all the Rights and Privileges of British Subjects', the gist of which is reflected fairly in the Māori translation.[9] Governor Thomas Gore Browne informed a conference of Māori chiefs at Kohimarama in 1860 that Queen Victoria had tasked him to 'watch over

Combat et prise de la Crête-à-Pierrot (Attack and take of the Crête-à-Pierrot), 1839.
Original illustration by Auguste Raffet, engraving by Hébert. From M. de Norvins, Histoire de Napoleon (Paris: Furne et Cie, éditeurs, 1839), p. 239. Courtesy of Wikimedia Commons

---

the interests and promote the advancement of her subjects without distinction of Race' and that 'New Zealand is the first country to be colonised on this new and humane system.'[10]

Browne had summoned friendly or neutral chiefs in response to two related developments: the Kīngitanga and the First Taranaki War (1860–61). The constant demand for Māori to sell their communally held land to satisfy the land hunger of streams of settlers was putting considerable pressure on Māori communities. Divisions between those who wished to hold their ancestral birthright and those who wanted to sell to Crown agents led, at times, to murders and armed conflict within and between tribal groups. So long as any violence did not spill over into settler-held land, however, the government did little except remonstrate with the combatants; with Māori tribes subject to little more than the governor's persuasive powers, its effective power was limited. But Māori leaders were well aware that their de facto independence would be at risk once their tribal land holdings were sold and occupied by settlers. In 1858, after considerable debate, and in an attempt to unite Māori in order to retain their lands and their rangatiratanga (chiefly authority), a number of North Island tribes selected the aged warrior chief Pōtatau Te Wherowhero to be the first Māori king. The King's authority over Māori was as tenuous as the governor's; several tribes remained loyal to the government, but the Kīngitanga, both as a concept and a territorial entity, held sway over much of the central North Island. When a botched land sale in Taranaki led to war in 1860, some Kīngitanga soldiers came south to assist local tribes against the British army. The war ended in a stalemate then truce in 1861, but with the military preparations of the new governor, Sir George Grey, it was obvious another clash was inevitable.[11]

Māori encountered niupepa almost from the very start of formal colonisation, with the government's first newspaper appearing in 1842. Although a Wesleyan missionary and several other Pākehā published their own titles, the government remained the key player for the first two decades and produced most of the niupepa content during this period, first just in Māori, then from 1849 bilingually. With very limited power to coerce Māori, these newspapers were part of a wider effort to persuade Māori that they would be better off adopting Pākehā ways, such as engaging in the market, accepting the governor's authority and British law, and selling land to enable Pākehā settlement. These Pākehā-run niupepa also sought to play down any influence the Kīngitanga might wield and heavily criticised Māori who resisted militarily in Taranaki.

From 1862 the Kīngitanga was able to respond in kind. Using a press that had been given to two Māori chiefs visiting the Austrian court in 1858, it published *Te Hokioi e Rere atu na*, a niupepa to project its own propaganda and counteract that of the government. Although comprising just 12 issues of one to four pages, *Te Hokioi* reflects a growing radicalism with direct criticisms of the government's actions and mana (power and authority). For example, it questioned the validity of the basis of the government's claim to rule, the Treaty of Waitangi, labelling it 'a covenant of the blind' that Māori had been duped into signing.[12] As the government built up its military strength, *Te Hokioi* asserted Māori mana over the Waikato River, declaring that it was not open to armed steamboats.[13] It also defended supporters of the King who ejected a group of Pākehā builders

OPPOSITE: *Tukaroto Matutaera Pōtatau Te Wherowhero Tāwhiao, the second Māori King (reigned 1860–1894).* F-50874-1/2. Courtesy of Alexander Turnbull Library, Wellington

constructing government barracks within the Kīngitanga boundary.[14] Despite 'kingship' and a unified Māori state being completely new creations emerging as a response to colonialism, *Te Hokioi* attempted to portray the Kīngitanga as a viable and legitimate entity, as the coming together of the enduring mana of many iwi (tribes), as well as through the orderly operation of its rūnanga (councils) and appointment of its own magistrates.[15]

Colonialism is constructed around difference, particularly in race and culture. As seen in the colonial discourses of Māori niupepa, these distinctions maintained racial hierarchies.[16] The term 'māori' denoted not merely 'natives' of New Zealand but could be applied to peoples of any part of the globe, as well as to any unbecoming behaviour that contrasted with that of the more civilised Pākehā. Even in accounts of ancient history in *Te Karere Maori*, the language used described Britons possessing 'māori' weapons and Romans wearing 'pākehā' clothes.[17] Niupepa might discuss specific physical racial differences – for example, that Melanesians, unlike Māori, 'belong to one of the black races of men'.[18] But race was also often defined ideologically rather than biologically, in terms of kiri mā (white skin) and kiri mangu (black skin). Māori belonged to the latter. When describing English law in 1858, *Te Karere Maori* stated, 'There is just one law for all, whether Māori or Pākehā, or white skin or black skin, it is the same.'[19] The very inclusiveness of the law is expressed through stark racial dichotomy. It is perhaps not surprising that Māori also used these terms. As one Māori said, in welcoming a Pākehā in 1858, 'Bring your white skin to me, to the black skin.'[20] But for the Kīngitanga, who sought an autonomous life separate from Pākehā control, adopting this language accentuated the division between coloniser and colonised. The King himself employed a racial identification when he addressed his fellow Māori as 'the black skins, whether on the Queen or King's side'.[21]

Haiti existed in the Māori imagination as an example of a black state that established itself in the face of white opposition. We cannot be sure how the editor of *Te Hokioi* came to know of the revolution, but it was possibly from Joseph Garavel, a French Catholic priest stationed within the Kīngitanga territory.[22] *Te Hokioi* introduced the story in March 1863 in an editorial titled 'The History of Haiti', which began with Columbus and the Spanish who encountered the 'Māori people' of the island, then moved on to explain that 'black-skinned people were attacked and killed, and the land was taken by the white-skinned people'. Soon after, the French took possession of the island, importing 'the blacks of Africa' as slaves for their coffee and sugar plantations. The account exemplified the cruelty of the 'Pākehā', especially to their 'half-caste' children. The use of God in the story lent greater righteousness to the revolt: 'So, God saw the great extent of the wickedness of the French, and he saw the pain of these people, and their cry reached God. Then God's anger turned on the French, and God allowed their half-caste children and the Māori to fight the French.' The last sentence is significant, too, as the black slaves had become 'Māori' (natives) in the story.

The Haitian Revolution was marked for its violence, but *Te Hokioi*'s discussion of the fighting was relatively brief. After 70,000 French were slain, the blacks 'announced their intention to separate from the French authority, to stop land selling practices, and establish their own policemen' – all aspirations shared by the Kīngitanga.[23] The account was short, omitting or glossing over many details, as the Kīngitanga itself was not keen to fight a war. The revolution's result – the Haitian state – was the main point, rather than the details. In the following month's issue, the niupepa returned to the story: 'Now that island has law, it has established its rangatiratanga [independence], its flags have been hoisted, and the rūnanga of that place are working for the good of their land. The chiefs of Haiti have unified their word, the law has mana, their many harbours are prosperous.' This was the vision *Te Hokioi* projected: 'Let the rūnanga peacefully operate, and perhaps the rangatiratanga of this island will be like Haiti, with prosperity, power and law, because we are struggling for a just cause. Perhaps God will look after his black-skinned children living here in Aotearoa.'[24]

Te Hokioi published one more issue in May, but by then hostilities had already reignited in Taranaki; the press was packed up and taken south as the Kīngitanga prepared for the anticipated attack.[25] On 9 July 1863 Governor Grey ordered Māori south of Auckland 'to take the Oaths of Allegiance to the Queen … or else retire up the Waikato'.[26] Most declined, choosing to abandon their homes and join their kin across the border. Then, on 11 July, General Cameron led the British army across the Mangatāwhiri Stream into Kīngitanga territory in order to crush the movement.[27] On 18 July, *Te Karere Maori* published a rebuttal to *Te Hokioi*'s Haiti story, 'in accordance with the wishes of our friends'. That it not only bothered but gave many pages to the task indicates that the government took the threat seriously. *Te Karere Maori* would have been preparing its copy alongside more martial preparations; the issue appeared after the Waikato War had begun (indeed, the opposing forces had already clashed at Koheroa). The timing indicates that the government's account of Haiti was not directed at the Kīngitanga but at other iwi as yet not involved in conflict.

In its account, *Te Karere Maori* provided a far more extended and systematic history, from the arrival of Columbus and the Spanish in 1492 to the Haitian payment to France for its independence, which was finally determined in 1838. Throughout, the emphasis was on violence, famine and instability.[28] In case its more comprehensive rendition was insufficient, an article immediately following provided a more subjective critique of the *Te Hokioi* account, using a series of extended metaphors, first comparing Māori stories to green glass or calabashes made with gourds (in contrast to the clear glass of Pākehā reasoning), which, 'like the weights and measures of dishonest traders, are only made, and intended, to deceive the buyer'.[29] It then turned directly to *Te Hokioi*: 'The crafty writer knew full well your aptitude and fondness for similitudes, and set his trap accordingly … so every ignorant and thoughtless Maori would, as an echo, surely say: "That island is like New Zealand, and its Maories are like us, and those Pakehas from Spain and France, are like these English Pakehas here."'[30] The paper then sought to compare the benefits brought by New Zealand's Pākehā missionaries, settlers and governors to the 'horrid cruelties of the Spaniards and the French' and invited disaffected Māori to return to the fold. The article concluded with a parable of a hungry wolf encountering a well-fed farm dog – unsubtle references to the Kīngitanga and more 'friendly' Māori. The wolf, unwilling to submit to a collar, 'bounded back to his barren solitude, there to idle and to hunger, as before', inevitably to die a miserable death.[31]

The Kīngitanga's reflection on the Haitian Revolution was short-lived. With the defeat at Ōrākau in the autumn of 1864, the King and his Waikato followers had effectively been driven from their lands to live as guests with Ngāti Maniapoto. Although the 'King Country' existed separately and beyond the government's authority, it was not, and could not be, the kind of state envisaged in 1863. The focus was first on survival, maintaining the mana of the King and his movement, and trying to get the confiscated Waikato lands returned. When King Tāwhiao made his peace with the government in 1881, the dream may still have been mana motuhake (self-determination), but the Kīngitanga now sat, albeit uncomfortably, under the mana of the Crown rather than separate from it; the movement found it more fruitful to argue its case on the basis of the Crown's breaches of the Treaty of Waitangi, rather than deny the validity of governmental authority.[32]

Prior to the outbreak of war in 1863, the Haitian Revolution had at least shown the possibility of a functioning anticolonial state. It also aligned with the colonial ideology of black and white skins, evident in both official and Māori debates. Like other imported ideas that nineteenth-century Māori used to critique or resist colonialism – such as the idea of Māori Jewishness, the abstract 'black' identity, or the Kīngitanga itself – the Haitian example was not a model to follow rigidly but a means to imagine a future manifestly different to what was on offer. Once it no longer fitted the Kīngitanga's goals, it was soon forgotten. In its account, *Te Hokioi* downplayed the revolution's violent history, as the Kīngitanga would have preferred more peaceful means to their desired end. Sadly, this was not to be.

Chapter 15

'A MISFORTUNE IN THE DISTANCE'

VIOLENCE AGAINST THE BUSH IN THE WRITINGS OF LOUISA ATKINSON

Grace Moore

In the 1870s botanist, journalist, taxidermist and novelist Louisa Atkinson warned of the catastrophic damage European settlers were causing to the Australian bush. Atkinson was a fierce critic of environmental violence and her works are remarkable for their vivid and sensitive depictions of the New South Wales landscape. She was a deeply respected nature-writer and published a regular column entitled 'A Voice from the Country', which appeared in both the *Sydney Morning Herald* and the *Sydney Mail* from 1859 until her untimely death in 1872. Atkinson's articles make fascinating reading, partly because of their detailed accounts of the flora and fauna of the bush, and partly because they mapped the violent changes wrought by settlers upon the Australian landscape. She was particularly concerned with how the settler community treated the bush as a resource to be plundered, and many of her newspaper columns sought to alert readers to the long-term effects of land clearance and farming. Above all, Atkinson wished to cultivate a respect for the environment and help her readers to understand Australia's ecology and the management practices of the land's traditional custodians.

Louisa Atkinson lived much of her life in the Kurrajong, northwest of Sydney, and her upbringing was highly unconventional. Her mother, Charlotte Barton – an accomplished woman who wrote the first Australian book for children – had fled an abusive second marriage, taking her young children to safety through the rugged Southern Highlands of New South Wales. A sickly child, Atkinson seems to have had little formal education but spent a great deal of time outdoors, sketching the plants and animals around her and recording her impressions in notebooks.¹ She became a skilled illustrator, and her botanical knowledge was so extensive that, as a young woman, she was consulted regularly by eminent botanists including W.S. Macleay, Ferdinand von Mueller and the Reverend William Woolls.

Atkinson contributed to the *Horticultural Magazine*, and her name appears often in the minutes of the New South Wales Horticultural Society. On 5 January 1865, for example, a report in the *Sydney Morning Herald* notes that 'Miss Atkinson, of the Kurrajong, sent a jar of jam of the Lisanthe sapida [*sic*]'. The account quotes her remarks about the 'native cranberry' and how it could be cultivated and put to use in preserves and cookery, before noting that Atkinson 'had made herself most remarkable for her endeavours to bring colonial productions into notice'.² Atkinson also attempted to introduce a 'Native Arts' column to the *Illustrated Sydney News* in the early 1850s; the feature, which aimed to introduce readers to Indigenous culture, ran just twice before it was discontinued. It was noteworthy for its attention to the environmental changes brought about by Europeans. Having grown up in the bush, Atkinson was fascinated by native plants and wildlife and, as the account of the Horticultural Society's meeting suggests, was committed to communicating their importance to the wider public. She was also keen to show her world through an Australian lens instead of bending it to a European aesthetic.³

Atkinson's seven novels offer fascinating insights into the settler impact upon Australia's ecology. Yet it is her journalism that marks her out as a pioneer conservationist. Her many columns discussed native animals and sea-life, plants, and the challenges associated with living in the bush. In her writing, she consistently took a stand against the settler community's efforts to turn the land to productivity. She was particularly vocal in her attacks on deforestation and wrote with a tone of confident expertise that belied her youth and gender. The fact that her column ran for more than a decade is testament to its popularity; it is also striking that she was known as the 'amiable and accomplished Miss Atkinson' despite her criticism of settler society's propensity to plunder the landscape.⁴

Atkinson's care for the Australian natural world is all the more remarkable if we consider her background. Her father James was a well-known pastoralist, and although he died when she was just a few weeks old, his writings must have cast a long shadow over his daughter's ecological thinking. He was the author of *An Account of the State of Agriculture and Grazing in New South Wales* (1826), a work that sought to address some of the 'problems' of farming in the Antipodes. The book contains a chapter dedicated to land clearance, or the killing of trees, which was of paramount importance to the ambitious settler:

> Some persons have preferred digging a deep hole on one side, and by throwing the stump down ... have succeeded in burying it out of the reach of the plough; others have taken off a belt of bark all round the tree, and killed it while standing ... Some have barked trees, and set fire to them standing; many will completely burn down, but a great many stumps and fragments will remain, and require as much or more trouble to be got rid of.[5]

James Atkinson's suggestions for wiping out native forests are devastating for their treatment of trees as obstacles to be removed as rapidly as possible. With his talk of stump burial, ringbarking, burning and killing trees while standing, this 'management' of the land – for which he was greatly admired – may appear to the modern reader as an act of ecocide.

James Atkinson was not alone in approaching the bush as a disorderly space to be hacked into submission. Writing of the stringy bark tree in a guide for would-be emigrants in 1839, John Stephens noted, 'It is estimated that, if twenty thousand persons emigrated to the Australian shores every year, for the next century, there would be enough for them all.'[6] Clearance was part of everyday life for settlers, whether they were making way for crops and grazing or thinking about the resource value of trees as timber. As historian Don Watson expresses it, 'By the middle of the nineteenth century much of the mighty bush had become a sheepwalk.'[7] Neither James Atkinson nor Stephens appears to give any thought to the need for renewal, nor do they offer any sense that forests might need to be nurtured rather than eradicated.

Unlike her father, Louisa Atkinson understood the damage that deforestation was causing, in particular its relationship to drought. She shows her insight into the discrepancy between her view of the bush and that of her broader community when she remarks, 'The tea tree or ironbark forests of parts of Cumberland, and the scrubs of Bargo leave an impression on the mind of more or less sterility; *to the botanist they may be interesting – to the woodman valuable*, but we rarely speak of them without the additional "barren".'[8] Here, Atkinson is recognising that the views of botanists and settler-farmers seldom aligned, while also registering the aesthetic challenges that native forests posed to those accustomed to European forests. Although she was never able to reconcile herself fully to the idea of culling trees, she understood that sustainable planting offered a way of satisfying the settler community's insatiable demand for timber. As she wrote in 1870, when advocating the planting of fast-growing species like cedar and walnut: 'It would seem advisable to plant suitable trees largely year by year; for, while the woodman's axe can fell the growth of a century in an hour, the forest springs up but slowly.'[9] Despite her great love of Australian native plants and creatures, she saw no difficulty in allowing imported varieties of trees. Given her professional friendships with proponents of acclimatisation like von Mueller, it is perhaps unsurprising that Atkinson was able to imagine native and introduced plant-life living happily alongside one another.

Elizabeth Lawson has remarked that Atkinson was 'unusual in noticing with alarm the decline of species in the districts she knows and treasures'.[10] This was at a time when, as Tim Bonyhady notes, artists like Eugene von Guérard elided the settler impact on the land by painting Australian landscapes that were apparently untouched.[11] Atkinson, by contrast, did not hold back in revealing the endangerment of the wilderness. Her illustrations embraced her wild surroundings but also recorded the presence and impact of colonial culture.

Several of Atkinson's novels – including *Gertrude, the Emigrant* (1857) and *Tom Hellicar's Children* (1871) – feature bleak, cleared landscapes, while her posthumously published work, *Tressa's Resolve* (1872), paid particular attention to the 'Herculean toil' required to tame the land for grazing.[12] Lawson highlights just how unusual Atkinson's voice was:

> Only implicitly does she recognise the value of keeping forest ecology intact, but a century and a half before the present crisis of native forests and, selecting her words carefully, she blames 'the extensive killing of the forests' for the loss of large flocks of birds and the making of 'deserts'.[13]

The article to which Lawson refers, 'Climatic Influences on the Habits of Birds' (16 June 1870), anticipates the dislocation that is all too familiar to us today as a result of climate change. According to Atkinson:

> During the late drought considerable disturbance occurred in the animal kingdom. Some birds forsook their usual haunts to wander – where, we know not; while others from a distance visited us, and, for a time, became residents in localities to which they had hitherto been strangers.[14]

These reluctant avian migrants had been displaced from their homes, and Atkinson was keen to make her readers understand their own role in the birds' removal. She was very conscious that human agency was accelerating

'A misfortune in the distance'

Louisa Calvert (née Atkinson), illustration of an Australian native forest.
FL1118746. Courtesy of Mitchell Library, State Library of New South Wales, Sydney

AFTERMATHS

Louisa Calvert (née Atkinson), forest scene with flying foxes.
FL1118749. Courtesy of Mitchell Library, State Library of New South Wales, Sydney

environmental change on an unprecedented scale in Australia. Writing in her regular column for the *Herald* on 24 May 1870 about an excursion she had taken to Cavan to gather bivalve specimens from the Murrumbidgee River, Atkinson noted that she was struck by this change and its implications for the future. She remarked that 'the scattered trees are evidently rapidly dying, pointing to a time when these ranges will be clear'.[15] Later in the column she commented, 'It needs no fertile imagination to foresee that in, say, half a century's time, tracts of hundreds of miles will be treeless.'[16]

It is impossible to put a figure on the exact scale of forest damage in the nineteenth century, but modellers suggest that Australia has lost 40 percent of its trees since European settlement. There were some attempts to slow the onslaught. As early as 1803, Philip Gidley King, the third governor of New South Wales, attempted to legislate against tree-felling on the banks of rivers and watercourses to prevent soil erosion. Yet as environmentalist and anthropologist Deborah Bird Rose has commented, 'Like many efforts to protect the land, this one was ignored.'[17]

In a piece that appeared in the *Sydney Morning Herald* on 3 February 1871, Atkinson attacked over-farming and suggested inexperience and ignorance might explain the relentlessness with which landowners cleared and planted. In a manner typical of her compassionate approach to landscape and people, she appealed to good sense and goodwill, earnestly believing that education would bring about change:

> Let us hope that a few good seasons will restore prosperity to the land; but it is very doubtful if the small landholder system can ever be permanent where a drought, or over-wet season, reduces the owner to want, unless a far more careful style of cultivation is pursued. 'I don't know how it is', said an old man to me, 'that that land's no good now, for I have known it grow wheat eighteen years running.' The reason seemed to me patent. But it does not follow because the Land Bill [The Crown Lands Occupation Act 1861 (NSW)] enables a man to secure a few acres of land that he should instinctively become a farmer. Some people argue that the earth was made for man and *must* support him, and that his instinct will teach him how to cultivate it. Many a ruined farmer has tried the truth of this hypothesis.[18]

In addition to her dismay at the way any man might come to Australia and reinvent himself as a farmer regardless of his skills and knowledge, Atkinson was highly critical of the entitlement with which settler-pastoralists approached the countryside. She deplored waste and, in the same article, hit out at farmers who killed native animals but made no use of their carcasses or skins. Still, the fact that she continued to pen her column, week after week, suggests she remained hopeful that her words would make a difference.

Settlers' ignorance of Country was a deep concern for Atkinson. While her fiction used catastrophic scenarios like bushfires to subtly initiate her readers into an understanding of Australia's difference, her journalism was much more direct. She highlighted some of the harm caused by settler ignorance in 'After Shells in the Limestone'. While she begins by discussing a landscape that is 'destitute of timber' as a result of insect attack and naturally occurring fungal diseases, she soon shifts her focus to human agency, depicting a landscape that is almost post-apocalyptic in its deadness:

> That various causes are killing the forests of New South Wales every traveller well knows. For some years past the black butts and flooded gums in the vicinity of Berrima have been dying, until now the 'floss' or treeless watersheds of that district are bordered by belts of dead timber. Even the woolly butts are now perishing, while in many localities miles of forest have died – apart from artificial means or ringbarking – that the ultimate consequence will be of a nature materially to affect those districts there can be no doubt. The immediate effect is to render them marshy and unfit for sheep pasturage.[19]

Noting the combination of disease and human intervention, Atkinson foresaw a future in which not only the vista but also the broader ecology would be affected. Ringbarking, or girdling (which involves removing a circular strip of bark from the tree trunk), had become a contentious issue in Australia, with some pastoralists deploying the technique to kill large numbers of trees swiftly. Novelist Anthony Trollope, who visited the colony twice in the early 1870s, described trees killed in this way as standing 'like troops of skeletons … very ugly to look at'.[20]

Atkinson's friend and fellow botanist William Woolls echoed her sentiments in an address to the Horticultural Society of New South Wales in September 1876: 'People may despise gum trees but I regard [them] as one of the wonders of Australian vegetation … that in the economy of nature they are absorbing that which is detrimental to animal life, and supplying in its place that which is necessary for health.'[21] Woolls went on to remark on the 'murderous process of ring-barking', while a newspaper account of his lecture went further still in emphasising the knock-on effects of

OPPOSITE: Percy F.S. Spence, 'A Forest: The Trees "Ring-barked" to Kill Them for Clearing', 1910.

From Frank Fox and Percy F.S. Spence, Australia: As Painted by Percy F.S. Spence and Described by Frank Fox (London: Adam & Charles Black, 1910), between pp. 68 and 69

'A misfortune in the distance'

violence against the bush, noting that 'the denudation of the soil of its indigenous gum-trees has been the opening of the sluice-valves of malaria'.[22] Despite these warnings from Atkinson and Woolls about the devastation caused by ring-barking, the practice persists to this day, although it remains a topic of deep controversy. Don Watson has compared ringing trees to an act of war and goes so far as to suggest that some of those who were complicit in the forest massacre experienced strong feelings of guilt and repentance for the remainder of their lives.[23]

Atkinson's work is remarkable for anticipating many of today's conversations about forests as the 'lungs of the world'. She offers a vision of Australia's future that is uncannily familiar to the modern reader when she comments:

> It would seem that the forests have acted as safety valves to carry off the superfluous moisture of the earth, and to attract that of the atmosphere, thus forming a circulating system. The minor vegetation is undergoing a considerable change. Rushes and aquatic plants present themselves in erstwhile dry regions. In time, there is much reason to fear, this excessive humidity will give place to the reverse; and like other treeless countries we shall suffer from an arid climate and soil. But our wide forests render such a catastrophe a misfortune in the distance.[24]

This prophecy of a 'misfortune in the distance' anticipates environmental theorist Rob Nixon's reminder of what he terms the 'slow violence' of the settler community against both the land and those who had tended it. Arguing that it is always the dispossessed – particularly Indigenous cultures – who first experience the adverse effects of reckless environmental policies, Nixon notes:

> When Europeans began to colonise Australia, some aborigines [sic] dubbed these unfathomable strangers 'the future eaters': the newcomers consumed without replacing, devouring the future at a speed bereft of foresight, hollowing out time by living as if the desert were a place of infinite, untended provision.[25]

As early as 1870, Atkinson showed her readers that they themselves were those 'future eaters', who take everything and replenish nothing while enacting what Nixon terms a 'delayed destruction that is dispersed across time and space'.[26] Atkinson's scope for environmental activism was inevitably limited by her gender, but she wrote against the grain of a community who saw themselves as improvers of the land, not destroyers.

Reading backwards from a present in which deforestation and global warming are extending fire seasons across the world, today's Australians – particularly those in rural and outlying areas – can be certain that this misfortune is no longer safely in the distance. Gamilaraay and Yuwalaraay elders from Walgett in northwest New South Wales say they have never seen conditions like today's droughts, and they doubt the changes can be reversed.[27] That Atkinson was able to foresee today's crisis is testament to her prescience, but also to her deep insight into ecological cause and effect. As Lawson has noted, 'Louisa knew that the greatest problem was forest felling', and she had an incisive understanding of the interdependency of the bush's flora and fauna.[28] For Atkinson, the forest was worthy of preservation not just because of the sustenance it offered but because it was both a home and a continuing source of wonder. The felling of trees became, for her, the epitome of casual waste; in both her fiction and her journalism, it was the root of all harm.

Parihaka, c. 1880.

Photograph by Josiah Martin, c. 1880. Courtesy of Auckland Art Gallery Toi o Tāmaki, Auckland

Chapter 16

'THE PIRATES OF PARIHAKA'
PARODY AS A RESPONSE TO VIOLENCE

Kirstine Moffat

On 30 October 2019, a Crown apology for the invasion and sacking of the pacifist community of Parihaka and the imprisonment of its people passed into law.[1] This came 138 years after government troops, on 5 November 1881, invaded the Taranaki community where the prophets Te Whiti-o-Rongomai and Tohu Kākahi had inspired a campaign of peaceful resistance to the confiscation of Māori land. A scathing 1996 Waitangi Tribunal report critiqued not only Crown action in 1881, but also the subsequent government suppression of the people of Parihaka through its 'forced removals, pass laws, and other suspensions of civil liberties'.[2]

The events at Parihaka have a long and complex history that continues to reverberate. For those seeking a more comprehensive account than the brief overview I provide here, I recommend the works of Dick Scott, Rachel Buchanan, Danny Keenan and Hazel Riseborough.[3] For Te Whiti, Tohu and their followers, Parihaka was a place of faith, sanctuary and community, but the Crown increasingly regarded Parihaka as what Native Minister John Bryce termed the 'headquarters of fanaticism and disaffection'.[4] When negotiations, arrests and the indefinite postponement of trials under the 1879 Māori Prisoners' Trials Act failed to stop the Māori passive resistance campaign, the Crown gathered a substantial military presence in Taranaki. On 5 November 1881 Bryce and Lieutenant Colonel John Roberts led 1589 heavily armed soldiers into Parihaka. About 2000 people, all dressed in their best clothes, sat on the marae waiting for them. The soldiers were met by singing children and women carrying loaves of bread. Buchanan writes that 'under the watch of an Armstrong canon mounted on Purepo … the soldiers arrested and exiled Parihaka leaders, they raped women and stole taonga, they evicted most of the 2000 residents and ransacked buildings and crops'.[5] Bryce claimed his campaign was a resounding success. For Māori, 5 November 1881 is remembered as 'te rā o te pāhua', 'the day of plunder'.[6]

This chapter explores the first creative response to the events at Parihaka, a parody called 'The Pirates of Parihaka', published in the Auckland weekly newspaper the *Observer* seven days after the invasion.[7] Through engaging with this previously undiscussed work, I reflect on the appropriateness of employing parody as a response to violence.

'The Pirates of Parihaka' reworks the hit comic opera *The Pirates of Penzance* by English duo W.S. Gilbert and Arthur Sullivan. First staged in London in 1879, *The Pirates of Penzance* had its Australasian debut in Melbourne in 1880. R.W. Cary's New Zealand production of the comic opera premiered in Wellington on 27 June 1881 and then toured throughout New Zealand, finishing a successful 10-night run in Auckland on 5 November 1881, the day of invasion.[8] The subtitle of the opera – *The Slave of Duty* – points to the protagonist Frederick's struggle between his allegiance to the infamous Pirates of Penzance and his desire to protect the woman he loves, Mabel. Her father, Major General Stanley, has antagonised the pirates by wrongfully claiming to be an orphan (the fearsome pirates are all orphans and sympathetic to anyone in the same situation). Learning of the Major General's lie, the pirates storm his mansion and defeat a timorous police force, only to yield when 'Queen Victoria's name' is evoked.[9]

This is a long way from the tragic events of Parihaka, but the comic opera inspired the unnamed 'imprisoned reporter' who penned 'The Pirates of Parihaka'. Given that Bryce had ordered what Scott terms a 'press blackout on his march', and that several journalists were arrested for trying to defy the ban, it is unsurprising that the parody is sympathetic to Te Whiti and Tohu and critical of Bryce.[10] I have been unable to identify the correspondent responsible for the parody, but a prior link between *The Pirates of Penzance* and Parihaka appeared in an article published in the *Auckland Star* on 4 November 1881. This satirises a reconnaissance mission by Bryce during which he was invited by Māori to enjoy 'the hospitalities of the place'. The unnamed correspondent declared that the 'closing scene between policemen and pirates in Gilbert and Sullivan's popular opera does not contain more exquisite elements of burlesque'.[11] The burlesque nature of 'The Pirates of Parihaka' is evident in the subtitle: 'Abridged from the Pirates of Pen's Aunts'. But beneath the clever pastiche, the obvious desire to capitalise on the phenomenal popularity of Gilbert and Sullivan's latest hit, and the imperial view of what the writer terms 'the natives', lies criticism of the Crown and empathy for Māori.

The parody jettisons the love plot of the original and focuses predominantly on three characters and their signature songs. The first of these is the Pirate King. In the Gilbert and Sullivan opera he is a flamboyant character who relishes his buccaneering life but possesses a patriotic love for Queen Victoria. 'The Pirates of Parihaka' uses the Pirate King as the model for Te Whiti, changing both the title of his signature song and the character's role from Pirate King to 'Maori Chief'. Within the restrictions of the beat-and-rhyme scheme of Gilbert and Sullivan's original, the parody achieves a remarkable shift in character. Gone is the flamboyance of the Pirate King, replaced by a dignified and heroic figure who castigates Pākehā greed and injustice:

> Oh, better far to live and die
> Under the rule of prophecy,
> And play the sly obstructive part,
> Than get a bullet through one's head and heart.
> Away to the cheating world go you,
> Where pakehas are well-to-do;
> But I'll be true to my own belief,
> And live and die a Maori chief.

'The Pirates of Parihaka' emphasises Te Whiti's prophetic and mythic qualities. His example restrains the aggression of some of his followers. These followers, who appear in the parody as the 'Native Chorus', long to 'pot Bryce with impunity' and speak of their desire to 'eat him with avidity' but relinquish this through loyalty to Te Whiti. Here, the work recycles reductive late Victorian clichés of both the cannibalistic ignoble savage (epitomised by the Chorus) and the Rousseauian noble savage (embodied by Te Whiti). Yet the Te Whiti of 'The Pirates of Parihaka' also shatters these kinds of colonial stereotypes. He is presented as a heroic leader of great mana. There is no ridicule in his portrayal, but respect for his restraint and his ability to maintain his peaceful doctrine in the face of violence.

Te Whiti is the one character who is multidimensional, having a role beyond that of leader. He is presented as a father, whose daughter comforts him when he wakes in the night anxious about the 'darksome dangers' that threaten his people. Unafraid of emotion, Te Whiti weeps 'glistening tears', the personal relationship

AFTERMATHS

'*The Invasion of Parihaka. – Mr. Bryce as He Appeared Leading the Way on His White Charger*'. Observer, *12 November 1881, p. 131*

of father and daughter circling out to encompass all of his people in a bond of connection and love.

The character and purpose of the Major General is also significantly altered in the parody, not least because the role of father that humanises him in the opera is shifted to Te Whiti. Absurdity is the key element of the Major General, his signature patter song revealing that he may be classically educated but knows nothing of military tactics. The gentle mockery meted out to the Major General is replaced, in 'The Pirates of Parihaka', with an eviscerating critique of John Bryce, who proclaims himself a 'model Native Minister'. A cartoon on the page of the newspaper immediately preceding 'The Pirates of Parihaka' prepares the reader for its lampooning tone, with the cartoon's title heralding Bryce's entrance on a 'white charger' but the accompanying image reducing his mount to a blinkered ass.[12]

Bryce's words reveal him to be opportunistic, devious and amoral, the ultimate hollow man:

> I am the very model of a model Native Minister;
> I can be either affable, or chaffable, or sinister;
> I know official dodges, and I can be oratorical,
> And write long memoranda in order categorical.
> I'm very well acquainted with matters diplomatical,
> I undertake decisions on some subjects problematical,
> About all Maori theories I am teeming a lot o' news …
> But if I prove a failure, what a devil of a pot I'll lose.

Bryce speaks openly about his campaign to smear political rival John Sheehan through leaking details of Sheehan's unpaid bills. He regards 'humbug' as a useful political tool and rejoices that he draws 'official pay' for a very slight political knowledge.

Reworking the 'ingenious paradox' song from *The Pirates of Penzance*, the author of the parody gives the lyrics a much darker turn; the paradox, as trumpeted by Bryce, is that due to a parliamentary sleight of hand, Māori are categorised as trespassers on their own land:

> Although you are living on your land, it has been confiscated,
> And therefore you are to be driven off, and your land appropriated.

The writer is full of disdain for Bryce and reduces him through parody to both a petty, self-serving bureaucrat and a grotesque monster who urges his troops not only to invade and plunder but also to 'slaughter' in order to fulfil his repellent aim of 'extermination'.

This castigation of Bryce is reinforced in the 'Reporter's Song', which adapts the mischievous spirit of the Major General's daughters sneaking off to dabble their toes in the sea to emphasise the lengths the press went to gain access to Parihaka in order to bear witness to the events. The press mock Bryce's 'autocratic capers' and promise that he and his fellow 'big officials' will get 'pepper from the papers', precisely what the 'imprisoned reporter' does in 'The Pirates of Parihaka'. A bond is established between the reporters and Māori, with Tohu praising the reporters for their 'learning … politeness … refinement' and his wife offering these 'poor wandering ones' '*kai*' in the form of 'spuds, pork and tea'. The reporters are as much at the mercy of Bryce and the colonial troops as Te Whiti and Tohu and, within the Gilbert and Sullivan universe, are joined to the wronged Māori through their link to the words of the original Pirates. In the climax to the parody, it is not Māori but the reporters who eventually 'yield in Queen Victoria's name' before being imprisoned by Bryce.

Perhaps the most beloved group of characters in the Gilbert and Sullivan canon are the inept police force in *The Pirates of Penzance*, who try to be manly and brave but are prone to running away when danger approaches. In the parody, the police become the armed constabulary who marched on Parihaka, led not by the Sergeant of Police of the original but by Colonel Roberts, the real-life army officer who commanded the troops. Like their counterparts in *The Pirates of Penzance*, the constabulary forces in 'The Pirates of Parihaka' would rather be watching nurses 'air their little babies in the sun'. They rally themselves with their marching song, 'Tarantara', congratulating themselves that they will 'make a splendid show' as they approach Parihaka. Yet the troops are also fearful. Roberts sings:

> For I've learned in many a brush,
>   Tarantara, tarantara,
> That a n—— in the bush,
>   Tarantara,
> Is as good as three of us.

Once again, the language betrays a distasteful nineteenth-century European patronage and bigotry towards Māori, yet Māori are also positioned as fundamentally superior to Roberts and his men in their valour, bravery and military skill, an ambivalence captured in a cartoon on the preceding page of the newspaper that shares something of the theatricality of 'The Pirates of Parihaka', with Te Whiti, Tohu and Hiroki and the two officers in the foreground posed like a dance line with the constabulary as a massed chorus behind.[13]

There is no record of 'The Pirates of Parihaka' ever being performed, but a fascinating archival find indicates that the work was read and appreciated. The Rolleston Family Papers, held by the Alexander Turnbull Library, includes a couple of Gilbert and Sullivan parodies.[14] The family are best known for their involvement in politics: William Rolleston was the Native Minister ousted by Bryce shortly before the invasion. The family were devotees of Gilbert and Sullivan, and after viewing the J.C. Williamson touring production of *The Pirates of Penzance* in 1882, the Rolleston children 'not only sang the tunes but also wrote

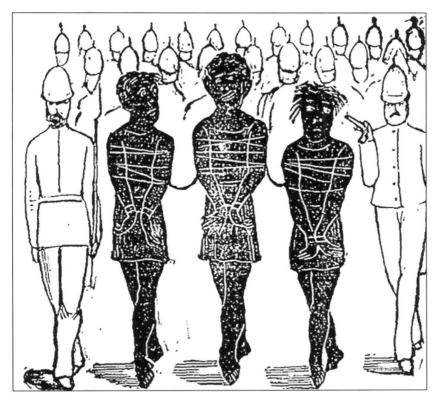

'Glorious Capture of Te Whiti, Tohu, and Hiroki'. Observer, *12 November 1881, p. 131*

parodies on the Policeman's Chorus'.[15] One of these children, Frank, painstakingly copied out 'The Pirates of Parihaka' by hand and signed the manuscript at the bottom. Given that Frank was born in 1873 and thus was only eight at the time of the Parihaka invasion, it is impossible that he could be the 'imprisoned reporter' who authored the piece. It is much more likely that a combination of his father's antipathy towards Bryce (William Rolleston believed in Māori self-determinism and worked for a peaceful resolution to events in Taranaki) and his love of Gilbert and Sullivan led Frank, possibly when he was a schoolboy at Christ's College in Christchurch, to transcribe the newspaper pastiche. Given the Rolleston family's love of theatre and the long-established British tradition of household theatrics, it is also possible that the transcription was made in preparation for a private performance.

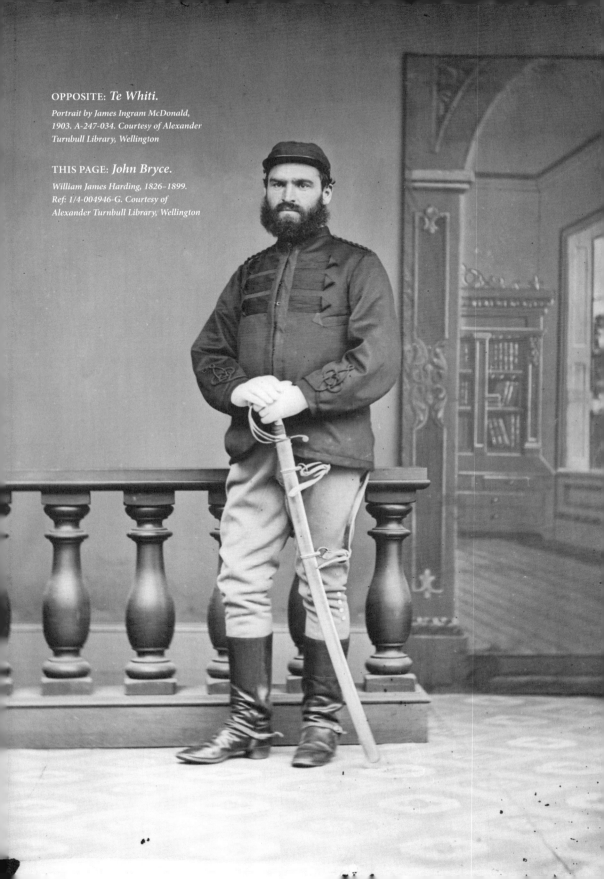

OPPOSITE: *Te Whiti.*
Portrait by James Ingram McDonald, 1903. A-247-034. Courtesy of Alexander Turnbull Library, Wellington

THIS PAGE: *John Bryce.*
William James Harding, 1826–1899. Ref: 1/4-004946-G. Courtesy of Alexander Turnbull Library, Wellington

Frank makes a few minor omissions in his transcript, but the only significant change comes at the end. After the constabulary's song about the unhappiness of their lot, Frank's transcript omits the stage direction 'Te Whiti, Tohu, and Horiki are seized' and Bryce's command to 'seize those reporters'. The final words in the transcript are almost the same as in the printed version of 'The Pirates of Parihaka':

> We yield with humble mien
> Because with all our faults, we love our Queen.

Yet the meaning is more ambiguous in Frank Rolleston's version. These lines are clearly attributed to the reporters in the published version, but in the transcript these final lines come on a page headed 'Colonel Robert's Song'. The probable reason for the change is that Frank was near the end of the page and wanted to bring his transcription to a swift resolution without wasting paper. But it is also possible to read Frank's version more subversively, with the Pākehā troops laying down their weapons in recognition that invading Parihaka was wrong and in contravention of the Queen's will. There are certainly the seeds of this interpretation in the work itself, with the script giving Te Whiti and his people both voice and presence. There is also ambiguity in the title – structurally, the pirates become the people of Parihaka, but thematically, they are Bryce and the constabulary, motivated by greed and self-interest. Both ways of reading the ending reduce the devastating impact of the invasion of Parihaka to a rhyming couplet. This failure to engage with actual events also speaks to the Pākehā cultural forgetting that has plagued Parihaka and its legacy.

Both versions of 'The Pirates of Parihaka' provoke a vital question: is parody an appropriate response to violence? Parody mimics the style of an author in a humorous or satirical way. To employ parody as a device to capture the violence, rape and looting at Parihaka is singularly inappropriate. There is something discordant in appropriating the burlesque comedy of Gilbert and Sullivan to these traumatic historical events. The discordancy is twofold: a lapse in sensitivity in evaluating how parody should be effectively employed and the dissonant use of a device that involves not only satire but humour. Ultimately, comic opera is too light, too trivial, too slight to do justice to a crime against humanity. Transporting the very English conventions of the Gilbert and Sullivan genre, with its reliance on issues of class, rank, absurd topsy-turvydom and an appreciation of the subtleties of British institutions, to the raw emotion of Parihaka – what Tonga Awhikau, a close advisor to Tohu, termed 'Kōharihari' (deep pain) – is jarring.[16] The prophetic and hopeful force of Te Whiti and Tohu's vision, what Tohu described in a speech as a 'foundation of Peace' that 'transcends' and 'inspires', is also absent, the themes too weighty for the medium.[17]

Despite this disjunct between parody and the tragedy of Parihaka, settler responses to the events repeatedly returned to this mode. A few days after the publication of 'The Pirates of Parihaka', on 21 November 1881, another parody of the events was printed in the *Lyttleton Times* by Frank Fudge (one of the pseudonyms of Thomas Bracken). 'The Battle of Parihaka' is a short poem that ridicules Bryce for claiming 'glory' after a 'battle' that is both a non-event and an injustice to the peaceful people of Parihaka.[18] In 1889 Jessie Mackay used Tennyson's 'The Charge of the Light Brigade' as the model for her ironic 'The Charge at Parihaka', while John Liddell's 'Skald Scott Sings' (1902) reworks Sir Walter Scott's 'Lochinvar' to ridicule Bryce.[19] This reliance on parody continued into the late twentieth century. Mervyn Thompson and William Dart's song-play, *Songs to the Judges* (1983), memorialises the trials following the invasion of Parihaka in the satirical song 'We Got It All Together Just for You', which takes 'the Gilbert-and-Sullivan' approach and features a judge performing 'a little skipping dance'.[20] Like 'The Pirates of Parihaka', these works are critical of Bryce and Crown actions, but tonally, they get it wrong.

What would be a more appropriate register? The wonderful collection *Parihaka: The art of passive resistance* (2001) contains a range of visual and written responses that acknowledge the trauma of the events.[21] To keep with the musical connection inherent in 'The Pirates of Parihaka', the many waiata composed by Māori to commemorate Parihaka and its legacy provide powerful, concentrated moments of intense emotion. Harry Dansey's play *Te Rakura: The feathers of the albatross* (1974) draws on these waiata to convey the ongoing cost of Parihaka:

> The men who broke, and bent, and turned the law
> Have done great evil, not alone to those
> Of that far time, but also to our own.[22]

Witi Ihimaera's 2011 novel, *The Parihaka Woman*, suggests that grand opera may provide an answer to the question of an appropriate musical and verbal response to violence. Ihimaera also turns to a pre-existing European work as a model, in this case Beethoven's 1805 *Fidelio*, which Ihimaera describes as 'political opera'.[23]

Ihimaera's narrative captures the two dominant emotions expressed through Beethoven's music: anger and hope. There is rage against colonial oppression in *The Parihaka Woman*, epitomised by the heroine Erenora's fight to free loved ones from wrongful imprisonment. Yet, in tracing the history of Parihaka from the nineteenth century to the present day, Ihimaera also looks forward to 'the arrival of Aranga, the day of resurrection and harvest' promised by Te Whiti and Tohu.[24] This, for me, is an appropriate response to Parihaka, an uncompromising anger at injustice, but also an honouring of the hopeful message of Parihaka – a new dawn after the dark night, following death, resurrection and new life.

> KO TE POO E TE IWI TE KAI HARI I TE RAA
> *The night O people is the bringer of the day*
> KO TE MATE TE KAI HARI I TE ORANGA E AU
> *Death is the bringer of life. I AM.*[25]

PART V
CREATIVE RESISTANCE

Chapter 17

GOORDBELAYIN

THE BEDFORD DOWNS MASSACRE PAINTINGS OF ROVER THOMAS

Rachel Burgess

> The white man history has been told and it's today in the book
> But our history is not there properly
> We've got to tell 'em through our paintings
> —Clifford Brooks, *Yiwarra Kuju: The Canning Stock Route*, 2010[1]

Rover Thomas is one of the most significant Aboriginal painters in the history of Australian art and one of the first to represent Australia at the Venice Biennale. His paintings have led to a greater appreciation of Aboriginal art, nationally and internationally, and provide a valuable Aboriginal perspective of Australian history. He is well known for his paintings of the Goorirr Goorirr Joonba and the Bedford Downs massacre, works that acknowledge the victims of an atrocity that occurred in the East Kimberley region of Western Australia nearly 100 years ago.

Born in the Great Sandy Desert, Rover Thomas worked in the East Kimberley region for over 30 years and is widely acknowledged as the founder of the East Kimberley or Warmun/Turkey Creek school of painting. His life was defined by the rapid cultural, historical and environmental changes that occurred in the early twentieth century in the Kimberley and Pilbara regions. As the pastoral industry expanded in northern Western Australia, Aboriginal people experienced forced migration, cultural stress and economic hardship, and Thomas's paintings document the historical trauma experienced by so many in this remote region. To fully appreciate his paintings, however, it is essential to understand his Aboriginal worldview and the inseparable links between Ninggoowoom/Family, Daam/Country and Ngarranggarni/the Dreaming.

Rover Thomas (c. 1926–1998), an Aboriginal man of Joolama skin, was born at Yalta on the Canning Stock Route in the Pilbara region of northern Western Australia. His mother, Ngakuyipa/Marrbi/Nyrrbi, also known as Nita, was an Aboriginal woman from the Kukatja cultural and language group in the Kutjungka region. His father, Lanikan Thomas was an Aboriginal man from the Wangkatjungka cultural and language group in the West Kimberley region.[2] Raised by two Wangkatjungka men – his father Lanikan and his father's relative, Sundown – Rover had a brother, Charlie Brooks, and two sisters, Nyuju Stumpy Brown and Kupi.[3] Aboriginal concepts of family and kinship are complex and shape social organisation and personal interactions. Kinship, moiety, totems and skin names determine how people relate to each other, and this dictates the roles, responsibilities and obligations people have to one another and the environment. These kinship ties form a vast network that extends throughout the Kimberley, Pilbara and Western Desert regions of Western Australia.

Thomas's Daam or Country is known as Kunawarritji/Well 33 and is located in the Pilbara region. Aboriginal people describe their Country as the place where they were born or grew up, or which they inherit from their parents and grandparents. This connection to Country is underpinned by cultural rights and responsibilities. Families who belong to and maintain rights of ownership over particular areas are interlinked through a matrix of Dreaming tracks, or Songlines, that trace the journeys of ancestral beings.[4]

Ngarranggarni is a concept also known as the Dreaming. It refers to the time of creation but transcends time as we know it. During the Ngarranggarni, ancestral beings – both animal and human – moved across the Country creating land features, plants and animals, performing ceremonies, singing, marrying and fighting. At the end of their journey the ancestral beings returned to earth to dwell in sacred sites such as hills, rocks, waterholes and salt lakes.[5]

Kunawarritji/Well 33 is an important Ngarranggarni/Dreaming site for Aboriginal people from the desert regions of Western Australia.[6] For desert people, water is far more than a vital resource essential to physical and economic survival. Jilla or freshwater springs are inhabited by ancestral beings that ensure the vitality and spiritual power of Country. Ceremonies, songs and stories come from the Ngarranggarni/Dreaming at these sites, and important aspects of Aboriginal cultural and religious practice depend on their maintenance.

Thomas's birthplace, Yalta, is a small Jumu or soakage close to the Canning Stock Route located in the Martu cultural and language area of the Great Sandy Desert. The soakage is situated amid an expanse of spinifex grasslands, low mulga woodlands and ti-tree bushes, and surrounded by vast undulating sand plains and dune fields in arid desert country. Jarntu was the name given to Thomas and it connects him to Yalta and to Kunawarritji/Well 33, the traditional land of his father and grandfathers. Jarntu is the Martu name for the dingo or wild dog found throughout Western Australia.[7]

Thomas left Kunawarritji/Well 33 after the death of his parents. He was about 10 years old and set out alone to walk along the Canning Stock Route. Drover Wally Dowling, who was living with Thomas's Gamelanyel/mother's sister at Mindibungu/Billiluna Station in the southeast Kimberley region, some 70 kilometres north of Wirrimanu/Balgo and 150 kilometres south of Yarilil/Halls Creek, was asked to keep an eye out for the young boy and bring him back. Dowling found Thomas in the Great Sandy Desert and took him north to Mindibungu/Billiluna Station where he was put to work in the stock camps with other Aboriginal people.[8] He acquired skills in fencing, yard-building, bore maintenance, saddle-making, ropework, horse-breaking, cattle-branding, mustering and animal husbandry. When Thomas turned 14, he was initiated into traditional Aboriginal Law by men from nearby Sturt Creek Station. In early adolescence he became a stockman, and during this time he was given the Gadiya/European name Rover Thomas.

During the 1940s, drovers from Mindibungu/Billiluna Station mustered large herds of cattle to Old Halls Creek (a former gold-mining town 15 kilometres from Yarilil/Halls Creek) along the northern section of the Canning Stock Route. They followed the disused Overland Telegraph Line and Old Halls Creek Track from Yarilil/Halls Creek to Yarrunga/Alice Downs Station, before crossing the Panton River and Great Northern Highway at Darrajayin/Springvale Station. The Springvale–Lansdowne Road took them past Doowoonan/Old Bedford directly to the Barangen/Bedford Downs Station homestead. The road from the homestead ran beside Garnanganyjel/Mt King and passed by the Goordbelayin/Bedford Downs massacre site. The drovers herded the cattle through deep gorges beside Garnanganyjel/Mt King or Joowarringayin/Mt Bedford onto the Bedford Stock Route, then followed this route along the Chamberlain River to the Durack and Saw Ranges. There they pushed the cattle through a gap in the Tier Ranges and moved along the King River Valley to the Wyndham Meatworks. As a young stockman, Rover Thomas regularly mustered cattle from Mindibungu/Billiluna Station to Wyndham along this route.[9]

Goordbelayin

Thomas eventually left Mindibungu/Billiluna Station to work as a fencing contractor on East Kimberley cattle stations such as Argyle, Alice Downs, Bedford Downs, Bow River, Lissadell, Mabel Downs, Moola Bulla, Springvale and Texas Downs. While working in the East Kimberley he formed close relationships with Gija people, including Paddy Jaminji, Queenie McKenzie-Garagarag, Timmy Timms-Gamaliny/Balmendarri, Jack Britten-Yalarrji/Warnngayirriny, George Mung Mung-Lirrmayirriny/Magany, Paddy Bedford-Nyoonkoony/Goowoomji, Hector Jandany, Henry Wambiny and Peggy Patrick-Barraddjil/Dirrmingali. These people were descendants of those who were killed, survived or witnessed the Bedford Downs massacre.[10]

ABOVE: *Rover Thomas,* Bedford Downs Massacre, *1985.*
Reproduced with kind permission of Jane Yalunga Tinmarie. Courtesy of the Holmes à Court Collection, Perth

OPPOSITE: *Rover Thomas,* Canning Stock Route, *1989.*
Reproduced with kind permission of Jane Yalunga Tinmarie. Courtesy of the Holmes à Court Collection, Perth

Bedford Downs Station was located in a rugged and inaccessible part of the East Kimberley region of Western Australia, 84 kilometres west of Warmun/Turkey Creek and 109 kilometres north of Yarilil/Halls Creek. The station was at the nexus of a group of small pastoral leases that included Adavale, Alice Downs, Bungle Bungle, Greenvale, Idamere, Mabel Downs, Mistake Creek and Tickalara. Other cattle stations located in the northwest Kimberley, such as Elgee Cliffs, Galway Downs, Karungie Downs and Tableland, also formed part of this network. This collective of stations was known as 'the back-blocks' or, more ominously, as 'the underworld', and was outside the patrol area covered by the Halls Creek and Fitzroy Crossing police.[11]

In 1917 the Quilty Brothers acquired the pastoral lease for Bedford Downs Station, and Patrick 'Paddy' Quilty (1888–1938) was the station's owner-manager until 1937. Bedford Downs was well established, with a homestead, 10,000 head of cattle and over 50 horses. The main workforce consisted of Aboriginal people from the Gija culture and language group, who were used as indentured labour and paid in rations such as bags of flour, sugar, tea, salt and sticks of tobacco. Most Aboriginal men engaged in cattle work – weaning, branding and earmarking, building and mending fences and constructing cattle yards. They were competent in all aspects of horsemanship, breaking in colts and fillies and mustering stock. Aboriginal women worked in the station homestead where they tended the kitchen garden, carted water from the wells and cooked, cleaned and washed for the manager and his four Gadiya/European workers. The women were often coerced into unwanted sexual contact with these men.[12] Aboriginal children were born into servitude and raised as indentured station workers.[13] Their lives were inextricably bound to the Gadiya/European station managers, and they lived in an environment where abuse and violence were normalised.[14] Aboriginal stockmen, domestic workers and their families tolerated these conditions to maintain their connection to traditional Country.

The area occupied by Bedford Downs Station was the traditional Country of Aboriginal people from the Gija culture and language group, and several highly significant Ngarranggarni/Dreaming sites were located on the station.[15] Barangen, the area immediately surrounding the Bedford Downs Station homestead, was a traditional campsite for the Gija people. Each year during Jadagen/Wet Season (November to March), those living on Bedford Downs would gather at a significant location for Ceremony.[16] At the beginning of Barnden/Dry Season (April to October), Gija people would return from Ceremony to work on Bedford Downs Station.

In late 1923 at the beginning of Jadagen/Wet Season, the older Gija and Worla men living on Bedford Downs Station speared a valuable milking cow that had strayed into their camp. Paddy Quilty and the station cook, Jack Smith, went looking for the cow and discovered that the Aboriginal men had butchered, cooked and eaten it. Quilty decided to assert his authority and contacted the Fitzroy Crossing police to have the men arrested. Then horse-mounted police, with the aid of armed Aboriginal men called native assistants, tracked, captured and detained the Gija and Worla men suspected of killing cattle, and removed them from the area. The prisoners were forced to march, in neck chains, 200 kilometres to Wyndham police station in the northeast Kimberley. Once the men arrived there they were summarily tried by the local Justice of the Peace or Resident Magistrate and charged with the offence of cattle stealing.

Aboriginal men found guilty of killing cattle were typically given lengthy prison sentences and could be gaoled for up to three years. Police identified the men using an identity 'tag' or 'ticket' fastened around their neck. They were usually imprisoned in Wyndham Goal or sent south by boat to Rottnest Island prison. However, the Gija and Worla men from Bedford Downs Station were set free still wearing their prison identification tags. The illiterate prisoners thought the 'tickets' were an official guarantee of safe passage home, but considering subsequent events, they should have been interpreted as a death warrant.

On hearing of their release, Quilty made an agreement with Gadiya/European pastoralists from nearby stations – Alexander 'Scotty' Sadler from Tableland Station, Patrick 'Barney' O'Leary from Galway Downs Station, William John 'Jack' Carey from Gibb River Station, James 'Scotty' Salmond and Paddy 'Scotty' Menmuir from Karunjie Station, and boundary rider Jack Callaghan – to kill the Aboriginal men on their return from Wyndham.[17] Some of these men had served together in the 10th Australian Light Horse Regiment during World War I and had been granted pastoral leases in the West Kimberley under the Australian Soldier Settlement Scheme.[18] The Gadiya/European men had earlier massacred groups of Aboriginal men, women and children in the northwest Kimberley region.[19]

In 1924, at the beginning of Barnden/Dry Season (April), the Gija and Worla men who had been sent to Wyndham returned to Bedford Downs Station. The Aboriginal men were assembled and went on a dray to collect wood for a bonfire. At lunchtime Jack Smith gave them tea, bread and jam that he had laced with strychnine. As the poison took effect, the Aboriginal men fell to the ground,

AFTERMATHS

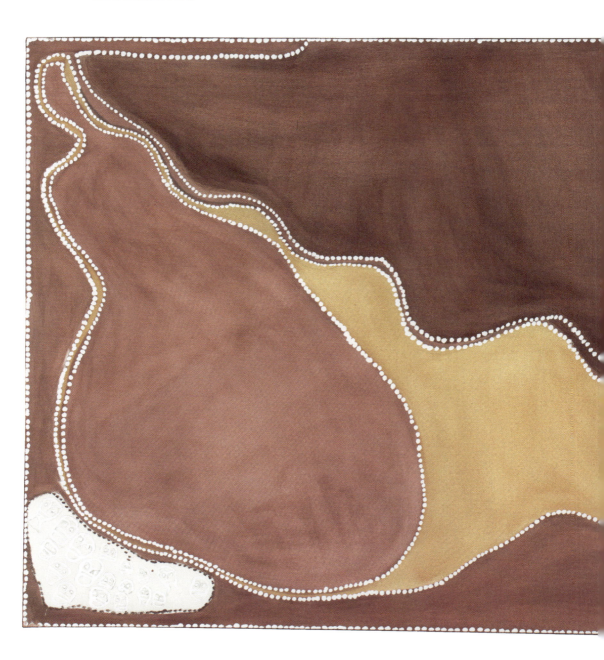

Rover Thomas, Bedford Downs Massacre, *1987.*
Reproduced with kind permission of Jane Yalunga Tinmarie. Courtesy of the Holmes à Court Collection, Perth

writhing, and the pastoralists bludgeoned them to death with sticks. Those who were injured or tried to escape were shot dead. The bodies were then carried to the woodheap, doused with kerosene and set on fire. One young man escaped by running to Garnanganyjel/Mt King, where he hid among the spinifex.[20]

After the massacre, Quilty and Smith returned to the homestead. The Aboriginal women had already noticed smoke billowing from the fire and asked Quilty why the Gija and Worla men had not returned with the dray. He claimed they had left to live at local stations and would not be coming back. Later in the afternoon the women walked to a small hill that overlooked the bonfire. As they came closer, they saw bodies burning among the flames and hurried back to the homestead to tell all the other Gija people about the atrocity. Early the next morning, the remaining Aboriginal workers and their families fled Bedford Downs for Violet Valley Station.[21]

Rover Thomas settled in the East Kimberley in the 1960s and was adopted into the Gija culture and language group. He married an Aboriginal woman named Rita Tinmarie and they had a daughter named Jane Yalunga Tinmarie.[22] Through his marriage to Rita, Thomas inherited the right to tell many of the Ngarranggarni/Dreaming stories about Gija Country. He lived with his family at Texas Downs, Lissadell and Bow River Station, and enjoyed a close relationship with Paddy Jaminji. Jaminji was born at Bedford Downs Station and had worked there all his adult life. He was 12 years old when the massacre occurred, and many of his immediate relatives had been killed. Jaminji was a Manambarrany/Senior Lawman and had a comprehensive understanding of his traditional Country coupled with great spiritual knowledge. He was an uncle to Thomas and encouraged him to engage fully with Gija ceremonial life.

In the 1960s the Pastoral Industry Award, which required station owners to pay their Aboriginal workers, was enforced in the northern cattle industry.[23] This development emerged with other changes, such as the use of helicopters for mustering and a drop in global beef prices that left the pastoral industry in freefall.[24] Many pastoralists in the Kimberley were either unwilling or unable to support the Aboriginal stockmen and their families who had come to depend on them, and these people were forced to move to regional centres like Wyndham, Halls Creek and Kununurra, where makeshift camps were constructed on Crown reserve land. The edges of those towns soon became clusters of humpies and tin shacks. Thomas and his family were taken to a camp outside of Wyndham called

Gooda Gooda/Nine Mile. During this tumultuous period of political change, forced migration, economic hardship and cultural stress, he had a prophetic dream.

In 1975, Thomas, Jaminji and their families moved from Gooda Gooda/Nine Mile to form an Aboriginal community in Warmun/Turkey Creek. Thomas shared the content of his prophetic dream with Jaminji and other Gija men, and together they worked to produce a Joonba/song and dance cycle. Joonba is a Gija word for a specific form of performance driven by spiritual and historical narratives. The narratives can be gifted to someone by a spirit through a series of dreams or developed by Manambarram/senior law people. Thomas became the custodian responsible for the direction, performance and circulation of the Goorirr Goorirr Joonba.

The Goorirr Goorirr Joonba chronicled the journey of a spirit woman to significant sites in Gija, Worla, Ngarinyin and Miriwoong Country. On this journey she encountered other beings who travelled with her to culturally significant sites. In the East Kimberley, the spirit woman travelled to Elgee Cliffs, Garnanganyjel/Mt King and the Goordbelayin/Bedford Downs Station massacre site, where she encountered the shade or shadows of the Gija and Worla men who were killed in the Bedford Downs massacre.

Thomas and Jaminji co-produced the first painted boards depicting the Bedford Downs massacre for the Goorirr Goorirr Joonba in 1979. The paintings were made in natural ochre on discarded offcuts of plywood from houses being constructed in the Warmun/Turkey Creek community. The two had painted in ochre in preparation for Ceremony throughout their lives, but the transition to painting on board was an innovation. The original Goorirr Goorirr Joonba had 31 verses, and each painting related to an individual element of the song cycle and was revealed sequentially. The boards were carried by dancers and accompanied by Songmen and a chorus that sang the verses.[25]

In the 1980s Thomas began painting in ochre on canvas for national and international exhibitions. Paintings produced during the early period of his career were presented in group exhibitions with other Australian Aboriginal artists. He developed a distinctive painting style characterised by sparse simplicity and an aerial perspective depicting maps of Country. The works did not contain obvious narrative elements, but recorded places where important spiritual and historic events had occurred and functioned as vehicles for the stories to be retold in the presence of others.

Michael O'Ferrall curated the exhibition *On the Edge: Five Aboriginal artists* (1989) at the Art Gallery of Western Australia (AGWA). The exhibition included a series of paintings by Thomas alongside works by Trevor Nickolls, an emerging Aboriginal artist from South Australia. By the late 1980s, Perth businessman Robert Holmes à Court had acquired a comprehensive body of works by Thomas for his private collection, including a series of extraordinary paintings that chronicled the Bedford Downs massacre.

In 1990, Thomas and Nickolls were both promoted through national exhibitions, including *Balance 1990* at the Queensland Art Gallery. They were also represented in state, national and international museum and art gallery collections. In the same year, the pair represented Australia at the Venice Biennale in Italy. The biennale included 13 paintings by Thomas, of which nine were from the AGWA collection, three from the Holmes à Court collection and one from the National Gallery of Australia. Thomas was promoted as a modern painter who represented the 'new wave' of Australian Aboriginal art at a time when it was still perceived as 'traditional'. International art critics hailed him as the 'star of the Venice Biennale'. But when the Bedford Downs massacre paintings were displayed in Venice, the exhibition catalogue referred to them only as Bedford Downs paintings, leaving out the violent historical reference. Many felt that this significantly altered the cultural importance of the artworks and silenced the retelling of a disturbing chapter of Australian history.

The National Gallery of Australia honoured Rover Thomas and his important role in the history of Australian art with an exhibition titled *Roads Cross* (1994). This included a series of works depicting the Goorirr Goorirr Joonba and the Bedford Downs massacre.[26] Australian art reviews and scholarly publications acknowledged Thomas as a central figure in the development of a new form of Australian modernism – an abstract, narrative-driven style of painting that had become synonymous with the East Kimberley region of Western Australia. There was, however, little acknowledgement of the settler colonial violence depicted throughout the exhibition.

In 1995 Thomas returned home to visit Yalta and his traditional Country at Kunawarritji/Well 33 on the Canning Stock Route. Almost 60 years had passed since he had left his birthplace in the Great Sandy Desert. He dedicated the rest of his life to painting Country located close to Kunawarritji/Well 33. When Thomas died in 1998, he was buried at Warmun/Turkey Creek in the East Kimberley region of Western Australia.

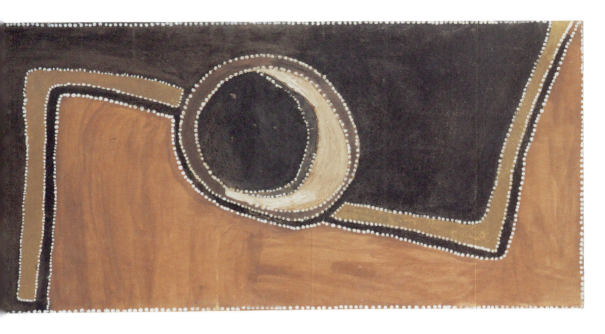

Rover Thomas, The Shade from the Hill Comes Over and Talks in Language, *1984.*
Reproduced with kind permission of Jane Yalunga Tinmarie. Courtesy of the Holmes à Court Collection, Perth

Chapter 18

MAPPING MASSACRES

ART, HISTORY AND ARTEFACTS IN JUDY WATSON'S *THE NAMES OF PLACES*

Anna Johnston

But when the statues come down, how might the atrocities themselves be publicly commemorated, rather than repressed?

—Ceridwen Dovey[1]

Every rock, every hill, every water, I know that place backwards and forwards, up and down, inside out. It's my country and I got names for every place.

—Queenie McKenzie[2]

How to recognise and appropriately memorialise the historical aftermath of colonialism remains a troubling question for contemporary societies globally. Visual symbols are particularly resonant. Statues of emblematic figures of imperial exploitation – Cecil Rhodes, Edward Colston and James Cook among others – have been toppled or defaced in Cape Town, Bristol and Gisborne. In Sydney in June 2020, a ring of police protected a Cook statue in Hyde Park, sparking media debate about the role of the state in protecting symbols as opposed to citizens.[3]

In response to these controversies, Australian writer Ceridwen Dovey has questioned whether the symbolic toppling of statues erases a past that should be assessed and accounted for instead. She considers two important projects that map the extent of violence in colonial Australia. The first is Lyndall Ryan's *Colonial Frontier Massacres* map, a collaboration between one of Australia's leading colonial historians, her research team, and IT and mapping specialists. The map provides detailed empirical data about precisely where and when skirmishes took place, supported with evidence from newspaper articles, published and private settler records and official reports.[4] Dovey suggests audiences who may be sceptical about frontier massacres can be confronted by the map 'with the gruesome truths recorded by their own ancestors – the magistrates and crown-lands commissioners,

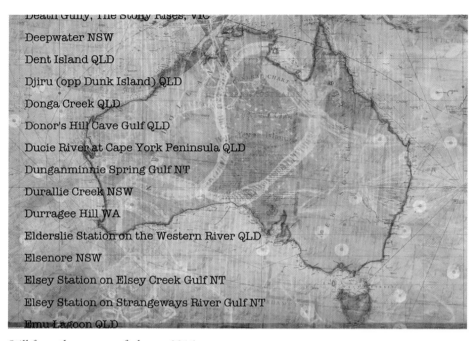

Still from the names of places, *2016.*
Reproduced with kind permission of Judy Watson. Courtesy of Milani Gallery

the settlers who wrote about killing sprees in their journals or correspondence'.[5]

The second project Dovey considers is Indigenous artist Judy Watson's *the names of places*. Watson draws on some of the same empirical research on massacres but redeploys this material into art: prints, paintings and installation pieces that sit in galleries alongside video works and online maps. *The names of places* uses creative methods to infuse the map of Australia with the record of colonial violence alongside Indigenous knowledge of place, people and history.

Indigenous histories, including of massacres, remain little known by the public.[6] Watson's work shows how Indigenous artistic forms can engage audiences and invites them to confront difficult parts of colonial history. The 2017 Uluru Statement from the Heart calls for truth-telling about the history of Aboriginal and Torres Strait Islander peoples because this is crucial to the ongoing process of healing and reconciliation in Australia. Artists such as Watson use Indigenous creative practices that seek to account for colonial histories of violence and to transform their meaning for Indigenous and non-Indigenous audiences.

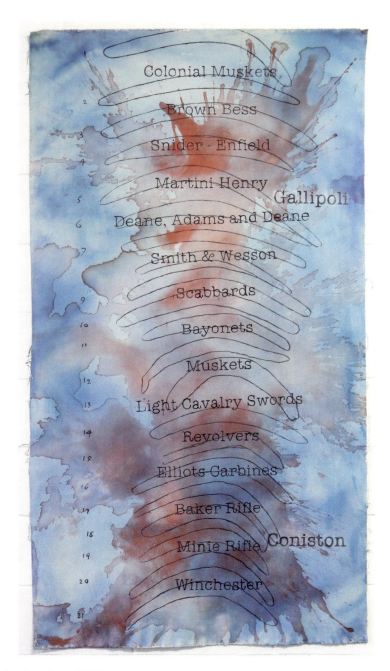

pale slaughter, *2015. Reproduced with kind permission of Judy Watson. Courtesy of Milani Gallery*

MAPPING AND TRUTH-TELLING

Watson's multimedia, research-based artwork *the names of places* (2016–) is part of an ongoing project that maps massacre sites across Australia. A 22-minute video work shows a scrolling list of the names of massacre sites set against an image of Matthew Flinders' map of Australia, 'Terra Australia, or Australia', from his 1801–03 *Investigator* voyage. The video was first exhibited at the Institute of Modern Art in Brisbane in 2016, then in the National Gallery of Australia's *Defying Empire: Third Indigenous triennial* a year later, and it continues to travel widely.[7] A website component of *the names of places* invites viewers to submit their own knowledge and stories of massacres to a database for the public documentation and retrieval of a 'forgotten' history.

In Watson's video artwork, the map of Australia becomes a layered visual record for other knowledge. English-language names drift across the shifting, shaky map background. At times the country seems to slide around under the map; at others, maps of colonial land allotments with their foreign names carve up the country, especially in the Gulf of Carpentaria and northwestern Queensland. This is Waanyi Country, where Watson's mother and grandmother lived.

On the website, often displayed on a touch screen beside the work, individual sites of violence are indicated by fine concentric black circles: a stylised version of the traditional mark for a campsite, a fireplace or a water source. From a Western perspective, they also look like target symbols. When clustered, the dense markings blacken particular colonial frontiers, especially on the eastern coastline and the Gulf of Carpentaria. Fine but intense blue dots spread out from individual sites, suggesting the movement of people, the traditional walking tracks of Country and the reverberations that flowed from each massacre. These also invoke the contested control of water on the colonial frontier.

Clicking on the site marker brings up information about the date and district of the massacre and brief information about the event. Original documentary sources in nineteenth-century handwriting pop up on the left-hand side of the screen if there is an archival document that refers specifically to the site. Images of Indigenous artefacts float across the map, stamping the document with different knowledges and different histories of occupation. As this chapter's epigraph from Gija artist Queenie McKenzie makes clear, Indigenous 'names for every place' tie together land, water and knowledge as complex cultural entities.[8] They also link artists working in traditional and contemporary styles.

Watson wants viewers of her video 'to be aware that any map is a slippery, contested artefact, and also to have a bodily response to the work'.[9] Audiences are presented with a rich portfolio of visual evidence that is both geographic and textual and draws on colonial and Indigenous knowledges. Across the surface of the digital map, the distressed patina of aged paper is marked with Watson's characteristic washes of pigment. Indigenous fibre crafts – which also resemble DNA spirals – make pale X-ray prints across land and sea. The animated tracery of artefacts suggests an enduring Indigenous presence that both precedes and transcends the colonial map. These different ways of knowing the land layer meaning and geography.

Other related works are usually installed alongside *the names of places*. *Pale slaughter* (Watson, 2015), for example, has exquisite layered washes – key elements of Watson's visual style that both reveal her print-making training and evoke the water and landscape of her traditional Country. In *pale slaughter* a numbered list in a hard typographic font marks the forms of military technology brought by the British Empire to colonial frontiers such as her family's Waanyi Country. The list is superimposed over shapes that suggest boomerangs and bodily scarification, and a wash of red against the blue background evokes the blood that accompanied colonial expansion.[10]

Partway through *the names of places*, an image of *pale slaughter* floats across the screen, briefly replacing the map. Collectively, these artworks juxtapose colonial documents, violence and cultural artefacts to produce a 'blood language' that is mapped onto place.[11] The audience experiences *the names of places* in a highly aestheticised yet powerfully political installation: neither the digital nor the print form allows the viewer to escape the consequences of colonial violence on Indigenous peoples and lands, and it is this that produces the intended 'bodily experience'.

The visual language of Watson's work creates a strong emotional effect. She describes showing the work to family members, who responded despairingly, 'Where *wasn't* there a massacre?'[12] When I screened the *names of places* video following a talk by the artist, audience members were mesmerised: they took seriously the process of witnessing the full 22-minute work as an aesthetic, historical and political immersion in complex knowledge.[13]

ART AND MASSACRES

Watson's map mirrors Indigenous practices in which place, story, law, philosophy, society and art form multilayered images of Country, in diverse art materials that might include sand, bark, cardboard, canvas and now the digital realm.[14] There is an established tradition of representing massacre sites in Indigenous art. The 2002–03 exhibition *Blood on the Spinifex*, held at the Ian Potter Museum of Art, University of Melbourne, and discussed by Rachel Burgess in this volume, demonstrated the strength of this tradition, with paintings by acclaimed Gija artists from the northeastern Kimberly region, including Paddy Bedford, Phyllis Thomas and Rusty Peters, part of the collective Jirrawun Arts.[15]

Blood on the Spinifex was a direct response to the Australian 'history wars' of the 2000s. Its artistic representations drew on oral history to counter conservative efforts to sanitise colonial history by diminishing Indigenous death and suffering under frontier conditions. Curator Tony Oliver put forward the exhibition as a direct rebuttal of Keith Windschuttle's book *The Fabrication of Aboriginal History* (2002), insisting that remote community artists had found new ways to tell their local stories: 'How is somebody who has an oral history meant to be involved in this debate? It's basically a European-dominated paradigm that these people haven't been able to enter … So they entered this debate through their own culture, through painting.'[16] The works also invoke modernist aesthetics and embody the Gija concept of 'Two-Way', which, Quentin Sprague argues:

> refers to the bringing together of two previously separate worlds … [but also] evokes the bringing together of settler-Australian, or settler-colonial, ways, with Aboriginal ways … The kind of ideal it expresses has often manifested in Australia as two worlds with largely antagonistic histories trying to find a means to move forward as one.[17]

These artists drew upon renowned northeastern Kimberley work related to Indigenous histories of massacres.

Queenie McKenzie's painting *Mistake Creek Massacre* (1997) epitomises the Australian controversies surrounding Indigenous art, violence and history. McKenzie's work responded to her friend and leading Kimberley artist, Rover Thomas. Thomas's *The Camp at Mistake Creek* (1980) was one of his series of works about local massacre sites. This knowledge circulated orally and locally, and seemingly without controversy. In 2001, Governor-General Sir William Deane acknowledged the suffering Gija people experienced because of the 1915 Mistake Creek massacre and related events. Windschuttle challenged the Indigenous account – he claimed the deaths of eight Gija people had been caused by Aboriginal perpetrators rather than police and settlers – and strongly criticised Deane in the media and also in the opening section of his widely publicised book.[18]

When the National Museum of Australia purchased McKenzie's *Mistake Creek Massacre* in 2005, the painting became caught up in debates about history. The museum was highly politicised during this period: Prime Minister John Howard was critical of its display of revisionist history, and political appointments were made to the museum council. McKenzie's painting was not displayed and council members ensured it was not entered in the National Historical Collection, which elevates the status of a work and ensures its longevity in the collection. According to museum director Craddock Morton, 'the council was of the view that this painting didn't satisfy that sort of historical factuality condition'.[19]

The museum finally exhibited *Mistake Creek Massacre* in July 2020 in the exhibition *Talking Blak to History*, suggesting a shift had taken place in the national narrative, at least in the cultural sector.[20] Head of the museum's Indigenous Knowledges Centre, Margo Neale, described the exhibition as amplifying Indigenous voices: '*Talking Blak to History* is a way of reclaiming our experiences in the story of Australian history and we're doing it in our own voices … You'll see and hear us through our objects, our art and our possessions. In other words, we're speaking through these things.'[21]

Oral history, artefacts and archival objects are resonant sources used by artists depicting colonial violence. They assist in reclaiming an Indigenous voice in history and countering the denial of Indigenous suffering under colonialism. These techniques link remote artists such as McKenzie and Thomas with new generations of often urban-based Indigenous artists.[22]

ARCHIVES, ARTEFACTS AND AFTERMATHS

Watson describes her practice as both archival and artistic: 'I often deal with concealed histories, revealing them and removing the whitewash.'[23] Art historian Lisa Chandler links Watson with several contemporary Indigenous artists who engage with museums and archival objects to reconnect with their appropriated cultural heritage and to critique colonial ideologies.[24] Like Watson, Vernon Ah Kee, Julie Gough, Fiona Foley and Brook Andrew (among others) use archives, photographs and Indigenous artefacts to inform their work.[25] Such artists transform cultural loss through artistic repatriation.[26] For example, Watson sketched Indigenous cultural objects she found in British collections that carried traces of past museum classification systems.²⁷ The titles of the subsequent etchings made clear her reclamation of intimate artefacts: *our bones in your collections* (1997); *our hair in your collections* (1997); *our skin in your collections* (1997). Watson describes the Indigenous presence she found in Waanyi objects far from Country and community:

> [They] have been rolled across the skin, so that they've taken those body oils with them. Then they have been worn against the skin so it's like that person is there … There they were in this very bland … space and yet they shimmered with life … almost like the energy of the artisan, the wearer, everybody else was in the room with me.²⁸

The creative transformation of these objects through art is personal and political. In converting her sketches of Waanyi artefacts to the 'in your collections' artworks, Watson placed them under a layer of fine paper 'because I was reticent about exposing them as baldly as my drawings. The chine collé is like a skin, and sets them back a bit, so they are not able to be too obviously "feasted upon" by the viewer.'²⁹ She later used the etchings in *museum piece* (2006) for the Musée du quai Branly in Paris. Watson's artefact sketches were etched into the museum's exterior glass: literal traces of Indigenous presence that were both visible and transparent.

Watson's subtle approach seeks to educate non-Indigenous audiences about appropriate cultural sensitivity: what can and cannot be explicitly seen and known. She engages with her subject matter not by 'replication, possession, or literal translation but rather [as] visual transformations influenced by her own sensibility, history and cultural understanding'.³⁰ Combining transformed artefacts and realist techniques into artistic forms is critical to Watson's memorialisation of Indigenous history. By incorporating cultural objects into *the names of places*, she imbues the map with rich and layered Indigenous knowledge.

Watson's *the names of places* and Ryan's map, *Colonial Frontier Massacres*, produce quite different effects, even though they share some historical sources and methods.³¹ The documentary function of historical mapping is crucial to Ryan's work. The map's imperative is to correct the deliberate obfuscation of colonial records during the history wars, which demands strong evidence of consistent colonial practices of violence that are verifiable and reproducible. In display, too, the approach is different. Ryan's map uses sophisticated spatial technologies for a hyper-realist visual display: viewers literally zoom in on an identified massacre site to view a high-resolution GIS (geographic information system) map produced by satellite imagery. It became apparent to Ryan's team, however, that revealing the exact locations to the general public could be disrespectful of local Indigenous knowledge of the sites. The specific locations were then 'purposefully … made imprecise' by rounding up the mapping algorithm in order to 'protect the sites from desecration, and [out of] respect for the wishes of Aboriginal communities to observe the site as a place of mourning'.[32]

Precise documentation is important but less visually central in Watson's map. Instead, her focus is on 'decolonising the map', first by decentring European names for existing geographical features; and second by using a First Nations perspective to record major historical events on the frontier and their ongoing aftermath.[33] Like the exhibition *Blood on the Spinifex*, Watson's project brings together oral histories and Indigenous creative practices to create new ways for Indigenous knowledge to speak to the public about difficult histories through art.

Other artworks that thicken traces of Indigenous presence and transform colonial artefacts are often displayed alongside Watson's *the names of places*. Family stories related by Watson's great-great-grandmother about massacres witnessed by her mother, Rosie, at Lawn Hill Station feature as part of her installation *salt in the wound* (2008). Wax sculptures of ears, fixed on walls as part of the larger installation piece, reference travellers' accounts of gruesome physical trophies collected by pastoralists and the Native Police.[34] This work makes interpersonal and gendered violence explicit. When installed alongside *the names of men* (2017) and *the names of places*, *salt in the wound* shows audiences that Watson is reflecting on a specific history of violence carried out by named individuals in familiar places, which must be witnessed as part of a truth-telling process.

The shock evoked by these graphic representations is measured by Watson's poetic reflection on the politics of listening that accompanies the artwork:

> I listen and hear those words
> a hundred years away
> that is my Grandmother's
> Mother's Country
> It seeps down through blood
> and memory
> and soaks
> into the ground.[35]

Judy Watson, salt in the wound, *2004.*
Reproduced with kind permission of Judy Watson. Courtesy of Milani Gallery

These sculptural elements are not merely colonial trophies or grotesque reminders of violence. They also connect Watson to distressing histories passed down by the women in her family.

Non-Indigenous audiences can also listen. They can engage with renderings of the violent colonial past through maps that use empirical approaches, like Ryan's map, and affective ones, such as Watson's art. For these audiences, and for Indigenous communities, Watson's artwork forms a compelling, if confronting, form of truth-telling and remapping of Country and history because it stages the intimate relationship between art and history, beauty and violence, documentary and interpretive modes, and colonial and Indigenous sources. Sprague suggests the 'idea that art might somehow reconcile the colonial inheritance of a nation is, of course, as admirable as it is impossible', yet this is the promise that Watson's dynamic and multilayered work allows audiences to explore through its immersive, experiential style.[36]

Chapter 19

ART, MEMORY AND THE AFTERMATHS OF IMPERIAL VIOLENCE

THE LIFE AND DEATH OF TE MARO

Tony Ballantyne

The acts of violence that underwrote the fundamentally unequal cultural order of empires have left an uneven imprint in art and visual culture.[1] It is true that abolitionists and humanitarians were adept at using visual culture to challenge slavery and to document Indigenous suffering, but such images were countercultural forces and generally had more purchase through the circulation of popular print culture than in high art.

Conversely, war – at least, in structured forms of ordered combat where European armies clashed with opposing forces of rival states and Indigenous kingdoms – did figure as significant material for the artists of empire. But those routine yet less ordered forms of imperial violence – kidnapping, hostage-taking, sexual violence, frontier raids, murders and reprisal killings – have left little or no imprint on the visual archives of empire.

The art of empire also demonstrated an uncanny ability to displace responsibility for killings. Take, for example, the arrival of HMS *Dolphin* in Tahiti in June 1767, a moment that was central in framing European perceptions of the wider Pacific and in enacting British territorial ambitions in the region. John Hawkesworth's influential 1773 compilation of Pacific voyage narratives featured an engraving showing the *Dolphin* under attack from Tahitians, a visual representation that emphasised Indigenous hostility and violence rather than imperial intrusion or the protracted use of violence by the British in response.[2] This image was repeatedly reproduced and recycled in European print culture over the ensuing decades and was later transformed into a painted screen, which is now held in the collection of the Australian Maritime Museum.[3] The willingness of officers of the *Dolphin* to deploy terror as a strategy not only shaped the strategies that Tahitians subsequently adopted in engaging with Europeans, but also underwrote the emergence of the mythic Tahiti of the European imagination.[4]

While art could serve as a powerful medium for imperial aspirations and ideologies, globally it also served as a powerful tool for anticolonial nationalists and Indigenous critics of empire. That has been the case within New Zealand, where the visual arts have been an important instrument for Māori arguments for mana motuhake (self-determination) and tino rangatiratanga (sovereignty). More generally still, over the last three decades empire-building and colonialism have become increasingly prominent preoccupations for New Zealand artists. They have turned to the past to pose questions about the nature of historical experience, to explore the connections between the brutality of empire and contemporary inequalities, and to think about how various aesthetic traditions are implicated in, or are able to break from, the cultural freight of colonialism. Curator Gaelen Macdonald, for example, has suggested that works that grapple with past historical actors, including those connected with Cook's voyages, have been important conduits for posing questions about the 'durability, diversity and on-going relevance of the portrait in New Zealand'.[5]

My focus in this chapter is an individual, Te Maro of Ngāti Rākai, a significant kin-group from Tūranganui-a-Kiwa (modern Gisborne) that would later become Ngāti Oneone. Te Maro was a high-ranking man, a skilled gardener and keeper of natural knowledge, and a kaitiaki (guardian) of the local environment. He was among a group of four men who emerged from the bush at the foot of the sacred maunga (mountain) Tītīrangi after seeing James Cook and his party of officers and sailors land at Tūranga in early October 1769. The *Endeavour*'s pinnace sat at the mouth of the Tūranganui River while Cook and his men attempted to engage with another group of locals on the south side of the river. According to Cook, the coxswain of the pinnace fired two warning shots with his musket over the heads of the four Ngāti Rākai men as they approached the yawl that had carried Cook and his colleagues across the river. When the second shot had no effect, the coxswain shot and killed Te Maro, whose three companions moved his body before retreating into the bush, perhaps ahead of the approach of Cook and his officers, who moved swiftly once they heard shots. Joseph Banks and the ship's surgeon Monkhouse studied Te Maro closely, treating him like an ethnographic specimen, and Monkhouse recorded that nails and beads were placed on Te Maro's body.[6]

The killing of Te Maro initiated a sequence of collisions with local peoples. The following day, the Rongowhakaata rangatira (chief) Te Rākau was shot after Cook ordered his men to open fire when Te Rākau seized the sword of Charles Green, the astronomer. Monkhouse and Banks fired upon Te Rākau, killing him, and Cook's party subsequently fired again, wounding at least three of Te Rākau's companions. In the wake of this incident, Cook determined that it would be a good strategy 'to surprise some of the natives and take them on board and by good treatment and presents endeavour to gain their friendship': in other words, use kidnapping and hostage-taking to demonstrate his positive intentions.[7] Not surprisingly, this strategy only produced more violence, as Cook ordered his men to fire over the heads of the crews of two waka (canoes) who were returning from fishing, after they tried to flee from the Europeans. When the crew of one waka resisted, Cook felt 'obliged' to shoot them, killing 'two or three' and wounding another, although Monkhouse noted that two were wounded and drowned and two wounded but escaped, and Banks suggested that all four were killed.[8] Three young men were taken onboard and were initially terrified; Banks noted that they were 'expecting no doubt instant death'.[9] These youths were Te Haurangi, Ikirangi and Marukauiti of Rongowhakaata. They were set ashore the following day prior to the *Endeavour*'s departure from Tūranganui-a-Kiwa, which Cook named 'Poverty Bay' because 'it afforded us no one thing we wanted'.[10]

These violence-studded cross-cultural collisions were long ignored by civic authorities and the Pākehā descendants of colonists in the region. Although the identities of Te Maro, Te Rākau, Te Haurangi, Ikirangi and Marukauiti were recorded and recalled by local historians in the late nineteenth century and early decades of the twentieth, as well as within the oral narratives of hapū (subtribes) and iwi (tribes) of the region, with time they were increasingly rendered marginal in popular narratives that celebrated the arrival of Cook and the *Endeavour*. By 1969, when the national bicentennial had its key set-piece celebrations with a 'Cook Week' in Tūranga/Gisborne, the victims of European violence had been rendered invisible in public history. The focus was firmly on Cook and on celebrating Gisborne as the first landing site of Europeans in New Zealand and its resulting status as a foundational site in national history.

But Te Maro, Te Rākau, Te Haurangi, Ikirangi and Marukauiti were never forgotten by hapū and iwi. In the last few decades there has been a broad shift within New Zealand, as the myth of the nation's supposedly superior race relations has been punctured and two generations of historical work has emphasised the violence, real and symbolic, that was deeply embedded in empire-building and colonialism. As Māori have increasingly challenged the celebration of Cook, public debate in Tūranga/Gisborne has been fraught and deeply contentious. Many local Māori see any commemoration of Cook and the *Endeavour* as re-enacting and celebrating a past that is deeply painful and directly implicated in the deprivation and marginalisation that many in their communities feel today.

Artist, historian and community leader Nick Tūpara of Ngāti Oneone has been a key player in these debates over public memory for the past decade. He saw the government-sponsored Tuia 250 programme as an opportunity to seek resources and cultural space to help tell Ngāti Oneone stories and ensure that the mana (status, authority) of his ancestors and kin was recognised locally.

Originally launched as 'Encounters 250', the Tuia programme evolved in response to numerous Māori critiques as well as the gradual and cautious engagement from a number of key iwi, who believed they could turn the initiative to serve their own ends. Tūpara explained that Tuia 250 was an opportunity to move the focus away from Cook, a project of vital important in Tūranga/Gisborne:

> A big part of these commemorations is an opportunity for us to articulate our place and find new strength to live in a Cook town … I come to celebrate Te Maro and that ancestor is my sole purpose for being involved in anything this year. And I'm only involved to the extent that I can successfully assist in putting our tipuna [ancestors] on our maunga.[11]

Living in the aftermath of empire, Tūpara did not want the collision with Europeans to define Te Maro's life and sought to avoid reducing his identity to that of a victim of British violence:

> The story of Te Maro gets a bit lost in the story of the last two seconds of his life, but he was a grower of food and feeder of people; he read the stars and the sun and the wind and advised people about what they needed to do to keep their families fed and well, and we wanted to tell that story. We have an understanding of a Māori chap killed by Cook's crew – now he has a name, a character and a story we can take some lessons from in terms of growing food and keeping people's well-being strong.[12]

Tūpara played a pivotal role in installing Te Maro at the centre of public memory in contemporary Tūranga/Gisborne. First, he led the redevelopment of Puhi Kai Iti/Cook Landing National Historic Reserve, a location that had marked Cook's arrival since a large obelisk was erected to Cook's memory in 1906. That

Sculpture of Te Maro by Nick Tūpara (Ngāti Oneone), Ruatanuika lookout, Tūranga/Gisborne. Photograph by Julia Rae. Reproduced with kind permission of Julia Rae

development itself was part of the marginalisation of Ngāti Oneone and its mana over the territory of the northern bank of the river and Tītīrangi. Over time, the river was re-routed and land reclaimed to support the development of the town's port, and key Ngāti Oneone sites were lost. The historic reserve was also increasingly hemmed in by a semi-industrial no-man's land. The sea now seems distant; a clutter of warehouses and vast piles of logs completely cut the site off from the water.

In 2019 the site was significantly redeveloped. Funding for this was provided though government bodies, and Ngāti Oneone played a pivotal role in the project. It offered a radical recontextualisation of the Cook memorial, so that the site now also acknowledges the landing of the waka *Te Ikaroa-a-Rauru* and its navigator and tohunga (skilled expert) Māia at Tawararo (Kaiti Beach). The waka is memorialised in a striking statue in the form of a steel frieze of *Te Ikaroa*, framed by representations of the other waka that connect Te Ika a Māui (the North Island of New Zealand) to the Pacific. The statue also marks the whare wānanga (house of learning) Puhi Kai Iti, established by Māia, a centre that helped transplant Pacific knowledge to a new location.[13]

Tūpara's design makes visible the long history of Māori settlement in the region and foregrounds a common thread of botanical knowledge that long predated the arrival of Cook's naturalist, Banks. *Te Ikaroa-a-Rauru* carried hue (gourd) seeds and traditional knowledge of gardening, and these are celebrated in the form of large sculptures on the western side of the redeveloped site. Physically, the site looks radically different, with a sequence of striking steel tukutuku panels woven together using the kaokao pattern, which gesture towards the importance of cooperation.[14]

A large sculpted installation was also erected featuring 23 pou (columns), nine of which are topped by hoe, or paddle-shaped forms, inlaid with tiki-figures – these commemorate the nine tangata whenua (people of the land) who were shot during those initial collisions with the crew of the *Endeavour*. Eight of these tiki are coloured a fiery orange-red, referring to musket-fire, while the ninth is an intense blue, referring to the trade beads left on the body of Te Maro by the British. The violence of empire and the pain and suffering it caused were now brought into dialogue with the 1906 obelisk, a marker of imperial memory.

For Tūpara, a flat stone platform in the centre of the redevelopment is pivotal to the whole redevelopment: this was designed for sitting upon and invites people to pause, reflect, come together and converse as they process the meaning of the forms that surround them and make sense of the juxtaposition of the new Māori elements and the stark imperial obelisk.

Tūpara led the development of the new Ruatanuika lookout on Tītīrangi, Kaiti Hill. Central here was a striking sculpture of Te Maro. Some 10 metres high, this finely worked nine-tonne steel disc makes Te Maro and the mana of Ngāti Oneone clearly visible across the landscape of Tūranga/Gisborne. It is a potent reminder of the weight of cultures and histories that long antedated the arrival of the *Endeavour*. This image of Te Maro rematerialises the mātauranga (knowledge) of Ngāti Oneone. The circular shape of Tūpara's work invokes seasonality and the cycles of time, the rhythms of nature that Te Maro gained a deep understanding of through the wānanga Puhi Kai Iti. Te Maro himself occupies the centre of the disc, grasping a hue, which gestures towards the utility of his knowledge and the importance of gardening in te ao Māori (the Māori world). He is surrounded by water and plant motifs, which not only allude to the specificity of the site, but also invoke the tight bonds that lace humans into the natural world within Māori knowledge traditions.¹⁵ This sculpture is an important part of the restoration of Tītīrangi and the local recognition of Ngāti Oneone's mana, and returns their presence to a landscape where colonisation and the drive for regional development had long rendered them marginal in the public imagination.

Leading Pacific New Zealand artist Michel Tuffery has also been drawn to Te Maro. In a striking dual portrait, *Te Maro and Solander, Two Intellectuals from Opposite Sides of the World, 1769* (2019), Tuffery has defined Te Maro not through his death but through his capacity, knowledge and social standing, identifying him as an 'intellectual'. Te Maro here is presented as an equal of Daniel Solander, the gifted botanist who trained at Uppsala University and became one of the so-called apostles of the great Swedish naturalist and classifier Carl Linnaeus. After returning from the Pacific to Britain, Solander produced the first detailed written study of New Zealand botany, the unpublished 'Primitiae Florae Novae Zelandiae', and served as Keeper of the Natural History Department of the British Museum.

Here Te Maro is Solander's peer. Tuffery himself notes Te Maro 'was a learned man, trained in the whare wānanga' Puhi Kai Iti and 'an expert in reading nature and a master producer of cultivated foods for his people'. Te Maro would have been an expert in the whakapapa (genealogy) of plants and the natural world, a knowledge system that also offered a powerful form of classification that traced the relationship between living things. This portrait suggests a kind of intellectual and cultural equivalence, but also to the opportunities lost because of imperial violence, which closed off the possibilities of constructive cross-cultural engagement in Tūranganui-a-Kiwa. Tuffery has been consistently interested in exploring the significance and aftermath of Cook's Pacific voyages through an aesthetic and cultural framework that is deeply anchored within the region; the figure of Te Maro enables him to underscore the richness and sophistication of Pacific knowledge traditions.

Nick Tūpara was Tuffery's model for his portrait of Te Maro, and Tūpara also played his Ngāti Oneone tipuna in Lala Rolls' rich documentary, *Tupaia's Endeavour* (2017, 2020). This offers a Pacific retelling of the *Endeavour* voyage, placing Tupaia, the 'arioi, artist, navigator, and diplomat from Raiātea', at the centre of the story. Although *Tupaia's Endeavour* does feature a re-enactment of the killing of Te Maro, it also includes extensive framing shots of the production of the scene, underlining the persistence of Ngāti Oneone as a people and allowing Tūpara to emphasise Te Maro's importance, his knowledge and mana.

AFTERMATHS

Michel Tuffery, Te Maro and Solander, Two Intellectuals from Opposite Sides of the World, 1769, *2019. Reproduced with kind permission of Michel Tuffery MNZM*

Nick Tūpara has wryly observed that whenever filmmakers want to make a documentary about Cook, they want to kill Te Maro again. Invariably, Tūpara or one of his kin takes on the role of Te Maro for the redramatisation of his death – a death which is frequently given meaning not because of Te Maro's own significance but because of his place in the story of Cook. While recalling, remembering and recognising the violence of empire is crucial, the history of Indigenous communities must not be reduced to the history of actions in the face of imperial intrusion, where the arrival of Europeans functions as what

Greg Dening called a 'zero-point', the defining historical moment that marks an irrevocable rupture.[16]

Tuffery and Tūpara seek to shift the ground of memory, recalling Te Maro for his capacity, for his place within a cultural and intellectual lineage, for the importance he had for his people. This framing recognises the importance of whakapapa: Te Maro is remembered in relation to his ancestors, especially those key knowledge-bearers who shaped the intellectual traditions he was heir to; he is remembered as a key leader of his people; he is remembered as a key source of knowledge.

In the aftermath of empire, however, these acts of memory are intensely political. Remembering Te Maro challenges longstanding narratives in Tūranga/Gisborne that define the history of the region and the history of 1769 primarily through the connection to Cook, traditions that have meant that many see it as what Tūpara calls a 'Cook town'. Tūpara's striking Te Maro sculpture at Ruatanuika offers another way of thinking about people and place, and place and history; it makes Te Maro literally visible to the whole community, reasserts his mana, and frames his story within traditional Māori knowledge. It is a potent statement about the power of cultural memory in the aftermath of empire, refusing to reduce the meaning of a life to a killing at the hands of incoming Europeans.

Chapter 20

TREATY-MAKER ON TRIAL
CONTESTING THE BATMAN MONUMENTS

Penelope Edmonds

Monuments are the telling of history made public. In recent years there has been a rush of protest and media debate, such as that seen in the #RhodesMustFall and #BlackLivesMatter movements, which highlight the problematic nature of public monuments that celebrate empire. Across the world protestors have toppled the bronze statues of men of empire in defiance of histories that celebrate or tacitly condone histories of slavery, Indigenous dispossession and colonialism. In Melbourne, sculptures and monuments to John Batman – widely lauded as the founder of Melbourne and known as the 'treaty-maker' with Kulin Aboriginal peoples – have been under similar scrutiny. After sustained public protest, along with threats to pull the statue down, the bronze figure of Batman was removed from the streets of Melbourne. Yet such wholesale removal erases along with it the possibility of any story to be told at all, or for examination of the violent realities of the colonial encounter in the southern colonies of Australia.

Other forms of protest allow for greater public engagement with historical narratives. I offer the example of a public performance that took place in 1991, in which Indigenous activists did not pull the figure of Batman down but sought to make him accountable to history and to Kulin Aboriginal peoples by putting his statue on trial, in a form of truth-telling and dynamic verbatim theatre. This Indigenous-led activist performance contested the entrenched settler myth of the 'great founder' to draw attention to the history of white settlement and violence against Indigenous peoples, and the afterlives of this violence that are with us today.

AFTERMATHS

Colonists like Batman were not lone pioneers, as depicted in memorial statues and other monuments. Batman travelled to Port Phillip with over 30 convicts and servants, some of whom were Aboriginal. He made a home for himself on Kulin Aboriginal lands with his wife, Eliza, and their children. Rather than pulling colonial monuments down, we might re-story them in ways that account for the tense and proximate relationships between settlers and Indigenous peoples on the colonial frontier.

BATMAN: THE MAN, THE MYTH

In 2017 just weeks after the widespread and violent toppling of Confederate sculptures in the United States, which, for many protestors, stood as monuments that served to condone or validate slavery, well-known Australian artist Ben Quilty commented:

> John Batman's sculpture stands proudly in a Melbourne carpark. My dad offered to help me pull it down this coming Australia Day … Changing the inscription to 'mass murderer' might slightly appease my sense of justice … This is Australia's [C]onfederate sculpture.[1]

John Batman is now a thoroughly contested figure. In the nineteenth and early twentieth centuries, sculptures and monuments, roads, parks and an electorate were named after Batman, the widely lauded founder of Melbourne. At one time it was proposed that what is now Melbourne be named 'Batmania' in his honour.

Batman was an Overstraiter from Tasmania (Van Diemen's Land), who, in 1835, crossed the Bass Strait to take up Indigenous Kulin lands on the southern shores of the mainland at Port Phillip. He led the entrepreneurial Port Phillip Association and sought to make a treaty with the ngurungaeta (chiefs or headmen) of the Kulin nation for over 600,000 acres (242,811ha) of land.[2] The Batman treaty with Kulin leaders was quickly declared null and void by Governor Richard Bourke to ensure the British Crown's complete claim over all land.

In 1935, on Melbourne's centenary, Batman was celebrated as the city's 'founding father'. By the late twentieth century, however, he had become a problematic figure: his syphilitic death had been politely glossed over and his dark deeds in Tasmania, as part of the 'Black War', had entered public consciousness and debate. Batman's attempted treaty with Kulin Aboriginal peoples has divided historians, who can't agree whether it was a genuine negotiation or a ruse to claim land. Some argue that he dressed his treaty language up with humanitarian rhetoric to effect a massive land grab and faked the signatures, or marks, of the Kulin chiefs. The inside cover of his original Port Phillip diary appears to show that he had practised writing the signs of Aboriginal Kulin leaders in advance.[3] Some support the case for 'Kulin Aboriginal knowing': that is, for Aboriginal political agency in this important treaty exchange.[4] Others have argued that the Kulin chiefs, who apparently marked the treaty documents with crosses, may have believed they were engaged in a Tanderrum ceremony, in which they gave Batman and his party temporary access to the land.[5] In this view, the Kulin regarded the treaty as a short-term land-use agreement and certainly not as a land sale or a commitment to give over lands in perpetuity.

Yet it is not only the 'Batman treaty' and the question of land rights and stolen lands that is under contestation. More recently there has been growing public awareness that the lands of the Kulin Nation were invaded largely by Europeans from Tasmania, or Overstraiters, and that their techniques of frontier warfare against Aboriginal peoples were part of a well-rehearsed repertoire that was imported with them. Batman had participated in and organised 'roving parties' from his property in Tasmania prior to and during the genocidal war against Aboriginal peoples. He also documented his participation in the Ben Lomond massacre, where at least 17 Aboriginal people died in a dawn attack.[6] Although historians of Tasmania and Victoria had known of his involvement for many decades, there had been little, if any, public acknowledgement of this until the 1990s.

The Batman Bridge near Launceston, Tasmania, has been under recent scrutiny as a monument to Batman. Long-time activist Michael Mansell, chair of the Aboriginal Land Council, commented in 2020 that Batman was 'a horrible man' and that his name should be removed from the bridge.[7] In Melbourne, the full standing sculpture of Batman has vanished from the city streets. In 2017 the Melbourne City Council gave official notice that, due to development in the city centre, the statue had to be removed; it was 'not known whether the statue will be returned to the site once construction is complete'.[8] In the same year, Darebin City Council sought to change the name of 'Batman Park' in consultation with the Wurundjeri Council, and in 2018 Darebin Council and the Greens lobbied successfully to rename the electorate of 'Batman', which was changed to 'Cooper' after Yorta Yorta activist and leader William Cooper.[9]

John Batman statue, Melbourne city, bronze. Photograph by David Keith Jones. Courtesy of Alamy Stock Photo

There is a profound shift taking place in Australia's understanding of its history of undeniable frontier violence, driven by Aboriginal activists and by the tireless work of historians such as Lyndall Ryan and her *Colonial Frontier Massacres* map project.[10] Accordingly, it is time for us to query the role of monuments to men like Batman within the public imagination. Historian Bruce Scates, among others, has argued that rather than removing the statues from our cities, it may be preferable to introduce 'dialogical memorialisation', where 'one view of the past takes issue with another'. Beyond tokenistic addendums to plaques, this approach demands a view of history 'not as some final statement, but [as] a contingent and contested narrative'.[11]

BATMAN ON TRIAL

In 1991 Aboriginal activists Gary Foley and Robbie Thorpe tried John Batman's statue for war crimes.[12] Unlike Ben Quilty's call to pull Batman's statue down, this Indigenous-led activist performance was a form of 'dialogical memorialisation' that was striking for the way it invoked a modern, twentieth-century human rights agenda to bring Batman and the state to account. It was, in every way, a potent and effective protest action.

On 6 October 1991, approximately 80 Koori and non-Aboriginal allies marched from Flinders Park (now Melbourne Park) on Batman Avenue to the Supreme Court of Victoria, in a protest that marked 161 years since Governor Arthur's declaration of war against the Tasmanian Aborigines on 7 October 1830 and the subsequent mobilisation of the 'Black Line'.[13] The Black Line was a military force made up of colonists who were deployed in a line across the settled colonies in Tasmania with the aim of pushing the local Aboriginal people onto the Tasman Peninsula, where they would then be surrounded, captured or killed.[14] The protest connected the two colonies – Van Diemen's Land (Tasmania) and Victoria – by exposing Batman's role in the Black War in Tasmania, where he had sizeable pastoral holdings – a 600-acre (242ha) property called Kingston.[15] The 'founder of Melbourne', wrote march organiser Brendan Condon, had participated in 'the attempted genocide of Tasmanian Aborigines before arriving in the Port Phillip region and continuing to dispossess and destroy Koori peoples' there.[16]

The protestors gathered outside the Supreme Court building where a barrister explained the relevance of the Genocide Convention of 1948 to Australian law and its violations of Indigenous human rights.[17] Koori activist Gary Foley spoke about how the law 'continues to work actively against the interests of Aborigines in their struggles for recognition and social justice'.¹⁸ After Foley had spoken, 'activists climbed the fence at the Supreme Court en masse to serve eviction notices on the building'. Through this action, the activists performed the eviction of the seat of European law from their own lands, making visible the contest of law and sovereignty between Aboriginal owners and newcomer Europeans.

At the statue of John Batman – at that time located 500 metres down the road from the Supreme Court, on Collins Street – Koori activist Robbie Thorpe tore up a copy of Batman's treaty of 1835 before placing the statue of John Batman on trial for war crimes. In this subversive action, the protestors performed the return of Batman's original treaty payment to Kulin peoples of tools, blankets and food, and then charged him with 'theft, trespass, rape and genocide'.¹⁹ The activists hung a sign for each of the crimes about the statue's neck and covered his hands with red tape to signify blood and the suffering he had caused. Condon records that 'as each charge was read, the crowd responded with a guilty verdict', themselves becoming participants and witnesses, or a jury, in the trial.²⁰ This dramatic anticolonial performance was a participatory event that called for public action. In placing Batman on trial and invoking the Genocide Convention, the protestors forcefully enlivened a modern twentieth-century human rights discourse, thus making Batman accountable to the past and to the present within local and global orders.

After the trial Foley and Thorpe invited non-Indigenous attendees to form their own treaty with Aboriginal people by signing up to 'pay the rent' for their use of Aboriginal land.²¹ 'Paying the rent' was a powerful reminder of stolen land and Indigenous land rights, and also of Indigenous sovereignty. Condon described the memorial protest performance as 'both educational and confrontational' in its attempt to 'reclaim the real history of Melbourne, and to challenge the wall of apathy, indifference and racism that still runs through the Gubbah [non-Indigenous] community in relation to Koori issues and struggle'.²²

THE LIMITS OF MEMORIALISATION

Rather than rehearsing the myth of the 'founding father of Melbourne' or celebrating Batman's heroic and apparently lone crossing from Tasmania to Port Phillip, we might instead aspire to a form of memorialisation that communicates the uncomfortable reality of the Batman family's relationships with Aboriginal people.²³ Lone heroic monuments rarely, if ever, convey the importance of the settler family in establishing or founding their new home while displacing

Aboriginal peoples from their existing lands and families. As white women such as Eliza Batman were making their homes in early Melbourne, Aboriginal women were losing their homes and lands. Part of the project of colonisation involved removing Aboriginal groups from their lands, at times by violent means such as massacres and reorganising family relationships. Often Aboriginal people were brought into European homesteads as domestic and pastoral labourers, leading to both tense and close family entanglements on these 'unhomely' frontiers.

Kingston homestead in Tasmania was situated on Plangermaireener Aboriginal land (the Ben Lomond region).[24] Here, the Batman family had around 30 servants, including convicts and Aboriginal people. This family had taken part in and profited from the 'Black War' between Aboriginal people and settlers in Tasmania (1828–34): their house was a depot and service point in the execution of orchestrated attacks against Aboriginal peoples.[25] Aboriginal boys were taken from massacres and used as labourers in the fields; one was named 'John Batman', and we do not know what became of him. The others were Rolepana, whom the Batmans named Benny or Ben Lomond, and Lurnerminner, who was named Jacky or Jack Allen.[26] The Batmans also worked with and lived alongside the so-called Sydney Natives, a group of around nine men who lived with the family in Tasmania and Port Phillip for well over 10 years. Rolepana and Lurnerminner ran away from Batman not long before he died; they took up work in Melbourne, where Rolepana later died. Lurnerminner went to sea and worked on whaling ships; he later travelled back to Tasmania where he lived at Oyster Cove Aboriginal Station, south of Hobart.[27]

Forced kinships were made and memorialised through the exchange of names. While Rolepana lost his Plangermaireener identity to be christened Benny or 'Ben Lomond', Eliza's seventh daughter was named Pelonemena Frances Darling Batman, after an Aboriginal woman from Ben Lomond, Tasmania, who had been incarcerated at Flinders Island Aboriginal station and placed under the direct guardianship of Commandant Darling there.[28] Pelonemena, or Pellenominer/Pellonymyna (the spelling varied), later died at Oyster Cove Aboriginal Station, south of Hobart. The transference of her name to Eliza's seventh daughter appears as a reciprocal, if disquieting, gesture to the Plangermaireener people, whose lands the Batmans had usurped. Perhaps they knew Pelonemena. This exchange of names is an unsettling accompaniment to the small Aboriginal boy who was christened 'John Batman'.

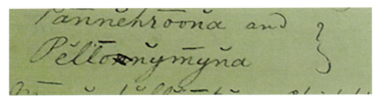

'Pellonymyna', also known as Pelonemena, or Pellenominer, as recorded in George Washington Walker's unpublished diary, Flinders Island, 1832.

Courtesy of Mitchell Library, State Library of NSW, Sydney

Bronze memorials that pay tribute to European 'founders' or settlers celebrate entrenched and official stories of colonisation and settler triumph, but they also tell us that this is all there *is* to be known. In this way, they reveal the limits of official public narratives, which obscure both violence and relationships across cultures and their close entanglements. In Melbourne, there might be memorials built to Rolepana or Ben Lomond and to Lurnerminner or Jack Allen, the young men who lived and travelled with the Batmans. This would offer a way to recount and memorialise their lives as survivors and Overstraiters who moved between Indigenous and European worlds and across colonies as voyagers.

In Tasmania, a monument to the Plangermaireener woman Pelonemena in the landscape would offer a powerful form of memorialisation. The Batman Bridge in Tasmania could be renamed the Pelonemena Bridge in honour of this Aboriginal woman and mother and would mark the violent and intimate entwined histories of Aboriginal people and settlers on the Australian frontier. In these ways, we might both create new memorials and re-story others in the name of truth-telling and public history.

Chapter 21

REWI'S LAST STAND AND DECOLONISING WAR HISTORY

Caitlin Lynch and Sian Smith

In late March 1864, British soldiers opened fire on a pā (fortified village) defended by Ngāti Maniapoto, Ngāti Raukawa, Ngāi Tūhoe, Tūwharetoa and Rongowhakaata. The colonial forces injured or killed as many as 200 defenders and the land was (and remains) confiscated by the Crown.[1] The battle of Ōrākau is simultaneously one of the most well-known and misunderstood events of the New Zealand Wars, due in part to the influence of *Rewi's Last Stand*.[2] The feature film, which was released in 1940, is loosely based on the events at Ōrākau, with an intercultural romance at the centre of its narrative. In 1949 the 112-minute film was cut down to 63 minutes for British television.[3] For several decades it was the most prominent screen representation of the New Zealand Wars and was used widely as an educational resource in schools. The British recut is the only version of the film remaining today. The prominence of *Rewi's Last Stand* and the mystery surrounding what was lost in the recut has fascinated history scholars, many of whom have discussed its significance in New Zealand's nation-building.

As scholars with a mutual passion for historical film, we have been captivated by this taonga and have spent countless hours considering its different interpretive layers.[4] We also feel a responsibility to this history as people whose families have indirectly benefited from the Crown's declaration of war against Māori in the 1860s, particularly in the Waikato. Writing for this collection reflects our mutual goal to contribute meaningfully and respectfully to the scholarship of our violent past. We also hope that by taking readers through different ways of understanding the film, we might shed light on historical narratives of colonial violence in Aotearoa.

In 1940, Pākehā society generally understood *Rewi's Last Stand* as progressive and historically authentic. While *Rewi's Last Stand* shows some empathy for the Māori defenders of Ōrākau, scholars have posed questions about the film's historical inaccuracies – namely, its assimilationist messages, romanticisation of a traumatic war and lack of Pākehā accountability. This chapter reflects on the limitations of colonial narrative and postcolonial critique of *Rewi's Last Stand* and advocates decolonising perspectives on audiovisual taonga.[5]

COLONIAL CONTEXT: A PROGRESSIVE PRODUCTION

In the context of 1940 colonial society, *Rewi's Last Stand* represents an effort to challenge amnesia around the New Zealand Wars. The film was released in the same year as the centenary of the signing of Te Tiriti o Waitangi. At that time, Pākehā recognition and historical knowledge of the New Zealand Wars was largely limited to James Cowan's chronicles, some inconsistently marked battle sites and monuments, and local myths.[6] In instances where the New Zealand Wars could not be forgotten, they were often grossly misrepresented. In *100 Crowded Years* (a film commissioned by the government to mark the centenary), the primary tragedy of the wars is the disruption to Pākehā farming when pioneering settlers are 'driv[en] from their land' by Māori violence.[7] There is no acknowledgment of colonial violence, nor that the settler characters' farm was Māori land in the first place. In comparison, *Rewi's Last Stand* presents a more balanced account of the wars, expressing sympathy for Māori and an admiration for the resilience demonstrated at Ōrākau.

Rewi's Last Stand's comparatively progressive approach to New Zealand Wars history reflects the collaborative nature of its production. Annabel Cooper's recent research reveals that the director, Rudall Hayward, relied heavily on input and support from Māori advisors, including Raureti Te Huia and Te Rongonui Paerata, whose whanaunga (relatives) defended Ōrākau.[8] Hayward and his collaborators filmed close to where the war at Ōrākau took place and at surrounding locations such as Rangiaowhia and Tūrangawaewae marae. This geographic accuracy and community engagement set the film apart from most other New Zealand 'historical' films – including Hayward's 1925 attempt to tell the history of Ōrākau (also titled *Rewi's Last Stand*), which was controversially made in Rotorua with a Te Arawa cast.[9]

In the prologue of Rewi's Last Stand, *an anonymous hand opens the cover of James Cowan's influential colonial narrative.* Film still courtesy of Ngā Taonga Sound & Vision, Wellington

Rewi's Last Stand emphasised the historical authenticity of its location shooting, cast of Ōrākau descendants and input from Cowan. The film's scrolling foreword explains that 'the townspeople [of Te Awamutu] filmed recently these pages from rough-hewn history, re-enacting on the actual locations the parts played by their pioneering forefathers'. The foreword is followed by a shot of a hand opening a history book: Cowan's *The New Zealand Wars: A history of Maori campaigns and the pioneering period*.[10] Promotional posters touted the film as 'a true and amazing epic' from 'New Zealand's storied past'.[11] This emphasis on authenticity challenged Pākehā historical amnesia and disassociation around the wars, casting New Zealand's colonial history and landscape in a new light.[12]

POSTCOLONIAL CRITIQUE: NARRATIVE AND ACCURACY

However, when we look closely at the narrative and representation in *Rewi's Last Stand*, its claim to historical truth starts to crumble.[13] While the film contains 'positive' representations of Māori, tropes of the dusky maiden and the noble savage propagate a romanticised version of 'one nation' assimilation. Meanwhile, Pākehā characters remain faultless and the Waikato War is represented as a display of good-natured chivalry, rather than a fundamentally imperialist venture that brought great trauma and intergenerational disenfranchisement to Te Rohe Pōtae and Kīngitanga Māori. In this critical light, *Rewi's Last Stand* appears more focused on Pākehā nation-building than genuinely addressing colonial history.[14]

Rewi's Last Stand's narrative devices reflect Pākehā desire for a unified New Zealand at the Treaty of Waitangi centenary. Aspects of nineteenth-century Waikato history are adapted to support this agenda. Early in the film, at the mission station in Te Awamutu, John Morgan speaks of the wheat seed as a metaphor for civilisation: 'All that wheat you see over there came from a few handfuls of seed we brought.' While it is true that Māori in the Waikato had developed a highly prosperous agricultural system, the film offers a kind of back-handed compliment, suggesting that the region's prosperity hinged upon the benevolent paternalism of Morgan and his religion-meets-agriculture agenda.[15] *Rewi's Last Stand* borrows from James Cowan's *The Old Frontier* for these narrative devices, suggesting that Cowan's role as Hayward's historical advisor also came with his agenda to affirm the legitimacy of Pākehā identity in Aotearoa.[16]

Cowan's *The Old Frontier* was also Hayward's source for his narrative's central character Ariana, played by Ramai Te Miha. Ariana was born into her maternal Ngāti Maniapoto whānau after her Pākehā father left her pregnant mother. When her mother passed away, Ariana was sent by her grandfather, Te Whatanui, to live with John Morgan at the Te Awamutu Mission station to be educated in a Pākehā system.[17] Although the film's Ariana is based on one of the survivors of Ōrākau with the same name, her narrative largely derives from a colonial fantasy that emphasises her dual heritage.

In *The Old Frontier*, Cowan copied a story about the survivor Ariana from an army chaplain's account, 'Life at Awamutu', published in London's *Fraser's Magazine*.[18] The story provides little insight into who Ariana actually was, instead romanticising her as a 'pretty half-caste girl' and the object of colonial male affection. *Rewi's Last Stand* maintains the chaplain's superficial representation of Ariana, focusing on her divided affection for two leading men rather than her experience of colonial violence at Ōrākau. Drawing from Cowan's version of history, Hayward's narrative compromises historical accuracy for romance.

In postcolonial critiques of *Rewi's Last Stand*, Ariana symbolises a unified nation through both her identity and her romantic affections. Her identity as someone of dual heritage comes to the fore when the film reveals her estranged father is Old Ben, one of the colonial soldiers. Recent scholarship on the film suggests that Ariana is a metaphor for the nation, and that her choice between Bob Beaumont (played by Leo Pilcher) and Tama Te Heu Heu (played by Henare Toka) presents two possibilities for the nation's future.[19] Tama Te Heu Heu is a sort of tragic antihero whose death, some argue, suggests the film had a fatalistic bent toward Māori who did not choose to assimilate to the one-nation paradigm.[20] Bob, on the other hand, represents the intercultural hero whose ability to adapt to te ao Māori while remaining true to his colonial gentility places him in an idealistic light. While he speaks a little te reo Māori and can wield a taiaha (fighting staff), he is ultimately loyal to the colonial cause and fights against the defenders of Ōrākau alongside Old Ben. The war presents Ariana with a choice between her desire to be with Bob and her duty to fight with Tama and her iwi (tribe/people). In a postcolonial analysis, Ariana must choose either to live and embrace colonial assimilation or to remain loyal to her Māori identity and die. In this critical light, Ariana is a symbol of colonial nation-building, and her agency is limited to this romanticised ultimatum.

The battle scene highlights how the film's desire to promote national unity and avoid affronting Pākehā and British audiences overshadows the atrocities committed at Ōrākau and in the wider Waikato War. The film deeply mischaracterises the context, strategy, motivations and aftermath of Ōrākau. One significant example is that the film does not acknowledge how prior events at Rangiriri and Rangiaowhia affected the defenders' decision to refuse to surrender. A few months before Ōrākau, at the battle of Rangiriri, Kīngitanga defenders raised a white flag to negotiate a truce with the British. When the British entered the pā, Kīngitanga released their weapons in good faith – only to be taken prisoner by the British and imprisoned in the hulk of a ship for 10 months.[21] In *Rewi's Last Stand*'s portrayal of the war, British forces raise a white flag to give their opponents the chance to surrender. Rewi Maniapoto, played by Raureti Te Huia, rejects the offer with a version of the famous line: 'Kāore e mau te rongo, ake, ake, ake!' (There will not be peace, never, never, never!) The film presents this response as an act of brave yet ultimately self-martyring stubbornness. In reality, however, knowing that the British forces could not be trusted to honour the code of truce, the defenders made a calculated decision.[22]

The massacre at Rangiaowhia in February 1864 also influenced events at Ōrākau. The Kīngitanga believed the British forces would not target Rangiaowhia as it was an 'agreed place of refuge' for women, children and the elderly.[23] Just over a month before the invasion of Ōrākau, Rangiaowhia was violently attacked. Oral histories tell of the soldiers burning down buildings with people inside and committing acts of murder and sexual violence.[24] The decision to stick together at Ōrākau rather than separate from the men was directly related to the recent violence experienced at Rangiaowhia.

Meanwhile, *Rewi's Last Stand* implies that women and children were accidentally caught up in the violence at Ōrākau, and that their refusal to leave their men was brave yet self-sacrificing. In the film's battle scene, Ariana asks an unnamed defender whether she and Rimi, a young boy, should 'go to the village' to shelter. 'No, it's too late now. Soldiers are coming,' he replies, as he ushers Ariana and Rimi into the trenches. Later in the scene Ahumai Te Paerata, another survivor of the Ōrākau invasion, stands atop the trenches and calls out, 'Ki te mate ngā tāne, me mate anō ngā wāhine me ngā tamariki!' (If the men are to die, the women and children will also). In response, Old Ben sentimentally remarks: 'What do we know of courage?', implying that the soldiers who would go on to kill those women and children were sympathetic and admiring of their resistance. While this representation may seem to cast Ahumai and her fellows in an admirable light, it romanticises the reasons behind their resistance. The film characterises their deaths and injuries as the result of willing self-sacrifice rather than brutal colonial invasion, demonstrating yet another example of how the film's narrative borrows from history to serve its own agenda.

Given all the ways *Rewi's Last Stand* misrepresents colonisation and Ōrākau, should we abandon it as a source of war history information and education? As one of the most visceral and widespread representations of the New Zealand Wars for many decades, perhaps its mythologisation of Ōrākau as a romantic, chivalrous event has done enough damage.[25]

DECOLONISING HISTORICAL FILM CRITIQUE

Although the narrative of *Rewi's Last Stand* does present some serious problems, a singular focus on narrative issues emphasises Pākehā storytelling and minimises the critical role of Māori authorship. Pākehā dominate key positions in cinematic narrative production – for example, as directors, cinematographers and scriptwriters. Even when narrative analysis is critical of Pākehā mythmaking, it still prioritises Pākehā authorship and risks ascribing Māori creativity to Pākehā. Postcolonial critiques, therefore, often continue the cycle of colonial thinking because they focus only on people who are in control of the narrative. This is evident in the way that most critical scholarship on *Rewi's Last Stand* is preoccupied with analysing Hayward's intentions.[26] In *Sleeps Standing: Moetū*, Witi Ihimaera and Hēmi Kelly suggest, 'Ngāti Maniapoto have the primary right to tell the story of Ōrākau. Others think they can tell it; historians trample all over their right, and some of the many accounts are despicable to the memory of the dead.'[27] How might our understanding of the messages and history of *Rewi's Last Stand* change when we listen to the Ngāti Maniapoto voices – such as those of Raureti Te Huia and his ancestors – involved in the film's production?

Te Huia Raureti, Raureti Paiaka and Rewi Maniapoto – father, grandfather and uncle of Raureti Te Huia – led the defence of Ōrākau against its colonial invaders.[28] Te Huia Raureti passed his memory of the battle on to his son who, in turn, gave the written account to Cowan as a key source for his Ōrākau narrative.[29] Although the film presents Cowan's voice as the historical authority (with the history book bearing his name in the prologue), Te Huia Raureti and other survivors who informed Cowan hold the primary authority on historical truth about the events at Ōrākau. The memory of Te Huia Raureti also comes through in his son's performance as Rewi Maniapoto. Raureti Te Huia prefers his father's wording of the famous phrase of resistance, 'kāore e mau te rongo', rather than the better-known 'ka whawhai tonu mātou'.[30] By speaking his father's words, Raureti Te Huia actively centres Ngāti Maniapoto experiences of the war in his performance.[31] This scene exemplifies the Māori creative and historical agency in *Rewi's Last Stand*.

This chapter's argument for a decolonising analysis is largely influenced by Ramai Te Miha Hayward's discussion of her involvement in the film. Te Miha Hayward (Ngāti Kahungunu, Ngāi Tahu) performed as the lead and collaborated with Rudall Hayward on post-production editing. She was attracted to performing in the film by the opportunity to sing on screen, but her waiata (songs), one of which featured in a scene where Ariana sings to children in the trenches at Ōrākau, were cut in the British edit.[32] It is possible that this lost scene may have expressed the sensitivity, fear of colonial violence and memory of Rangiaowhia not present in the British cut of the battle. Hayward found watching the recut process too difficult, but Te Miha Hayward stayed on as witness while the film was edited to appease British audiences. In a 1994 radio interview she recalled, 'I saw all the bits that were cut out … Rudall couldn't bear to see it cut. He just couldn't bear it.'[33] Later she worked tirelessly to have the film preserved and shared through the Hayward Historical Film Trust. Te Miha Hayward's care for *Rewi's Last Stand* throughout the twentieth century affirms its status as a taonga, and its continued value and relevance.

It seems Te Miha Hayward did not want the narrative inaccuracies of *Rewi's Last Stand* to overshadow the film's potential to engage audiences with history. Instead, she wanted the film to be shown with educational resources explaining why the history it portrayed was wrong. In the radio interview she corrected some of the film's mistakes, such as that Governor Grey was deliberately seeking to acquire land in the Waikato, and that Ariana 'didn't die as the film seemed to indicate; she lived'.[34] While the film's narrative might try to restrict Ariana to a romantic device, if we take heed of Te Miha Hayward's perspective, her character reminds audiences of the real Ariana, her resistance, and her survival.

To suggest that the problems with the film's narrative discredit its importance undermines the work of Māori in it, such as Te Huia and Te Miha Hayward, and the significance of the war itself. The contributions of Māori collaborators, including the uncredited descendants and performers, are critical to the story of Ōrākau being told from Māori perspectives, even though they are presented in a colonial narrative. Te Miha Hayward described the descendants who performed in *Rewi's Last Stand* as artists, not actors, reliving the battle of their ancestors.[35] Perhaps acting implies pretence, whereas artists channel their creative force to express their realities.

Ultimately, no matter what the narrative says, the film records Māori performances imbued with meaning of the past in which their land, people and identities were threatened through the brutality of colonial military, legislative and psychological violence. Māori performers and collaborators involved in the film's production contributed to the acknowledgement of their ancestors' resistance. Their contribution represents a continued resistance to colonial narratives of cultural warfare. Moving beyond the romance narrative brings to the

A battle scene from Rewi's Last Stand, *filmed near the Ōrākau war site, shows performers running to their defensive trenches.* Film still courtesy of Ngā Taonga Sound & Vision, Wellington

---

fore a story of resistance and survival of one of the 'darkest days' in Aotearoa.[36]

Te Whare Taonga o Otawhao Te Awamutu/Te Awamutu Museum demonstrates how *Rewi's Last Stand* might contribute to New Zealand Wars education within a decolonising framework. With permission through the film's kaipupuri organisation, Ngā Taonga Sound and Vision, the museum screens the film as part of its exhibition *Resistance, Resilience and Remembrance*, which opened in October 2020 ahead of Rā Maumahara (the national day of commemoration for the New Zealand Wars).[37] In the exhibition, the film plays amid display boards featuring information about Ōrākau and the Waikato War, enhancing audience understanding of the film in the wider context of violence at Ōrākau and subsequent raupatu (land confiscation).

According to Te Whare Taonga exhibitions coordinator Henriata Nicholas, the film is not glamorised in its display.[38] Rather, locals and visitors are given an opportunity to watch the film in a contextualised space. Nicholas suggests that showing *Rewi's Last Stand* in this forum presents an opportunity for descendants to connect with their ancestors in the film, as well as their history at Ōrākau. The geographic and historical proximity of Te Awamutu to Ōrākau makes Te Whare Taonga o Otawhao Te Awamutu a powerful place to view *Rewi's Last Stand*. The history of missionary settlement at Te Awamutu is implicated in the colonial politics that led to war. Watching the film in this place encourages viewers to engage with the ongoing consequences of the Waikato invasion and consider their own place in the history of Aotearoa. Perhaps the museum's exhibition aligns with the contextualised approach that Ramai Te Miha Hayward envisaged to correct the film's history.

Navigating colonial and postcolonial readings of *Rewi's Last Stand* reveals that they do not do enough to understand Māori perspectives of the past and in film media. The colonial view presented in the film sanitised historical colonial violence in favour of romance and nation-building, and the focus of postcolonial critique on deconstructing such inaccuracies tends to reproduce Eurocentric notions of film authorship and historical authority.

Listening to how Māori voices speak in *Rewi's Last Stand* effects a vital shift in perspective in the interpretation of history. Such interpretation should reflect an understanding that strives for the ethical imperative of partnership established under Te Tiriti o Waitangi and will open up more meaningful insight on historical narratives and their role in navigating the present and future. Interrogating our own modes of analysis and centring Māori perspectives in our histories will be crucial for the vision of history education in Aotearoa, especially concerning our colonial wars.

CONCLUSION

Lyndall Ryan and Camille Nurka

Historians have too often been unwilling to name and describe the violence of settler colonialism, which has typically been characterised in terms of abstract legacies. Yet Indigenous writers, activists and artists recognise it as a violent process that shapes Indigenous realities in the present. *Aftermaths* not only acknowledges colonial violence as foundational to the creation of modern settler states but also demonstrates the patchy and uneven qualities of public and private memory today. The weight of memory, the burden of its emotional freight, is mostly carried by Indigenous communities and families. Our purpose has been to bring home to the reader the impact the loss of ceremonies has had on Indigenous peoples, the ruthlessness of the colonisers, and the failure of the latter to understand the horrors of dispossession. Colonisers can no longer turn a blind eye to the consequences.

This volume has sought to break the settler code of silence by placing Indigenous sovereignty at the centre of historical storytelling. One example of this work of centring Indigenous experience is the growing support for recognition of the frontier wars in Australia and New Zealand. The process is much further advanced in New Zealand with the establishment of the Waitangi Tribunal, which has investigated historic injustices since 1985, and the introduction of a compulsory history curriculum in New Zealand schools from 2023. In Australia, the federal government elected in 2022 has promised to acknowledge the 2017 Uluru Statement from the Heart, which advocates a constitutionally enshrined First Nations voice, along with a Makarrata Commission for truth-telling and agreement-making on treaties. In support of this response, Indigenous writer

AFTERMATHS

Thomas Mayor published *Finding the Heart of the Nation* in October 2019, just before the symposium that led to the collection of chapters in this book.[1] Mayor contested the policy of the Australian War Memorial in Canberra that although it honours Australia's war dead, it only represents those who died in Australian military campaigns overseas.[2] In promoting this policy, the Australian War Memorial denies the existence of the frontier wars and also elides the involvement of British regiments that fought in the first stage of the Australian frontier wars, 1788–1843, and were the leading protagonists in the New Zealand Wars in the 1840s and 1860s. Upon discharge, most of the soldiers remained in Australia and New Zealand as settlers and became a critical component of local militia forces, which parried attempts by Indigenous people to claim their sovereignty. We still await comprehensive studies of the regiments that served for extended periods in the frontier wars in Australia and New Zealand.[3]

The reclamation of Indigenous sovereignty is confronting for settler Australians and Pākehā New Zealanders. Indigenous Australian scholar Chelsea Watego notes the coincidence in the year 2020 of the 'global Black Lives Matter movement after the murder of African-American man George Floyd at the hands of a Minneapolis police officer' and the 250th anniversary of Captain Cook's voyage along the east coast of Australia. According to Watego, the latter was to be 'commemorated with a lavish year-long party courtesy of a $50 million tab covered by the federal government, which included sailing a replica of Cook's *Endeavour* around the continent in some sort of sordid victory lap, which Cook never actually sailed'.[4] Watego continues: 'As fate would have it, Covid-19 intervened. The ship never did set sail, let alone reach its scheduled thirty-nine locations, which included Bedanug or, as they refer to it, "Possession Island" where Captain Cook is alleged to have "claimed" Australia for the British Crown.'[5]

The exhibition *Endeavour Voyage: The untold stories of Cook and first Australians*, held at the National Museum in Canberra, told a different story. Prepared by Bana Yirriji Artists Group in conjunction with Margo Neale, the museum's senior Indigenous curator, the exhibition was planned over three years with Indigenous communities along Australia's east coast and included *The Message: The story from the shore* by Indigenous filmmaker Alison Page.[6] The film followed Indigenous accounts of the *Endeavour* as it sailed up Australia's east coast from Point Hicks to Cape York over 126 days. It also queried whether Cook had ever visited Bedanug ('Possession Island') and planted a flag claiming Eastern Australia for Britain. Cook did not mention the island or the flag-planting in his journal as the *Endeavour* sailed around the tip of Cape York and only included the claim in his journal several weeks later when the *Endeavour* reached Batavia (Jakarta) in the Dutch East Indies.[7] Without the replica *Endeavour* and other planned settler celebrations taking centre stage, the exhibition and the film gained an ascendancy in truth-telling about Cook and the origins of Australia's violent colonial past. The film is available on YouTube through the National Museum of Australia website and has been widely screened in schools across Australia.

A further challenge to the settler celebration of overseas war service took place in Hobart, Tasmania, in 2022. The Returned Services League (RSL), which plays a leading role in the organisation of official marches across Australia on Anzac Day, 25 April, for the first time included a contingent of Aboriginal descendants of the survivors of the Black War of the 1820s in the march in Hobart. The RSL also actively supports the construction of an official memorial to the Black War.[8]

In other projects, Indigenous and non-Indigenous artists have come together to represent their family origins and experiences of settler colonialism. In the exhibition *the red thread of history, loose ends*, held at the National Gallery of Australia in Canberra in 2022, Indigenous artist Judy Watson (whose work is the subject of Anna Johnston's chapter) and settler artist Helen Johnson draw on the role of women within the legacies of colonialism. This exhibition is a truth-telling exercise and visual dialogue between the two female artists, who seek to 'explore the ways in which colonial systems of exclusion continue to impact culture and politics today'.[9] The 'red thread' references Australian politician Henry Parkes' portrayal of the federated settler colonies as united by a 'crimson thread of kinship'; and buried beneath this story is the 'red thread' of ochre connecting far older kinships between First Nations peoples and their interconnected lands. The 'loose ends' are suggestive of the ongoing effects of colonialism in Australia and the unfinished business of recognising and respecting Indigenous sovereignty. In an interview alongside Johnson, Watson discusses the importance of family in understanding the temporal 'layers' of place, and how her own intimate, matrilineal connections refute the myth of settler property.[10] This comes through strongly in her collaborative artworks, created with family and friends, which make use of natural fibres such as string, calico and muslin to represent the transmission of cultural knowledge and also of shared pain in the creation of material objects that represent Indigenous resilience and trauma in the aftermath of colonialism. Watson's *veil of tears*, for instance, features painted calico stitched onto muslin veils that hang in front of the names of 51 Aboriginal people who have died in police custody. The stitches pierce and repair the 'open wounds' of the fabric of colonial history that continue to cause harm to Indigenous communities today. Watson's veils point to the submerged histories revealed to the observer behind the transparent muslin, a theme that is recapitulated from the settler perspective in the large screens painted by Johnson that hang in the middle of the room. As Johnson explains, her artworks 'reference theatre backdrops. The colonial logic they engage likes to present itself as an immersive reality.'[11] Her large square panels occupy the very centre of the room, perhaps reflecting the dominance of white settler symbology in defining the historical narrative, crafted through layers of violence and denial. Severed hands, disembodied women, eyes without faces and a preponderance of layered textual elements evoke a sense of psychic and semantic fracture that comes from settler denial and guilt.

Womanhood and maternity are the themes that bring the artists together. While Johnson grapples with the settler state's need for white women's reproductive power in its attempted erasure of Indigenous bodies and languages, Watson quietly insists upon Indigenous presence, pain and survival. While Watson prioritises specific women in her family, Johnson focuses on the symbology of the white woman in the birth of the white nation and woman's role as moral guardian and mistress of the domestic space. The effect of this somewhat disjunctive artistic dialogue is jarring and uncomfortable – but perhaps it could not be otherwise – in its effort to explore the intimate relationships formed in, through and against the institutional and symbolic structures of colonialism.

Like *the red thread of history* exhibition – which opened after our symposium was held at Te Papa Tongarewa in Wellington, New Zealand, in November 2019 – *Aftermaths* is a dialogue between the authors that explores the hidden and terrible intimacies of violence within the larger machine of colonialism. The key elements of settler colonialism – the violence of dispossession and the code of silence that prevailed in the aftermath, and the dishonourable policy of assimilation that attempted to make Indigenous people disappear into settler society – have now been exposed across the Pacific rim, enabling Indigenous claims of sovereignty to grow in strength. The editors hope this collection will trigger further exploration of the critical themes of colonisation and its lasting impact upon the traditional Indigenous owners of colonised lands, including the violent attempts to make them disappear.

NOTES

INTRODUCTION

1. Keith Sinclair used the term 'aftermath' in *Kinds of Peace: Maori people after the wars, 1870–85* (Auckland: Auckland University Press, 1991), p. 7.
2. Moana Jackson, 'Where to next? Decolonisation and the stories in the land', in Bianca Elkington, Moana Jackson, Rebecca Kiddle, Ocean Ripeka Mercier, Mike Ross, Jennie Smeaton and Amanda Thomas (eds), *Imagining Decolonisation*, (Wellington: Bridget Williams Books, 2020), p. 134.
3. Susan Sleeper-Smith, Jeffrey Ostler and Joshua L. Reid, 'Introduction', in Susan Sleeper-Smith, Jeffrey Ostler and Joshua L. Reid (eds), *Violence and Indigenous Communities: Confronting the past and engaging the present* (Evanston: Northwestern University Press, 2021), p. 1.
4. Chelsea Watego, *Another Day in the Colony* (Brisbane: University of Queensland Press, 2021), p. 8.
5. Jackson, 'Where to next?', p. 133.
6. Shino Konishi, 'First Nations scholars, settler colonial studies, and Indigenous history', *Australian Historical Studies 50*, no. 3, 2019, p. 286.
7. This volume emerged from the symposium 'Afterlives: Intimacy, violence and colonialism', held at Museum of New Zealand Te Papa Tongarewa in November 2019. This was the final event of the Australian Research Council Discovery Project 'Intimacy and violence in settler societies on the anglophone Pacific Rim 1830–1930', led by Professor Lyndall Ryan.
8. Antoinette Burton, *The Trouble with Empire: Challenges to modern British imperialism* (Oxford: Oxford University Press, 2015); Philip Dwyer and Amanda Nettelbeck (eds), *Violence, Colonialism and Empire in the Modern World* (Basingstoke: Palgrave Macmillan, 2018).
9. Amanda Nettelbeck, 'Proximate strangers and familiar antagonists: Violence on an intimate frontier', *Australian Historical Studies 47*, no. 2, 2016, pp. 209–24.
10. Joanna Kidman, Vincent O'Malley, Liana MacDonald, Tom Roa and Keziah Wallis, *Fragments from a Contested Past: Remembrance, denial and New Zealand history* (Wellington: Bridget Williams Books, 2022).
11. Annabel Cooper, *Filming the Colonial Past: The New Zealand Wars on screen* (Dunedin: Otago University Press, 2018).
12. There is a growing scholarship on critical family history within a settler colonial context. See the special issue of *Genealogy* dedicated to critical settler family history, edited by Avril Bell: www.mdpi.com/journal/genealogy/special_issues/critical_family_history

CHAPTER 1

1. Research for this chapter was carried out as part of the project 'He taonga te wareware? Remembering and forgetting difficult histories in Aotearoa/New Zealand', supported by a grant from the Marsden Fund, Royal Society Te Apārangi. It draws on two earlier papers: Joanna Kidman,

'He taonga te wareware: Mātauranga Māori and education', in Jacinta Ruru and Linda Waimarie Nikora (eds), *Ngā Kete Mātauranga: Māori scholars at the research interface* (Dunedin: Otago University Press, 2020), pp. 81–87; and Vincent O'Malley, '"Recording the incident with a monument": The Waikato War in historical memory', *Journal of New Zealand Studies 19*, 2015, pp. 79–97.
2. Paul Meredith and Robert Joseph, *The Battle of Ōrākau: Māori veterans' accounts* (Waikato: Ōrākau Heritage Society and the Maniapoto Māori Trust Board, 2014), p. 30.
3. Vincent O'Malley, *The Great War for New Zealand: Waikato 1800–2000* (Wellington: Bridget Williams Books, 2016).
4. Waitangi Tribunal, *Te Mana Ahuru: Report on Te Rohe Pōtae claims* (pre-publication version) (Wellington: Waitangi Tribunal, 2018), p. 511.
5. Hitiri Te Paerata, *Description of the Battle of Orakau, as Given by the Native Chief Hitiri Te Paerata of the Ngatiraukawa Tribe, at the Parliament Buildings, 4th August 1888* (Wellington: Government Printer, 1888), p. 9.
6. *New Zealander*, cited in *New Zealand Herald*, 14 April 1864.
7. 'Jubilee of Orakau', *Waipa Post*, 3 April 1914; 'Orakau Jubilee', *King Country Chronicle*, 4 April 1914.
8. 'Orakau celebrations', *New Zealand Herald*, 30 March 1914.
9. 'The fruit of Orakau', *New Zealand Herald*, 31 March 1914.
10. Gilbert Mair, *Jubilee Souvenir of Battle of Orakau, Fought March 31st, April 1st, and 2nd, 1864, and in Commemoration of 50 Years of Peace, 1864–1914* (Hamilton: Waikato Times, 1914).
11. Translation of draft inscription, n.d. [c. January 1917], IA 1 7/4/38, Archives New Zealand.
12. E.M. Statham to J. Hislop, 15 January 1917, IA 1 7/4/38, Archives New Zealand.
13. J. Allan Thomson, Director, Dominion Museum, to Under Secretary, Internal Affairs, 20 January 1917, IA 17/4/38, Archives New Zealand.
14. James Cowan, *The New Zealand Wars and the Pioneering Period*, vol. 1 (Wellington: Government Printer, 1983), p. 3.
15. Annabel Cooper, *Filming the Colonial Past: The New Zealand Wars on screen* (Dunedin: Otago University Press, 2018), pp. 42–45, 90–91.
16. *Orakau Commemoration, 1864–1964: Kihikihi centenary* (Te Awamutu: Te Awamutu Jaycees, 1964).
17. Harry Dansey, 'Reflections on battle centenaries', *Te Ao Hou 48*, 1964, pp. 34–35.
18. Trish Dunleavy, '"Magnificent failure" or subversive triumph? *The Governor*', in James E. Bennett and Rebecca Beirne (eds), *Making Film and Television Histories: Australia and New Zealand* (London: I.B. Tauris, 2012), pp. 67–72.
19. 'Potshots fired over Belich's wars', *Evening Post*, 8 July 1998.
20. Vincent O'Malley and Joanna Kidman, 'Settler colonial history, commemoration and white backlash: Remembering the New Zealand Wars', *Settler Colonial Studies 8*, no. 3, 2018, pp. 298–313.

CHAPTER 2

1. Gabrielle Appleby and Megan Davis, 'The Uluru Statement and the promises of truth', *Australian Historical Studies 49*, no. 4, 2018, pp. 501–9.
2. 'Uluru Statement from the Heart', 2017: https://ulurustatement.org/; Reconciliation Australia and Healing Foundation, 'Truth-telling symposium report' (Canberra: Reconciliation Australia and Healing Foundation, 2018): www.reconciliation.org.au/wp-content/uploads/2019/02/truth-telling-symposium-report1.pdf
3. Stuart Macintyre and Anna Clark, *The History Wars* (Melbourne: Melbourne University Press, 2003).

4. 'Australia Day: What do Australians think about celebrating the nation on January 26?', ABC News, 26 January 2019: www.abc.net.au/news/2019-01-26/what-do-australians-think-about-australia-day-this-year/10753278; Lyndall Ryan et al., *Colonial Frontier Massacres, Australia, 1788–1930* (Newcastle: University of Newcastle, 2017–2020), funded by Australian Research Council, Discovery Project 140100399: https://c21ch.newcastle.edu.au/colonialmassacres/map.php; Judy Watson, *the names of places*, 2016, Institute of Modern Art, Brisbane: http://thenamesofplaces.com/tnop/; 'The killing times', *Guardian*: www.theguardian.com/australia-news/series/the-killing-times
5. Jack Farrugia, Peta Dzidic and Lynne Roberts, '"It is usually about the triumph of the coloniser": Exploring young people's conceptualisations of Australian history and the implications for Australian identity', *Journal of Community Applied Social Psychology* 28, 2018, pp. 483–94.
6. Polity Research & Consulting (for Reconciliation Australia), '2018 Australian reconciliation barometer' (Sydney: Polity Research, 2018), 80, 121: www.reconciliation.org.au/wp-content/uploads/2019/02/final_full_arb-full-report-2018.pdf
7. Polity Research & Consulting, '2018 Australian reconciliation barometer', p. 96.
8. For instance, Kate Darian-Smith, 'Australia Day, Invasion Day, Survival Day: A long history of celebration and contestation', *The Conversation*, 26 January 2017: https://theconversation.com/australia-day-invasion-day-survival-day-a-long-history-of-celebration-and-contestation-70278; Timothy Bottoms, 'Why we ought to be remembering the frontier wars on Anzac Day', *Sydney Morning Herald*, 23 April 2015: www.smh.com.au/opinion/why-we-ought-to-be-remembering-the-frontier-wars-on-anzac-day-20150423-1mrwtp.html
9. Alternatively, Tony Birch argues that the date of Australia Day does not have practical power to advance genuine change or national remorse. Tony Birch, 'A change of date will do nothing to shake Australia from its colonial-settler triumphalism', *IndigenousX*, 21 January 2018: https://indigenousx.com.au/tony-birch-a-change-of-date-will-do-nothing-to-shake-australia-from-its-colonial-settler-triumphalism/
10. Paul Daley, 'Australia's frontier war killings still conveniently escape official memory', *Guardian*, 8 June 2018: www.theguardian.com/australia-news/postcolonial-blog/2018/jun/08/australias-frontier-war-killings-still-conveniently-escape-official-memory
11. Polity Research & Consulting, '2018 Australian reconciliation barometer', p. 117.
12. Manu Vimalassery, Alyosha Goldstein, Juliana Hu Pegues, 'On colonial unknowing', *Theory and Event* 19, no. 4, special issue, 2016
13. Jon Altman and Melinda Hinkson (eds), *Coercive Reconciliation: Stabilise, normalise, exit Aboriginal Australia* (Melbourne: Arena, 2007).
14. Ravi de Costa, 'Two kinds of recognition: The politics of engagement in settler societies', in Sarah Maddison, Tom Clark and Ravi de Costa (eds), *The Limits of Settler Colonial Reconciliation* (Singapore: Springer, 2016), p. 49.
15. Penelope Edmonds, *Settler Colonialism and (Re)conciliation: Frontier violence, affective performances, and imaginative refoundings* (London: Palgrave, 2016).
16. Tracy Ireland, 'Captain Cook is a contested national symbol, so why spend more money on him?', *The Conversation*, 11 May 2018: www.abc.net.au/news/2018-05-11/captain-james-cook-who-discovered-australia-indigenous-ownership/9750772
17. 'Controversy over ACT Reconciliation Day', SBS News, 25 May 2018: www.sbs.

com.au/news/controversy-over-act-reconciliation-day
18. For instance, Djon Mundine, OAM, conceptual producer, *The Aboriginal Memorial*, 1987–88, National Gallery of Australia; Fiona Foley, *Witnessing to Silence*, 2004, Brisbane Magistrates Court forecourt; Yhonnie Scarce and Meryl Ryan in consultation with the Aboriginal Reference Group, curators, *(in)visible: The First Peoples and war*, 2015, Lake Macquarie City Art Gallery; Brook Andrew and Trent Walter, *Standing by Tunnerminnerwait and Maulboyheenner*, 2016, City of Melbourne; Paul Bong, *Shields*, 2017, Cairns CBD public art installation; Tjyllyungoo/Lance Chadd in collaboration with Trish Robinson and Stuart Green, *Wirin*, 2018, Yagan Square, Perth; Myles Russell-Cook, curator, *Colony: Frontier wars*, 2018, National Gallery of Victoria.
19. See Monument Australia, 2010–2020: http://monumentaustralia.org.au/themes/conflict/indigenous
20. Mark McKenna, *Looking for Blackfella's Point: An Australian history of place* (Sydney: UNSW Press, 2002); Skye Krichauff, *Memory, Place and Aboriginal–Settler History* (London: Anthem Press, 2017).
21. William Stanner, 'The Great Australian Silence' (1968), in *The Dreaming and Other Essays* (Melbourne: Black Inc, 2009), pp. 182–92.
22. Henry Reynolds, *The Other Side of the Frontier* (Ringwood: Penguin, 1981).
23. Fiona Skyring and Sarah Yu with the Karajarri Native Title Holders, '"Strange strangers": First contact between Europeans and Karajarri people on the Kimberley coast of Western Australia', in Peter Veth, Peter Sutton and Margo Neale (eds), *Strangers on the Shore* (Canberra: National Museum of Australia, 2008).
24. Maitland Brown, 'Journal of an expedition in the Roebuck Bay district under the command of Maitland Brown, Esq.', *Perth Gazette and WA Times*, 24 May 1865; Bruce Scates, 'A monument to murder: Celebrating the conquest of Aboriginal Australia', *Studies in Western Australian History 10*, 1989, pp. 21–31.
25. Public Action Project, 'Unmasking the monument: The other side of the pioneer myth', in Rae Frances and Bruce Scates (eds), *The Murdoch Ethos* (Melbourne: Murdoch University, 1989), p. 222.
26. James Young, 'The counter-monument: Memory against itself in Germany today', *Critical Inquiry 18*, no. 2, 1992, pp. 267–96.
27. Interview with Joe Edgar, Vanessa Mills and Ben Collins, 'The controversial statue that was added to, not torn down or vandalised', ABC News, 29 August 2017: www.abc.net.au/news/2017-08-29/explorers-monument-added-to-not-torn-down-or-vandalised/8853224
28. Bruce Scates, 'Monumental errors: How Australia can fix its racist colonial statues', *The Conversation*, 27 August 2017: https://theconversation.com/monumental-errors-how-australia-can-fix-its-racist-colonial-statues-82980
29. Elizabeth Strakosch, 'Counter-monuments and nation-building in Australia', *Peace Review 22*, no. 3, 2010, pp. 268–75.
30. For a review of such debates, see Bronwyn Batten and Paul Batten, 'Memorialising the past: Is there an Aboriginal way?', *Public History Review 15*, 2008, p. 93; Andreas Huyssen, 'Monumental seduction', *New German Critique 69*, 1996, pp. 181–200.
31. Julie Marcus, 'Bicentenary follies: Australians in search of themselves', *Anthropology Today 4*, no. 3, 1988, pp. 4–6.
32. Ray Kerkhove, 'Multuggerah (c. 1820–1846)', from the Australian Dictionary of Biography: http://ia.anu.edu.au/biography/multuggerah-29904

33. William Charles Wilkes, 'The raid of the Aborigines', *Bell's Life in Sydney and Sporting Reviewer*, 4 and 11 January 1845.
34. Frank Uhr, *Multuggerah and the Sacred Mountain* (Tingalpa: Boolarong Press, 2019); Stephen Muecke, Alan Rumsey and Banjo Wirrunmarra, 'Pigeon the outlaw: History as texts', *Aboriginal History 9*, nos 1–2, 1985, pp. 81–100; Chilla Bulbeck, 'Memorials and the history of the frontier', *Australian Historical Studies 24*, no. 96, 1991, pp. 168–78.
35. Marie-Louise Ayres, 'A picture asks a thousand questions', *NLA Magazine 5*, no. 2, 2011, p. 11.
36. 'St Luke's Reconciliation Cross', Doing Justice, 2016: www.doingjustice.org.au/st-lukes-reconciliation-cross/
37. For instance, memorials to the 1928 Coniston massacre (Northern Territory, established 2003), 1816 Appin massacre (New South Wales, established 2007), and Aboriginal Massacres Monument (Victoria, established 2011).
38. Vanessa Mills, 'Women recognised for love and death in Broome pearling', ABC News, 29 November 2010.
39. Stephen Gilchrist, 'Surfacing histories: Memorials and public art in Perth', *Artlink*, 1 June 2018, pp. 42–47.
40. An earlier campaign for a memorial on the site by Bingara resident Len Payne dates back to the 1960s. For a timeline of the memorial plans, see 'Memorial story – Living history', Friends of Myall Creek, 2020: www.myallcreek.org/index.php/memorial-story
41. 'Hundreds gather for Myall Creek commemorations', *Inverell Times*, 10 June 2019: www.inverelltimes.com.au/story/6208100/hundreds-gather-for-myall-creek-commemorations/; Jane Lydon and Lyndall Ryan (eds), *Remembering the Myall Creek Massacre* (Sydney: NewSouth, 2018).
42. Mark McKenna, *From the Edge: Australia's lost histories* (Melbourne: Melbourne University Publishing, 2016).

CHAPTER 3

1. Arini Loader, 'Te Pūtake o Te Riri', *The Briefing Papers*, 6 November 2018: https://briefingpapers.co.nz/te-putake-o-te-riri/
2. Nēpia Mahuika, 'A brief history of whakapapa: Māori approaches to genealogy', *Genealogy 3*, no. 2, 2019, p. 32.
3. Takirirangi Smith, 'Nga tini ahuatanga o whakapapa korero', *Educational Philosophy and Theory 32*, no. 1, 2000, p. 53.
4. Joseph Selwyn Te Rito, 'Whakapapa: A framework for understanding identity', *MAI Review*, no. 2, 2007, p. 9.
5. Joseph Selwyn Te Rito, 'Whakapapa and whenua: An insider's view', *MAI Review*, no. 3, 2007, pp. 1–8.
6. A few of these submissions, though not many, are accessible through the Waitangi Tribunal website: https://forms.justice.govt.nz/search/WT/
7. Loader, 'Te Pūtake o Te Riri'.
8. Rachel Buchanan, *Ko Taranaki Te Maunga* (Wellington: Bridget Williams Books, 2018), pp. 102–03. On the ceremony and Bill, see Shannon Haunui-Thompson, 'Tears as Crown apologises for Parihaka atrocities', *Te Manu Korihi*, RNZ, 9 June 2017: www.rnz.co.nz/news/te-manu-korihi/332613/tears-as-crown-apologises-for-parihaka-atrocities; Te Aniwa Hurihanganui, 'Parihaka reach milestone to reconcile relationship with Crown', *Te Manu Korihi*, RNZ, 24 October 2019: www.rnz.co.nz/news/te-manu-korihi/401714/parihaka-reach-milestone-to-reconcile-relationship-with-crown
9. Buchanan, *Ko Taranaki Te Maunga*, p. 103.
10. Leah Bell, 'Difficult histories: In conference', *New Zealand Journal of Public History 7*, no. 1, 2020, pp. 9, 10.

Notes: Chapter 3

11. Tim Watkin, 'Podcast: Waitara and one family's journey', RNZ, 17 March 2020 [50:46]: www.rnz.co.nz/programmes/nzwars-waitara/story/2018738836/taranaki-wars-waitara-and-one-family-s-journey
12. Amanda Thomas, 'Pākehā and doing the work of decolonisation', in Rebecca Kiddle, Bianca Elkington, Moana Jackson, Ocean Ripeka Mercier, Mike Ross, Jennie Smeaton, and Amanda Thomas, *Imagining Decolonisation* (Wellington: Bridget Williams Books, 2020), pp. 110–12, 120.
13. Alison Jones, *This Pākehā Life: An unsettled memoir* (Wellington: Bridget Williams Books, 2020), p. 173–81.
14. Miranda Johnson, 'Knotted histories', *Journal of New Zealand Studies*, no. NS29, 2019, pp. 89–96.
15. Hugh Campbell, *Farming Inside Invisible Worlds: Modernist agriculture and its consequences* (London: Bloomsbury Academic, 2020), pp. 59–79.
16. For example, Christine Sleeter, 'Critical family history: Situating family within contexts of power relationships', *Journal of Multidisciplinary Research* 8, no. 1, 2016, 11–23; Sleeter, 'Becoming white: Reinterpreting a family story by putting race back into the picture', *Race, Ethnicity and Education 14*, no. 1, 2011, pp. 421–33; Sleeter, 'Inheriting footholds and cushions: Family legacies and institutional racism', in Judith Flores Carmona and Kristen V. Luschen (eds), *Crafting Critical Stories: Toward pedagogies and methodologies of collaboration, inclusion and voice* (New York: Peter Lang Publishing, 2014), pp. 11–26.
17. Belinda Borell, Helen Moewaka Barnes and Tim McCreanor, 'Conceptualising historical privilege: The flip side of historical trauma, a brief examination', *AlterNative: An International Journal of Indigenous Peoples 14*, no. 1, 2018, p. 31. Cited in Avril Bell, 'Reverberating historical privilege of a "middling" sort of settler family', *Genealogy 4*, no. 2, 2020, p. 5.
18. Bell, 'Reverberating historical privilege', p. 15.
19. Richard Shaw, *The Forgotten Coast* (Palmerston North: Massey University Press, 2021). Rachel Buchanan responded by reviewing the book for *The Spinoff*, 'The forgotten coast: A Pākehā wrestles with his family history', *The Spinoff*, 23 Nov 2021: https://thespinoff.co.nz/books/23-11-2021/the-forgotten-coast-a-pakeha-wrestles-with-his-family-history-at-parihaka
20. For example, Rebecca Ream, 'Composting layers of Christchurch history', *Genealogy 5*, no. 3, 2021, https://doi.org/10.3390/genealogy5030074; Esther Fitzpatrick, 'A story of becoming: Entanglement, settler ghosts, and postcolonial counterstories, *Cultural Studies – Critical Methodologies 18*, no. 1, pp. 43–51.
21. Pickering's family history research will be published in a forthcoming special issue of *Genealogy* under the working title 'From clearance to coloniser: A Scottish Gael's journey to becoming Pākehā'.
22. Hēmi Kelly's Te Māhuri 1 class, Semester 1, 2018, Auckland University of Technology.
23. 'Wyndham and Josephine Wills, wedding', Puke Ariki Heritage Collections: https://collection.pukeariki.com/objects/168665
24. Buchanan, *Ko Taranaki Te Maunga*, p. 82.
25. Stanley Cohen, *States of Denial: Knowing about atrocities and suffering* (Cambridge: Polity Press, 2001), p. 1.
26. Cohen, *States of Denial*, 139.
27. Maria Haenga-Collins, 'Closed stranger adoption, Māori and race relations in Aotearoa New Zealand, 1955–1985' (PhD thesis, Australian National University, 2017), pp. vii, 21, 201. Available at https://openresearch-repository.anu.edu.au/handle/1885/132619

28. Haenga-Collins refers to the way colonial patterns are repeated in the institution and practices of closed stranger adoption of Māori children into Pākehā families. See Haenga-Collins, 'Closed stranger adoption', 39. Some other stark recent examples have been the way the police raids in Te Urewera in 2007 mirrored a notorious raid on Maungapōhatu in 1917, and the way the Foreshore and Seabed Act 2004, like the New Zealand Settlements Act 1863, removed vast tracts of land from Māori with the stroke of a pen.
29. Glenn Colquhoun, cited in Rebecca Kiddle, 'Colonisation sucks for everyone', in Kiddle, Elkington, Jackson et al., *Imagining Decolonisation*, p. 86.
30. Lydia Wevers, 'Being Pakeha: The politics of location', *Journal of New Zealand Studies* 4/5, 2006, p. 8.

CHAPTER 4

1. Arthur Herbert Messenger, 'Children of the Forest: A frontier tale of old Taranaki', *School Journal 46*, no. 2, part 4, March 1952, p. 37.
2. Arthur Herbert Messenger, 'Children of the Forest: A frontier tale of old Taranaki', *School Journal 46*, no. 4, part 4, June 1952, p. 100.
3. 'The art of the Burton Brothers', *Dunedin Weekender,* 12 June 1983.
4. James Cowan, *The New Zealand Wars and the Pioneering Period*, vol. 2 (Wellington: R.E. Owen Government Printer, 1923), p. 310.
5. Ibid., p. 542.
6. 'Massacre at the White Cliffs', *Taranaki Herald*, 20 February 1869.
7. William Morley, *The History of Methodism in New Zealand* (Wellington: McKee and Co., 1900), p. 166.
8. Graham Brazendale, 'John Whiteley: Land sovereignty and the land wars of the 19th century', *Proceedings of the Wesley Historical Society of New Zealand 64*, 1997, p. 34.
9. Ibid., p. 35.
10. Ibid.
11. 'Massacre at the White Cliffs', *Taranaki Herald*, 20 February 1869.
12. Cowan, *The New Zealand Wars*, p. 542.
13. Morley, *The History of Methodism in New Zealand*, p. 167.
14. Ibid.
15. 'The White Cliff Massacre', *Taranaki Herald*, 3 April 1869.
16. 'The Maori rebellion', *Taranaki Herald*, 27 February 1869.
17. Ranginui Walker, *Ka Whawhai Tonu Matou: Struggle without end* (Auckland: Penguin Books, 1990), p. 124; Cowan, *The New Zealand Wars*, p. 400.
18. G.E.J. Hammer, 'A pioneer missionary: Raglan to Mokau, 1844–1880: Cort Henry Schnackenberg', *Proceedings of the Wesley Historical Society of New Zealand 57*, 1991, p. 78.
19. George G. Carter, 'John Whiteley: Missionary martyr', *Proceedings of the Wesley Historical Society of New Zealand 10*, no. 3, 1952; Morley, *The History of Methodism in New Zealand*, p. 168.
20. Morley, *The History of Methodism in New Zealand*, pp. 167–69; William F.F. Thomas, 'William Morley – Lecture for the AGM of the Wesley Historical Society', *Proceedings of the Wesley Historical Society of New Zealand 80*, 2005, p. 10.
21. Morley, *The History of Methodism in New Zealand*.
22. Paul Keresztes, 'Tertullian's Apologeticus: A historical and literal study', in *Latomus 25*, 1966, p. 129.
23. 'Native version of the murder of the Rev. Mr. Whiteley', *Daily Southern Cross*, 12 March 1869.
24. 'Taranaki', *Otago Daily Times*, 30 May 1871; Cowan, *The New Zealand Wars*, p. 540.
25. 'The Whiteley memorial', *Otago Daily Times*, 2 December 1897.

26. 'Revd. and Dear Sirs, North Shore, Auckland, New Zealand, 8 May 1869', Benjamin Ashwell Papers, 1834–1869, MSS-Archives-A-172, Special Collections, University of Auckland Library, Auckland; Cort Schnackenberg, *Manuscripts and Typescripts of Letter Books*, 27 March 1869, Methodist Theological Archives, St John's Theological College, Auckland.
27. Paul Thomas, 'The Crown and Māori in Mōkau 1840–1911: A report commissioned by the Waitangi Tribunal for Te Rohe Potae Inquiry', Waitangi Tribunal, 2011, Wai 898 #A28, p. 157.
28. Cowan, *The New Zealand Wars*, p. 540.
29. Thomas, 'The Crown and Māori in Mōkau 1840–1911', p. 157.
30. Cowan, *The New Zealand Wars*, p. 541.
31. 'Mr Civil Commissioner Parris' visit to Mokau', *Taranaki Herald*, 13 May 1871; 'Taranaki', *Otago Daily Times*, 30 May 1871.
32. Cowan, *The New Zealand Wars*, p. 305.
33. Ibid., p. 540.
34. 'Interprovincial', *Waikato Times*, 10 August 1882.
35. 'New Plymouth', *Bay of Plenty Times*, 18 September 1882.
36. 'Te Wetere telegram scandal', *Hawera & Normanby Star*, 1 September 1882.
37. Amnesty Act 1882 (46 VICT, 1882, No. 70).
38. C.J. Hutchinson, 'Wetere Te Rerenga', *New Zealand Herald*, 14 March 1889.
39. 'An amnesty', *Colonist*, 27 September 1882.
40. 'The murder of the Rev. Mr Whiteley', *New Zealand Herald*, 18 August 1882.
41. Cowan, *The New Zealand Wars*, p. 309.
42. Heeni Wharemaru and Mary Katharine Duffie, *Heeni: A Tainui elder remembers* (Auckland: HarperCollins, 1997).
43. Wharemaru and Duffie, *Heeni*, p. 78.
44. Ibid., p. 20.
45. Walker, *Ka Whawhai Tonu Matou*.
46. Hammer, 'A pioneer missionary', p. 92; Thomas, 'The Crown and Māori in Mōkau 1840–1911', p. 158.
47. 'Native affairs at Kawhia', *Taranaki Herald*, 21 April 1866.
48. 'The surveyors' story', *Star*, 29 March 1883; 'Presentations', *New Zealand Herald*, 4 January 1886.
49. 'Wellington', *Nelson Evening Mail*, 14 February 1883; Thomas, 'The Crown and Māori in Mōkau 1840–1911', p. 278.
50. 'The new Maori members', *Bay of Plenty Times*, 2 August 1884; 'Land settlement', *Auckland Star*, 1 April 1889; 'The pension list', *Thames Advertiser*, 23 September 1880.
51. Morley, *The History of Methodism in New Zealand*, p. 166; Reverend and Dear Sirs, Taupiri C.M. Station, Waikato, New Zealand, 26 November 1864. Benjamin Ashwell Papers, 1834–1869, MSS-Archives-A-172. Special Collections, University of Auckland Library, Auckland.
52. Morley, *The History of Methodism in New Zealand*, p. 167.

CHAPTER 5

1. David Helvarg, 'Island of resilience: The Wiyot reclaim their land and culture from a dark past', *American Indian 21*, no. 1, 2020: www.americanindianmagazine.org/story/wiyot
2. Llewellyn L. Loud, 'Ethnogeography and archaeology of the Wiyot territory', *University of California Publications in American Archaeology and Ethnology 14*, no. 3, 23 December 1918, p. 335; Benjamin Madley, *An American Genocide: The United States and the California Indian catastrophe* (New Haven: Yale University Press, 2016), pp. 281–82; Jack Norton, *Genocide in Northwestern California: When our worlds cried* (San Francisco: Indian Historian Press, 1979), pp. 82–90; Ray Raphael and Freeman House, *Two Peoples, One Place: Humboldt history, volume one*, rev. edn (Eureka: Humboldt County

Historical Society, 2011), pp. 164–70; Jerry Rohde, 'Genocide and extortion', *North Coast Journal*, 25 February 2010: https://www.northcoastjournal.com/humboldt/genocide-and-extortion/Content?oid=2130748; William B. Secrest, *When the Great Spirit Died: The destruction of the California Indians 1850–1860* (Fresno: Craven Street Books, 2003), pp. 326–31.

3. Gladys Reichard, 'Wiyot grammar and texts', *University of California Publications in American Archaeology and Ethnology 22*, no. 1, 26 June 1925, p. 141.

4. Cutcha Risling Baldy, *We Are Dancing for You: Native feminisms and the revitalization of women's coming-of-age ceremonies* (Seattle: University of Washington Press, 2018), p. 52.

5. Kerry J. Malloy, 'Remembrance and renewal at Tuluwat: Returning to the center of the world,' in Ajlina Karamehić-Muratović and Laura Kromják (eds), *Remembrance and Forgiveness: Global and interdisciplinary perspectives on genocide and mass violence* (London: Routledge, 2021), pp. 20–33, 26. Helvarg, 'Island of resilience'; Heidi Walters, 'Renewal', *North Coast Journal*, 20 March 2014: www.northcoastjournal.com/Humboldt/renewal/Content?oid=2515790

6. Cheryl Seidner, in William S. Kowinski, 'In 1860 six murderers nearly wiped out the Wiyot Indian Tribe – in 2004 its members have found ways to heal', *SFGate*, 28 February 2004: www.sfgate.com/entertainment/article/In-1860-six-murderers-nearly-wiped-out-the-Wiyot-2816476

7. I am grateful to have been able to consult with Ted Hernandez of the Wiyot Tribe and Tom Torma, former cultural director (non-Native) for the tribe, in the writing of this chapter, and appreciate their advice and encouragement. I also thank Marnie Atkins, of the Wiyot Cultural Center, for her assistance. I am indebted to Terry Snowball, Ho-Chunk/Prairie Band Potawatomi, Repatriation Coordinator at the NMAI, for pointing me in the direction of the dress to begin with, and for his advice and assistance since. Any errors or misjudgements are entirely mine.

8. 'History of the collections', Smithsonian National Museum of the American Indian: https://americanindian.si.edu/explore/collections/history; Douglas Cole, *Captured Heritage: The scramble for northwest coast artifacts* (Vancouver: UBC Press, 1995), pp. 216–17; Ira Jaknis, 'A new thing? The NMAI in historical and institutional perspective', *American Indian Quarterly 30*, nos 3/4, 2006, p. 516, pp. 532–33; Lawrence M. Small, 'A passionate collector', *Smithsonian Magazine*, November 2000: www.smithsonianmag.com/history/a-passionate-collector-33794183/

9. Wiyot skirt, Catalogue Card NMAI #086522.00: National Museum of the American Indian. G. Heye to G. Nicholson, 29 October 1918: Folder 'Heye, George G.', Box 3, Correspondence 1898–1951, Grace Nicholson Papers and Addenda, Huntington Library, San Marino, California; Maria Galban, archivist NMAI, email to author, 15 October 2020.

10. Susan Bernardin, 'Capturing and recapturing culture: Trailing Grace Nicholson's legacy in northwestern California', in Susan Bernardin, Melody Graulich, Lisa MacFarlane and Nicole Tonkovich (eds), *Trading Gazes: Euro-American women photographers and Native North Americans, 1880–1940* (New Brunswick: Rutgers University Press, 2003), pp. 150–85; Erika Marie Bsumek, 'Exchanging places: Virtual tourism, vicarious travel, and the consumption of southwestern Indian artifacts', in Hal K. Rothman (ed.), *The Culture of Tourism,*

the Tourism of Culture: Selling the past to the present in the American southwest (Albuquerque: University of New Mexico Press, 2003), p. 131; Marvin Cohodas, *Basket Weavers for the California Curio Trade: Elizabeth and Louise Hickox* (Tucson: University of Arizona Press & the Southwest Museum, 1997), p. 89.
11. Department of the Interior National Park Service, 'Notice of Intent to Repatriate Cultural Items: Peabody Museum of Archaeology and Ethnology, Harvard University, Cambridge, MA', *Federal Register 83*, no. 98, 21 May 2018: www.govinfo.gov/content/pkg/FR-2018-05-21/pdf/2018-10781.pdf; Tom Torma, 'Lhatsik Houmoulu'l "House of Tradition": Sacred items to be returned from Peabody Museum', *The Da'Luk: Wiyot Tribe 17*, no. 3 (2017), p. 5: https://docplayer.net/191319314-The-da-luk-wiyot-tribe-march-1-happy-102nd-birthday-evelyn-horn-volume-17-issue-3.html. Department of the Interior National Park Service, 'Notice of Intent to Repatriate Cultural Items: Brooklyn Museum, Brooklyn NY', *Federal Register 82*, no. 165, 28 August 2017: www.govinfo.gov/content/pkg/FR-2017-08-28/html/2017-18188.htm
12. Margaret Duckett, 'Bret Harte and the Indians of Northern California', *Huntington Library Quarterly 18*, no. 1 (Nov. 1954), pp. 59–83, 64. Raphael and House, *Two Peoples, One Place*, pp. 164–70.
13. Marnie Atkins, cited in Paul McHugh, 'Robust resilience of the Wiyot Tribe', *San Francisco Chronicle California North Coast Series*, 17 September 2005: http://paulmchugh.net/2005/09/robust-resilience-of-the-wiyot-tribe/
14. Nealis Hall and Brittany Britton, 'Newest community loan for women's ceremonial dresses: Long ago to today', *Clarke Museum Blog*, 28 April 2019: www.clarkemuseum.org/blog/newest-community-loan-for-womens-ceremonial-dresses-long-ago-to-today; Helvarg, 'Island of resilience'.
15. Helvarg, 'Island of resilience'.
16. Cohodas, *Basket Weavers for the California Curio Trade*, p. 125; Les W. Field (with Merv George), *Abalone Tales: Collaborative explorations of sovereignty and identity in Native California* (Durham: Duke University Press, 2008), pp. 129, 132 (referring to Hupa traditions).
17. Thadeus Greenson, 'The island's return: The unprecedented repatriation of the center of the Wiyot universe', *North Coast Journal*, 24 October 2019: www.northcoastjournal.com/humboldt/the-islands-return/Content?oid=15494902
18. Baldy, *We Are Dancing for You*; Malloy, 'Remembrance and renewal at Tuluwat'.
19. Shomik Mukherjee, 'Wiyot Tribe raising funds for 2020 World Renewal Ceremony', *Times Standard*, 8 April 2019: www.times-standard.com/2019/04/08/wiyot-tribe-raising-funds-for-2020-world-renewal-ceremony/

CHAPTER 6

1. I am grateful to Sue Dinsdale who helped me track Nathaniel and Margaret's movements, thank Rebecca Schwartz and Zoë Laidlaw for taking time to talk to me about this project and the place of St Helena in the British imperial world, and acknowledge Charlotte Macdonald who pointed me to new scholarship detailing the history of slavery on St Helena. The research for this chapter was support by a Rutherford Discovery Fellowship funded by the Royal Society Te Apārangi.
2. Harding's photograph appears in William Main, *Maori in Focus* (Wellington: Millwood Press, 1976), p. 48. On interracial marriage, see Angela Wanhalla, *Matters of the Heart: A history*

of interracial marriage in New Zealand (Auckland: Auckland University Press, 2013).
3. See Hugh Hughes and Lyn Hughes, *Discharged in New Zealand: Soldiers of the imperial foot regiments who took their discharge in New Zealand 1840–1870* (Auckland: New Zealand Society of Genealogists, 1988).
4. See the Soldiers of Empire Marsden Project led by Charlotte Macdonald for further details about this cohort of men: www.soldiersofempire.nz
5. Nathaniel was 23 and Margaret was 21. St James Church Banns of Marriage, 1849–1924, p. 21. EAP524/2/3/1, British Library Endangered Archives Project: https://eap.bl.uk/archive-file/EAP524-2-3-1
6. Charlotte Macdonald and Rebecca Lenihan, 'Paper soldiers: The life, death and reincarnation of nineteenth-century military files across the British Empire', *Rethinking History 22*, no. 2, 2018, p. 376. These imperial connections are the focus of Charlotte Macdonald's Marsden-funded project, Soldiers of Empire: www.soldiersofempire.nz
7. Myna Trustram, *Women of the Regiment: Marriage and the Victorian army* (Cambridge: Cambridge University Press, 1984), p. 1.
8. Ibid., p. 18.
9. Letter to the Undersecretary of State for War, 22 January 1857, WO 43/713 St Helena Regiment (Correspondence) re garrison, National Archives, Kew (hereafter NA).
10. Numbers from Letter to the Undersecretary of State for War, 22 January 1857, WO 43/713 St Helena Regiment (Correspondence) re garrison, NA.
11. Trustram, *Women of the Regiment*, p. 32.
12. Ibid., p. 38.
13. See Stephen Royale, *The Company's Island: St Helena, company colonies and the colonial endeavour* (London: I.B. Tauris, 2008).
14. John McAleer, '"The Key to India": Troop movements, southern Africa, and Britain's Indian Ocean world, 1795–1820', *International History Review 35*, no. 2, 2013, p. 296.
15. Ben Jeffs, Helen MacQuarrie, Andrew Pearson and Annsofie Witkin, *Infernal Traffic: Excavation of a liberated African graveyard in Rupert's Valley, St Helena* (London: Council for British Archaeology, 2012).
16. John McAleer, 'Looking east: St Helena, the South Atlantic and Britain's Indian ocean world', *Atlantic Studies 13*, no. 1, 2013, pp. 78–98.
17. Daniel A. Yon, 'Race-making/race-mixing: St Helena and the South Atlantic world', *Social Dynamics: A Journal of African Studies 33*, no. 2, 2007, p. 146.
18. Andrew Pearson, *Distant Freedom: St Helena and the abolition of the slave trade, 1840–1872* (Liverpool: University of Liverpool Press, 2016), p. 3.
19. 'Daniel Domingues da Silva, David Eltis, Philp Misevich and Olatunji Ojo, 'The diaspora of Africans liberated from slave ships in the nineteenth century', *Journal of African History 55*, no. 3, 2014, p. 350.
20. Pearson, *Distant Freedom*, p. 110.
21. Ibid., pp. 201–43.
22. McAleer, 'Looking east', p. 81; Yon, 'Race-making/race-mixing', p. 152.
23. Yon, 'Race-making/race-mixing', p. 151.
24. Muster for month ended 31 January 1849, St Helena Muster Roll, 1847–49, WO 12/11045, NA.
25. Muster roll for 1 July–30 September 1849, St Helena Muster Roll, 1849–51, WO 12/11046, NA.
26. He left for London from Melbourne in March 1878 on board the *Somersetshire* (Victoria Outward Passenger Lists, 1852–1915: findmypast.co.uk) and

Notes: Chapter 7

returned to New Zealand in June 1879 (*Wanganui Chronicle*, 21 June 1879, p. 2).
27. Pearson, *Distant Freedom*, p. 274.
28. Nathaniel regularly collected good conduct pay from July to March 1856. St Helena Muster Roll, 1853–55, WO 12/11048, NA; St Helena Muster Roll, 1855–57, WO 12/11050, NA.
29. Nathaniel petitioned the governor in 1868 for a small pension to be awarded until he recovered his health and could return to work. AD1 75 CD1868/5234, Reporting on the case of Nathaniel Flowers, Archives New Zealand, Wellington.
30. He advertised regularly in the local papers. The earliest advertisement found so far appeared in the *Wanganui Herald*, 14 March 1870, p. 3.
31. One of the most invisible dimensions of the New Zealand Wars is sexual violence committed against Māori women by troops. See Angela Wanhalla, 'Interracial sexual violence in 1860s New Zealand', *New Zealand Journal of History* 45, no. 1, 2011, pp. 71–84.

CHAPTER 7

1. Peter France, *The Charter of the Land: Custom and colonisation in Fiji* (Melbourne: Oxford University Press, 1969), chaps. 5 and 6; Deryck Scarr, *Fragments of Empire: A history of the Western Pacific High Commission 1877–1914* (Canberra: ANU Press, 1967); Nicholas Thomas, *Colonialism's Culture: Anthropology, travel and government* (Princeton: Princeton University Press, 1994); Lorenzo Veracini, '"Emphatically not a white man's colony": Settler colonialism and the construction of colonial Fiji', *Journal of Pacific History* 43, no. 2, 2008, pp. 189–205.
2. Vijay Naidu, *The Violence of Indenture in Fiji* (Lautoka: Fiji Institute of Applied Studies, 2004 [1980]); Brij Lal, *Chalo Jahaji: On a journey through indenture in Fiji* (Canberra and Suva: ANU and Fiji Museum, 2000).
3. The Bose Vakaturaga was itself a colonial institution. Colin Newbury, '*Bose Vakauraga*: Fiji's Great Council of Chiefs, 1875–2000', *Pacific Studies* 29, nos. 1/2, 2006, pp. 82–127.
4. Tracey Banivanua Mar and Nadia Rhook, 'Counter networks of empires: Reading unexpected people in unexpected places,' *Journal of Colonialism and Colonial History* 19, no. 2, 2018.
5. James Whitelaw, 'People, land and government in Suva, Fiji' (PhD diss., Australian National University, 1966), p. 51.
6. Scarr, *Fragments of Empire*, pp. 7–8; Lauren Benton, *Law and Colonial Cultures: Legal regimes in world history, 1400–1900* (Cambridge: Cambridge University Press, 2002); Lisa Ford, 'Law', in David Armitage and Alison Bashford (eds), *Pacific Histories: Land, Ocean, People* (Basingstoke and London: Palgrave Macmillan, 2014), pp. 220–26; Sally Engle Merry, *Colonizing Hawai`i: The cultural power of law* (Princeton: Princeton University Press, 2000).
7. Kate Stevens, *Gender, violence and criminal justice in the colonial Pacific, 1880–1920* (London: Bloomsbury, 2023), chap. 2; see also Margaret Rodman, *Houses Far from Home: British colonial space in the New Hebrides* (Honolulu: University of Hawai`i Press, 2001).
8. Norman Etherington, 'The gendering of indirect rule: Criminal law and colonial Fiji, 1875–1900', *Journal of Pacific History* 31, no. 1, 1996, pp. 45–46.
9. The Criminal Procedure Ordinance 1875 ensured that any cases involving Fijians were tried by assessors, as the impartiality of a European jury in judging crimes involving non-Europeans was deemed dubious at best. See Peter Duff, 'The evolution of trial by judge and assessors in

Fiji', *Journal of Pacific Studies 21*, 1997, pp. 189–213. Trial by assessor was extended to Indian, Chinese and Pacific Islanders in 1883; Bridget Brereton, *Law, Justice and Empire: The colonial career of John Gorrie, 1829–1892* (Barbados: University of the West Indies Press, 1997), p. 127; *Unsworn Testimony Ordinance 1875* (No. X) and Criminal Procedure Ordinance 1875 (No. 23), Fiji Certified Copies of Acts, CO 84/1, and Native Witness Protection Ordinance 1883 (No. 3), Certified Copies of Acts of the Fiji Islands 1881–1887, CO 84/2, National Archives Kew, London (hereafter NAK).
10. Thomas, *Colonialism's Culture*, p. 116.
11. Lord Stanmore, *Fiji: Records of private and public life 1875–1880*, vol. 1 (Edinburgh: Printed by R. and R. Clark, 1897), p. 302: '[A]ll criminal offences of any gravity, with, perhaps, a few trifling exceptions, might at once be brought under the operation of English law.'
12. Martin Wiener explains that interracial murder – like sexual crime – trials provide 'revealing episodes in the ordinary operation of the criminal law across the Empire, cases in which this underlying conflict [between liberalism and inequality] could not simply be argued in the abstract but had to be resolved by a courtroom decision over the fate of an actual defendant'. Martin Wiener, *An Empire on Trial: Race, murder, and justice under British rule, 1870–1935* (Cambridge: Cambridge University Press, 2009), p. 5.
13. See Supreme Court Ordinance 1875 (No. 14); Criminal Procedure Ordinance 1875 (No. 23); Summary Offences Ordinance 1876 (No. 17). Fiji Certified Copies of Acts 1875–1880, CO 84/1, NAK. While sodomy (sexual intercourse between men) and bestiality (sexual relations with an animal) appear rarely in the Supreme Court, they involved a different gendered dynamic and are not considered here.
14. Given the demographics of the colony, fewer European women appeared in court. For more on the voices of the colonised in Fiji's courts, see John Kelly, '"Coolie" as labour commodity: Race, sex, and European dignity in colonial Fiji', *Journal of Peasant Studies 19*, nos. 3–4, 1992, p. 262; John Kelly, 'Gaze and grasp: Plantations, desires, indentured Indians, and colonial law in Fiji', in Lenore Manderson and Margaret Jolly (eds), *Sites of Desire, Economies of Pleasure: Sexualities in Asia and the Pacific* (Chicago: University of Chicago Press, 1997), pp. 73–98.
15. Case 30/1910, Criminal Sittings, Fiji Supreme Court, National Archives of Fiji, Suva (hereafter NAF). See also Case 1/1881. The names of victims, defendants and witnesses are not used in full.
16. Case 89/1917, Criminal Sittings, Fiji Supreme Court, NAF.
17. Case 7/1881, Criminal Sittings, Fiji Supreme Court, NAF.
18. Case 21/1907, Criminal Sittings, Fiji Supreme Court, NAF.
19. Case 16[?]/1879, Criminal Sittings, Fiji Supreme Court, NAF.
20. Case 13/1881, Criminal Sittings, Fiji Supreme Court, NAF.
21. Case 6/1891, Criminal Sittings, Fiji Supreme Court, NAF.
22. *The Fiji Times*, Wednesday 9 April 1884, microfilm, NAF. Brij Lal, 'Kunti's cry: Indentured women on Fiji's plantations', *Indian Economic and Social History Review 22*, no. 1, 1985, pp. 55–71; Brij Lal, 'Veil of dishonour: Sexual jealousy and suicide on Fiji plantations', *Journal of Pacific History 20*, no. 3, 1985, pp. 135–55; Claudia Knapman, *White Women in Fiji, 1835–1930: The ruin of empire?* (London: Allen and Unwin, 1986).
23. Matthew Hale, cited in Susan Estrich, 'Rape', *The Yale Law Journal 95*, no. 6,

1986, pp. 1094–95. Note this statement was published posthumously.
24. See Joanna Bourke, *Rape: A history from 1860 to the present* (London: Virago, 2007); Louise A. Jackson, *Child Sexual Abuse in Victorian England* (London: Routledge, 1999); Anna Clark, *Women's Silence, Men's Violence: Sexual assault in England, 1770–1845* (London: Pandora Press, 1987); Durba Ghosh, 'Household crimes and domestic order: Keeping the peace in colonial Calcutta, c. 1770–c. 1840', *Modern Asian Studies* 38, 2004, pp. 599–623; Jonathan Saha, 'The male state: Colonialism, corruption and rape investigations in the Irrawaddy Delta c. 1900', *Indian Economic and Social History Review* 48, no. 3, 2010, pp. 343–76.
25. Lal, 'Veil of dishonour'; Carolyn Strange, 'Masculinities, intimate femicide and the death penalty in Australia, 1890–1920', *British Journal of Criminology* 43, 2003, p. 335.
26. Memo for the Assistant Colonial Secretary, SM Valia, 13/1/93 CSO 304/1893, in CSO 2320/1985, NAF; Bourke, *Rape*, pp. 390–94; Robert Nicole, *Disturbing History: Resistance in early colonial Fiji* (Honolulu: University of Hawai`i Press, 2010), p. 164.
27. Elizabeth Kolsky, '"The body evidencing the crime": Rape on trial in colonial India, 1860–1947', *Gender & History* 22, no. 1, 2010, p. 111.
28. Nancy Stepan, *The Idea of Race in Science: Great Britain 1800–1960* (London: Macmillan, 1982).
29. Salesa makes this statement with references to policies of racial amalgamation, but it can equally be applied to law. Damon Salesa, *Racial Crossings: Race, intermarriage, and the Victorian British Empire* (Oxford: Oxford University Press, 2011), p. 42.
30. Stevens, *Gender, violence and criminal justice*, chap. 3.
31. All material related to this trial found in Case 74/1910 Criminal Sittings, Fiji Supreme Court, NAF.
32. Rape and sexual assault were considered criminal if proven to be against the will of an adult woman, but criminal regardless of consent in a minor. In other cases, determining the age of the victim was both difficult for officials and crucial in deciding what charges to press. See also Case 9/1906 and Case 29/1906, Criminal Sittings, Fiji Supreme Court, NAF.
33. Thomas, *Colonialism's Culture*, pp. 108–12; Nicholas Thomas, 'Sanitation and seeing: The creation of state power in early colonial Fiji', *Comparative Studies in Society and History* 32, no. 1, 1990, pp. 149–70; Nicole, *Disturbing History*, chaps. 5 and 7.

CHAPTER 8

1. Alice Edith Tonge, 'The Youngs of Umbercollie: The first white family in South-West Queensland, 1845', typescript, n.d., ML MSS 3821, Mitchell Library, State Library of New South Wales, Sydney, p. 23.
2. Ibid., p. 15.
3. Lyndall Ryan et al., *Colonial Frontier Massacres, Australia, 1788–1930* (Newcastle: University of Newcastle, 2017–2020), funded by Australian Research Council, Discovery Project 140100399: https://c21ch.newcastle.edu.au/colonialmassacres/map.php
4. Tonge, 'The Youngs of Umbercollie', p. 24.
5. Ibid.
6. Mark Copland, 'A system of assassination: The Macintyre River frontier 1837–1850' (Honours thesis, University of Queensland, 1990); Heather Goodall, 'Authority under challenge: Pikampul land and Queen Victoria's law during the British invasion of Australia', in Martin Daunton and Rick Halpern (eds), *Empire and Others: British encounters*

with Indigenous peoples, 1600–1850 (Philadelphia: University of Pennsylvania Press, 1999), pp. 260–78.
7. Ryan et al., *Colonial Frontier Massacres, Australia, 1788–1930*.
8. *Sydney Morning Herald*, 15 October 1847, p. 3; Copland, 'A system of assassination', p. 52.
9. *Maitland Mercury,* 13 October 1847, p. 3; Richard Bligh to Colonial Secretary A. Deas Thomson, 29 February 1848, in F. Watson (ed.), *Historical Records of Australia* (Sydney: Parliament of the Commonwealth of Australia, 1925), series 1, vol. 26, pp. 396–98; Copland, 'A system of assassination', p. 58, note 19.
10. Tonge, 'The Youngs of Umbercollie', p. 22.
11. Copland, 'A system of assassination', p. 53.
12. Tonge, 'The Youngs of Umbercollie', p. 23.
13. Richard Bligh to Chief Commissioner of Crown Lands, 10 January 1849, in Copland, 'A system of assassination', p. 53.
14. William Telfer, *The Wallabadah Manuscript: The early history of the northern districts of New South Wales. Recollections of the early days* (Kensington: New South Wales University Press, 1980), p. 39.
15. Tonge, 'The Youngs of Umbercollie', p. 23.
16. Copland, 'A system of assassination', p. 66.
17. Goodall, 'Authority under challenge', p. 266.
18. Evidence of Jonathan Young, Maitland District Court Depositions, March/April 1849, in Copland, 'A system of assassination', p. 66.
19. Evidence of Margaret Young, Maitland District Court Depositions, March/April 1849, in Copland, 'A system of assassination', p. 66.
20. Warialda Letterbook CPS Justices 1847–1855, 4 September 1848, in Copland, 'A system of assassination', p. 67.
21. Copland, 'A system of assassination', p. 59.
22. Maitland District Court Depositions, March/April 1849, in Copland, 'A system of assassination', p. 67.
23. Copland, 'A system of assassination', p. 68.
24. Ibid., pp. 67–68; Goodall, 'Authority under challenge', p. 266.
25. Copland, 'A system of assassination', p. 69.
26. Ibid.
27. Ibid., pp. 69–70.
28. Goodall, 'Authority under challenge', p. 267.
29. Ibid., p. 266.
30. Ibid., p. 267.
31. Ibid.
32. Ibid., p. 268.
33. Copland, 'A system of assassination', pp. 70–71.
34. Tonge, 'The Youngs of Umbercollie', p. 20.

CHAPTER 9

1. Miriel Lenore, 'Cootachah', in Miriel Lenore and Louise Crisp, *Travelling Alone Together/Ruby Camp* (North Melbourne: Spinifex Press, 1997), p. 149. Lenore's collection *Travelling Alone Together* appears alongside Crisp's collection *Ruby Camp* in a single volume.
2. Lenore, 'The boys', in *Travelling Alone Together*, p. 150.
3. Edward John Eyre, *Autobiographical Narrative of Residence and Exploration in Australia, 1832–1839*, ed. Jill Waterhouse (London: Caliban Books, 1984), p. 105.
4. Jill Waterhouse, 'Edward John Eyre: Queanbeyan district landowner, overlander and explorer, especially his relationships with local Aboriginal people and convicts', *Canberra Historical Journal* 41, 1998, pp. 15, 21–22.
5. Eyre, *Autobiographical Narrative*, p. 105.
6. See Dane Kennedy for a discussion of Indigenous boys and explorers in Australian and African expeditions. Dane Kennedy, *The Last Blank Spaces: Exploring Africa and Australia* (Cambridge: Harvard University Press, 2013), pp. 171–79.
7. Eyre, *Autobiographical Narrative*, p. 105.
8. Ibid., p. 115.

9. Ibid., p. 116.
10. Ibid., p. 121.
11. Ibid., p. 123.
12. Ibid., p. 124. Shirleene Robinson highlights the prevalence of Aboriginal children being removed from their families, not just by the state but also unofficially by individual settlers. She acknowledges that some 'settlers attempted to negotiate directly with Indigenous people to obtain their children', but these cases were outnumbered by 'kidnapping[s] and forced removal[s]'. Shirleene Robinson, 'Regulating the race: Aboriginal children in private European homes in colonial Australia', *Journal of Australian Studies 37*, no. 3, 2013, pp. 308–09.
13. Eyre, *Autobiographical Narrative*, p. 127.
14. Kennedy, *The Last Blank Spaces*, pp. 171–79.
15. Eyre, *Autobiographical Narrative*, p. 177.
16. Ivan Rudolph, *Eyre: The forgotten explorer* (Sydney: HarperCollins, 2014), chap. 5.
17. Ibid., chap. 10.
18. Edward John Eyre, *Journals of Expeditions of Discovery into Central Australia, and Overland from Adelaide to King George's Sound, in the Years 1840–1, including an Account of the Manners and Customs of the Aborigines, and the State of Their Relations with Europeans*, 2 vols (London: T. and W. Boone, 1845), vol. 1, p. 294.
19. Julie Evans, *Edward Eyre: Race and colonial governance* (Dunedin: Otago University Press, 2005), p. 21.
20. Eyre, *Journals*, vol. 1, pp. 297–99.
21. Ibid., pp. 234–35.
22. Ibid., p. 386.
23. Ibid., p. 388.
24. Jill Waterhouse points out that cutting rations had been Eyre's usual disciplinary technique in managing the convict labourers at his Molonglo property. Waterhouse, 'Edward John Eyre', p. 21.
25. Eyre, *Journals*, vol. 1, p. 389.
26. In April 1838 on his first overlanding expedition, his crew had threatened mutiny. Eyre was worried that Unmallie would leave with them: 'I was greatly afraid that if any of the men really did go he would be induced to go with them, nor did I know how to prevent this, so silent and cunning are the Australian blacks in all they do.' Eyre, *Autobiographical Narrative*, p. 147.
27. Eyre, *Journals*, vol. 1, pp. 389–91; Edward John Eyre, *Reports of the Expedition to King George's Sound 1841 and the Death of Baxter* (Adelaide: Sullivan's Cove, 1983), pp. 39–40.
28. Eyre, *Journals*, vol. 1, pp. 392–93.
29. Ibid., p. 402. He wore 'nothing but his shirt', so Eyre assumed he had been asleep. Eyre, *Reports of the Expedition*, p. 43.
30. Eyre, *Journals*, vol. 2, p. 1.
31. Ibid., pp. 2–3.
32. Ibid., p. 4.
33. Ibid., p. 9.
34. Ibid., pp. 11–12.
35. Ibid., p. 21.
36. Ibid., p. 24.
37. Eyre, *Reports of the Expedition*.
38. Malcolm Uren and Robert Stephens, *Waterless Horizons: The first full-length study of the extraordinary life of Edward John Eyre, explorer, overlander, and pastoralist in Australia* (Melbourne: Robertson and Mullens, 1942), p. 176.
39. 'Relics of Eyre's expedition', *South Australian Register*, 18 February 1882, p. 1.
40. Daisy Bates, *My Natives and I*, ed. P.J. Bridge (Victoria Park: Hesperian Press, 2004), p. 116.
41. Geoffrey Dutton, 'Eyre, Edward John (1815–1901)', from the Australian Dictionary of Biography: http://adb.anu.edu.au/biography/eyre-edward-john-2032/text2507
42. Robinson, 'Regulating the race'.
43. Kennedy, *The Last Blank Spaces*, pp. 166, 175.

CHAPTER 10

1. Office of Environment and Heritage, 'Cootamundra Aboriginal Girls Home', NSW Department of Planning, Industry and Environment: www.environment.nsw.gov.au/heritageapp/ViewHeritageItemDetails.aspx?ID=5061346
2. Heather Radi, 'Ardill, George Edward (1857–1945)', from the Australian Dictionary of Biography: http://adb.anu.edu.au/biography/ardill-george-edward-5048
3. Human Rights and Equal Opportunity Commission, 'Bringing them home: Report of the National Inquiry into the Separation of Aboriginal and Torres Strait Islander Children from Their Families' (Sydney: HREOC, 1997), p. 141: www.humanrights.gov.au/sites/default/files/content/pdf/social_justice/bringing_them_home_report.pdf
4. Bridget Brennan, 'The stolen children of Cootamundra: "Years later, what's changed?"', ABC News, 12 February 2018: www.abc.net.au/news/2018-02-11/stolen-generations-cootamundra-girls-home-whats-changed/9408132
5. Office of Environment and Heritage, 'Cootamundra Aboriginal Girls Home', NSW Department of Planning, Industry and Environment: www.environment.nsw.gov.au/heritageapp/ViewHeritageItemDetails.aspx?ID=5061346
6. Brennan, 'The stolen children of Cootamundra'.
7. Human Rights and Equal Opportunity Commission, 'Bringing them home', p. 161.
8. Cootamundra is in southwest rural New South Wales and is extremely cold during the winter months.
9. Office of Environment and Heritage, 'Cootamundra Aboriginal Girls Home', NSW Department of Planning, Industry and Environment: www.environment.nsw.gov.au/heritageapp/ViewHeritageItemDetails.aspx?ID=5061346.
10. Victoria Haskins, 'A better chance? Sexual abuse and the apprenticeship of Aboriginal girls under the NSW Aborigines Protection Board', *Aboriginal History 28*, 2004, p. 42.
11. Haskins, 'A better chance?'
12. Human Rights and Equal Opportunity Commission, 'Bringing them home: Report of the National Inquiry into the Separation of Aboriginal and Torres Strait Islander Children from Their Families' (Sydney: HREOC, 1997), p. 5: www.humanrights.gov.au/sites/default/files/content/pdf/social_justice/bringing_them_home_report.pdf
13. Parliament of Australia, Department of Parliamentary Services, 'Prime Minister Kevin Rudd, MP – Apology to Australia's Indigenous peoples', recorded 13 February 2008: https://info.australia.gov.au/about-australia/our-country/our-people/apology-to-australias-indigenous-peoples
14. ABC Education, 'Prime Minister Keating's Redfern address, 1992', ABC Education, first broadcast 10 December 1992: www.abc.net.au/education/paul-keatings-1992-redfern-speech/13889050
15. 'About the National Redress Scheme', a national scheme for people who have experienced institutional child sexual abuse: www.nationalredress.gov.au/about/about-scheme; Jens Korff, 'Compensation for Stolen Generation members', 8 February 2019: www.creativespirits.info/aboriginalculture/politics/stolen-generations/compensation-for-stolen-generation-members; 'Redress scheme', Aboriginal and Torres Strait Islander Legal Services (Qld): www.atsils.org.au/wp-content/uploads/2014/11/FACT-SHEET_Redress-Scheme.pdf; 'Stolen Generations Reparations Scheme', Government of South Australia: www.

dpc.sa.gov.au/responsibilities/aboriginal-affairs-and-reconciliation/reconciliation/stolen-generations-reparations-scheme; 'Stolen Generations Reparations Scheme and Funeral Assistance Fund', NSW government: www.aboriginalaffairs.nsw.gov.au/healing-and-reparations/stolen-generations/reparations-scheme; 'The National Redress Scheme', knowmore: https://knowmore.org.au/about-us/redress-and-royal-commission/redress-scheme/
16. 'Victoria's Stolen Generations Redress Scheme is a step on a journey towards justice', Victorian Aboriginal Legal Service: www.vals.org.au/victorias-stolen-generations-redress-scheme-is-a-step-on-a-journey-towards-justice/
17. Stephanie Gilbert, 'Living with the past: The creation of the stolen generation positionality', *AlterNative: An International Journal of Indigenous Peoples 15*, 2019, pp. 226–33.
18. Achille Mbembe, *Critique of Black Reason* (Durham and London: Duke University Press, 2017), p. 121.
19. Ibid., p. 122.
20. Ibid., p. 123.

CHAPTER 11

1. Brij V. Lal (ed.), *Bittersweet: The Indo-Fijian experience* (Canberra: Pandanus Books, 2004), p. 10.
2. Janak Pandey, 'India', in James Georgas, John W. Berry, Fons J.R. van de Vijver, Çigdem Kagitçibasi, & Ype H. Poortinga (eds), *Families Across Cultures: A 30-nation psychological study* (Cambridge: Cambridge University Press, 2006), p. 369.
3. Kenneth Lowell Gillon, *Fiji's Indian Migrants: A history to end of indenture in 1920* (Oxford: Oxford University Press, 1962), pp. 59–67; Lal (ed.), *Bittersweet*, p. 10; Hugh Tinker, *A New System of Slavery: The export of Indian labour overseas 1830–1920* (London: Oxford University Press, 1974), p. 118.
4. Erica Newman, 'Colonial intervention on guardianship and "adoption" practices in Fiji 1874–1970' (PhD diss., University of Otago, 2018), p. 73.
5. 'Forwarding Draft Ordinance – Care and Maintenance of Orphan Indian Immigrants', Colonial Secretary Office, 84/2813, Fiji National Archives, Suva.
6. William Gordon Bryce, 'An ordinance with regard to Indian immigration', *The Laws of Fiji: Containing the ordinances of Fiji and subsidiary legislation thereunder, enacted on or before the 16th day of April 1955* (London: C.F. Roworth, 1956).
7. Newman, 'Colonial intervention on guardianship', p. 75.
8. John Ernest Popins, *Delight to the Heart: A short story of the Dudley Orphanage for Indian Girls at Dilkusha 'Delight to the heart'* (Melbourne: Spectator Publishing, 1935).
9. Andrew Thornley, 'The Methodist mission and the Indians in Fiji 1900–1920' (Master's thesis, University of Auckland, 1973), p. 136.
10. Newman, 'Colonial intervention on guardianship', p. 104.
11. Thornley, 'The Methodist mission and the Indians in Fiji 1900–1920', p. 137.
12. Cited in Ibid., p. 138.
13. Ibid.
14. Ibid.
15. Ibid.
16. Ibid., pp. 140–41.
17. Ibid., p. 141; Newman, 'Colonial intervention on guardianship', p. 106.
18. Example retrieved from MMSA file Nausori/A/1 (Indian) Correspondence re: Indian Orphanages, Fiji National Archives, Suva (hereafter FNA).
19. Newman, 'Colonial intervention on guardianship', p. 107.
20. Ibid., pp. 107–08.
21. Thornley, 'The Methodist mission and the

Indians in Fiji 1900–1920', p. 142.
22. Information retrieved from MMSA file Nausori/A 1 (Indian) Correspondence re: Indian Orphanages, FNA.
23. Example retrieved from MMSA file Nausori/A/1 (Indian) Correspondence re: Indian Orphanages, FNA.
24. Newman, 'Colonial intervention on guardianship', p. 108.
25. Thornley, 'The Methodist mission and the Indians in Fiji 1900–1920', pp. 143–44.
26. Ibid., p. 144.
27. The use of orphanages as a boarding home during difficult times had been a common occurrence since their establishment in Europe, America and within British colonies, so this idea was not an unusual arrangement.
28. Newman, 'Colonial intervention on guardianship', pp. 209–25.

CHAPTER 12

1. T.T. Flynn was the founding professor of biology at the University of Tasmania.
2. Errol Flynn, *My Wicked Wicked Ways* (New York: G.P. Putnam, 1959), p. 33.
3. 'Young, Edward', Pitcairn Islands Study Center: https://library.puc.edu/pitcairn/bounty/crew5.shtml; Sir George Young, *Facsimile for a Proposal for a Settlement on the Coast of New South Wales 1785* (Sydney: Angus and Robertson, 1888): http://handle.slv.vic.gov.au/10381/108487
4. Patty O'Brien, *The Pacific Muse: Exotic femininity and the colonial Pacific* (Seattle: University of Washington Press, 2006), pp. 121–29.
5. Marelle Flynn, letter to Earl Conrad, cited in Earl Conrad, *Errol Flynn: A memoir* (New York: Dodd, Mead and Company, 1978), pp. 52–53.
6. 'Outrages in the Western Pacific', *Sydney Morning Herald*, 26 April 1882, p. 6. Ambae was also known as Aobe and Leper Island in the nineteenth century.
7. Thomas Harrisson, *Savage Civilisation* (New York: Alfred Knopf, 1937), pp. 210–11; Death notice for Robert Young, *Sydney Morning Herald*, 4 January 1879; Marelle Flynn, letter to Earl Conrad, cited in Conrad, *Errol Flynn*, pp. 52–53.
8. Debra Fasano, *Young Blood: The making of Errol Flynn* (Whitefield: Debra Fasano, 2009).
9. Tony Thomas (ed.), *From a Life of Adventure: The writings of Errol Flynn* (Secaucus: Citadel Press, 1980), p. 43.
10. John Hammond Moore reproduced the remaining diary in full in *The Young Errol Flynn Before Hollywood* (Sydney: Angus and Robertson, 1975), pp. 109–18.
11. Alice Allen Innes is the person who censored Flynn's diary. Stuart Inder, 'His wicked wicked ways: Leaves from Errol Flynn's New Guinea diary', *Pacific Islands Monthly*, November 1960, pp. 80–83; Alice Allen Innes to Chas Hamilton Inc. NY, 25 August 1969, MSS 1408, Mitchell Library, State Library of New South Wales, Sydney.
12. Patricia O'Brien, 'Wild colonial boy: Errol Flynn's rape case, Pacific pasts and the making of Hollywood', *Australian Historical Studies 52*, no. 4, 2021, pp. 591–610.
13. Inder, 'His wicked wicked ways', p. 80.
14. Flynn, *My Wicked Wicked Ways*, p. 103.
15. Ibid., pp. 69, 71.
16. Ibid., p. 95.
17. Amirah Inglis, *Not a White Woman Safe: Sexual anxiety and politics in Port Moresby, 1920–1934* (Canberra: Australian National University Press, 1975); Roger Thompson, *Australian Imperialism in the Pacific* (Carlton: University of Melbourne Press, 1980); 'Making a mandate: The formation of Australia's New Guinea policies 1919–1925', *Journal of Pacific History 25*, no. 1, 1990, pp. 68–84.
18. Flynn, *My Wicked Wicked Ways*, p. 105.
19. David Steen, 'It happened one night at MGM', *Vanity Fair*, 1 April 2003:

www.vanityfair.com/news/2003/04/mgm200304; Pamela Hutchinson, 'Moguls and starlets: 100 years of Hollywood's corrosive, systemic sexism', *Guardian*, 19 October 2017: www.theguardian.com/film/2017/oct/19/moguls-and-starlets-100-years-of-hollywoods-corrosive-systemic-sexism

20. 'Girl on stand describes meeting Flynn at party', *Los Angeles Times*, 15 January 1943, II, p. 10.
21. 'New Flynn story aired', *Los Angeles Times*, 22 January 1943, II, p. 1.
22. Flynn, *My Wicked Wicked Ways*, pp. 315, 325.

CHAPTER 13

1. Robert Fairbairn, *Government Gazette of Western Australia*, no. 53, 5 December 1882, p. 520.
2. *Inquirer*, 17 February 1886.
3. Robinson to Secretary of State, 9 March 1881, in Correspondence relating to the question of police protection to settlers in outlying districts, promulgation of pearl shell fishery regulations and protection of the Aboriginal natives, Western Australian Legislative Council (WALC), Parliamentary Papers, 1881, no. 13, p. 5.
4. Western Australian Legislative Council, *Instructions to and reports from the resident magistrate despatched by direction of His Excellency on special duty to the Murchison and Gascoyne districts* (Perth: Richard Pether, Government Printer, 1882).
5. New land regulations in 1864 raised the maximum lease area to 100,000 acres (40,468ha) and offered a generous rent concession to those willing to pioneer new northern districts. *Western Australian Government Gazette*, 24 August 1864, chapter VIII, paras 1–7.
6. Neville Green, 'Aboriginal sentencing in Western Australia in the late 19th century with reference to Rottnest Island prison', *Records of the Western Australian Museum*, Supplement 79, 2011, pp. 77–85. See also Ann Curthoys and Jessie Mitchell, *Taking Liberty: Indigenous rights and settler self-government in colonial Australia, 1830–1890* (Cambridge: Cambridge University Press, 2019), pp. 361–84.
7. *Inquirer and Commercial News*, 1 March 1876, p. 4.
8. As Ann Curthoys has recently pointed out, this system ensured a docile frontier population as well as securing coerced labour.
9. WALC, *Instructions to and reports from the resident magistrate*, p. 7.
10. Ibid., p. 9.
11. Ibid., p. 7.
12. Ibid., pp. 7, 12.
13. Ibid., p. 9.
14. Ibid. Gifford commented that the Aboriginal men were not at war, as evidenced by their allowing their women to be taken – however, this, too, accounted for their 'stealing sheep for some kind of reparation', pp. 12–13.
15. 'The native difficulty (Mr Fairbairn's report)', *Herald,* 12 August 1882, p. 1; Robert M. Walcott was Charles (and John) Brockman's partner at Minilya Station, Gascoyne, until December 1884. The partnership was dissolved in December 1884. *West Australian*, 20 December 1884, p. 1.
16. *Government Gazette of Western Australia*, no. 53, 5 December 1882, p. 520.
17. Ibid.
18. Kay Forrest, *The Challenge and the Chance: The colonisation and settlement of north west Australia 1861–1914* (Victoria Park: Hesperian Press, 1996), pp. 142–43.
19. Green, 'Aboriginal sentencing in Western Australia', pp. 77–85.
20. Ibid.
21. 'The native labour system on the Gascoyne, by the Rev. J.B. Gribble, F.C.S. Missionary to the Natives', *Inquirer and Commercial News*, 20 January 1886, p. 5.

22. Jane Lydon, 'Christian heroes? John Gribble, Exeter Hall and antislavery on Western Australia's frontier', *Studies in Western Australian History 30*, 2016, pp. 59–72; Su-Jane Hunt, 'The Gribble affair: A study in colonial politics', *Studies in Western Australian History 8*, 1984, pp. 42–51; John Brown Gribble, *Dark Deeds in a Sunny Land* (Perth: Stirling Bros, 1886); *West Australian*, 18 December 1885.
23. See Stephen Churches, 'Put not your faith in princes (or courts) – Agreements made from asymmetrical power bases: The story of a promise made to Western Australia's Aboriginal people', in Peter Read, Gary Meyers and Bob Reece (eds), *What good condition? Reflections on an Australian Aboriginal treaty, 1986–2006*, (Canberra: ANU Press, 2006), pp. 1–14; Ann Curthoys and Jane Lydon (eds), 'Governing Western Australian Aboriginal people: Section 70 of WA's 1889 Constitution', special issue, *Studies in Western Australian History 30*, 2016; Jane Lydon, 'Introduction: Section 70 of the Western Australian Constitution Act 1889, or, "Throwing dust in the eyes of the people"', *Studies in Western Australian History 30*, 2016, pp. 1–7.
24. 'The Aborigines in Western Australia', *The Times*, 4 February 1905, p. 12; 'The Aborigines in West Australia', *The Times*, 8 March 1905, p. 2; 'The treatment of Australian natives', *The Times*, 14 April 1905, p. 4; 'Dr Roth's report', *The Times*, 1 May 1905, p. 14.
25. 'The Aborigines question. Dr Roth's report: Interview with Sir John Forrest. The difficulty of the native question. The police defended', *West Australian*, 4 February 1905, p. 7. See also 'Alleged ill-treatment of Australian natives', *The Times*, 11 January 1907, p. 3.
26. Douglas Lockwood, *Herald* (Melbourne), 19 March 1958.
27. I explore this transition in Jane Lydon, *Anti-slavery and Australia: No slavery in a free land?* (New York: Routledge, 2021).
28. Larissa Behrendt, 'Aboriginal women and the white lies of the feminist movement: Implications for Aboriginal women in rights discourse', *Australian Feminist Law Journal 1*, 1993, pp. 27–44; Hannah McGlade, Bronwyn Carlson and Marlene Longbottom, 'An open letter in response to the lack of public concern or response to the killings of Aboriginal and Torres Strait Islander women', *Croakey*, 9 March 2021: www.croakey.org/an-open-letter-in-response-to-the-lack-of-public-concern-or-response-to-the-killings-of-aboriginal-and-torres-strait-islander-women/; Bronwyn Carlson, 'No public outrage, no vigils: Australia's silence at violence against Indigenous women', *The Conversation*, 16 April 2021: https://theconversation.com/no-public-outrage-no-vigils-australias-silence-at-violence-against-indigenous-women-158875
29. Sally Morgan, *My Place* (Perth: Fremantle Press, 1987), p. 618.

CHAPTER 14

1. Joseph L. Celusien, '"The Haitian turn": An appraisal of recent literary and historiographical works on the Haitian Revolution', *Journal of Pan-African Studies 5*, no. 6, 2012, p. 39.
2. Adom Getachew, 'Universalism after the post-colonial turn: Interpreting the Haitian Revolution', *Political Theory 44*, no. 6, 2016, pp. 823, 830.
3. Christian Cantir, '"Savages in the midst": Revolutionary Haiti in international society (1791–1838)', *Journal of International Relations and Development 20*, no. 1, 2017, p. 238; Kofi Barima, 'Militancy and spirituality: Haiti's revolutionary impact on Jamaica's Africans and Afro-Creoles, 1740–1824',

Wadabagei: A journal of the Caribbean and its diaspora 14, nos 1/2, 2013, pp. 78, 81; Mitch Cachun, 'Antebellum African Americans, public commemoration, and the Haitian Revolution: A problem of historical mythmaking', *Journal of the Early Republic 26*, no. 2, 2006, pp. 250, 252; Matt Clavin, 'Race, rebellion, and the Gothic: Inventing the Haitian Revolution', *Early American Studies 5*, no. 1, 2007, p. 2.
4. David P. Geggus, 'Epilogue', in David P. Geggus (ed.), *The Impact of the Haitian Revolution in the Atlantic World* (Columbia: University of South Carolina Press, 2001), p. 247; see also Celusien, '"The Haitian turn"', pp. 44–45.
5. For example, Celusien, '"The Haitian turn"', pp. 37–54; Doris L. Garraway, *Tree of Liberty: Cultural legacies of the Haitian Revolution in the Atlantic world* (Charlottesville: University of Virginia Press, 2008); Geggus, *The Impact of the Haitian Revolutionary in the Atlantic World*; Paul Gilroy, *The Black Atlantic: Modernity and double consciousness* (London: Verso, 1993).
6. Bronwyn Elsmore, *Like Them That Dream: The Maori and the Old Testament* (Auckland: Reed, 2000).
7. Richard Boast, 'Vanished Theocracies: Christianity, war and politics in New Zealand, 1830–80', in Lisa Ford and Tim Rowse (eds) *Between Indigenous and Settler Governance* (Abingdon: Routledge, 2013), p. 72; Vincent O'Malley, *The Great War for New Zealand: Waikato 1800–2000* (Wellington: Bridget Williams Books, 2016), pp. 77–78; Pei Te Hurinui, *King Pōtatau: An account of the life of Pōtatau Te Wherowhero the first Māori King* (Wellington: Huia Publishers, [1959] 2010), pp. 176–77.
8. Hazel Petrie, *Outcasts of the Gods?: The struggle over slavery in Māori New Zealand* (Auckland: Auckland University Press, 2015).
9. Claudia Orange, *The Treaty of Waitangi* (Wellington: Bridget Williams Books, 1987), pp. 42–43.
10. *Te Karere Maori*, 14 July 1863, pp. 6, 9; see also Lachy Paterson, 'The Kohimarama Conference of 1860: A contextual reading', *Journal of New Zealand Studies*, 12 (2012), pp. 29–46.
11. James Belich, *The New Zealand Wars and the Victorian Interpretation of Racial Conflict* (Auckland: Auckland University Press, [1989] 2015), pp. 119–25.
12. *Te Hokioi*, 15 February 1863, p. 2.
13. *Te Hokioi*, 8 December 1862, p. 1.
14. *Te Hokioi*, 24 March 1863, p. 1.
15. See Lachy Paterson, '*Te Hokioi* and the legitimization of the Māori nation', in Brendan Hokowhitu and Vijay Devdas (eds), *The Fourth Eye: Māori media in Aotearoa New Zealand* (Minneapolis: University of Minnesota Press, 2013), pp. 124–42.
16. See Lachy Paterson, 'Kiri Mā, Kiri Mangu: The terminology of race and civilisation in the mid-nineteenth-century Maori-language newspapers', in Jenifer Curnow, Ngapare Hopa and Jane McRae (eds), *Rere atu, taku manu! Discovering history, language and politics in the Maori-language newspapers* (Auckland: University of Auckland Press, 2002), pp. 78–97.
17. *Te Karere Maori*, 30 November 1857, p. 6; 15 March 1859, p. 4.
18. *Te Karere Maori*, 1 February 1855, p. 21.
19. *Te Karere Maori*, 22 November 1858, p. 1.
20. *Te Whetu o te Tau*, 1 September 1858, p. 3.
21. *Te Hokioi*, 15 January 1863, p. 1.
22. E.R. Simmons, 'Garavel, Joseph Marie', from the Dictionary of New Zealand Biography: https://teara.govt.nz/en/biographies/1g2/garavel-joseph-marie
23. 'Te Korero o Haiti', *Te Hokioi*, 24 March 1863, pp. 1–2.
24. *Te Hokioi*, 26 April 1863, p. 2.
25. 'The Hokioi Press', *Journal of the Te*

Awamutu Historical Society 6, no. 1, 1971, p. 22.
26. Sir George Grey to the Duke of Newcastle, 1 August 1863, *Appendix to the Journals of the House of Representatives*, E-03A (1863), p. 1: https://paperspast.natlib.govt.nz/parliamentary/appendix-to-the-journals-of-the-house-of-representatives/1863/I/890
27. Belich, *The New Zealand Wars*, p. 133.
28. 'St. Domingo, or Hayti; Hana Tomingo, ko Haiti tetahi o ona ingoa', *Te Karere Maori*, 18 July 1863, pp. 6–8.
29. 'A voice from afar, with more "talk about Hayti"; He reo no tawhiti, me etahi atu "Korero mo Haiti"', *Te Karere Maori*, 18 July 1863, pp. 8–14. Quotation from p. 9.
30. *Te Karere Maori*, 18 July 1863, p. 9.
31. Ibid., pp. 8–14.
32. Michael Belgrave, *Dancing with the King: The rise and fall of the King Country, 1864–1885* (Auckland: Auckland University Press, 2017).

CHAPTER 15

1. Patricia Clarke, *Pioneer Writer: The life of Louisa Atkinson, novelist, journalist, naturalist* (Sydney: Allen & Unwin, 1990), pp. 62–63.
2. 'Horticultural society of Sydney', *Sydney Morning Herald*, 5 January 1865, p. 5.
3. Elizabeth Lawson, *The Natural Art of Louisa Atkinson* (Sydney: State Library of New South Wales Press, 1995), p. 31.
4. 'The late Mrs. J.S. Calvert', *Australian Town and Country Journal*, 30 November 1878, p. 17.
5. James Atkinson, *An Account of the State of Agriculture and Grazing in New South Wales*, 2nd edn (London: J. Cross, [1826] 1844), p. 128.
6. John Stephens, *The History of the Rise and Progress of the New British Province of South Australia*, 2nd edn (London: Smith, Elder & Co., 1839), pp. 62–63.
7. Don Watson, *The Bush: Travels in the heart of Australia* (Melbourne: Hamish Hamilton, 2014), p. 219.
8. L.A. [Louisa Atkinson], 'A voice from the country: Mount Tomah', *Sydney Morning Herald*, 28 January 1861, p. 2. Atkinson's columns appeared under the initials 'L.A.' until her marriage to James Snowden Calvert in 1869, when she became 'L.C.'
9. L.C. [Louisa Atkinson], 'A voice from the country: After shells in the limestone', *Sydney Morning Herald*, 24 May 1870, p. 5.
10. Lawson, *The Natural Art of Louisa Atkinson*, p. 85
11. See Tim Bonyhady, *Images in Opposition: Australian landscape painting, 1801–1890* (Oxford: Oxford University Press, 1984).
12. Louisa Atkinson, 'Tressa's resolve, A tale by the late Mrs. Calvert', *Sydney Mail and New South Wales Advertiser*, 2 November 1872, p. 569.
13. Lawson, *The Natural Art of Louisa Atkinson*, p. 85.
14. L.C. [Louisa Atkinson], 'Climatic influences on the habits of birds', *Sydney Mail*, 16 June 1870, p. 12.
15. Atkinson, 'A voice from the country', p. 5.
16. Ibid.
17. Deborah Bird Rose, *Nourishing Terrains: Australian Aboriginal views of landscape and wilderness* (Canberra: Australian Heritage Commission, 1996), p. 7.
18. L.C. [Louisa Atkinson], 'Hanging Rock on the Southern Road', *Sydney Morning Herald*, 3 February 1871, p. 5.
19. Atkinson, 'A voice from the country', p. 5.
20. Anthony Trollope, *Harry Heathcote of Gangoil* (London: Folio Society, 1998), p. 6.
21. William Woolls, 'Wonders of Australian vegetation', *Sydney Morning Herald*, 15 September 1876, p. 2.
22. Ibid.; 'Don't ring-bark or cut down gum trees', *Warwick Examiner and Times*, 30 September 1876, p. 3.
23. Watson, *The Bush*, pp. 191–92.

24. Louisa Atkinson, 'The Fitzroy waterfalls' (1871), in Louisa Atkinson, *Excursions from Berrima and a Trip to Manaro and Molonglo in the 1870s* (Canberra: Mulini Press, 1980), p. 18.
25. Rob Nixon, *Slow Violence and the Environmentalism of the Poor* (Boston: Harvard University Press, 2011), p. 96.
26. Ibid., p. 2.
27. Michael Slezak, 'Scorched country: The destruction of Australia's native landscape', *Guardian*, 7 March 2018: www.theguardian.com/environment/2018/mar/07/scorched-country-the-destruction-of-australias-native-landscape; Lorena Allam and Carly Earl, 'For centuries the rivers sustained Aboriginal culture. Now they are dry, elders despair', *Guardian*, 21 January 2019: www.theguardian.com/australia-news/2019/jan/22/murray-darling-river-aboriginal-culture-dry-elders-despair-walgett
28. Lawson, *The Natural Art of Louisa Atkinson*, pp. 85–86.

CHAPTER 16

1. Te Ture Haeata ki Parihaka 2019/Parihaka Reconciliation Act 2019, Public Act 2019 No. 60: www.legislation.govt.nz/act/public/2019/0060/latest/versions.aspx
2. Waitangi Tribunal, *The Taranaki Report: Kaupapa Tuatahi* (Wellington: Legislation Direct, 1996), Wai 143, p. 206.
3. Dick Scott, *Ask the Mountain: The story of Parihaka* (Auckland: Raupo, 2008); Rachel Buchanan, *The Parihaka Album: Lest we forget* (Wellington: Huia, 2009); Danny Keenan, *Te Whiti O Rongomai and the Resistance of Parihaka* (Wellington: Huia, 2015); Hazel Riseborough, *Days of Darkness: Taranaki, 1878–1884* (Wellington: Allen and Unwin, 1989).
4. Cited in Hazel Riseborough, 'Te Pāhuatanga o Parihaka', in Te Miringa Hohaia, Gregory O'Brien and Lara Strongman (eds), *Parihaka: The art of passive resistance* (Wellington: City Gallery, Victorian University Press, Parihaka Pā Trustees, 2001), p. 31.
5. Buchanan, *The Parihaka Album*, p. 24.
6. Cited in Hazel Riseborough, 'Te Pāhuatanga o Parihaka', p. 19.
7. 'The Pirates of Parihaka', *Observer*, 12 November 1881, p. 132.
8. 'The Pirates of Penzance', *Lyttleton Times*, 28 June 1881, p. 5; 'Theatre Royal – Cary's Opera Company', 4 November 1881, p. 5.
9. W.S. Gilbert and Arthur Sullivan, *The Complete Gilbert and Sullivan*, ed. Ed Glinert (London: Penguin, 2006), p. 190.
10. Scott, *Ask the Mountain*, p. 115.
11. 'The Evening Star', *Auckland Star*, 4 November 1881, p. 2.
12. 'The Invasion of Parihaka. – Mr. Bryce as He Appeared Leading the Way on His White Charger', *Observer*, 12 November 1881, p. 131.
13. 'Glorious Capture of Te Whiti, Tohu, and Hiroki', *Observer*, 12 November 1881, p. 131.
14. Rolleston family: Further papers, 1873–1903, MS79-287-1, Alexander Turnbull Library, Wellington.
15. Rosamund Rolleston, *William and Mary Rolleston: An informal biography* (Wellington: Reed, 1971), p. 81.
16. Keenan, *Te Whiti O Rongomai*, p. 143.
17. Tohu Kākahi, 1895 speech, cited in Te Miringa Hohaia, 'Ngaa Puutaketanga Koorero Moo Parihaka', in Hohaia, O'Brien and Strongman, *Parihaka*, p. 59.
18. Frank Fudge, 'The Battle of Parihaka', *Lyttleton Times*, 21 November 1881, p. 5.
19. Jane Stafford, '"To sing this Bryce and bunkum age": Colonial poetry and Parihaka', in Hohaia, O'Brien and Strongman, *Parihaka*, pp. 179–85.
20. Mervyn Thompson, with music by William Dart, *Songs to the Judges* (Wellington: Playmarket, 1983), p. 11.

21. Hohaia, O'Brien and Strongman, *Parihaka*.
22. Harry Dansey, *Te Raukura: The feathers of the albatross* (Auckland: Longman Paul, 1974), p. 56. In his introduction to the play, Dansey records that this waiata is 'an authentic Parihaka chant … The approval of a Parihaka elder was gained before it was used', p. xii.
23. Witi Ihimaera, 'Author's note', *The Parihaka Woman* (Auckland: Vintage, 2011), p. 299.
24. Ihimaera, *The Parihaka Woman*, pp. 291–92.
25. Haka verses recorded by Wiremu Te Kāhui Kararehe, 'Haka verse for Te Whiti', cited in Hohaia, 'Ngaa Puutaketanga Koorero Moo Parihaka', p. 56.

CHAPTER 17

1. Clifford Brooks, in John Carty, Carly Davenport and Monique La Fontaine, *Yiwarra Kuju: The Canning Stock Route* (Canberra: National Museum of Australia, 2010), p. 1.
2. Wally Caruana, 'Rover Thomas Dreams the Krill Krill', in *Roads Cross: The paintings of Rover Thomas* (Canberra: National Gallery of Australia, 1994), p. 4; Will Christensen, in *Rover Thomas: I want to paint* (Perth: Holmes à Court Gallery, 2003), p. 54.
3. John Carty, 'Drawing a line in the sand: The Canning Stock Route and contemporary art', in Carty, Davenport and La Fontaine, *Yiwarra Kuju*, p. 65.
4. Curtis Taylor Parnngurr, in Carty, Davenport and La Fontaine, *Yiwarra Kuju*, p. 38.
5. Carty, Davenport and La Fontaine, *Yiwarra Kuju*, p. 49.
6. Roley Williams, in Carty, Davenport and La Fontaine, *Yiwarra Kuju*, p. 81.
7. Eubena Nampitjin, in Carty, Davenport and La Fontaine, *Yiwarra Kuju*, p. 84.
8. Caruana, 'Rover Thomas Dreams the Krill Krill', p. 4; Carty, 'Drawing a line in the sand', p. 65.
9. John Echo, interview by Rachel Burgess, 15 August 2019; Francis Kofod, 'Gija glossary', in Paddy Bedford, Russell Storer and Museum of Contemporary Art, *Paddy Bedford* (Sydney: Museum of Contemporary Art, 2006), pp. 136–37.
10. Kofod, 'Gija Glossary', 136–37; Jane Yalunga Tinmarie, interview by Rachel Burgess, 24 January 2019.
11. Cathie Clement, 'Historical notes relevant to impact stories of the East Kimberley', *East Kimberley Working Paper No. 2* (Canberra: Australian National University, 1989), pp. 3–4.
12. Mary Ann Jebb, *Blood, Sweat and Welfare* (Perth: UWA Publishing, 2002), pp. 125–26; Charlie McAdam, in Elizabeth Tregenza, *Boundary Lines* (Victoria: Penguin Books, 1995), pp. 6–13.
13. Jebb, *Blood, Sweat and Welfare*, pp. 125–26.
14. Ibid.; John Echo, interview by Rachel Burgess, 15 August 2019.
15. Francis Kofod, 'Paddy Bedford's stories', in Bedford, Storer and Museum of Contemporary Art, *Paddy Bedford*, p. 72.
16. Phyllis Kaberry, *Aboriginal Woman Sacred and Profane* (London: Routledge, 2004).
17. Cathie Clement, submission to the Review of Exhibitions and Public Programs at the National Museum of Australia, 2003: www.nma.gov.au/about/corporate/review-of-exhibitions-and-programs/review-submissions; Cathie Clement, 'The Humpty Dumpty factor in Aboriginal history', *Teaching History 37*, no. 4, 2003, pp. 26–32; Kate Auty, 'Patrick Bernard O'Leary and the Forrest River massacres', *Aboriginal History 28*, 2004, pp. 122–55.
18. Jebb, *Blood, Sweat and Welfare*, p. 104.
19. Ibid., p. 38.
20. Bob Nyalcas and Dotty Whatebee, in Ross and Bray, 'Impact Stories of the East Kimberley', pp. 56–62; McAdam, in Tregenza, *Boundary Lines*, pp. 6–13.

21. Ryan, 'Oral histories from the Turkey Creek area, WA'; Nyalcas and Whatebee, in Ross and Bray, 'Impact Stories of the East Kimberley', pp. 56–62; McAdam, in Tregenza, *Boundary Lines*, pp. 6–13.
22. Jane Yalunga Tinmarie, interview by Rachel Burgess, 24 January 2019.
23. Sister Theresa Morinelli, interview by Rachel Burgess, 5 June 2019.
24. Bill Bunbury, *It's Not the Money It's the Land: Aboriginal stockmen and the equal wages case* (Fremantle: Fremantle Arts Centre Press, 2002), p. 67.
25. Ibid., p. 67.
26. Rover Thomas in Caruana, *Roads Cross*, pp. 25–27.

CHAPTER 18

1. Ceridwen Dovey, 'The mapping of massacres', *New Yorker*, 6 December 2017: www.newyorker.com/culture/culture-desk/mapping-massacres
2. Cited in Patricia Vinnicombe, 'Queenie McKenzie: Tribute', *Artlink 20*, no. 1, 2000: www.artlink.com.au/articles.cfm?id=1389
3. 'Two women charged over alleged defacing of Captain Cook statue in Sydney's Hyde Park', ABC, 14 June 2020: www.abc.net.au/news/2020-06-14/nsw-women-charged-over-defacing-captain-cook-statue-in-sydney/12353598
4. Lyndall Ryan et al., *Colonial Frontier Massacres, Australia, 1788–1930* (Newcastle: University of Newcastle, 2017–2020), funded by Australian Research Council, Discovery Project 140100399: https://c21ch.newcastle.edu.au/colonialmassacres/map.php The map can be accessed here, along with the research and technical information
5. Dovey, 'The mapping of massacres'.
6. See the Uluru Statement from the Heart, 2017: https://ulurustatement.org/. Wide consultation with Indigenous groups led to the recommendation for a Makarrata Commission. In March 2018 Parliament appointed the Joint Select Committee on Constitutional Recognition relating to Aboriginal and Torres Strait Islander Peoples. Agreement-making and truth-telling are canvassed in Section 6 of the committee's final report. See Joint Select Committee on Constitutional Recognition relating to Aboriginal and Torres Strait Islander Peoples Commonwealth of Australia, *Final Report* (Canberra: Commonwealth of Australia, 2018).
7. The video work is included in the *Defying Empire* travelling exhibition (most recently at Mildura Arts Centre in 2019), which also links to the online map: http://thenamesofplaces.com/tnop/
8. McKenzie is referring to the East Kimberley, but see also Marcia Langton on Cape York Peninsula, where land and water work together as 'a unitary cultural phenomenon': 'Earth, wind, fire and water: The social and spiritual construction of water in Aboriginal societies', in Bruno David, Bryce Barker and Ian J. McNiven (eds), *The Social Archaeology of Australian Indigenous Societies* (Canberra: Aboriginal Studies Press, 2006), pp. 139–60.
9. Dovey, 'The mapping of massacres'.
10. Thanks to Lisa Chandler for pointing out the multiple potential meanings of the background Indigenous images. The link between marking on (museum) artefacts and cicatrices on Aboriginal skin is made by Watson herself in relation to a 2014 exhibition: see Diana Young and Judy Watson, *Written on the Body* (St Lucia: Anthropology Museum, University of Queensland, 2014), cover note.
11. See Judy Watson and Louise Martin-Chew, *Blood Language* (Melbourne: Miegunyah-Melbourne University Press, 2009).
12. Dovey, 'The mapping of massacres'.
13. Judy Watson and Lyndall Ryan (with Bill Pascoe, Greg Hooper, Jonathan Richards;

chaired by Michael Aird), 'Mapping massacre: History, art, place', public panel discussion, 2 December 2018, UQ Anthropology Museum, 'Unsettling Australia', International Association for Australian Studies conference, University of Queensland, 3–5 December 2018: https://iash.uq.edu.au/event/session/1464

14. On sand stories, see Jennifer Green, *Drawn from the Ground: Sound, sign and inscription in Central Australian sand stories* (Cambridge: Cambridge University Press, 2014). On the disjunction between Western mapping technologies and Indigenous deep knowledge of place, see Richard J. Martin and David Trigger, '"Nothing Never Change": Mapping land, water and Aboriginal identity in the changing environments of Northern Australia's Gulf Country', *Settler Colonial Studies 5*, no. 4, 2015, pp. 317–33.

15. See Quentin Sprague's excellent catalogue essay on this exhibition when it travelled to the Bathurst Art Gallery in 2018, reproduced in 2020 as part of a major art auction catalogue: 'How to describe broken landscapes', Deutscher and Hackett, 18 March 2020: www.deutscherandhackett.com/important-paintings-jirrawun-artists-helene-teichmann-collection-lots-23-%E2%80%93-29. See also Rachel Burgess, this volume.

16. 'Landscapes in blood', *Sydney Morning Herald*, 14 December 2002: www.smh.com.au/national/landscapes-in-blood-20021214-gdfysp.html. Keith Windschuttle, *The Fabrication of Aboriginal History. Volume 1: Van Diemen's Land 1803–1847* (Sydney: Macleay Press, 2002). For an early rebuttal of Windschuttle's spurious claims, see Robert Manne (ed.), *Whitewash: On Keith Windschuttle's fabrication of Aboriginal history* (Melbourne: Black Inc., 2003), which includes Cathie Clement's chapter 'Mistake Creek', pp. 199–213.

17. Sprague, 'How to describe broken landscapes'.

18. See William Deane, 'Decrying the memories of Mistake Creek is yet further injustice', *Sydney Morning Herald*, 27 November 2002: www.smh.com.au/national/decrying-the-memories-of-mistake-creek-is-yet-further-injustice-20021127-gdfvkb.html

19. Bernard Lagan, 'Black ban', *Bulletin 124*, no. 6520, 2006, p. 39.

20. Interestingly, McKenzie's related painting, *The Horse Creek Massacre (1880s)*, has featured on the National War Memorial website since 2017. It formed part of the exhibition *For Country, for Nation*, which focused on traditions of Aboriginal and Torres Strait Islanders in protecting country, and the blogpost was explicit about McKenzie's reference to massacres: 'Queen of the desert', 14 July 2017, Australian War Memorial: www.awm.gov.au/articles/blog/queen-of-the-desert

21. Niki Burnside, 'Queenie Mckenzie's "Mistake Creek Massacre" displayed by National Museum after years of controversy', ABC, 22 July 2020: www.abc.net.au/news/2020-07-22/talking-blak-to-history-indigenous-exhibition-at-national-museum/12472370

22. For example, the exhibition *Myall Creek and Beyond*, curated by Bianca Beetson, New England Regional Art Museum (NERAM), Armidale, June 2018, which included work by Judy Watson and other contemporary artists: www.neram.com.au/myall-creek-and-beyond/

23. Watson and Martin-Chew, *Blood Language*, p. 20.

24. Lisa Chandler, 'The reclaimed object: Transformations of museum artefacts by Indigenous Australian artists,' in G.U. Grossmann and P. Krutisch (eds), *The Challenge of the Object. Die Herausforderung des Objekts. 33rd*

Congress of the International Committee of the History of Art, Nuremburg 15–20 July 2012 (conference proceedings), (Nuremburg: Germanisches National Museum, 2013), pp. 566–69.
25. See Vernon Ah Kee's artwork referencing family photos from the Tindale collection *Fantasies of the Good* (2004) series and *neither pride nor courage* (2006), featured in *Transforming Tindale*, State Library of Queensland (2016): www.slq.qld.gov.au/showcase/transforming-tindale/gallery; Fiona Foley, *Biting the Clouds: A Badtjala perspective on the Aboriginals Protection and Restriction of the Sale of Opium Act, 1897* (St Lucia: University of Queensland Press, 2020); Brook Andrew and Katie Dyer (eds), *Evidence: Brook Andrew* (Ultimo: Museum of Applied Arts and Sciences Media, 2015); on Julie Gough, see her solo exhibition *Julie Gough: Tense past*, Tasmanian Museum and Art Gallery, 7 June–3 November 2019: www.tmag.tas.gov.au/whats_on/exhibitions/current_upcoming/info/julie_gough_tense_past
26. Chandler, 'The reclaimed object', p. 566.
27. The Musée du quai Branly has been subject to various critiques. See Sally Price, *Paris Primitive: Jacques Chirac's museum on the Quai Branly* (Chicago: University of Chicago Press, 2007); Margaret Jolly, 'Becoming a "new" museum? Contesting oceanic visions at Musée du quai Branly', *The Contemporary Pacific 23*, no. 1, 2011, pp. 108–39; Geoffrey White, 'Civilizations on the Seine: Sally Price's *Paris Primitive*', *Museum Anthropology Review* 6, no. 1, 2012, pp. 38–62.
28. Watson, cited in Chandler, 'The reclaimed object', p. 568.
29. Watson and Martin-Chew, *Blood Language*, p. 172.
30. Chandler, 'The reclaimed object', p. 569.
31. For details of their methodology, see Greg Hooper, Jonathan Richards and Judy Watson, 'Mapping colonial massacres and frontier violence in Australia: "the names of places"', *Cartographica 55*, no. 3, 2020, pp. 193–98.
32. For a detailed discussion of their method, see the introduction to Ryan et al., *Colonial Frontier Massacres, Australia, 1788–1930*.
33. Hooper et al., 'Mapping colonial massacres', p. 198.
34. 'Mr Watson has 40 prs of blacks' ears nailed round the walls, collected during raiding parties after the loss of many cattle speared by the blacks.' Cited in Watson and Martin-Chew, *Blood Language*, p. 141. The historical Jack Watson is not related to the artist.
35. Watson and Martin-Chew, *Blood Language*, p. 141.
36. Sprague, 'How to describe broken landscapes'.

CHAPTER 19

1. The author would like to acknowledge the importance of his conversations with Michel Tuffery and Nick Tūpara in writing this chapter.
2. John Hawkesworth, *An Account of the Voyages Undertaken by the Order of His Present Majesty for Making Discoveries in the Southern Hemisphere: and successively performed by Commodore Byron, Captain Wallis, Captain Carteret, and Captain Cook, in the Dolphin, the Swallow, and the Endeavour*, vol. 1 (London: Printed for W. Strahan and T. Cadell in the Strand, 1773), inserted before p. 223.
3. *Captain Samuel Wallis and the DOLPHIN attacked by Otahitians*, c. 1800, object no. 00006125, Australian National Maritime Museum, Sydney: http://collections.anmm.gov.au/objects/42869/captain-samuel-wallis-and-the-dolphin-attacked-by-otahitians?ctx=32bb0a98-8404-4140-acd2-255daf63e332&idx=3

4. W.H. Pearson, 'European intimidation and the myth of Tahiti', *Journal of Pacific History* 4, no. 1, 1969, pp. 199–217.
5. Gaelen Macdonald, 'Introduction: Tranquillity disturb'd', *Tranquillity Disturbed: A contemporary look at historical New Zealand, 12 March–31 March 2015* (Wellington: New Zealand Portrait Gallery/Te Pukenga Whakaata, 2015), unpaginated.
6. Journal of James Cook, 9 October 1769 and Journal of William Brough Monkhouse, 8 October 1769, in *The Journals of Captain James Cook on His Voyages of Discovery: The voyage of the Endeavour, 1768–1771*, ed. J.C. Beaglehole (Cambridge: Cambridge University Press, 1955), pp. 169, 565–66; Joseph Banks, Journal 8 October 1769, in *The Endeavour Journal of Joseph Banks 1768–1771*, ed. J.C. Beaglehole (Sydney: Angus and Robertson, 1962), p. 400.
7. Journal of James Cook, 9–10 October 1769, in Beaglehole, *The Voyage of the Endeavour*, p. 170.
8. Journal of James Cook, 10 October 1769, and Journal of William Brough Monkhouse, 9 October 1769, in Beaglehole, *The Voyage of the Endeavour*, pp. 170, 568; Banks, Journal 9 October 1769, in Beaglehole, *The Endeavour Journal of Joseph Banks*, p. 403.
9. Banks, Journal 9 October 1769, in Beaglehole, *The Endeavour Journal of Joseph Banks*, p. 403.
10. Journal of James Cook, 11 October 1769, in Beaglehole, *The Voyage of the Endeavour*, p. 172.
11. 'Capt. Cook: A "genocidal murderer" – Indigenous scholar Tina Ngata', *Te Ao Māori News*, 16 July 2019: www.teaomaori.news/capt-cook-genocidal-murderer-indigenous-scholartina-ngata
12. Sally Blundell, 'Tuia 250: The effects of Captain James Cook's arrival on tangata whenua', *Listener*, 8 October 2019.
13. 'Tipuna Te Maro', *Gisborne Herald*, 25 September 2019: www.gisborneherald.co.nz/local-news/20190925/tipuna-te-maro/
14. 'Reserve transformed with stunning installation', *Waterford Press*: www.waterfordpress.co.nz/business/currie-construction/
15. 'Telling stories of Tairawhiti', *Gisborne Herald*, 30 September 2019: www.gisborneherald.co.nz/local-news/20190930/two-sculptures-unveiled-on-saturday-on-titirangi-kaiti-hill-celebrate-important-figures-and-voyaging/
16. Greg Dening, 'Empowering imaginations', *The Contemporary Pacific* 9, no. 2, 1997, p. 427.

CHAPTER 20

1. Ben Quilty, Facebook, 24 August 2017: www.facebook.com/290611141314/posts/for-the-last-few-days-i-have-listened-to-people-i-admire-and-people-i-dont-talk-/10154553460831315/
2. 'Ngurungaeta' is a Woiwurrung word meaning 'head man' or 'tribal leader'. Gary Presland, *First People: The Eastern Kulin of Melbourne, Port Phillip and Central Victoria* (Melbourne: Museum Victoria Publishing, 2010).
3. Bain Attwood, *Possession: Batman's treaty and the matter of history* (Melbourne: Miegunyah Press, 2009).
4. Robert Kenny, 'Tricks or treats?: A case for Kulin knowing in Batman's treaty', *History Australia* 5, no. 2, 2011, pp. 1–38.
5. Bain Attwood has suggested that they may have misconstrued the English 'twig and turf' ceremony – walking the boundary and passing a twig – for Tanderrum, which can also involve the giving of small branches of gumtrees. Attwood, *Possession*.
6. Penelope Edmonds and Michelle Berry, 'Eliza Batman's house: Unhomely frontiers and intimate Overstraiters in Van Diemen's Land and Port Phillip', in Penelope Edmonds and Amanda Nettelbeck (eds),

Intimacies of Violence in the Settler Colony: Economies of dispossession around the Pacific Rim (New York: Palgrave Macmillan, 2018), pp. 115–37.
7. Belinda King, 'Should we rename the Batman Bridge in Tasmania?', ABC, 15 June 2020: www.abc.net.au/news/2020-06-15/should-we-rename-batman-bridge-in-tasmania/12355404
8. Joe Hinchliffe, 'Call to remove statue of John Batman', *Age*, 26 August 2017: www.theage.com.au/national/victoria/call-to-remove-statue-of-john-batman-founder-of-melbourne-over-role-in-indigenous-killings-20170826-gy4snc.html
9. Aisha Dow, 'Bye bye Batman', *Age*, 16 February 2017: www.theage.com.au/national/victoria/bye-bye-batman-melbourne-founders-name-to-be-erased-from-electorate-history-20170216-guepuj.html; Calla Wahlquist and Paul Karp, 'Melbourne electorate of Batman renamed after Indigenous activist', *Guardian*, 20 June 2018: www.theguardian.com/australia-news/2018/jun/20/melbourne-electorate-of-batman-renamed-after-indigenous-activist
10. Lyndall Ryan et al., *Colonial Frontier Massacres, Australia, 1788–1930* (Newcastle: University of Newcastle, 2017–2020), funded by Australian Research Council, Discovery Project 140100399: https://c21ch.newcastle.edu.au/colonialmassacres/map.php
11. Bruce Scates, 'Call to topple monuments is an opportunity for debate', *Age*, 11 June 2020: www.theage.com.au/national/call-to-topple-monuments-is-an-opportunity-for-debate-20200611-p551qs.html
12. Brendan Condon, 'John Batman's statue tried for war crimes', *Nonviolence Today 25*, March/April 1992: http://dkeenan.com/NvT/
13. Ibid.
14. 'The Black Line', National Museum Australia: www.nma.gov.au/defining-moments/resources/the-black-line
15. P.L. Brown, 'Batman, John (1801–1839)', from the Australian Dictionary of Biography: http://adb.anu.edu.au/biography/batman-john-1752
16. Condon, 'John Batman's statue tried for war crimes'.
17. The Convention on the Prevention and Punishment of the Crime of Genocide (Genocide Convention) is an instrument of international law that codified for the first time the crime of genocide: www.un.org/en/genocideprevention/genocide-convention.shtml
18. Condon, 'John Batman's statue tried for war crimes'.
19. Ibid.
20. Ibid.
21. Ibid.
22. Ibid.
23. See Penelope Edmonds, 'Batmans Hill', eMelbourne, 2008: www.emelbourne.net.au/biogs/EM00164b.htm; Penelope Edmonds, 'Founding myths', eMelbourne, 2008: www.emelbourne.net.au/biogs/EM00603b.htm. See also Agnes Paton Bell, *Melbourne: John Batman's village* (Melbourne: Cassell, 1965); James Bonwick, *John Batman: Founder of a city* (Hobart: Education Department, 1971).
24. Michael Cannon and Ian McFarlane, *Historical Records of Victoria*, vol. 3 (Melbourne: Victorian GPO, 1981–2002).
25. Henry Reynolds, *Fate of a Free People: A radical re-examination of the Tasmanian wars* (Melbourne: Penguin, 1995); Lyndall Ryan, *Tasmanian Aborigines: A history since 1803* (Sydney: Allen and Unwin, 2012).
26. Edmonds and Berry, 'Eliza Batman's house'.
27. Ibid.
28. For information on Pellenominer, see Julie Gough, 'Forgotten lives – The first photographs of Tasmanian Aboriginal people', in Jane Lydon (ed.), *Calling the Shots: Indigenous photographies* (Canberra: Aboriginal Studies Press,

2014), pp. 37–38. See also N.J.B. Plomley (ed.), *Friendly Mission: The Tasmanian journals and papers of George Augustus Robinson, 1829–1834*, 2nd edn (Hobart: Quintus Publishing, 2008), Appendices, p. 1026.

CHAPTER 21

1. *Te Mana Whatu Ahuru: Report on te Rohe Potae claims. Pre-publication version, parts I & II* (Wellington: Waitangi Tribunal, 2018), Wai 898, p. 524.
2. Rudall C. Hayward, dir., *Rewi's Last Stand* (Frontier Films, 1940).
3. Virginia Callanan, 'The last stand', *Gauge: The Blog of New Zealand's Audiovisual Archives*, 15 May 2014: https://ngataonga.org.nz/
4. Taonga are tangible and intangible treasures of significance in te ao Māori. Paul Tapsell discussed the association of taonga with ancestors and tribal lands, stating that taonga 'can be tangible, like a greenstone pendant, a geothermal hot pool, or a fishing ground, or they can be intangible, like the knowledge to weave, or to recite genealogy, and even the briefest of proverbs'. Paul Tapsell, 'The flight of Pareraututu: An investigation of taonga from a tribal perspective', *The Journal of the Polynesian Society 106*, no. 4, 1997, | p. 331.
5. Although colonial and postcolonial are adjectives used to describe our first two scholarly approaches, we use the verb 'decolonising' (as opposed to decolonial critique) for our third approach intentionally. Our analysis of *Rewi's Last Stand* is influenced by decolonising scholarship, Linda Tuhiwai Smith's *Decolonizing Methodologies* in particular. We seek to demonstrate how earlier approaches we have taken in considering *Rewi's Last Stand* – colonial and postcolonial – are not enough to advocate for history that takes seriously Indigenous sovereignty and tino rangatiratanga. As such, active decolonising analysis should be distinguished from 'decolonial' – a term that implies both a finished state of being and a continuity from colonial and postcolonial scholarly forms. In our view, decolonising approaches to history reject this kind of descriptive continuity and instead embody active and ongoing work against colonisation.
6. Pākehā reluctance to engage with colonisation history is evident in the director Rudall Hayward's difficulty finding extras for his film: Pākehā in Te Awamutu, many of whom would have been descendants of soldiers and beneficiaries of raupatu (land confiscation), were not interested in playing their forebears, reflecting a reluctance to engage with the problematic history of the area. In an interview with the *King Country Chronicle* (17 November 1937, p. 7), Hayward commented: 'I must say that I am very disappointed at the response from young men of Te Awamutu and neighbourhood made to our invitation for them to assist by being cast as soldiers … there has been a lamentable lack of enthusiasm, or even interest, in the important undertaking.' Many of the extras ended up being inmates from Waikeria prison. We do not know whether their participation was due to a personal interest in history or simply reflective of the limited opportunities to leave prison and be involved in something creative.
7. H.H. Bridgman, dir., *100 Crowded Years* (Wellington: Government Film Studios, 1941).
8. Annabel Cooper, *Filming the Colonial Past: The New Zealand Wars on screen* (Dunedin: Otago University Press, 2018), pp. 69–70.
9. Though the 1925 and 1940 *Rewi's Last Stand* films share a title and draw

inspiration from the Waikato War, their focus, narrative and tone are distinct. Only fragments of the 1925 film survive today but they (along with documentation) show the earlier film focused more on the experience of a colonial soldier and his Pākehā wife than on Māori experiences. The 1925 version of *Rewi's Last Stand* was originally intended to be shot in the Waikato/Waipā area, with support from Waikato–Tainui leader Te Puea Hērangi. However, Hayward could not provide adequate compensation for the services and resources provided by Hērangi, so instead found a cheaper option in Rotorua with cast from Te Arawa. This displacement of Waikato–Tainui history caused a major grievance between Hērangi and Hayward that lasted many years. When Hayward was filming the 1940 *Rewi's Last Stand*, Hērangi allowed scenes to be shot at Tūrangawaewae marae but would not let Hayward himself inside to direct them. Hayward's insult was only settled when he and Ramai Te Miha Hayward donated funds toward a wharekai (dining hall) for the marae after the making of *To Love a Maori* (1972), where Te Arikinui Dame Te Ataairangikaahu honoured the couple at Tūrangawaewae. See 'Ngā Puna Waihanga 1986 – Part 5', Ngā Taonga Sound and Vision, Wellington (hereafter NgTSV): www.ngataonga.org.nz/collections/catalogue/catalogue-item?record_id=232198. See also Cooper, *Filming the Colonial Past*, pp. 40–41.
10. James Cowan, *The New Zealand Wars: A history of the Māori campaigns and the pioneering period, vol. 1 (1845–64)* (Wellington: R.E. Owen, Government Printer, 1922).
11. 'Rewi's Last Stand' poster (1939), P03899, NgTSV: https://ngataonga.org.nz/
12. This is reflected in a review from the *Dominion*: 'Few could remain unmoved by the sense of danger lurking in scenes familiar to all of us as peaceful holiday spots, or quiet bush and farm lands. To feel like that is to get a new insight into and genuine patriotic understanding of the New Zealand countryside.' See 'Around the theatres: Films showing in Wellington', *Dominion*, 27 July 1940, p. 16. *Rewi's Last Stand*, Vertical Files, Jonathan Dennis Library, NgTSV.
13. New Zealand film and history scholars such as Alistair Fox, Annabel Cooper, Martin Blythe and Bruce Babington have provided rigorous postcolonial critique of *Rewi's Last Stand*, drawing attention to the colonial codings embedded in the film's narrative. Bruce Babington, *A History of the New Zealand Fiction Feature Film: Staunch as?* (Manchester: University Press, 2007); Martin Blythe, *Naming the Other: Images of the Māori in New Zealand film and television* (Metuchen: Scarecrow Press, 1994); Cooper, *Filming the Colonial Past*; Alistair Fox, 'Rudall Hayward and the Cinema of Maoriland: Genre-mixing and counter-discourses in *Rewi's Last Stand* (1925), *The Te Kooti Trail* (1927) and *Rewi's Last Stand/The Last Stand* (1940)', in Barry Keith, Alistair Fox and Hilary Radner (eds), *New Zealand Cinema: Interpreting the past* (Bristol: Intellect Books, 2011).
14. This aligns with Pierre Sorlin's view that historical films are merely 'instrument[s] for talking about the present'. Pierre Sorlin, *The Film in History: Restaging the past* (Oxford: Blackwell, 1980), p. 35.
15. *Te Mana Whatu Ahuru: Report on te Rohe Potae claims. Pre-publication version, parts I & II* (Wellington: Waitangi Tribunal, 2018), Wai 898, pp. 190, 331.
16. James Cowan, *The Old Frontier: Te Awamutu, the story of the Waipa Valley* (Te Awamutu: The Waipa Post Printing and Publishing Company, 1922).

17. In the film Morgan attempts to suggest that Ariana is 'one of us', and that he had adopted her as one of his own children. However, a later scene between Te Whatanui and Ariana affirms that the arrangement made for her was one consistent with whāngai, where she lived with them for a time and particular purpose. This is an example of how the narrative does not fully come to grips with Māori culture and tikanga (Māori epistemological values and practices), despite their presence in it. Sian Smith, '"It came from me" – Māori representation in Ramai Te Miha Hayward's authorship' (Master's thesis, Te Herenga Waka Victoria University of Wellington, 2020), p. 15.
18. The army chaplain, credited as P.C.B., was most likely Patrick Beaton, known for his other colonial literary forays. Smith, '"It came from me"', pp. 25–26.
19. Notably, Cooper gives greater attention to Ariana's agency than other scholars of the film. Cooper, *Filming the Colonial Past*, p. 76; Melissa Cross, 'The forgotten soundtrack of Maoriland: Imagining the nation through Alfred Hill's songs for *Rewi's Last Stand*' (Master's thesis, Massey University, 2015), pp. 69–70.
20. Smith, '"It came from me"', p. 15.
21. *Te Mana Whatu Ahuru*, pp. 469–72.
22. Ibid., pp. 471, 516, 521; Rewi Maniapoto to Hon. Native Minister, Mr. J. Ballance, 3 February 1885. Translated by Mr. G.T. Wilkinson, Government Native Agent, Waikato, *Otago Daily Times*, Issue 8284, 10 September 1888. In Witi Ihimaera and Hēmi Kelly, *Sleeps Standing: Moetū* (New Zealand: Vintage, 2017), p. 185.
23. *Te Mana Whatu Ahuru*, pp. 490, 504.
24. Ibid., pp. 503–08.
25. *Rewi's Last Stand* was the most prominent audio-visual representation of the New Zealand Wars until the late 1970s, when the television series *The Governor* (1977) and then *Utu* (1983) brought revisionist histories of the wars to screen. During the 1950s, 1960s and 1970s, *Rewi's Last Stand* was screened to school groups and broadcast on state television.
26. We, too, in previous work, have fallen into the auteur trap of spending so much time ruminating on Hayward that we neglected the work of other creatives involved in the film's planning, production and preservation.
27. Ihimaera and Kelly, *Sleeps Standing*, p. 87.
28. Cooper, *Filming the Colonial Past*, p. 86.
29. See the 1920 account of Ōrākau by Te Huia Raureti in Ihimaera and Kelly, *Sleeps Standing*, p. 191.
30. The film includes both phrases. Immediately following the delivery of 'kāore e mau te rongo' by Te Huia Raureti, a young man rephrases the words, shouting 'ka whawhai tonu mātou' to the British troops.
31. This analysis draws heavily on Cooper's in-depth research into the 'whakapapa and genealogy of knowledge' involved in this scene (see Cooper, *Filming the Colonial Past*, p. 86). However, Cooper interprets the variation in phrasing as a sign of Hayward's sensitivity toward Māori and his desire to appease popular audiences, which, we believe, gives Hayward too much credit. Considering the urgency with which the film was made, and its limited resourcing, it seems unlikely that Hayward would have given these words so much attention. It is more likely that Te Huia himself, having a much deeper understanding of Ōrākau and its history, would have spoken these words as they were expressed according to his father's account.
32. Ramai Hayward, recorded interview with Ramai Hayward, interview by Alwyn Owen, mp3, circa 1994, audio tape, side 2, Wairarapa Archive, Masterton District Library. We have questioned between us the extent to which the British editor

removed content because it showed the British troops in an unfavourable light. It seems to us that the removal of scenes where children appeared in the fortification during fighting might be understood as an act of silencing.
33. Hayward, recorded interview with Ramai Hayward, interview by Owen, side 2.
34. Hayward, recorded interview with Ramai Hayward, interview by Owen, side 1.
35. Hayward, recorded interview with Ramai Hayward, interview by Owen, side 2.
36. Ōrākau is described as one of the 'darkest days' by Te Rohe Pōtae claimants. *Te Mana Whatu Ahuru*, p. 516.
37. Ngā Taonga Sound and Vision is a kaipupuri organisation, acting as an archival protector of audio-visual taonga, and seeks appropriate permissions for taonga use. The framework Tiakina guides the organisation to connect kaitiaki individuals, whānau, hapū and iwi with the taonga of their ancestors that are held in its taonga Māori collection: https://ngataonga.org.nz/
38. Personal communication with Henriata Nicholas, 7 October 2020, Wellington and Te Awamutu.

CONCLUSION

1. Thomas Mayor, *Finding the Heart of the Nation* (Melbourne: Hardie Grant, 2019).
2. Statement by Australian War Memorial, in Paul Daley, 'Why does the Australian War Memorial ignore the frontier war?', *Guardian Australia,* 12 September 2013: www.theguardian.com/world/2013/sep/12/australian-war-memorial-ignores-frontier-war
3. Charlotte Macdonald explores the economic, cultural and social impact of the imperial regiments stationed in New Zealand from the 1840s to the 1870s. See 'Soldiers of empire: Garrison and empire in the 19th century', 2021: www.soldiersofempire.nz
4. Chelsea Watego, *Another Day in the Colony* (Brisbane: University of Queensland Press, 2021), p. 3.
5. Ibid., p. 4.
6. *Endeavour Voyage: The untold stories of Cook and the First Australians* (exhibition), 2 June 2020–26 April 2021, National Museum of Australia, Canberra: https://nma.gov.au /exhibitions/endeavour-voyage; National Museum of Australia, *The Message: The story from the shore*, YouTube, uploaded 28 January 2021: www.youtube.com/watch?v=hoU65yHWikA
7. National Museum of Australia, *The Message*.
8. Rachel Knowles and Sarah Maunder, 'Aboriginal marchers join Hobart's Anzac Day celebration for the first time', *NITV News*, 25 April 2022: www.sbs.com.au/nitv/article/2022/04/25/aboriginal-marchers-join-hobarts-anzac-day-celebration-first-time
9. Wall label, *Judy Watson & Helen Johnson: the red thread of history, loose ends* (exhibition), the Balnaves Contemporary Series, 19 February–5 June 2022, National Gallery of Australia, Canberra.
10. Tina Baum, interview with Judy Watson and Helen Johnson, 'The Balnaves Contemporary Series: the red thread of history', National Gallery of Australia: https://nga.gov.au/stories-ideas/the-red-thread-of-history/
11. Ibid.

BIBLIOGRAPHY

ARCHIVAL MATERIAL

Alexander Turnbull Library, Wellington:
Rolleston family: Further papers, 1873–1903, MS79-287-1

Archives New Zealand, Wellington:
E.M. Statham to J. Hislop, 15 January 1917, IA 1 7/4/38
J. Allan Thomson, Director, Dominion Museum, to Under Secretary, Internal Affairs, 20 January 1917, IA 17/4/38
Reporting on the case of Nathaniel Flowers, AD1 75 CD1868/5234

Methodist Theological Archives, St John's Theological College, Auckland:
Cort Schnackenberg, Manuscripts and Typescripts of Letter Books, 27 March 1869

Mitchell Library, State University of New South Wales, Sydney:
Tonge, Alice Edith, 'The Youngs of Umbercollie: The first white family in South-West Queensland, 1845', typescript, n.d., ML MSS 3821

National Archives, Kew, London:
Letter to the Undersecretary of State for War, 22 January 1857, WO 43/713 St Helena Regiment (Correspondence) re garrison
Unsworn Testimony Ordinance 1875 (No. X) and Criminal Procedure Ordinance 1875 (No. 23), Fiji Certified Copies of Acts, CO 84/1, and Native Witness Protection Ordinance 1883 (No. 3), Certified Copies of Acts of the Fiji Islands 1881–1887, CO 84/2

National Archives of Fiji, Suva:
Cases 30/1910, 89/1917, 7/1881, 21/1907, 16[?]/1879, 13/1881, 6/1891, Criminal Sittings, Fiji Supreme Court
'Forwarding Draft Ordinance – Care and Maintenance of Orphan Indian Immigrants', Colonial Secretary Office, 84/2813

Special Collections, University of Auckland Library, Auckland:
Benjamin Ashwell Papers, 1834–1869, MSS-Archives-A-172
'Revd. and Dear Sirs, North Shore, Auckland, New Zealand, 8 May 1869', Benjamin Ashwell Papers, 1834–1869, MSS-Archives-A-172

NEWSPAPERS

Auckland Star
Australian Town and Country Journal
Bay of Plenty Times
Colonist
Daily Southern Cross
Dunedin Weekender
Evening Post
Government Gazette of Western Australia
Hawera & Normanby Star
Herald
Inquirer and Commercial News
King Country Chronicle
Listener

Los Angeles Times
Lyttleton Times
Nelson Evening Mail
New Zealand Herald
Observer
Otago Daily Times
Perth Gazette and WA Times
South Australian Register
Sydney Mail and New South Wales Advertiser
Sydney Morning Herald
Taranaki Herald
Te Hokioi
Te Karere Maori
Te Whetu o te Tau
Thames Advertiser
The Fiji Times
The Times
Waikato Times
Waipa Post
West Australian
Western Australian Government Gazette

BOOKS AND REPORTS

Altman, Jon and Melinda Hinkson (eds), *Coercive Reconciliation: Stabilise, normalise, exit Aboriginal Australia* (Melbourne: Arena, 2007)

Andrew, Brook and Katie Dyer (eds), *Evidence: Brook Andrew* (Ultimo: Museum of Applied Arts and Sciences Media, 2015)

Atkinson, James, *An Account of the State of Agriculture and Grazing in New South Wales*, 2nd edn (London: J. Cross, [1826] 1844)

Attwood, Bain, *Possession: Batman's treaty and the matter of history* (Melbourne: Miegunyah Press, 2009)

Babington, Bruce, *A History of the New Zealand Fiction Feature Film: Staunch as?* (Manchester: University Press, 2007)

Baldy, Cutcha Risling, *We Are Dancing for You: Native feminisms and the revitalization of women's coming-of-age ceremonies* (Seattle: University of Washington Press, 2018)

Bates, Daisy and P.J. Bridge (ed.), *My Natives and I* (Victoria Park: Hesperian Press, 2004)

Beaglehole, J.C., *The Endeavour Journal of Joseph Banks 1768–1771* (Sydney: Angus and Robertson, 1962)

Belgrave, Michael, *Dancing with the King: The rise and fall of the King Country, 1864–1885* (Auckland: Auckland University Press, 2017)

Belich, James, *The New Zealand Wars and the Victorian Interpretation of Racial Conflict* (Auckland: Auckland University Press, [1989] 2015)

Bell, Agnes Paton, *Melbourne: John Batman's village* (Melbourne: Cassell, 1965)

Benton, Lauren, *Law and Colonial Cultures: Legal regimes in world history, 1400–1900* (Cambridge: Cambridge University Press, 2002)

Blythe, Martin, *Naming the Other: Images of the Māori in New Zealand film and television* (Metuchen: Scarecrow Press, 1994)

Bonwick, James, *John Batman: Founder of a city* (Hobart: Education Department, 1971)

Bonyhady, Tim, *Images in Opposition: Australian landscape painting, 1801–1890* (Oxford: Oxford University Press, 1984)

Bourke, Joanna, *Rape: A history from 1860 to the present* (London: Virago, 2007)

Brereton, Bridget, *Law, Justice and Empire: The colonial career of John Gorrie, 1829–1892* (Barbados: University of the West Indies Press, 1997)

Bryce, William Gordon, 'An ordinance with regard to Indian immigration', *The Laws of Fiji: Containing the ordinances of Fiji and subsidiary legislation thereunder, enacted on or before the 16th day of April 1955* (London: C.F. Roworth, 1956)

Buchanan, Rachel, *Ko Taranaki Te Maunga* (Wellington: Bridget Williams Books, 2018)

Buchanan, Rachel, *The Parihaka Album: Lest we forget* (Wellington: Huia, 2009)

Bunbury, Bill, *It's Not the Money It's the Land: Aboriginal stockmen and the equal wages case* (Fremantle: Fremantle Arts Centre Press, 2002)

Burton, Antoinette, *The Trouble with Empire: Challenges to modern British imperialism* (Oxford: Oxford University Press, 2015)

Campbell, Hugh, *Farming Inside Invisible Worlds: Modernist agriculture and its consequences* (London: Bloomsbury Academic, 2020)

Cannon, Michael and Ian McFarlane, *Historical Records of Victoria, vol. 3* (Melbourne: Victorian GPO, 1981–2002)

Carty, John, Carly Davenport and Monique La Fontaine, *Yiwarra Kuju: The Canning Stock Route* (Canberra: National Museum of Australia, 2010)

Clark, Anna, *Women's Silence, Men's Violence: Sexual assault in England, 1770–1845* (London: Pandora Press, 1987)

Clarke, Patricia, *Pioneer Writer: The life of Louisa Atkinson, novelist, journalist, naturalist* (Sydney: Allen & Unwin, 1990)

Cohen, Stanley, *States of Denial: Knowing about atrocities and suffering* (Cambridge: Polity Press, 2001)

Cohodas, Marvin, *Basket Weavers for the California Curio Trade: Elizabeth and Louise Hickox* (Tucson: University of Arizona Press & the Southwest Museum, 1997)

Cole, Douglas, *Captured Heritage: The scramble for northwest coast artifacts* (Vancouver: UBC Press, 1995)

Conrad, Earl, *Errol Flynn: A memoir* (New York: Dodd, Mead and Company, 1978)

Cooper, Annabel, *Filming the Colonial Past: The New Zealand Wars on screen* (Dunedin: Otago University Press, 2018)

Cowan, James, *The New Zealand Wars and the Pioneering Period*, vol. 1 (Wellington: Government Printer, 1983)

Cowan, James, *The New Zealand Wars and the Pioneering Period*, vol. 2 (Wellington: R.E. Owen Government Printer, 1923)

Cowan, James, *The New Zealand Wars: A history of the Māori campaigns and the pioneering period*, vol. 1 (1845–64) (Wellington: R.E. Owen, Government Printer, 1922)

Cowan, James, *The Old Frontier: Te Awamutu, the story of the Waipa Valley* (Te Awamutu: The Waipa Post Printing and Publishing Company, 1922)

Curthoys, Ann and Jessie Mitchell, *Taking Liberty: Indigenous rights and settler self-government in colonial Australia, 1830–1890* (Cambridge: Cambridge University Press, 2019)

Dansey, Harry, *Te Raukura: The feathers of the albatross* (Auckland: Longman Paul, 1974)

Dwyer, Philip and Amanda Nettelbeck (eds), *Violence, Colonialism and Empire in the Modern World* (Basingstoke: Palgrave Macmillan, 2018)

Edmonds, Penelope, *Settler Colonialism and (Re)conciliation: Frontier violence, affective performances, and imaginative refoundings* (London: Palgrave, 2016)

Elsmore, Bronwyn, *Like Them That Dream: The Maori and the Old Testament* (Auckland: Reed, 2000)

Evans, Julie, *Edward Eyre: Race and colonial governance* (Dunedin: Otago University Press, 2005)

Eyre, Edward John, *Autobiographical Narrative of Residence and Exploration in Australia, 1832–1839*, ed. Jill Waterhouse (London: Caliban Books, 1984)

Eyre, Edward John, *Journals of Expeditions of Discovery into Central Australia, and Overland from Adelaide to King George's Sound, in the Years 1840–1, including an Account of the Manners and Customs of the Aborigines, and the State of Their Relations with Europeans,* 2 vols (London: T. and W. Boone, 1845)

Bibliography: Books and reports

Eyre, Edward John, *Reports of the Expedition to King George's Sound 1841 and the Death of Baxter* (Adelaide: Sullivan's Cove, 1983)

Fasano, Debra, *Young Blood: The making of Errol Flynn* (Whitefield: Debra Fasano, 2009)

Field, Les W. (with Merv George), *Abalone Tales: Collaborative explorations of sovereignty and identity in Native California* (Durham: Duke University Press, 2008)

Flynn, Errol, *My Wicked Wicked Ways* (New York: G.P. Putnam, 1959)

Foley, Fiona, *Biting the Clouds: A Badtjala perspective on the Aboriginals Protection and Restriction of the Sale of Opium Act, 1897* (St Lucia: University of Queensland Press, 2020)

Forrest, Kay, *The Challenge and the Chance: The colonisation and settlement of north west Australia 1861–1914* (Victoria Park: Hesperian Press, 1996)

France, Peter, *The Charter of the Land: Custom and colonisation in Fiji* (Melbourne: Oxford University Press, 1969)

Frances, Rae and Bruce Scates, *The Murdoch Ethos* (Melbourne: Murdoch University, 1989)

Garraway, Doris L., *Tree of Liberty: Cultural legacies of the Haitian Revolution in the Atlantic world* (Charlottesville: University of Virginia Press, 2008)

Geggus, David P., *The Impact of the Haitian Revolution in the Atlantic World* (Columbia: University of South Carolina Press, 2001)

Gilbert, W.S. and Arthur Sullivan, *The Complete Gilbert and Sullivan*, ed. Ed Glinert (London: Penguin, 2006)

Gillon, Kenneth Lowell, *Fiji's Indian Migrants: A history to end of indenture in 1920* (Oxford: Oxford University Press, 1962)

Gilroy, Paul, *The Black Atlantic: Modernity and double consciousness* (London: Verso, 1993)

Green, Jennifer, *Drawn from the Ground: Sound, sign and inscription in Central Australian sand stories* (Cambridge: Cambridge University Press, 2014)

Gribble, John Brown, *Dark Deeds in a Sunny Land* (Perth: Stirling Bros, 1886)

Harrisson, Thomas, *Savage Civilisation* (New York: Alfred Knopf, 1937)

Hawkesworth, John, *An Account of the Voyages Undertaken by the Order of His Present Majesty for Making Discoveries in the Southern Hemisphere: and successively performed by Commodore Byron, Captain Wallis, Captain Carteret, and Captain Cook, in the Dolphin, the Swallow, and the Endeavour, vol. 1* (London: Printed for W. Strahan and T. Cadell in the Strand, 1773)

Hughes, Hugh and Lyn Hughes, *Discharged in New Zealand: Soldiers of the imperial foot regiments who took their discharge in New Zealand 1840–1870* (Auckland: New Zealand Society of Genealogists, 1988)

Ihimaera, Witi and Hēmi Kelly, *Sleeps Standing: Moetū* (New Zealand: Vintage, 2017)

Ihimaera, Witi, *The Parihaka Woman* (Auckland: Vintage, 2011)

Inglis, Amirah, *Not a White Woman Safe: Sexual anxiety and politics in Port Moresby, 1920–1934* (Canberra: Australian National University Press, 1975)

Jackson, Louise A., *Child Sexual Abuse in Victorian England* (London: Routledge, 1999)

Jebb, Mary Ann, *Blood, Sweat and Welfare* (Perth: UWA Publishing, 2002)

Jeffs, Ben, Helen MacQuarrie, Andrew Pearson and Annsofie Witkin, *Infernal Traffic: Excavation of a liberated African graveyard in Rupert's Valley, St Helena* (London: Council for British Archaeology, 2012)

Joint Select Committee on Constitutional Recognition relating to Aboriginal and Torres Strait Islander Peoples Commonwealth of Australia, Final Report

(Canberra: Commonwealth of Australia, 2018)
Jones, Alison, *This Pākehā Life: An unsettled memoir* (Wellington: Bridget Williams Books, 2020)
Kaberry, Phyllis, *Aboriginal Woman Sacred and Profane* (London: Routledge, 2004)
Keenan, Danny, Te Whiti O Rongomai and the Resistance of Parihaka (Wellington: Huia, 2015)
Kennedy, Dane, *The Last Blank Spaces: Exploring Africa and Australia* (Cambridge: Harvard University Press, 2013)
Kidman, Joanna, Vincent O'Malley, Liana MacDonald, Tom Roa and Keziah Wallis, *Fragments from a Contested Past: Remembrance, denial and New Zealand history* (Wellington: Bridget Williams Books, 2022)
Knapman, Claudia, *White Women in Fiji, 1835–1930: The ruin of empire?* (London: Allen and Unwin, 1986)
Krichauff, Skye, *Memory, Place and Aboriginal–Settler History* (London: Anthem Press, 2017)
Lal, Brij V. (ed.), *Bittersweet: The Indo-Fijian experience* (Canberra: Pandanus Books, 2004)
Lal, Brij V., *Chalo Jahaji: On a journey through indenture in Fiji* (Canberra and Suva: ANU and Fiji Museum, 2000)
Lawson, Elizabeth, *The Natural Art of Louisa Atkinson* (Sydney: State Library of New South Wales Press, 1995)
Lenore, Miriel and Louise Crisp, *Travelling Alone Together/Ruby Camp* (North Melbourne: Spinifex Press, 1997)
Lydon, Jane and Lyndall Ryan (eds), *Remembering the Myall Creek Massacre* (Sydney: NewSouth, 2018)
Lydon, Jane, *Anti-slavery and Australia: No slavery in a free land?* (New York: Routledge, 2021)
Macintyre, Stuart and Anna Clark, *The History Wars* (Melbourne: Melbourne University Press, 2003)

Madley, Benjamin, *An American Genocide: The United States and the California Indian catastrophe* (New Haven: Yale University Press, 2016)
Main, William, *Maori in Focus* (Wellington: Millwood Press, 1976)
Manne, Robert (ed.), *Whitewash: On Keith Windshuttle's fabrication of Aboriginal history* (Melbourne: Black Inc., 2003)
Mayor, Thomas, *Finding the Heart of the Nation* (Melbourne: Hardie Grant, 2019)
Mbembe, Achille, *Critique of Black Reason* (Durham and London: Duke University Press, 2017)
McKenna, Mark, *From the Edge: Australia's lost histories* (Melbourne: Melbourne University Publishing, 2016)
McKenna, Mark, *Looking for Blackfella's Point: An Australian history of place* (Sydney: UNSW Press, 2002)
Meredith, Paul and Robert Joseph, *The Battle of Ōrākau: Māori veterans' accounts* (Waikato: Ōrākau Heritage Society and the Maniapoto Māori Trust Board, 2014)
Merry, Sally Engle, *Colonizing Hawai`i: The cultural power of law* (Princeton: Princeton University Press, 2000)
Morgan, Sally, *My Place* (Perth: Fremantle Press, 1987)
Morley, William, *The History of Methodism in New Zealand* (Wellington: McKee and Co., 1900)
Naidu, Vijay, *The Violence of Indenture in Fiji* (Lautoka: Fiji Institute of Applied Studies, 2004 [1980])
Nicole, Robert, *Disturbing History: Resistance in early colonial Fiji* (Honolulu: University of Hawai`i Press, 2010)
Nixon, Rob, *Slow Violence and the Environmentalism of the Poor* (Boston: Harvard University Press, 2011)
Norton, Jack, *Genocide in Northwestern California: When our worlds cried* (San Francisco: Indian Historian Press, 1979)
O'Brien, Patty, *The Pacific Muse: Exotic femininity and the colonial Pacific* (Seattle:

University of Washington Press, 2006)
O'Malley, Vincent, *The Great War for New Zealand: Waikato 1800–2000* (Wellington: Bridget Williams Books, 2016)
Orange, Claudia, *The Treaty of Waitangi* (Wellington: Bridget Williams Books, 1987)
Pearson, Andrew, *Distant Freedom: St Helena and the abolition of the slave trade, 1840–1872* (Liverpool: University of Liverpool Press, 2016)
Petrie, Hazel, *Outcasts of the Gods?: The struggle over slavery in Māori New Zealand* (Auckland: Auckland University Press, 2015)
Plomley, N.J.B. (ed.), *Friendly Mission: The Tasmanian journals and papers of George Augustus Robinson, 1829–1834, 2nd edn* (Hobart: Quintus Publishing, 2008)
Popins, John Ernest, *Delight to the Heart: A short story of the Dudley Orphanage for Indian Girls at Dilkusha 'Delight to the heart'* (Melbourne: Spectator Publishing, 1935)
Presland, Gary, *First People: The Eastern Kulin of Melbourne, Port Phillip and Central Victoria* (Melbourne: Museum Victoria Publishing, 2010)
Raphael, Ray and Freeman House, *Two Peoples, One Place: Humboldt history, volume one*, rev. edn (Eureka: Humboldt County Historical Society, 2011)
Reichard, Gladys, 'Wiyot grammar and texts', *University of California Publications in American Archaeology and Ethnology* 22, no. 1, 26 June 1925
Reynolds, Henry, *Fate of a Free People: A radical re-examination of the Tasmanian wars* (Melbourne: Penguin, 1995)
Reynolds, Henry, *The Other Side of the Frontier* (Ringwood: Penguin, 1981)
Riseborough, Hazel, *Days of Darkness: Taranaki, 1878–1884* (Wellington: Allen and Unwin, 1989)
Rodman, Margaret, *Houses Far from Home: British colonial space in the New Hebrides* (Honolulu: University of Hawai`i Press, 2001)
Rolleston, Rosamund, *William and Mary Rolleston: An informal biography* (Wellington: Reed, 1971)
Rose, Deborah Bird, *Nourishing Terrains: Australian Aboriginal views of landscape and wilderness* (Canberra: Australian Heritage Commission, 1996)
Royale, Stephen, *The Company's Island: St Helena, company colonies and the colonial endeavour* (London: I.B. Tauris, 2008)
Rudolph, Ivan, *Eyre: The forgotten explorer* (Sydney: HarperCollins, 2014)
Ryan, Lyndall, *Tasmanian Aborigines: A history since 1803* (Sydney: Allen and Unwin, 2012)
Salesa, Damon, *Racial Crossings: Race, intermarriage, and the Victorian British Empire* (Oxford: Oxford University Press, 2011)
Scarr, Deryck, *Fragments of Empire: A history of the Western Pacific High Commission 1877–1914* (Canberra: ANU Press, 1967)
Scott, Dick, *Ask the Mountain: The story of Parihaka* (Auckland: Raupo, 2008)
Secrest, William B., *When the Great Spirit Died: The destruction of the California Indians 1850–1860* (Fresno: Craven Street Books, 2003)
Shaw, Richard, *The Forgotten Coast* (Palmerston North: Massey University Press, 2021)
Sinclair, Keith, *Kinds of Peace: Maori people after the wars, 1870–85* (Auckland: Auckland University Press, 1991)
Sleeper-Smith, Susan, Jeffrey Ostler and Joshua L. Reid (eds), *Violence and Indigenous Communities: Confronting the past and engaging the present* (Evanston: Northwestern University Press, 2021)
Sorlin, Pierre, *The Film in History: Restaging the past* (Oxford: Blackwell)
Stanmore, Lord, *Fiji: Records of private and public life 1875–1880, vol. 1* (Edinburgh: Printed by R. and R. Clark, 1897)

Stepan, Nancy, *The Idea of Race in Science: Great Britain 1800–1960* (London: Macmillan, 1982)

Stephens, John, *The History of the Rise and Progress of the New British Province of South Australia*, 2nd edn (London: Smith, Elder & Co., 1839)

Stevens, Kate, *Gender, Violence and Criminal Justice in the Colonial Pacific, 1880–1920* (London: Bloomsbury, 2023)

Te Hurinui, Pei, *King Pōtatau: An account of the life of Pōtatau Te Wherowhero, the first Māori King* (Wellington: Huia Publishers, [1959] 2010)

Telfer, William, *The Wallabadah Manuscript: The early history of the northern districts of New South Wales. Recollections of the early days* (Kensington: New South Wales University Press, 1980)

Thomas, Nicholas, *Colonialism's Culture: Anthropology, travel and government* (Princeton: Princeton University Press, 1994)

Thomas, Paul, 'The Crown and Māori in Mōkau 1840–1911: A report commissioned by the Waitangi Tribunal for Te Rohe Potae Inquiry', Waitangi Tribunal, 2011, Wai 898 #A28

Thomas, Tony (ed.), *From a Life of Adventure: The writings of Errol Flynn* (Secaucus: Citadel Press, 1980)

Thompson, Roger, *Australian Imperialism in the Pacific* (Carlton: University of Melbourne Press, 1980)

Tinker, Hugh, *A New System of Slavery: The export of Indian labour overseas 1830–1920* (London: Oxford University Press, 1974)

Tranquillity Disturbed: A contemporary look at historical New Zealand, 12 March–31 March 2015 (Wellington: New Zealand Portrait Gallery/Te Pukenga Whakaata, 2015)

Trollope, Anthony, *Harry Heathcote of Gangoil* (London: Folio Society, 1998)

Trustram, Myna, *Women of the Regiment: Marriage and the Victorian army* (Cambridge: Cambridge University Press, 1984)

Uren, Malcolm and Robert Stephens, *Waterless Horizons: The first full-length study of the extraordinary life of Edward John Eyre, explorer, overlander, and pastoralist in Australia* (Melbourne: Robertson and Mullens, 1942)

Uhr, Frank, *Multuggerah and the Sacred Mountain* (Tingalpa: Boolarong Press, 2019)

Waitangi Tribunal, *Te Mana Ahuru: Report on Te Rohe Pōtae claims* (pre-publication version) (Wellington: Waitangi Tribunal, 2018)

Waitangi Tribunal, *The Taranaki Report: Kaupapa Tuatahi* (Wellington: Legislation Direct, 1996)

Walker, Ranginui, *Ka Whawhai Tonu Matou: Struggle without end* (Auckland: Penguin Books, 1990)

Wanhalla, Angela, *Matters of the Heart: A history of interracial marriage in New Zealand* (Auckland: Auckland University Press, 2013)

Watego, Chelsea, *Another Day in the Colony* (Brisbane: University of Queensland Press, 2021)

Watson, Don, *The Bush: Travels in the heart of Australia* (Melbourne: Hamish Hamilton, 2014)

Watson, F. (ed.), *Historical Records of Australia* (Sydney: Parliament of the Commonwealth of Australia, 1925), series 1, vol. 26

Watson, Judy and Louise Martin-Chew, *Blood Language* (Melbourne: Miegunyah-Melbourne University Press, 2009)

Wharemaru, Heeni and Mary Katharine Duffie, *Heeni: A Tainui elder remembers* (Auckland: HarperCollins, 1997)

Wiener, Martin, *An Empire on Trial: Race, murder, and justice under British rule, 1870–1935* (Cambridge: Cambridge University Press, 2009)

Windschuttle, Keith, *The Fabrication of Aboriginal History. Volume 1: Van Diemen's Land 1803–1847* (Sydney: Macleay Press, 2002)

Young, Diana and Judy Watson, *Written on the Body* (St Lucia: Anthropology Museum, University of Queensland, 2014)

BOOK CHAPTERS

Atkinson, Louisa, 'The Fitzroy waterfalls' (1871), in Louisa Atkinson (ed.), *Excursions from Berrima and a Trip to Manaro and Molonglo in the 1870s* (Canberra: Mulini Press, 1980), pp. 17–19

Bernardin, Susan, 'Capturing and recapturing culture: Trailing Grace Nicholson's legacy in northwestern California', in Susan Bernardin, Melody Graulich, Lisa MacFarlane and Nicole Tonkovich (eds), *Trading Gazes: Euro-American women photographers and Native North Americans, 1880–1940* (New Brunswick: Rutgers University Press, 2003), pp. 150–85

Boast, Richard, 'Vanished theocracies: Christianity, war and politics in New Zealand 1830–80', in Lisa Ford and Tim Rowse (eds), *Between Indigenous and Settler Governance* (Abingdon: Routledge, 2013) pp. 70–82

Bsumek, Erika Marie, 'Exchanging places: Virtual tourism, vicarious travel, and the consumption of southwestern Indian artifacts', in Hal K. Rothman (ed.), *The Culture of Tourism, the Tourism of Culture: Selling the past to the present in the American southwest,* (Albuquerque: University of New Mexico Press, 2003), pp. 118–139

Carty, John, 'Drawing a line in the sand: The Canning Stock Route and contemporary art', in John Carty, Carly Davenport and Monique La Fontaine, *Yiwarra Kuju: The Canning Stock Route* (Canberra: National Museum of Australia, 2010), pp. 23–31

Caruana, Wally, 'Rover Thomas Dreams the Krill Krill', in *Roads Cross: The paintings of Rover Thomas* (Canberra: National Gallery of Australia, 1994), p. 22

Chandler, Lisa, 'The reclaimed object: Transformations of museum artefacts by Indigenous Australian artists,' in G.U. Grossmann and P. Krutisch (eds), *The Challenge of the Object. Die Herausforderung des Objekts. 33rd Congress of the International Committee of the History of Art, Nuremburg 15–20 July 2012 (conference proceedings)* (Nuremburg: Germanisches National Museum, 2013), pp. 566–69

Christensen, Will, in *Rover Thomas: I want to paint* (Perth: Holmes à Court Gallery, 2003), p. 54

Churches, Stephen, 'Put not your faith in princes (or courts) – Agreements made from asymmetrical power bases: The story of a promise made to Western Australia's Aboriginal people', in Peter Read, Gary Meyers and Bob Reece (eds), *What good condition? Reflections on an Australian Aboriginal treaty, 1986–2006* (Canberra: ANU Press, 2006), pp. 1–14

de Costa, Ravi, 'Two kinds of recognition: The politics of engagement in settler societies', in Sarah Maddison, Tom Clark and Ravi de Costa (eds), *The Limits of Settler Colonial Reconciliation* (Singapore: Springer, 2016), pp. 49–66

Dunleavy, Trish, '"Magnificent failure" or subversive triumph? The Governor', in James E. Bennett and Rebecca Beirne (eds), *Making Film and Television Histories: Australia and New Zealand* (London: I.B. Tauris, 2012), pp. 67–72

Edmonds, Penelope and Michelle Berry, 'Eliza Batman's house: Unhomely frontiers and intimate Overstraiters in Van Diemen's Land and Port Phillip', in Penelope Edmonds and Amanda Nettelbeck (eds), *Intimacies of Violence in the Settler Colony: Economies of dispossession around the Pacific Rim* (New York: Palgrave Macmillan, 2018), pp. 115–37

Ford, Lisa, 'Law', in David Armitage and Alison Bashford (eds), *Pacific Histories:*

Land, Ocean, People (Basingstoke and London: Palgrave Macmillan, 2014), pp. 220–26

Fox, Alistair, 'Rudall Hayward and the Cinema of Maoriland: Genre-mixing and counter-discourses in *Rewi's Last Stand* (1925), *The Te Kooti Trail* (1927) and *Rewi's Last Stand/The Last Stand* (1940)', in Barry Keith, Alistair Fox and Hilary Radner (eds), *New Zealand Cinema: Interpreting the past* (Bristol: Intellect Books, 2011), pp. 45–65

Goodall, Heather, 'Authority under challenge: Pikampul land and Queen Victoria's law during the British invasion of Australia', in Martin Daunton and Rick Halpern (eds), *Empire and Others: British encounters with Indigenous peoples, 1600–1850* (Philadelphia: University of Pennsylvania Press, 1999), pp. 260–78

Gough, Julie, 'Forgotten lives – The first photographs of Tasmanian Aboriginal people', in Jane Lydon (ed.), *Calling the Shots: Indigenous photographies* (Canberra: Aboriginal Studies Press, 2014), pp. 20–52

Jackson, Moana, 'Where to next? Decolonisation and the stories in the land', in Bianca Elkington, Moana Jackson, Rebecca Kiddle, Ocean Ripeka Mercier, Mike Ross, Jennie Smeaton and Amanda Thomas (eds), *Imagining Decolonisation*, (Wellington: Bridget Williams Books, 2020), pp. 133–55

Kelly, John, 'Gaze and grasp: Plantations, desires, indentured Indians, and colonial law in Fiji', in Lenore Manderson and Margaret Jolly (eds), *Sites of Desire, Economies of Pleasure: Sexualities in Asia and the Pacific* (Chicago: University of Chicago Press, 1997), pp. 73–98

Kidman, Joanna, 'He taonga te wareware: Mātauranga Māori and education', in Jacinta Ruru and Linda Waimarie Nikora (eds), *Ngā Kete Mātauranga: Māori scholars at the research interface* (Dunedin: Otago University Press, 2020), pp. 81–87

Kofod, Francis, 'Gija glossary', in Russell Storer (ed.), *Paddy Bedford* (Sydney: Museum of Contemporary Art, 2006), pp. 136–37

Kofod, Francis, 'Paddy Bedford's stories', in Russell Storer (ed.), *Paddy Bedford* (Sydney: Museum of Contemporary Art, 2006), pp. 72–98

Malloy, Kerry J., 'Remembrance and renewal at Tuluwat: Returning to the center of the world,' in Ajlina Karamehić-Muratović and Laura Kromják (eds), *Remembrance and Forgiveness: Global and interdisciplinary perspectives on genocide and mass violence* (London: Routledge, 2021), pp. 20–33

Pandey, Janak, 'India', in James Georgas, John W. Berry, Fons J.R. van de Vijver, Çigdem Kagitçibasi and Ype H. Poortinga (eds), *Families Across Cultures: A 30-nation psychological study* (Cambridge: Cambridge University Press, 2006), pp. 362–69

Paterson, Lachy, 'Kiri Mā, Kiri Mangu: The terminology of race and civilisation in the mid-nineteenth-century Maori-language newspapers', in Jenifer Curnow, Ngapare Hopa and Jane McRae (eds), *Rere atu, taku manu! Discovering history, language and politics in the Maori-language newspapers* (Auckland: University of Auckland Press, 2002), pp. 78–97

Paterson, Lachy, 'Te Hokioi and the legitimization of the Māori nation', in Brendan Hokowhitu and Vijay Devdas (eds), *The Fourth Eye: Māori media in Aotearoa New Zealand* (Minneapolis: University of Minnesota Press, 2013), pp. 124–42

Riseborough, Hazel, 'Te Pāhuatanga o Parihaka', in Te Miringa Hohaia, Gregory O'Brien and Lara Strongman (eds), *Parihaka: The art of passive resistance* (Wellington: City Gallery, Victorian

University Press, Parihaka Pā Trustees, 2001), p. 31

Skyring, Fiona and Sarah Yu with the Karajarri Native Title Holders, '"Strange strangers": First contact between Europeans and Karajarri people on the Kimberley coast of Western Australia', in Peter Veth, Peter Sutton and Margo Neale (eds), *Strangers on the Shore* (Canberra: National Museum of Australia, 2008), pp. 60–75

Sleeter, Christine, 'Inheriting footholds and cushions: Family legacies and institutional racism', in Judith Flores Carmona and Kristen V. Luschen (eds), *Crafting Critical Stories: Toward pedagogies and methodologies of collaboration, inclusion and voice* (New York: Peter Lang Publishing, 2014), pp. 11–26

Stafford, Jane, '"To sing this Bryce and bunkum age": Colonial poetry and Parihaka', in Te Miringa Hohaia, Gregory O'Brien and Lara Strongman (eds), *Parihaka: The art of passive resistance* (Wellington: City Gallery, Victorian University Press, Parihaka Pā Trustees, 2001), pp. 179–85

Stanner, William, 'The Great Australian Silence' (1868), in *The Dreaming and Other Essays* (Melbourne: Black Inc, 2009), pp. 182–92

Thomas, Amanda, 'Pākehā and doing the work of decolonisation', in Rebecca Kiddle, Bianca Elkington, Moana Jackson, Ocean Ripeka Mercier, Mike Ross, Jennie Smeaton, and Amanda Thomas, *Imagining Decolonisation* (Wellington: Bridget Williams Books, 2020), pp. 42–54.

JOURNALS AND JOURNAL ARTICLES

'The Hokioi Press', *Journal of the Te Awamutu Historical Society 6*, no. 1, 1971, p. 21–26

Appleby, Gabrielle and Megan Davis, 'The Uluru Statement and the promises of truth', *Australian Historical Studies 49*, no. 4, 2018, pp. 501–09

Auty, Kate, 'Patrick Bernard O'Leary and the Forrest River massacres', *Aboriginal History 28*, 2004, pp. 122–55

Ayres, Marie-Louise, 'A picture asks a thousand questions', *NLA Magazine 5*, no. 2, 2011, pp. 8–11

Banivanua Mar, Tracey and Nadia Rhook, 'Counter networks of empires: Reading unexpected people in unexpected places', *Journal of Colonialism and Colonial History 19*, no. 2, 2018

Barima, Kofi, 'Militancy and spirituality: Haiti's revolutionary impact on Jamaica's Africans and Afro-Creoles, 1740–1824', *Wadabagei: A journal of the Caribbean and its diaspora 14*, nos (1/2), 2013

Batten Bronwyn and Paul Batten, 'Memorialising the past: Is there an Aboriginal way?', *Public History Review 15*, 2008, pp. 92–116

Behrendt, Larissa, 'Aboriginal women and the white lies of the feminist movement: Implications for Aboriginal women in rights discourse', *Australian Feminist Law Journal 1*, 1993, pp. 27–44

Bell, Avril, 'Reverberating historical privilege of a "middling" sort of settler family', *Genealogy 4*, no. 2, 2020

Bell, Leah, 'Difficult histories: In conference', *New Zealand Journal of Public History 7*, no. 1, 2020, pp. 9–10

Brazendale, Graham, 'John Whiteley: Land sovereignty and the land wars of the 19th century', *Proceedings of the Wesley Historical Society of New Zealand 64*, 1997

Bulbeck, Chilla, 'Memorials and the history of the frontier', *Australian Historical Studies 24*, no. 96, 1991, pp. 168–78

Cachun, Mitch, 'Antebellum African Americans, public commemoration, and the Haitian Revolution: A problem of historical mythmaking', *Journal of the Early Republic 26*, no. 2, 2006, pp. 249–73

Cantir, Christian, '"Savages in the midst": Revolutionary Haiti in international society (1791–1838)', *Journal of International Relations and Development* 20, no. 1, 2017, pp. 238–61

Carter, George G., 'John Whiteley: Missionary martyr', *Proceedings of the Wesley Historical Society of New Zealand 10*, no. 3, 1952

Celusien, Joseph L., '"The Haitian turn": An appraisal of recent literary and historiographical works on the Haitian Revolution', *Journal of Pan-African Studies* 5, no. 6, 2012, pp. 37–55

Clavin, Matt, 'Race, rebellion, and the Gothic: Inventing the Haitian Revolution', *Early American Studies* 5, no. 1, 2007, pp. 1–29

Clement, Cathie, 'Historical notes relevant to impact stories of the East Kimberley', *East Kimberley Working Paper No. 2* (Canberra: Australian National University, 1989), pp. 3–4

Clement, Cathie 'The Humpty Dumpty factor in Aboriginal history', *Teaching History* 37, no. 4, 2003, pp. 26–32

Curthoys, Ann and Jane Lydon, 'Governing Western Australian Aboriginal people: Section 70 of WA's 1889 Constitution', special issue, *Studies in Western Australian History 30,* 2016

da Silva, Daniel Domingues, David Eltis, Philp Misevich and Olatunji Ojo, 'The diaspora of Africans liberated from slave ships in the nineteenth century', *Journal of African History* 55, no. 3, 2014, pp. 347–69

Dansey, Harry, 'Reflections on battle centenaries', *Te Ao Hou 48,* 1964, pp. 34–35

Dening, Greg, 'Empowering imaginations', *The Contemporary Pacific* 9, no. 2, 1997, pp. 419–29

Duckett, Margaret, 'Bret Harte and the Indians of Northern California', *Huntington Library Quarterly 18*, no. 1, (Nov. 1954), pp. 59–83

Duff, Peter, 'The evolution of trial by judge and assessors in Fiji', *Journal of Pacific Studies 21*, 1997, pp. 189–213

Estrich, Susan, 'Rape', *The Yale Law Journal 95*, no. 6, 1986, pp. 1087–184

Etherington, Norman, 'The gendering of indirect rule: Criminal law and colonial Fiji, 1875–1900', *Journal of Pacific History 31*, no. 1, 1996, pp. 42–57

Farrugia, Jack, Peta Dzidic and Lynne Roberts, '"It is usually about the triumph of the coloniser": Exploring young people's conceptualisations of Australian history and the implications for Australian identity', *Journal of Community Applied Social Psychology 28*, 2018, pp. 483–94

Fitzpatrick, Esther, 'A story of becoming: Entanglement, settler ghosts, and postcolonial counterstories', *Cultural Studies – Critical Methodologies 18*, no. 1, pp. 43–51

Getachew, Adom, 'Universalism after the post-colonial turn: Interpreting the Haitian Revolution', *Political Theory 44*, 2016, pp. 821–45

Ghosh, Durba, 'Household crimes and domestic order: Keeping the peace in colonial Calcutta, c. 1770–c. 1840', *Modern Asian Studies 38*, 2004, pp. 599–623

Gilbert, Stephanie, 'Living with the past: The creation of the stolen generation positionality', *AlterNative: An International Journal of Indigenous Peoples 15*, 2019, pp. 226–33

Gilchrist, Stephen, 'Surfacing histories: Memorials and public art in Perth', *Artlink*, June 2018, pp. 42–47

Green, Neville, 'Aboriginal sentencing in Western Australia in the late 19th century with reference to Rottnest Island prison', *Records of the Western Australian Museum, Supplement 79,* 2011, pp. 77–85

Hammer, G.E.J, 'A pioneer missionary: Raglan to Mokau, 1844–1880: Cort Henry Schnackenberg', *Proceedings of the Wesley Historical Society of New Zealand 57,* 1991

Haskins, Victoria, 'A better chance? Sexual abuse and the apprenticeship of Aboriginal girls under the NSW

Aborigines Protection Board', *Aboriginal History 28*, 2004, pp. 33–58

Hooper, Greg, Jonathan Richards and Judy Watson, 'Mapping colonial massacres and frontier violence in Australia: "the names of places"', *Cartographica 55*, no. 3, 2020, pp. 193–98

Hunt, Su-Jane, 'The Gribble affair: A study in colonial politics', *Studies in Western Australian History 8*, 1984, pp. 42–51

Huyssen, Andreas, 'Monumental seduction', *New German Critique 69*, 1996, pp. 181–200

Inder, Stuart, 'His wicked wicked ways: Leaves from Errol Flynn's New Guinea diary', *Pacific Islands Monthly*, November 1960, pp. 80–83

Jaknis, Ira, 'A new thiNgā The NMAI in historical and institutional perspective', *American Indian Quarterly 30*, nos 3/4, 2006, pp. 511–42

Johnson, Miranda, 'Knotted histories', *Journal of New Zealand Studies (NS29)*, 2019, pp. 89–96

Kelly, John, '"Coolie" as labour commodity: Race, sex, and European dignity in colonial Fiji', *Journal of Peasant Studies 19*, nos 3–4, 1992, pp. 246–67

Kenny, Robert, 'Tricks or treats?: A case for Kulin knowing in Batman's treaty', *History Australia 5*, no. 2, 2011, pp. 1–38

Keresztes, Paul, 'Tertullian's Apologeticus: A historical and literal study', *Latomus 25*, 1966, pp. 124–33

Kolsky, Elizabeth, '"The body evidencing the crime": Rape on trial in colonial India, 1860–1947', *Gender & History 22*, no. 1, 2010, pp. 109–30

Konishi, Shino, 'First Nations scholars, settler colonial studies, and Indigenous history', *Australian Historical Studies 50*, no. 3, 2019, pp. 285–304

Lagan, Bernard, 'Black ban', *Bulletin 124*, no. 6520, 2006, p. 39

Lal, Brij V., 'Kunti's cry: Indentured women on Fiji's plantations', *Indian Economic and Social History Review 22*, no. 1, 1985, pp. 55–71

Lal, Brij V., 'Veil of dishonour: Sexual jealousy and suicide on Fiji plantations', *Journal of Pacific History 20*, no. 3, 1985, pp. 135–55

Loud, Llewellyn L., 'Ethnogeography and archaeology of the Wiyot territory', *University of California Publications in American Archaeology and Ethnology 14*, no. 3, 23 December 1918, pp. 221–436

Lydon, Jane, 'Christian heroes? John Gribble, Exeter Hall and antislavery on Western Australia's frontier', *Studies in Western Australian History 30*, 2016, pp. 59–72

Lydon, Jane, 'Introduction: Section 70 of the Western Australian Constitution Act 1889, or, "Throwing dust in the eyes of the people"', *Studies in Western Australian History 30,* 2016, pp. 1–7

Macdonald, Charlotte and Rebecca Lenihan, 'Paper soldiers: The life, death and reincarnation of nineteenth-century military files across the British Empire', *Rethinking History 22*, no. 2, 2018, pp. 375–402

Mahuika, Nēpia, 'A brief history of whakapapa: Māori approaches to genealogy', *Genealogy 3*, no. 2, 2019, p. 32

Marcus, Julie, 'Bicentenary follies: Australians in search of themselves', *Anthropology Today 4*, no. 3, 1988, pp. 4–6

Martin, Richard J. and David Trigger, '"Nothing Never Change": Mapping land, water and Aboriginal identity in the changing environments of Northern Australia's Gulf Country', *Settler Colonial Studies 5*, no. 4, 2015, pp. 317–33

McAleer, John, 'Looking east: St Helena, the South Atlantic and Britain's Indian ocean world', *Atlantic Studies 13*, no. 1, 2013, pp. 78–98

McAleer, John, '"The Key to India": Troop movements, southern Africa, and Britain's Indian Ocean world, 1795–1820', *International History Review 35*, no. 2, 2013, pp. 294–316

Messenger, Arthur Herbert, 'Children of the Forest: A frontier tale of old Taranaki', *School Journal 46*, no. 2, part 4, March 1952

Muecke, Stephen, Alan Rumsey and Banjo Wirrunmarra, 'Pigeon the outlaw: History as texts', *Aboriginal History 9*, nos 1–2, 1985, pp. 81–100

Nettelbeck, Amanda, 'Proximate strangers and familiar antagonists: Violence on an intimate frontier', *Australian Historical Studies 47*, no. 2, 2016, pp. 209–24

Newbury, Colin, 'Bose Vakauraga: Fiji's Great Council of Chiefs, 1875–2000', *Pacific Studies 29*, nos. 1/2, 2006, pp. 82–127

O'Malley, Vincent and Joanna Kidman, 'Settler colonial history, commemoration and white backlash: Remembering the New Zealand Wars', *Settler Colonial Studies 8*, no. 3, 2018, pp. 298–313

O'Malley, Vincent, '"Recording the incident with a monument": The Waikato War in historical memory', *Journal of New Zealand Studies 19*, 2015, pp. 79–97

Paterson, Lachy, 'The Kohimarama Conference of 1860: A contextual reading', *Journal of New Zealand Studies 12*, 2012, pp. 29–46

Pearson, W.H., 'European intimidation and the myth of Tahiti', *Journal of Pacific History 4*, no. 1, 1969, pp. 199–217

Robinson, Shirleene, 'Regulating the race: Aboriginal children in private European homes in colonial Australia', *Journal of Australian Studies 37*, no. 3, 2013, pp. 302–15

Saha, Jonathan, 'The male state: Colonialism, corruption and rape investigations in the Irrawaddy Delta c. 1900', *Indian Economic and Social History Review 48*, no. 3, 2010, pp. 343–76

Scates, Bruce, 'A monument to murder: Celebrating the conquest of Aboriginal Australia', *Studies in Western Australian History 10*, 1989, pp. 21–31

Sleeter, Christine, 'Becoming white: Reinterpreting a family story by putting race back into the picture', *Race, Ethnicity and Education 14*, no. 1, 2011, pp. 421–33

Sleeter, Christine, 'Critical family history: Situating family within contexts of power relationships', *Journal of Multidisciplinary Research 8*, no. 1, 2016, pp. 11–23

Smith, Takirirangi, 'Nga tini ahuatanga o whakapapa korero', *Educational Philosophy and Theory 32*, no. 1, 2000, pp. 53–60

Strakosch, Elizabeth, 'Counter-monuments and nation-building in Australia', *Peace Review 22*, no. 3, 2010, pp. 268–75

Strange, Carolyn, 'Masculinities, intimate femicide and the death penalty in Australia, 1890–1920', *British Journal of Criminology 43*, 2003, pp. 310–39

Tapsell, Paul, 'The flight of Parerautututu: An investigation of taonga from a tribal perspective', *The Journal of the Polynesian Society 106*, no. 4, 1997, pp. 323–74

Thomas, Nicholas, 'Sanitation and seeing: The creation of state power in early colonial Fiji', *Comparative Studies in Society and History 32*, no. 1, 1990, pp. 149–70

Thomas, William F.F., 'William Morley – Lecture for the AGM of the Wesley Historical Society', *Proceedings of the Wesley Historical Society of New Zealand 80*, 2005

Torma, Tom, 'Lhatsik Houmoulu'l "House of Tradition": Sacred items to be returned from Peabody Museum', *The Da'Luk: Wiyot Tribe 17*, no. 3, 2017, p. 5

Veracini, Lorenzo, '"Emphatically not a white man's colony": Settler colonialism and the construction of colonial Fiji', *Journal of Pacific History 43*, no. 2, 2008, pp. 189–205

Vimalassery, Manu, Alyosha Goldstein, Juliana Hu Pegues, 'On colonial unknowing', *Theory and Event 19*, no. 4, special issue, 2016

Wanhalla, Angela, 'Interracial sexual violence in 1860s New Zealand', *New Zealand Journal of History 45*, no. 1, 2011, pp. 71–84

Waterhouse, Jill, 'Edward John Eyre: Queanbeyan district landowner, overlander and explorer, especially his relationships with local Aboriginal people and convicts', *Canberra Historical Journal 41*, 1998, pp. 15–24

Wevers, Lydia, 'Being Pakeha: The politics of location', *Journal of New Zealand Studies (4/5)*, 2006, pp. 1–9

Yon, Daniel A., 'Race-making/race-mixing: St Helena and the South Atlantic world', *Social Dynamics: A Journal of African Studies 33*, no. 2, 2007, pp. 144–63

Young, James, 'The counter-monument: Memory against itself in Germany today', *Critical Inquiry 18*, no. 2, 1992, pp. 267–96

THESES

Copland, Mark, 'A system of assassination: The Macintyre River frontier 1837–1850' (Honours thesis, University of Queensland, 1990)

Cross, Melissa, 'The forgotten soundtrack of Maoriland: Imagining the nation through Alfred Hill's songs for Rewi's Last Stand' (Master's thesis, Massey University, 2015)

Haenga-Collins, Maria, 'Closed stranger adoption, Māori and race relations in Aotearoa New Zealand, 1955–1985' (PhD thesis, Australian National University, 2017)

Newman, Erica, 'Colonial intervention on guardianship and "adoption" practices in Fiji 1874–1970' (PhD thesis, University of Otago, 2018)

Thornley, Andrew, 'The Methodist mission and the Indians in Fiji 1900–1920' (Master's thesis, University of Auckland, 1973)

Whitelaw, James, 'People, land and government in Suva, Fiji' (PhD thesis, Australian National University, 1966)

ONLINE SOURCES

ABC Education, 'Prime Minister Keating's Redfern address, 1992', *ABC Education*, first broadcast 10 December 1992: www.abc.net.au/education/paul-keatings-1992-redfern-speech/13889050

'About the National Redress Scheme', a national scheme for people who have experienced institutional child sexual abuse: www.nationalredress.gov.au/about/about-scheme

Allam, Lorena and Carly Earl, 'For centuries the rivers sustained Aboriginal culture. Now they are dry, elders despair', *Guardian*, 21 January 2019: www.theguardian.com/australia-news/2019/jan/22/murray-darling-river-aboriginal-culture-dry-elders-despair-walgett

Appendix to the Journals of the House of Representatives, E-03A (1863), p. 1: https://paperspast.natlib.govt.nz/parliamentary/appendix-to-the-journals-of-the-house-of-representatives/1863/I/890

'Australia Day: What do Australians think about celebrating the nation on January 26?', *ABC News*, 26 January 2019: www.abc.net.au/news/2019-01-26/what-do-australians-think-about-australia-day-this-year/10753278

Baum, Tina, interview with Judy Watson and Helen Johnson, 'The Balnaves Contemporary Series: the red thread of history', National Gallery of Australia: https://nga.gov.au/stories-ideas/the-red-thread-of-history/

Birch, Tony, 'A change of date will do nothing to shake Australia from its colonial-settler triumphalism', *IndigenousX*, 2 January 2018: https://indigenousx.com.au/tony-birch-a-change-of-date-will-do-nothing-to-shake-australia-from-its-colonial-settler-triumphalism/

Brennan, Bridget, 'The stolen children of Cootamundra: "Years later, what's changed?"', *ABC News,* 12 February 2018: www.abc.net.au/news/2018-02-11/stolen-generations-cootamundra-girls-home-whats-changed/9408132

Brown, P.L., 'Batman, John (1801–1839)', from the *Australian Dictionary of Biography*: http://adb.anu.edu.au/biography/batman-john-1752

Burnside, Niki, 'Queenie McKenzie's "Mistake Creek Massacre" displayed by National Museum after years of controversy', *ABC News,* 22 July 2020: www.abc.net.au/news/2020-07-22/talking-blak-to-history-indigenous-exhibition-at-national-museum/12472370

Callanan, Virginia, 'The last stand', *Gauge: The Blog of New Zealand's Audiovisual Archives*, 15 May 2014: https://ngataonga.org.nz

'Capt. Cook: A "genocidal murderer" – Indigenous scholar Tina Ngata', *Te Ao Māori News*, 16 July 2019: www.teaomaori.news/capt-cook-genocidal-murderer-indigenous-scholartina-ngata

Carlson, Bronwyn, 'No public outrage, no vigils: Australia's silence at violence against Indigenous women', *The Conversation*, 16 April 2021: https://theconversation.com/no-public-outrage-no-vigils-australias-silence-at-violence-against-indigenous-women-158875

Clement, Cathie, submission to the Review of Exhibitions and Public Programs at the National Museum of Australia, 2003: www.nma.gov.au/about/corporate/review-of-exhibitions-and-programs/review-submissions

Condon, Brendan, 'John Batman's statue tried for war crimes', *Nonviolence Today* 25, March/April 1992: http://dkeenan.com/NvT/

'Controversy over ACT Reconciliation Day', *SBS News*, 25 May 2018: www.sbs.com.au/news/controversy-over-act-reconciliation-day

Daley, Paul, 'Australia's frontier war killings still conveniently escape official memory', *Guardian*, 8 June 2018: www.theguardian.com/australia-news/postcolonial-blog/2018/jun/08/australias-frontier-war-killings-still-conveniently-escape-official-memory

Daley, Paul, 'Why does the Australian War Memorial ignore the frontier war?', *Guardian Australia*, 12 September 2013: www.theguardian.com/world/2013/sep/12/australian-war-memorial-ignores-frontier-war

Deane, William, 'Decrying the memories of Mistake Creek is yet further injustice', *Sydney Morning Herald*, 27 November 2002: www.smh.com.au/national/decrying-the-memories-of-mistake-creek-is-yet-further-injustice-20021127-gdfvkb.html

Department of the Interior National Park Service, 'Notice of Intent to Repatriate Cultural Items: Peabody Museum of Archaeology and Ethnology, Harvard University, Cambridge, MA', Federal Register 83, no. 98, 2 May 2018: www.govinfo.gov/content/pkg/FR-2018-05-21/pdf/2018-10781.pdf

Department of the Interior National Park Service, 'Notice of Intent to Repatriate Cultural Items: Brooklyn Museum, Brooklyn NY', Federal Register 82, no. 165, 28 August 2017: www.govinfo.gov/content/pkg/FR-2017-08-28/html/2017-18188.htm

Dovey, Ceridwen, 'The mapping of massacres', *New Yorker*, 6 December 2017: www.newyorker.com/culture/culture-desk/mapping-massacres

Dow, Aisha, 'Bye bye Batman', *Age*, 16 February 2017: www.theage.com.au/national/victoria/bye-bye-batman-melbourne-founders-name-to-be-erased-from-electorate-history-20170216-guepuj.html

Bibliography: Online sources

Dutton, Geoffrey, 'Eyre, Edward John (1815–1901)', from the *Australian Dictionary of Biography*: http://adb.anu.edu.au/biography/eyre-edward-john-2032/text2507

Edmonds, Penelope, 'Batmans Hill', eMelbourne, 2008: www.emelbourne.net.au/biogs/EM00164b.htm

Edmonds, Penelope, 'Founding myths', eMelbourne, 2008: www.emelbourne.net.au/biogs/EM00603b.htm

Endeavour Voyage: The untold stories of Cook and the First Australians (exhibition), 2 June 2020–26 April 2021, National Museum of Australia, Canberra: https://nma.gov.au/exhibitions/endeavour-voyage

Gough, Julie, *Tense past*, Tasmanian Museum and Art Gallery, 7 June–3 November 2019: www.tmag.tas.gov.au/whats_on/exhibitions/current_upcoming/info/julie_gough_tense_past

Greenson, Thadeus, 'The island's return: The unprecedented repatriation of the center of the Wiyot universe', *North Coast Journal*, 24 October 2019: www.northcoastjournal.com/humboldt/the-islands-return/Content?oid=15494902

Hall, Nealis and Brittany Britton, 'Newest community loan for women's ceremonial dresses: Long ago to today', *Clarke Museum Blog*, 28 April 2019: www.clarkemuseum.org/blog/newest-community-loan-for-womens-ceremonial-dresses-long-ago-to-today

Haunui-Thompson, Shannon, 'Tears as Crown apologises for Parihaka atrocities', *Te Manu Korihi*, RNZ, 9 June 2017: www.rnz.co.nz/news/te-manu-korihi/332613/tears-as-crown-apologises-for-parihaka-atrocities

Helvarg, David, 'Island of resilience: The Wiyot reclaim their land and culture from a dark past', *American Indian 21(1)*, 2020: www.americanindianmagazine.org/story/wiyot

Hinchliffe, Joe, 'Call to remove statue of John Batman', *Age*, 26 August 2017: www.theage.com.au/national/victoria/call-to-remove-statue-of-john-batman-founder-of-melbourne-over-role-in-indigenous-killings-20170826-gy4snc.html

'History of the collections', Smithsonian National Museum of the American Indian: https://americanindian.si.edu/explore/collections/history

Human Rights and Equal Opportunity Commission, 'Bringing them home: Report of the National Inquiry into the Separation of Aboriginal and Torres Strait Islander Children from Their Families' (Sydney: HREOC, 1997): www.humanrights.gov.au/sites/default/files/content/pdf/social_justice/bringing_them_home_report.pdf

'Hundreds gather for Myall Creek commemorations', *Inverell Times*, 10 June 2019: www.inverelltimes.com.au/story/6208100/hundreds-gather-for-myall-creek-commemorations/

Hurihanganui, Te Aniwa, 'Parihaka reach milestone to reconcile relationship with Crown', Te Manu Korihi, *RNZ*, 24 October 2019: www.rnz.co.nz/news/te-manu-korihi/401714/parihaka-reach-milestone-to-reconcile-relationship-with-crown

Hutchinson, Pamela, 'Moguls and starlets: 100 years of Hollywood's corrosive, systemic sexism', *Guardian*, 19 October 2017: www.theguardian.com/film/2017/oct/19/moguls-and-starlets-100-years-of-hollywoods-corrosive-systemic-sexism

Ireland, Tracy, 'Captain Cook is a contested national symbol, so why spend more money on him?', *The Conversation*, 11 May 2018: www.abc.net.au/news/2018-05-11/captain-james-cook-who-discovered-australia-indigenous-ownership/9750772

Kerkhove, Ray, 'Multuggerah (c. 1820–1846)', from the *Australian Dictionary of Biography*: http://ia.anu.edu.au/biography/multuggerah-29904

King, Belinda, 'Should we rename the Batman Bridge in Tasmania?', *ABC*, 15 June 2020: www.abc.net.au/news/2020-06-15/should-we-rename-batman-bridge-in-tasmania/12355404

Knowles, Rachel and Sarah Maunder, 'Aboriginal marchers join Hobart's Anzac Day celebration for the first time', *NITV News*, 25 April 2022: www.sbs.com.au/nitv/article/2022/04/25/aboriginal-marchers-join-hobarts-anzac-day-celebration-first-time

Korff, Jens, 'Compensation for Stolen Generation members', 8 February 2019: www.creativespirits.info/aboriginalculture/politics/stolen-generations/compensation-for-stolen-generation-members

Kowinski, William S., 'In 1860 six murderers nearly wiped out the Wiyot Indian Tribe – in 2004 its members have found ways to heal', *SFGate*, 28 February 2004: www.sfgate.com/entertainment/article/In-1860-six-murderers-nearly-wiped-out-the-Wiyot-2816476

'Landscapes in blood', *Sydney Morning Herald*, 14 December 2002: www.smh.com.au/national/landscapes-in-blood-20021214-gdfysp.html

Lawrence M. Small, 'A passionate collector', *Smithsonian Magazine*, November 2000: www.smithsonianmag.com/history/a-passionate-collector-33794183/

Loader, Arini, 'Te Pūtakeo Te Riri', *The Briefing Papers*, 6 November 2018: https://briefingpapers.co.nz/te-putake-o-te-riri/

McGlade, Hannah, Bronwyn Carlson and Marlene Longbottom, 'An open letter in response to the lack of public concern or response to the killings of Aboriginal and Torres Strait Islander women', *Croakey*, 9 March 2021: www.croakey.org/an-open-letter-in-response-to-the-lack-of-public-concern-or-response-to-the-killings-of-aboriginal-and-torres-strait-islander-women/

McHugh, Paul, 'Robust resilience of the Wiyot Tribe', *San Francisco Chronicle California North Coast Series*, 17 September 2005: http://paulmchugh.net/2005/09/robust-resilience-of-the-wiyot-tribe/

Monument Australia, 2010–2020: http://monumentaustralia.org.au/themes/conflict/indigenous

Mukherjee, Shomik, 'Wiyot Tribe raising funds for 2020 World Renewal Ceremony', *Times Standard*, 8 April 2019: www.times-standard.com/2019/04/08/wiyot-tribe-raising-funds-for-2020-world-renewal-ceremony/

National Museum of Australia, The Message: The story from the shore, YouTube, uploaded 28 January 2021: www.youtube.com/watch?v=hoU65yHWikA

Office of Environment and Heritage, 'Cootamundra Aboriginal Girls Home', NSW Department of Planning, Industry and Environment: www.environment.nsw.gov.au/heritageapp/ViewHeritageItemDetails.aspx?ID=5061346

Parliament of Australia, Department of Parliamentary Services, 'Prime Minister Kevin Rudd, MP – Apology to Australia's Indigenous peoples', recorded 13 February 2008: https://info.australia.gov.au/about-australia/our-country/our-people/apology-to-australias-indigenous-peoples

Polity Research & Consulting (for Reconciliation Australia), '2018 Australian reconciliation barometer' (Sydney: Polity Research, 2018), 80, 121: www.reconciliation.org.au/wp-content/uploads/2019/02/final_full_arb-full-report-2018.pdf

Radi, Heather, 'Ardill, George Edward (1857–1945)', from the *Australian Dictionary of Biography*: http://adb.anu.edu.au/biography/ardill-george-edward-5048

Ream, Rebecca, 'Composting layers of Christchurch history', *Genealogy*

5(3), 2021, https://doi.org/10.3390/genealogy5030074

'Redress scheme', Aboriginal and Torres Strait Islander Legal Services (Qld): www.atsils.org.au/wp-content/uploads/2014/11/FACT-SHEET_Redress-Scheme.pdf; 'Stolen Generations Reparations Scheme', Government of South Australia: www.dpc.sa.gov.au/responsibilities/aboriginal-affairs-and-reconciliation/reconciliation/stolen-generations-reparations-scheme

'Reserve transformed with stunning installation', Waterford Press: www.waterfordpress.co.nz/business/currie-construction/

'Rewi's Last Stand' poster (1939), P03899, NgTSV: https://ngataonga.org.nz/

Rohde, Jerry, 'Genocide and extortion', *North Coast Journal*, 25 February 2010: https://www.northcoastjournal.com/humboldt/genocide-and-extortion/Content?oid=2130748

Ryan, Lyndall et al., *Colonial Frontier Massacres, Australia, 1788–1930* (Newcastle: University of Newcastle, 2017–2020), funded by Australian Research Council, Discovery Project 140100399: https://c21ch.newcastle.edu.au/colonialmassacres/map.php

Scates, Bruce, 'Call to topple monuments is an opportunity for debate', *Age*, 11 June 2020: www.theage.com.au/national/call-to-topple-monuments-is-an-opportunity-for-debate-20200611-p551qs.html

Scates, Bruce, 'Monumental errors: How Australia can fix its racist colonial statues', *The Conversation*, 27 August 2017: https://theconversation.com/monumental-errors-how-australia-can-fix-its-racist-colonial-statues-82980

Simmons, E.R., 'Garavel, Joseph Marie', from the *Dictionary of New Zealand Biography*: https://teara.govt.nz/en/biographies/1g2/garavel-joseph-marie

Sir George Young, Facsimile for a Proposal for a Settlement on the Coast of New South Wales 1785 (Sydney: Angus and Robertson, 1888): http://handle.slv.vic.gov.au/10381/108487

Sir George Young, Facsimile for a Proposal for a Settlement on the Coast of New South Wales 1785 (Sydney: Angus and Robertson, 1888): http://handle.slv.vic.gov.au/10381/108487

Slezak, Michael, 'Scorched country: The destruction of Australia's native landscape', *Guardian*, 7 March 2018: www.theguardian.com/environment/2018/mar/07/scorched-country-the-destruction-of-australias-native-landscape

Small, Lawrence M., 'A passionate collector', *Smithsonian Magazine*, November 2000: www.smithsonianmag.com/history/a-passionate-collector-33794183/

Steen, David 'It happened one night at MGM', *Vanity Fair*, April 2003: www.vanityfair.com/news/2003/04/mgm200304

'St Luke's Reconciliation Cross', Doing Justice, 2016: www.doingjustice.org.au/st-lukes-reconciliation-cross/

'Stolen Generations Reparations Scheme and Funeral Assistance Fund', NSW government: www.aboriginalaffairs.nsw.gov.au/healing-and-reparations/stolen-generations/reparations-scheme; 'The National Redress Scheme', https://knowmore.org.au/about-us/redress-and-royal-commission/redress-scheme/

'Telling stories of Tairawhiti', *Gisborne Herald*, 30 September 2019: www.gisborneherald.co.nz/local-news/20190930/two-sculptures-unveiled-on-saturday-on-titirangi-kaiti-hill-celebrate-important-figures-and-voyaging/

Te Ture Haeata ki Parihaka 2019/Parihaka Reconciliation Act 2019, Public Act 2019 No. 60: www.legislation.govt.nz/act/public/2019/0060/latest/versions.aspx

'The Black Line', National Museum Australia: www.nma.gov.au/defining-moments/resources/the-black-line

'The controversial statue that was added to, not torn down or vandalised', *ABC News*, 29 August 2017: www.abc.net.au/news/2017-08-29/explorers-monument-added-to-not-torn-down-or-vandalised/8853224

'The Killing Times', *Guardian*: www.theguardian.com/australia-news/series/the-killing-times

'Tipuna Te Maro', *Gisborne Herald*, 25 September 2019: www.gisborneherald.co.nz/local-news/20190925/tipuna-te-maro/

'Two women charged over alleged defacing of Captain Cook statue in Sydney's Hyde Park', *ABC*, 14 June 2020: www.abc.net.au/news/2020-06-14/nsw-women-charged-over-defacing-captain-cook-statue-in-sydney/12353598

'Uluru Statement from the Heart', 2017: https://ulurustatement.org/; Reconciliation Australia and Healing Foundation, 'Truth-telling symposium report' (Canberra: Reconciliation Australia and Healing Foundation, 2018): www.reconciliation.org.au/wp-content/uploads/2019/02/truth-telling-symposium-report1.pdf

'Victoria's Stolen Generations Redress Scheme is a step on a journey towards justice', Victorian Aboriginal Legal Service: www.vals.org.au/victorias-stolen-generations-redress-scheme-is-a-step-on-a-journey-towards-justice/

Wahlquist, Calla and Paul Karp, 'Melbourne electorate of Batman renamed after Indigenous activist', *Guardian*, 20 June 2018: www.theguardian.com/australia-news/2018/jun/20/melbourne-electorate-of-batman-renamed-after-indigenous-activist

Watkin, Tim, 'Podcast: Waitara and one family's journey', *RNZ*, 17 March 2020 [50:46]: www.rnz.co.nz/programmes/nzwars-waitara/story/2018738836/taranaki-wars-waitara-and-one-family-s-journey

Watson, Judy, *The Names of Places*, 2016, Institute of Modern Art, Brisbane: http://thenamesofplaces.com/tnop/

'Wyndham and Josephine Wills, wedding', Puke Ariki Heritage Collections: https://collection.pukeariki.com/objects/168665

'Young, Edward', Pitcairn Islands Study Center: https://library.puc.edu/pitcairn/bounty/crew5.shtml

INDEX

Bold denotes illustrations and tables

100 Crowded Years (movie) 236

Aboriginal Australians *see* Indigenous Australian peoples
Aborigines Protection Act **123**, 153, 155
Aborigines Protection Board 118, 155
activism/activists 24, 25, 32, 176, 227–29, 231–32, 245, 246
aftermath definition 19
An Account of the State of Agriculture and Grazing in New South Wales (Atkinson) 168–69
Aotearoa New Zealand
    botany 223
    colonialism, settler 49, 79, 162, 165, 218, 220
    farming 53, 236
    Gisborne (Tūranganui-a-Kiwa) 218–19, 220–21, **221**, 223
    governments 36, 38, 49, 53, 56, 65, 159–60, 163, 179, 221, 236
    history in education curricula 38, 52, 56, 245
    land dispossession 54, 56, 159–60, 243
    Ōrākau 29, 30–36, **32**, **33**, **35**, **37**, **38**, 63, 164, 235–44, **243**
    Parihaka 24, 51–52, 54–55, **178**, 179–90, **182**, **185**, 189
    police force 54–55, 184
    Pukearuhe 59, 60, 64
    Rangiaowhia 63, 239, 240, 242
    reconciliation 51–52
    Te Awamutu 237, 238, 243, 244
    Te Papa Tongarewa Museum of New Zealand 15, 248
    Te Pōrere 53
    Treaty of Waitangi/Te Tiriti o Waitangi 158–59, 160, 164, 236, 244

    Waitangi Tribunal 51, 54, 179, 245
    Whanganui 79, 80, 83, 84
    see also battles; iwi; Māori; massacres/murders; Pākehā; *individual people*
Appleby, Gabrielle 39
Arbuckle, Roscoe (Fatty) 143
Ardill, George 118
Arnold, Gilbert Emerson 94–95
art, Indigenous
    Balance 1990 (exhibition) 204
    Endeavour Voyage: The untold stories of Cook and first Australians (exhibition) 246
    Goorirr Goorirr Joonba (performance) 193, 203, 204
    Holmes à Court, Robert 204
    McKenzie, Queenie 207, 210, 212–13
    Nickolls, Trevor 204
    O'Ferrall, Michael 204
    On the Edge: Five Aboriginal artists (exhibition) 204
    Roads Cross (exhibition) 204
    Talking Blak to History (exhibition) 213
    the red thread of history, loose ends (exhibition) 247
    Thomas, Rover 24, 193–97, **196**, **197**, **200–201**, 202–4, **205**
    Tuffery, Michael 24–25, 223, 224, 225
    Tūpara, Nick 24–25, 220, **221**, 222, 223–25
    Venice Biennale 204
    Watson, Judy 24, **208**, **209**, 210–11, 213–15, **216**
    see also individual artworks
Ashwell, Benjamin 63
assimilation 20–21, 23, 25, 236, 238, 239, 248
Atkins, Marnie 74–75
Atkinson, James 168–69

Atkinson, Louisa 24, 167–77, **171**, **172**
Auckland Star (newspaper) 180
Australia
    assimilation 23
    Australia Day 39, 40, 228
    Australian Capital Territory (ACT) **123**
    'Change the Date' campaign 39, 40
    environmental damage from colonisation 24, 167–77
    expeditions 107–16, **111**, **115**
    governments 41, 46, 110, 149, 152, 154–55, 245–46
    Macintyre River 97–100, **98**, **99**, 103
    Melbourne (Port Phillip) 25, 108, 227, 228, 229, **230**, 231–33, 234
    Murchison–Gascoyne region 149–53, **151**
    New South Wales 48, 103, 108, 117–21, **119**, **123**, 167, 168–69, 173, 174, 177
    Northern Territory **123**
    public opinion/trends 40
    Queensland 42, **47**, 97, 119–20, **124**, 125, 140, 204, 210
    reconciliation 39–41, 48, 121, 208
    South Australia 108, 109–10, 115, **124**, 204
    Stolen Generations 23, 117–26, **123–24**
    Sydney 98, 102, 118, 140, 207
    Tasmania 108, **124**, 228, 229, 231, 232–33, 234, 247
    Western Australia 24, 42, 110, **124**, 149–56, 193–95, 198, 204
    see also frontier wars, Australian; Indigenous Australian peoples; *individual people*
Awhikau, Tonga 189
Ayres, Marie-Louise 46

Balance 1990 (exhibition) 204
Banks, Joseph 218–19, 222
Batman, Eliza 228, 233
Batman, John 25, 227–34, **230**
battles
    One Tree Hill 45, **45**, 46, **47**
    Ōrākau battle/pā 29, 30–36, **32**, **33**, **35**, **37**, **38**, 63, 164, 235–44, **243**
    Parihaka 24, 51–52, 54–55, **178**, 179–90, **182**, **185**, 189
    Pukearuhe 59, 60, 64
    Te Pōrere 53

see also frontier wars, Australian; massacres; New Zealand Wars
Bavin, Cyril 131–32, 133
Baxter, John 108, 109–10, 112, 113–15
Bedford Downs/Goordbelayin massacre 193, 195, 197–204, **197**, **200–201**, **205**
Beethoven, Ludvig von 189–90
Belich, James 38
Bell, Avril 54–55, 58
Bell, Leah 52
Ben Lomond massacre 229
Black Lives Matter movement 227, 246
blackbirding *see* kidnapping
Bligh, Richard 100–103
Blood on the Spinifex (exhibition) 212
Borell, Belinda 54
Bounty, HMS 139, 140, 141
Bracken, Thomas 189
British Army 79–82, 84
British Army/forces 30, 32, 64, 79–82, 84, 85–86, 160, 163, 217, 220, 235, 239–40, 246
British Empire 66, 83, 92–93, 96, 140, 155, 158, 217–18, 222, 225, 227, 228, 246
    see also imperialism
Brockman, Charles 149, 150, 152
Brockman/Corunna, Daisy 156
Brooks, Clifford 193
Brown, Maitland 43
Browne, Thomas Gore 81, 158–59
Bryce, John 179–89, **182**, **187**
Buchanan, Rachel 51–52, 55, 56, 179
Burton, John 130

Calvert, Louisa (née Atkinson) *see* Atkinson, Louisa
Cameron, Duncan 30–31, 163
Camp at Mistake Creek, The (Thomas) 212
Campbell, Hugh 53
Canning Stock Route 193, 194–95, **196**, 204
Captain Blood (movie) 139
Caribbean 82, 83, 139, 140, 157
Chandler, Lisa 213
children/young people 23
    abuse in care 117–26, **123–24**
    National Inquiry into the Separation of Aboriginal and Torres Strait Islander Children from Their Families 118, 120, 121

orphanages 127, 129–37, **135**
    sexual violence/abuse 23, 93–95, 117–26, **123–24**
    violence towards 60, 63, 71, 77, 101, 240
Christian, Fletcher 139, 140
Coates, A.R. 132, 133
Cockburn, David 63
code of silence, colonial 22, 97–104, 150, 153, 245, 248
Cohen, Stanley 56–57
Colonial Frontiers Massacres digital map 98, 100, 207, 214–15, 216, 231
colonial legal systems 87, 88–90
    Australia 100–03, 104, 151–52, 155–56
    bias against Indigenous peoples/non-Europeans 93, 94–96, 101, 103–04, 125
    Fiji 87, 88–96
    see also legal cases
colonialism, settler 17, 19–23, 24, 41, 158, 207, 213, 227, 248
    Aotearoa New Zealand 49, 79, 162, 165, 218, 220
    Australia 127, 247
    Caribbean 139
    Fiji 89
Colquhoun, Glenn 58
Combat et prise de la Crête-à-Pierrot (Raffet) **159**
Condon, Brendan 231
Cook, Captain James 24–25, 41, 207, 218–21, 223–25, 246–47
Cooper, Annabel 229, 236
Cootachah (Indigenous Australian) 107–10, 112, 113–16
Cootamundra Aboriginal Girls' Home 117–21, **119**
Copland, Mark 99–100, 101, 103
Costa, Ravi de 41
Cowan, James 36, 236–37, **237**, 238–39, 241
Crown Lands Occupation Act 173

Daily Southern Cross (newspaper) 64
Damita, Lili 139, 141, 143
Dansey, Harry 189
Dark Deeds in a Sunny Land (Gribble) 154
Dart, William 189
Davis, Megan 39
Deane, William 212–13

decolonisation 55, 215, 236, 241–44
denial, historical 50, 56–57, 213, 246, 248
Dening, Greg 224
dialogical memorialisation 44, 231
Dilkusha Children's Home (orphanage) 130–31, 131, 135–36
Dolphin, HMS 217–18
Domville Taylor, Thomas 46, **47**
Dovey, Ceridwen 207–08
Drake-Brockman, Howden 156
Dreaming/Ngarranggarni 193–94, 198, 202, 203
Dunedin Weekender (newspaper) 60

East India Company 81, 82
education curricula, New Zealand 38, 52, 56, 245
Eketone, Anaru 22, 59–60, 66, 68
Endeavour, HMS 218, 219–20, 222, 223, 246–47
Endeavour Voyage: The untold stories of Cook and first Australians (exhibition) 246
environmental damage from colonisation 24, 167–77
Explorers' Monument (Fremantle) 42–45, 43
Eyre, Edward 107–16, **115**

Fabrication of Aboriginal History (Windschuttle) 212
Fairbairn, Robert 149, 150–55
family histories, Pākehā 50, 52–56
farming 53, 167, 168–69, 173–74, 236
    see also pastoralism
Field, Les 75
Fiji 21, 23, 87–96, **88, 89, 92**, 127–37, **128, 131, 135**
film industry 139, 143, 145
Finding the Heart of the Nation (Mayor) 246
First Nations peoples 215, 245, 247
    see also Indigenous Australian peoples
Fitzpatrick, Esther 55
Flinders Island (Walker) **234**
Flowers, Margaret **78**, 79–80, 83–86
Flowers, Nathaniel **78**, 79–80, 81, 83–86
Flynn, Errol 24, 139–45
Flynn, Theodore 142
Foley, Gary 231–32
Forest: The Trees 'Ring-barked' to Kill Them for Clearing, A (Spence) 175

Forgotten Coast, The (Shaw) 54–55
Forrest, John 155
France/French 157, 162–63, 164
frontier wars, Australian 39–40
    Australian War Memorial 246
    code of silence 22, 97, 99, 101, 102–03, 150, 153
    Colonial Frontiers Massacres digital map 98, 100, 207, 214–15, 216, 231
    Kulin Nation 229
    local historical memory 41
    Macintyre River 97–100, **98, 99**, 103
    memorials/commemorations 22, 40, 41–47, **43, 45**, 48
    Murchison–Gascoyne region 149–53, **151**
    Myall Creek massacre 48
    One Tree Hill, Battle of 45, **46, 47**
    public opinion 40
    'Uluru Statement from the Heart' 39, 40, 208, 245
    see also massacres/murders
Fudge, Frank 189

Gale, Charles 152
Garavel, Joseph 162–63
Getachew, Adom 157
Gija peoples 197, 198–99, 202–03, 210, 212–13
Gilbert and Sullivan (dramatist/composer) 180–81, 184–85, 188–89
Gilbert, Stephanie 23
Gilchrist, Stephen 48
Gilhooly, Andrew 54–55
Gisborne (Tūranganui-a-Kiwa) 218–19, 220–21, **221**, 223
Goodall, Heather 99–100, 103
Goordbelayin *see* Bedford Downs/Goordbelayin massacre
Goorirr Joonba (performance) 193, 203, 204
Gordon, Arthur 128
Government Gazette of Western Australia (newspaper) 149
governments
    Australian 41, 46, 110, 149, 152, 154–55, 245–46
    British 83, 87–88
    Fiji 88, **89**, 129, 132
    New Zealand 36, 38, 49, 53, 56, 65, 159–60, 163, 179, 221, 236

Grandmother Dress 71, 72–77, **73**
Great Britain/British 82, 83, 87–88, 89, 90, **92**, 128, 149, 158, 223, 239, 246
Grey, George 160, 163, 242
Gribble, John 149, 150, 154–55
Guardian, The (newspaper) 39

Haenga-Collins, Maria 58
Haiti 24, 157–58, 162–65
Hale, Matthew 92–93
half-caste people 65, 163, 238–39
Harris, George 102
Hartman, Carroll 74
Haskins, Victoria 120
Hawkesworth, John 217
Hayward, Ramai Te Miha **37**, 238, 241–42, 244
Hayward, Rudall 25, 36, **37**, 236, 238, 239, 241–42
    see also Rewi's Last Stand (movie)
Heald, Susan 71
Hernandez, Michelle 75, **76**
Heye, George 73
historical privilege 52, 54
history in New Zealand schools 38, 245
Holden, Stephen 101, 103
Hollywood 139, 143, 145
Holmes à Court, Robert 204

Ihimaera, Witi 189–90, 241
Ikirangi 219
Illustrated Sydney News (newspaper) 168
imperialism 86, 87, 90, 157, 181, 207, 217–18, 222, 225, 238
    see also British Empire
indentured labour 22, 23
    Indigenous Australians 116, 149–56, 198
    Indians 87–88, 128–29, **128**, 132–34, 136
    Pacific peoples 21, 87–88, 141
    sexual violence against labourers 91–92
    see also slavery/slave trade
India/Indians
    Indian orphans 129–37, **135**
    indentured labour 87–88, 128–29, **128**, 132–34, 136
Indigenous Australian peoples
    Aborigines Protection Board 118, 155
    Bigambul 97, 98, 100–01, 102

children taken from families 23, 107–16, 117–26, **123–24**
Eyre's expeditions 107–16
First Nations 215, 245, 247
Gamilaraay 177
Gija 197, 198–99, 202–03, 210, 212–13
indentured/coerced labour 116, 149–56, 198
Jagera 45–46
Karajarri 43, 44
Koori 231–32
Kulin 25, 227–29, 232
land dispossession 228, 232
Maimie, murder of 97–104
Ngarranggarni/Dreaming 193–94, 198, 202, 203
Plangermaireener 233–34
resistance to settlers 45–46
sexual violence/abuse 117–26, **123–24**, 150, 152–53, 154, 155–56, 198
Stolen Generations 23, 107–16, 117–26, **123–24**
'Uluru Statement from the Heart' 39, 40, 208, 245
Waanyi 24, 210, 211, 214; *see also* Watson, Judy
Wangkatjungka peoples 193
worldview 193–95, 202–03, 212
Yuwalaraay 177
see also art, Indigenous; *individual people*
Indigenous peoples/settler relationships/friendships 23, 42, 79, 103–04, 151, 219, 228
In the Wake of the Bounty (movie) 139, 141
Innes, Alice 141
Isaacs, Uncle Colin 46–47
iwi
Ngāi Tūhoe 235
Ngāti Maniapoto 34, 35, 59, 60, **61**, 63, 64, 65, 164, 235, 238, 241
Ngāti Oneone 218, 220–25, **221**
Ngāti Rākai 218; *see also* Te Maro
Ngāti Raukawa 31, **32**, **33**, 34, 235
Rongowhakaata 219, 235
Tainui 60
Tūwharetoa 235
Waikato 59, 60

Jackson, Moana 19, 20
Jagera peoples 45–46
Jager, Frank 75
Jaminji, Paddy 202–03
Johnson, Helen 247–48
Johnson, Miranda 53
Johnston, Anna 24
Jones, Alison 53
Joshuing (Indigenous Australian) 107, 108–09

Kākahi, Tohu 179, 180, 183–84, **185**, 188–89, 190
Karajarri peoples 43, 44
Keating, Paul 121
Kelly, Hēmi 241
Kenny, Dane 116
Kidman, Joanna 19, 22
kidnapping 48, 128, 141, 152, 153, 155, 217, 219
Kimberley region 47–48, 193–204
King, John Whiteley 65
King, Michael 58
King, Philip 173
Kīngitanga movement 24, 35, 158–64, **161**, 165, 238, 239–40
knowledge, Indigenous 208, 210, 214–15, 218, 222–23, 225
Ko Taranaki Te Maunga (Buchanan) 52
Konishi, Shino 20, 23
Kulin peoples 25, 227–29, 232

La Grange Bay massacre 43, 44
land dispossession, Māori/Indigenous Australians 54, 56, 159–60, 228, 232, 243
Lawson, Elizabeth 170, 177
legal cases
Rex v RB 93–94
The People of the State of California vs Errol Flynn 143–44
see also colonial legal systems
legislation **88**
Aborigines Protection Act 118, **123**, 153, 155
Crown Lands Occupation Act 173
Māori Prisoners' Trials Act 179
Master and Servant Act 150
Ordinance to Provide for the Care and Maintenance of Orphan Indian Immigrants 129–30
Slavery Abolition Act 83

Lenihan, Rebecca 80
Lenore, Miriel 107
Loader, Arini 50, 51, 55, 58
local vs national historical memory 41–42, 44–47
Los Angeles Times (newspaper) 144
Lurnerminner (Indigenous Australian) 233, 234
Lydon, Jane 24
Lyttleton Times (newspaper) 189

Macdonald, Charlotte 80
Macdonald, Gaelen 218
Mackay, Jessie 189
Maclean, Daniel 101–02
Māia 221–22
Maihiati (New Guinea girl) 142
Maimie (indigenous Australian), murder of 97–104
Maitland Mercury (newspaper) 100
mana motuhake (self-determination) 164, 185, 218
   see also sovereignty, Indigenous
Maniapoto, Rewi 34, 35, 64, 239–40, 241
Mansell, Michael 229
Māori
   art 218, 221–25, **221**, **224**
   Kīngitanga movement 24, 35, 158–64, **161**, 238, 239–40
   land dispossession 54, 56, 159–60, 243
   mana motuhake (self-determination) 164, 185, 218
   mātauranga Māori 222–23, 225
   niupepa (newspapers) 24, 158, 160–64, 165
   Parihaka 24, 51–52, 54–55, **178**, 179–90, **182**, **185**, 189
   perspectives/memories, historical 30, 32, **32**, 34–38, **35**, **37**, 66–68, 236–44
   sovereignty, Indigenous 158, 160, 162, 163, 185, 218, 232, 245, 246, 247, 248
   sexual violence/abuse against 23, 180, 188, 240
   te reo Māori 49–50, 55
   tino rangatiratanga (sovereignty) 160, 162, 163, 185, 218
   waiata (songs) 34, 189, 241–42
   whakapapa/kin-based histories 50–51, 66, 223, 225
   see also iwi; massacres/murders; New Zealand Wars; *individual people*

Māori Prisoners' Trials Act 179
Mark, James 100, 101, 102–03
Mark, Johnny 100
Marshall, Anaru 52
Marukauiti 219
masculinity, white/colonial 23, 139, 140, 144–45
massacres/murders
   Bedford Downs/Goordbelayin 193, 195, 197–204, **197**, **200–01**, **205**
   Ben Lomond 229
   Blood on the Spinifex (exhibition) 212
   Colonial Frontiers Massacres digital map 98, 100, 207, 214–15, 216, 231
   Fiji 90
   La Grange Bay 43, 44
   Macintyre River 97–100, **98**, **99**, 103
   Maimie (indigenous Australian), murder of 97–104
   Mistake Creek 212–13
   Murchison–Gascoyne region 152
   Myall Creek 48
   names of places, the (Watson) 24, 208, **208**, 210–11, 214–15
   Ōrākau pā 29, 30–36, **32**, **33**, **35**, **37**, **38**, 63, 164, 235–44, **243**
   pale slaughter (Watson) **209**, 211
   Rangiaowhia 63, 239, 240, 242
   salt in the wound (Watson) 215, **216**
   Tasmania 231
   Whiteley, John 60–68, **61**, **62**, **67**
   Wiyot Tribe 71–72, 77
Master and Servant Act 150
Mayor, Thomas 246
Mbembe, Achille 126
McKenna, Mark 48
McKenzie, Queenie 207, 210, 212–13
Melbourne (Port Phillip) 25, 108, 227, 228, 229, **230**, 231–33, 234
memorials/monuments 32–34, **35**, 36
   Australian War Memorial 246
   counter-monuments 44
   dialogical memorialisation 44, 231
   Explorers' Monument 42–45, **43**
   Myall Creek Memorial Site 48
   Puhi Kai Iti/Cook Landing National Historic Reserve 220–22
   Reconciliation Cross 45–47, **45**, **47**

statues/monuments, colonial 44, 207, 227–28, 229, **230**, 231–33, 234
'Women in Pearling' 47–48
memory
   collective amnesia 22
   dialogical memorialisation 44, 231
   family 22
   local vs national historical memory 41–42, 44–47
   Pākehā historic perspective/memory 49–56, 58, 63–65, 188, 225, 236–44, 241, 246
   popular 22
   private 22
   sensory 126
Message: The story from the shore, The (movie) 246–47
Messenger, A.H. 59
Methodist Church 63, 66, 127, 130, 132–35
Mills, Keri 20, 22, 49, 55–56
missionaries/missionary work 60–68, **62**, 135–36, 154–55, 160
Mistake Creek massacre 212–13
Mistake Creek Massacre (McKenzie) 212–13
Mitchell Library 98
Moffatt, Kirstine 24
Monkhouse, William 218–19
Moore, Grace 24
Morgan, Sally 156
Morley, William 63, 68
movies/documentaries
   100 Crowded Years 236
   Captain Blood 139
   In the Wake of the Bounty 139, 141
   Message: The story from the shore, The 246–47
   New Zealand Wars 38
   Rewi's Last Stand 25, 36, **37**, 235–44, **237**, **243**
   Tupaia's Endeavour 223–24
   see also film industry; Flynn, Errol; television programmes/series
Multuggerah (Jagera peoples) 45–46
Murchison–Gascoyne region 149–53, **151**
My Place (Morgan) 156
My Wicked Wicked Ways (Flynn & Conrad) 141–42, 144
Myall Creek Memorial Site 48

mythmaking 22, 32, 34, 35, 36, 139, 141, 144, 219, 227, 232, 236, 240–41
   see also truth-telling

names of places, the (Watson) 24, 208, **208**, 210–211, 214–15
nation building 34, 39, 44, 235, 238, 239, 244, 245
National Inquiry into the Separation of Aboriginal and Torres Strait Islander Children from Their Families 118, 120, 121
National Museum of Australia 213, 247
Native Americans *see* North American Indigenous peoples
Neale, Margo 213, 246
Neramberein (Indigenous Australian) 107, 109–10, 112–16
Nettelbeck, Amanda 22
New Guinea 141–44
New Zealand *see* Aotearoa New Zealand
New Zealand Herald (newspaper) 34
New Zealand Wars
   100 Crowded Years (movie) 236
   contested memories 22
   Governor, The (TV series) 38
   Māori perspectives/memories 30, 32, **32**, 34–38, **35**, **37**, 66–68, 236–44
   memorials/anniversaries 32–34, **35**, 36
   Pākehā commentary/historiography 30, **32**, 34–38, **35**, **37**, 51–53, 55–56, 63–65, 188, 236–44
   Rewi's Last Stand (movie) 25, 36, **37**, 235–44, **237**, **243**
   Taranaki Wars 55–56, 59–63, 159–60
   Waikato War 30, 36, 38, 63, 163, 238, 239, 243
New Zealand Wars (documentary/TV series) 38
New Zealand Wars: A history of Maori campaigns and the pioneering period, The (Cowan) **237**
Newman, Erica 23
Ngā Taonga Sound and Vision 243
Ngāi Tūhoe 235
Ngakuyipa/Marrbi/Nyrrbi (Indigenous Australian) 193
Ngarranggarni/Dreaming 193–94, 198, 202, 203

Ngāti Maniapoto 34, 35, 59, 60, **61**, 63, 64, 65, 164, 235, 238, 241
Ngāti Oneone 218, 220–25, **221**
Ngāti Rākai 218
  see also Te Maro
Ngāti Raukawa 31, **32**, **33**, 34, 235
Nicholas, Henriata 244
Nicholson, Grace 73–74
Nickolls, Trevor 204
Nixon, Rob 176
niupepa (newspapers) 24, 158, 160–64, 165
Nixon, Rob 176
North American Indigenous peoples
  Wiyot Tribe 71–77, **73**, **76**
  World Renewal Ceremony 71, 72, 75, 77

O'Brien, Patricia 23–24
O'Ferrall, Michael 204
O'Malley, Vincent 19, 22
Observer (newspaper) 180
Old Frontier, The (Cowan) 238–39
Oliver, Tony 212
On the Edge: Five Aboriginal artists (exhibition) 204
One Tree Hill, Battle of 45, **45**, 46, **47**
Ōrākau battle/pā 29, 30–36, **32**, **33**, **35**, **37**, **38**, 63, 164, 235–44, **243**
oral histories 36, 58, 115, 212, 213, 215, 219, 240
Ordinance to Provide for the Care and Maintenance of Orphan Indian Immigrants 129–30
orphanages 127, 129–37, **135**

Pacific peoples
  Fiji 21, 23, 87–96, **88**, **89**, **92**, 127–37, **128**, **131**, **135**
  indentured labour 21, 87–88, 141
  New Guinea 141–44
  Papua 21, 142, 143
  Western Pacific 140, 143
  see also Māori
Page, Alison 246–47
Paiaka, Raureti 241
Pākehā
  family histories 50, 52–56
  historic perspective/memory 49–56, 58, 63–65, 68, 188, 225, 236–44, 246

New Zealand Wars commentary/historiography 30, **32**, 34–38, **35**, **37**, 51–53, 55–56, 63–65, 188, 236–44
This Pākehā Life (Jones) 53
pale slaughter (Watson) **209**, 211
Parihaka 24, 51–52, 54–55, **178**, 179–90, **182**, **185**, 189
Parihaka: The art of passive resistance (Hohaia & Strongman) 189
Parihaka Woman, The (Ihimaera) 189–90
Parkes, Henry 247
parody 24, 180–84, 188–89
passive resistance see Parihaka
pastoralism 43, 149, 150, 152–53, 155, 156, 168–69, 173–74, 193, 195, 198–99, 202
  see also farming
Paterson, Lachy 24
pearling industry 47–48, 149, 150–51
Pelonemena/Pellenominer/Pellonymyna (Indigenous Australian) 233–34, **234**
Phillips, Henry 65
Pickering, Dani 55
Pilbara region 156, 193–94
'Pirates of Parihaka, The' 180–89
Pirates of Penzance, The (Gilbert and Sullivan) 180, 183, 184–85
police forces
  Armed Constabulary 54–55, 184
  Australia 99–100, 102, 151–52, 153, 198, 199, 207, 215
  Fiji 90, **92**, 93–94, 95
  Native Police 215
  New Zealand 54–55, 184
  Pirates of Penzance, The (Gilbert and Sullivan) 180, 183, 184–85
  police violence 95, 247–48
Port Jackson see Sydney *under* Australia
Port Phillip see Melbourne (Port Phillip)
prisons/prisoners, Indigenous peoples **43**, 149, 153, 155, 179, 199, 239
Public Action Project 44
Puhi Kai Iti/Cook Landing National Historic Reserve 220–22
Pukearuhe 59, 60, 64

Quilty, Ben 228, 231
Quilty, Patrick 198, 199, 202

Radio New Zealand 52
Raffet, Auguste **159**
Rangiaowhia massacre 63, 239, 240, 242
Raureti, Te Huia 241
Ream, Rebecca 55
Reardon, John 101, 103
reconciliation
    Aotearoa New Zealand 51–52
    Australia 39–41, 48, 121, 208
    North America 75–77
    'Uluru Statement from the Heart' 39, 40, 208, 245
Reconciliation Australia 39, 40
Reconciliation Cross 42, **45**, 46, 47
redress/redress schemes 72, 122, **123–24**, 125
    see also reconciliation
Resistance, Resilience and Remembrance (exhibition) 243
Returned Services League (RSL) 247
Rewi's Last Stand (movie) 25, 36, 37, 235–44, 237, 243
Rex v RB (legal case) 93–94
Rhodes, Cecil 44, 207, 227
Roads Cross (exhibition) 204
Roberts, John 179, 184
Robinson, Governor 150, 152, 153
Rolepana (Indigenous Australian) 233, 234
Rolleston, Frank 188
Rolleston, William 184–85
Rongowhakaata (iwi) 219, 235
Rose, Deborah 173
Royal Navy, British 82–83
Rudd, Kevin 121
Ryan, Lyndall 207, 214–15, 216, 231

Saint-Domingue 157
salt in the wound (Watson) 215, **216**
Scates, Bruce 44, 231
Scott, Edward 110
Seidner, Cheryl 71, 72
self-determination (mana motuhake) 164, 185, 218
    see also sovereignty, Indigenous
sexual violence/abuse
    bias against Indigenous peoples/non-Europeans 93, 94–96, 125
    children 93–95, 117–26, **123–24**
    Flynn, Errol 141–45

historiography, lack of 23, 87
Indigenous Australians 117–26, **123–24**, 150, 152–53, 154, 155–56, 198
Māori 23, 180, 188, 240
rape 23, 90–96, 120, 126, 153, 156
redress schemes 122, **123–24**, 125
statutory rape 141, 142, 143–44
Stolen Generations (Australia) 117–26, **123–24**
underreporting 93, 96
Shaw, Richard 54–55
Slavery Abolition Act 83
slavery/slave trade 82–83, 149–50, 154–55, 157–58, 162–63
    see also indentured labour
Sleeps Standing: Moetū (Kelly and Ihimaera) 241
Sleeter, Christine 54, 55
Smith, Jack 199–202
Smith, Takirirangi 50
Smithsonian National Museum of the American Indian 71, 72, 73, 74–75, 77
Solander, Daniel 223, **224**
Songs to the Judges (Dart and Thompson) 189
South America 82, 83
sovereignty, Indigenous 158, 160, 162, 163, 185, 218, 232, 245, 246, 247, 248
Spence, Percy F.S. **175**
Sprague, Quentin 212
St Helena 79–86, **85**
Statham, Edith 34–35
statues/monuments 44, 207, 227–28, 229, **230**, 231–33, 234
Stolen Generations (Australia) 23, 107–16, 117–26, **123–24**
Strakosch, Elizabeth 44
Suva 88–90, **88**, **89**, 95
Sydney (Australia) 98, 102, 118, 140, 207
Sydney Mail (newspaper) 167
Sydney Morning Herald (newspaper) 153, 167, 168, 173

Tahiti/Tahitian people 140, 144, 217–18
Tainui (iwi) 60
Talking Blak to History (exhibition) 213
Taranaki Wars 55–56, 59–63, 159–60
Tāwhiao, Tukaroto Matutaera Pōtatau Te Wherowhero 34, **161**

Te Awamutu 237, 238, 243, 244
Te Haurangi 219
Te Heuheu (whānau) 34, 35
Te Hokioi e Rere Atu na (newspaper) 24, 158, 160–64, 165
Te Huia, Raureti 241
Te Ikaroa-a-Rauru (waka) 221–22
Te Karere Maori (newspaper) 162, 163–64
Te Maro 24–25, 218–25, **221**, **224**
Te Maro and Solander, Two Intellectuals from Opposite Sides of the World, 1769 (Tuffery) 223, **224**
Te Paerata, Ahumai 31, **32**, **33**, 240
Te Paerata, Hitiri 31
Te Papa Tongarewa Museum of New Zealand 15, 248
'Te Pūtake o te Riri' (Loader) 51
Te Rākau 219
Te Rakura: The feathers of the albatross (Dansey) 189
te reo Māori 49–50, 55
Te Rerenga, Wētere 59–68, **61**, **67**
Te Rito, Joseph 50–51
Te Tiriti o Waitangi *see* Treaty of Waitangi/Te Tiriti o Waitangi
Te Whare Taonga o Otawhao Te Awamutu/Te Awamutu Museum 243
Te Wherowhero, Pōtatau 34, 160
Te Whiti-o-Rongomai 179, 180, 181–82, 183–84, **185**, **186**, 188, 189, 190
television programmes/series 38, 235
Tertullian 63
'The Charge at Parihaka' (Mackay) 189
'The Battle of Parihaka' (Fudge) 189
The People of the State of California vs Errol Flynn (legal case) 143–44
the red thread of history, loose ends (exhibition) 247
theatre
 Gilbert and Sullivan (dramatist/composer) 180–81, 184–85, 188–89
 'Pirates of Parihaka, The' 180–89
 Pirates of Penzance, The (Gilbert and Sullivan) 180, 183, 184–85
This Pākehā Life (Jones) 53
Thomas, Amanda 52–53
Thomas, Lanikan 193

Thomas, Rover 24, 193–97, **196**, **197**, **200–01**, 202–4, **205**
Thompson, Mervyn 189
Thorpe, Robbie 231, 232
Times, The (newspaper) 62
tino rangatiratanga (sovereignty) 160, 162, 163, 185, 218
 see also sovereignty, Indigenous
Tonge, Alice 98
treaties with Indigenous peoples 25, 51, 54, 158–59, 160, 164, 179, 228, 236, 244, 245
Treaty of Waitangi/Te Tiriti o Waitangi 158–59, 160, 164, 236, 244
Tressa's Resolve (Atkinson) 170
Trollope, Anthony 174
truth-telling 39–40, 41, 48, 208, 210, 215–16, 227, 234, 245
 see also mythmaking; reconciliation
Tuffery, Michael 24–25, 223, **224**, 225
Tuia 250 programme 220
Tupaia's Endeavour (documentary) 223–24
Tūpara, Nick 24–25, 220–21, **221**, 222, 223–25
Tupersalai (New Guinea girl) 142–43
Tūranganui-a-Kiwa (Gisborne) 218–19, 220–21, **221**, 223
Tūwharetoa (iwi) 235

'Uluru Statement from the Heart' 39, 40, 208, 245
United States of America 157, 246
 see also North American Indigenous peoples

Van Diemen's Land *see* Tasmania *under* Australia
veil of tears (Watson) 247–48
Venice Biennale 204
Violence and Indigenous Communities: Confronting the past and engaging the present (Sleeper-Smith, Ostler & Reed) 19

Waanyi peoples 24, 210, 211, 214
 see also Watson, Judy
waiata (songs) 34, 189, 241–42
Waikato (iwi) 59, 60
Waikato War 30, 36, 38, 63, 163, 238, 239, 243
 see also New Zealand Wars
Waitangi Tribunal 51, 54, 179, 245

Walcott, Robert 152–53
Walker, George **234**
Wangkatjungka peoples 193
Wanhalla, Angela 79
Watego, Chelsea 19–20, 246
Watkin, Tim 52
Watson, Don 176
Watson, Judy 24, **208**, **209**, 210–11, 213–15, **216**
Webster, Doreen 120
West Australian (newspaper) 154
Wetere, Rongo 66
Wevers, Lydia 58
whakapapa/kin-based histories, Māori 50–51, 66, 223, 225
Whanganui 79, 80, 83, 84
Wharemaru, Heeni 66
Whiteley, John 60–68, **62**
Wills, Martha 55, **56**, **57**
Wills, Thomas 55–56, **56**, **57**

Windschuttle, Keith 212–13
Wittenoom, Frank 151, 152, 153, 156
Wiyot Tribe 71–77, **73**, **76**
'Women in Pearling' 47–48
women, violence against 60, 63, 71, 77, 97–104, 154, 240, 248
  see also sexual violence/abuse
Woolls, William 174, 176
World Renewal Ceremony 71, 72, 75, 77
Wylie (Indigenous Australian) 110, **111**, 112–16

Yiwarra Kuju: The Canning Stock Route (Brooks) 193
Young, Edward 139–40
Young, Fredrick 140
Young, Jonathan 97, 100–01, 102, 103
Young, Margaret 97–100, 101, 102, 103–04
Young, Robert 140–41